THINKING LIKE AN ECONO

Thinking like an Economist

How Efficiency Replaced Equality in U.S. Public Policy

Elizabeth Popp Berman

PRINCETON UNIVERSITY PRESS

PRINCETON AND OXFORD

Published by Princeton University Press
41 William Street, Princeton, New Jersey 08540
99 Banbury Road, Oxford OX2 6JX

press.princeton.edu

First paperback printing, 2023
Paper ISBN 978-0-691-24888-2

The Library of Congress has cataloged the cloth edition as follows:

Names: Berman, Elizabeth Popp, 1975– author.
Title: Thinking like an economist : how efficiency replaced equality
    in U.S. public policy / Elizabeth Popp Berman.
Description: Princeton : Princeton University Press, [2022] |
    Includes bibliographical references and index.
Identifiers: LCCN 2021042133 (print) | LCCN 2021042134 (ebook) |
    ISBN 9780691167381 (hardback) | ISBN 9780691226606 (ebook)
Subjects: LCSH: United States—Economic policy. | United States—Social policy. |
    Equality—United States. | Policy sciences—United States. | United States—Politics
    and government. | BISAC: SOCIAL SCIENCE / Sociology / General |
    POLITICAL SCIENCE / Public Policy / General
Classification: LCC HC106.84 .B47 2022 (print) | LCC HC106.84 (ebook) |
    DDC 330.973–dc23
LC record available at https://lccn.loc.gov/2021042133
LC ebook record available at https://lccn.loc.gov/2021042134

British Library Cataloging-in-Publication Data is available

Editorial: Meagan Levinson and Jacqueline Delaney
Production Editorial: Kathleen Cioffi
Jacket/Cover Design: Lauren Smith
Production: Erin Suydam
Publicity: James Schneider and Kathryn Stevens
Copyeditor: Jennifer Harris

This book has been composed in Adobe Text and Gotham

For Daniel, Nova, and Naomi

CONTENTS

THINKING LIKE AN ECONOMIST

1

Thinking like an Economist

In 2008, Barack Hussein Obama was elected to the presidency of the United States on a promise of "hope and change." The first Black president, born fifteen years after Bill Clinton and George W. Bush, Obama's election represented for many the turning of a page: the arrival of a new, multiracial America that would be able to transcend its racist past and build a brighter, more inclusive future.

Beyond the symbolic importance of breaking what the *New York Times* called the "last racial barrier," many of Obama's supporters anticipated that he would usher in substantial policy change.[1] After eight years of the George W. Bush presidency, these voters hoped Obama would find a way to ensure that all Americans had healthcare, rein in Wall Street, and finally address the mounting crisis of climate change. Progressive Democrats, in particular, were excited and energized by the results of an election that had once seemed so unlikely.

Obama did oversee the resolution of the 2008 financial crisis and the nation's long, slow climb out of the Great Recession. He had some major legislative accomplishments, which included the Affordable Care Act (ACA), the Dodd-Frank financial reforms, and a massive economic stimulus package. Yet even before 2010, many progressives began expressing disappointment with Obama's policy leadership.[2]

What stands out in retrospect about the Obama presidency is its continuity with the recent past. The truly ambitious new policies—ones that might have been top-of-mind for Democrats in 1970, or 1935—never materialized.

This is not because such possibilities were pursued unsuccessfully; they were never even seriously considered. And the policies that *were* proposed tended to share some characteristics more commonly associated with Republican administrations: a focus on leveraging choice, competition, incentives, and the power of markets in the pursuit of outcomes that would be not just effective, but efficient.

Take healthcare policy. Obama's signal accomplishment in social policy, "Obamacare," was modeled after Republican Mitt Romney's 2006 Massachusetts healthcare reform bill. Obama's version combined elements from both Republican and Democratic health reform plans of the early 1990s.[3] The ACA increased the number of people with insurance, but it did not establish universal coverage or a right to healthcare. It established a complex system that sought to harness competition between insurers to keep costs down and incentivized the purchase of insurance with subsidies for those with lower incomes. The law also levied penalties against those who chose to forgo insurance. While some Democrats mentioned the possibility of universal, single-payer healthcare—which had been the party's platform in the 1970s—the insider consensus was that such an approach was not only politically unrealistic but also actively undesirable because it would fail to keep costs down.[4]

Financial reform offers another example. The Dodd-Frank Act, passed in the aftermath of the 2008 financial crisis, was meant to ensure that banks deemed "too big to fail" could never again threaten to bring down the entire financial system with them. Yet while the bill introduced new regulatory requirements and created the Consumer Financial Protection Bureau, Dodd-Frank did little to take on the power of the banks.[5] In the late 1990s, a bipartisan deregulatory impulse had led to the repeal of the Glass-Steagall Act, which had separated commercial and investment banking, and to rapid expansion of the biggest banks.[6] But even after the 2008 crisis, policymakers never seriously reconsidered reinstating the division between commercial and investment banks. The idea of using antitrust policy to break up the banks was never on the table.[7]

Or consider policies to address climate change, a core plank of Obama's 2008 campaign. The administration originally supported the Waxman-Markey Bill, a 2009 cap-and-trade bill that would have limited greenhouse gas emissions for the first time, but the proposal died in the Senate.[8] Obama then turned to regulation as a next-best option. New fuel economy standards and a plan to reduce power plant emissions tried to use the authority of the Clean Air Act to address climate change, with very modest success.[9] Both the cap-and-trade and regulatory approaches built on an economic framework that sought to use market forces (in the former case) or cost-benefit calculations (in the latter) to achieve efficient policy results. The strategy of simply instructing government to determine safe levels of emissions and requiring firms to meet them, as Democrats might have proposed in the 1970s, was not even discussed.

Obama was, of course, faced with many constraints that shaped both the options he considered and what he could actually accomplish: Republicans in Congress, more conservative members of his own party, the particular scrutiny he received as a Black man in the White House, and, notably, the worst recession in seventy years. The limits on what he was able to realize as president are not solely explained by a failure of imagination. But what is so striking about Obama's time in Washington is not that he sought to achieve fundamental change and failed. It is how constricted the very horizons of possibility seemed to be.

Moments of crisis like 2008 can be moments of political transformation. As Rahm Emanuel, Obama's chief of staff, suggested that year, "You never want a serious crisis to go to waste."[10] So why, then, did the Obama administration not produce, or even seek, more fundamental change, despite coming to power during just such a crisis and having, for two full years, control of both the House and the Senate? Why did it remain committed to an incrementalist, modestly ambitious vision of government, even as the country faced unprecedented challenges? And should we expect the same from the Biden administration, which inherited much of Obama's legacy (and many of his advisors), and came to power during a global pandemic, but also at a time of greater mobilization on the political left?

There is no single right answer to this question. The Democratic Party's enduring commitment to a market-friendly, technocratic approach to policy since 1990 has many sources, including the influence of the tech and finance industries within the national Democratic Party, the ever-rightward shift of Republicans, the relative weakness of organized movements on the left, and the depth and complexity of interest-group politics in domains like healthcare and climate policy. Any one of these makes transformative change hard; combined, they can make it feel impossible.

This book addresses a critical, yet underappreciated, historical change that helps explain Democrats' apparent lack of ambition, among other political shifts: the rise of a distinctive way of *thinking* about policy—what I call the "economic style of reasoning"—that has become prevalent in Washington. The economic style of reasoning is a loose approach to policy problems that is grounded in the academic discipline of economics, but has traveled well beyond it. It is often perceived as politically neutral, but it nevertheless contains values of its own—values like choice, competition, and, especially, efficiency. Today, its dominance as a framework for thinking about policy problems is often taken for granted, but this has not always been the case.

In the chapters that follow, I provide an account of where the economic style of reasoning came from, how it spread and was institutionalized in Washington, and what its political effects have been. Between the 1960s and the 1980s, two intellectual communities—both initially led by liberal technocrats who thought government could solve social problems and improve the working of markets—introduced this distinctive style to new parts of the policymaking process. One was a group of systems analysts who came from the RAND Corporation and offered new answers to the age-old question, "How should government make decisions?" The other was a loose network of industrial organization economists who came to Washington to ask, "How should we govern markets?" I follow the movement of these economists and their fellow-travelers into a variety of policy domains and show how they helped to institutionalize an economic style of reasoning through law, regulation, and organizational change.

I also demonstrate the political effects of this change. The high value that the economic style placed on efficiency, incentives, choice, and competition frequently conflicted with competing political claims grounded in values of rights, universalism, equity, and limiting corporate power. As the influence of the economic style became more durable, it became harder for those competing claims to gain political purchase. While the economic style had the potential to conflict with conservative as well as liberal values, in practice, its predominant political effect has been to reinforce the conservative turn that began in American politics in the 1970s. For Republicans, economic reasoning remained a means to an end; for Democrats, the values of economics became an end in themselves.

The results of this turn continue to play out in politics today. Material interests play an undeniable role in determining which ideas get political attention in the first place. But once a particular intellectual framework is institutionalized, it can take on a life of its own, defining the boundaries of what is seen as politically reasonable. For Democrats, the institutionalization of the economic style has limited political options over the last thirty years, even as social movements and an increasingly organized left have introduced new voices and a new level of dissatisfaction with the status quo. Whether those voices will gain greater influence will, once again, depend on collective action as well as ordinary interest group politics. But their success will also depend on their ability to reform or dislodge a way of thinking about policy that has become thoroughly naturalized, and that is much less politically neutral than it appears.

The Economic Style of Reasoning and Its Importance

Philosopher Ian Hacking initially proposed the term "style of reasoning" to capture the distinctive ways of thinking made possible with the emergence of statistics.[11] But styles of reasoning are not scientific paradigms, nor are they particular theories or models. Instead, they are collections of orienting concepts, ways of thinking about problems, causal assumptions, and approaches to methodology.[12]

The economic style of reasoning is a loose approach that began turning up in Washington as early as the 1950s, but that really spread in policymaking between about 1965 and 1985. It starts with basic microeconomic concepts, like incentives, various forms of efficiency, and externalities. It takes a distinctive approach to policy problems that includes using models to simplify, quantifying, weighing costs and benefits, and thinking at the margin.[13] It also includes causal policy stories linked to economic theories—that, for example, investing in education will increase human capital and raise incomes.[14]

The style is grounded in the authority of PhD-producing economics departments, which reproduce it, certify those credentialed to use it, and, over time, gradually drive its evolution. These departments are at the center of what microbiologist and philosopher Ludwik Fleck called an "esoteric circle," one made up of those who publish in top economics journals and create new knowledge in the discipline.[15]

A weaker version of the style circulates well beyond the rarified air of elite economics departments. Economics PhDs teach in law, policy, and business schools, where graduate students in other disciplines are exposed to the basics of the style. Indeed, as sociologists Tim Hallett and Matt Gougherty show in their ethnography of a public affairs program, learning to "think like an economist (without becoming one)" is integral to pursuit of the master's degree.[16] An even broader set of people learn the style's elementary concepts in Econ 101 classes, or in other undergraduate courses grounded in economic reasoning.

This much larger group of people, who lack PhDs in economics but are familiar with the basic principles of economic reasoning, make up concentric "exoteric circles" of those influenced by the economic style. Their numbers include faculty in professional schools oriented toward it, producers of policy knowledge who apply it, and policymakers and advocates who adopt its approach, sometimes unawares.[17] While the inhabitants of these exoteric circles may not be familiar with the cutting edge of the discipline, what's happening at the frontiers of knowledge may not matter much for policy purposes. As economist Alain Enthoven, one of Robert McNamara's whiz kids, wrote in 1963—and others have reaffirmed—"the tools of analysis that we use [in policymaking] are the simplest, most fundamental concepts of economic theory [that] most of us learned as sophomores."[18]

In practice, the economic style is a loose and flexible approach to analyzing policy problems that has evolved gradually over time. But the style does reflect two core stances whose implications can be seen playing out in a variety of policy domains. First, it maintains a deep appreciation of markets as efficient allocators of resources. This does not mean that its adherents believe that markets are perfect, that deregulation is always the answer, or that market failures are not a problem. But it does mean that they tend to see government's role as creating the legal framework that will facilitate well-functioning markets and correct for any market failures. It also means that they tend to view policy domains through a market lens. They display an affinity for introducing market-like elements—like choice and competition—into areas, such as education or healthcare, that are not governed primarily or solely as markets.

Second, the economic style places a very high value on efficiency as the measure of good policy. Once a particular objective has been democratically chosen, adherents of the economic style regard a good policy as the most cost-effective means to reach that objective. Policy goals themselves can also be evaluated through the lens of efficiency: an appropriate level of regulation, for example, is the one that will maximize net benefits to society. The economic style portrays efficiency as a politically neutral value. Any objective can be achieved in a more or less efficient manner, and who would advocate for inefficiency? Yet, as we will see, centering efficiency often means displacing other political values, or ignoring the politics behind the process of identifying efficient policy decisions.

———

A brief foray into the rise of the economic style in environmental policy between 1970 and 1990 can put some empirical flesh on this abstract description. The years around 1970 saw Washington enact a major wave of environmental policies in response to growing public concern with pollution and the rise of a powerful environmental movement. These policies, which included President Richard Nixon's creation of the Environmental Protection Agency (EPA, 1970) and Congress's passage of laws like the National Environmental Policy Act (NEPA, 1969), the Clean Air Act (1970), and the Clean Water Act (1972), had broad, bipartisan support.[19]

This wave of policy change was motivated by a complex mix of factors. NEPA, for example, emphasized ecological interrelations. The law declared that it would "encourage productive and enjoyable harmony between man and his environment."[20] The Clean Air Act focused on "the effects of air pollutants on public health and welfare."[21] Both the Clean Air and Water Acts were influenced by political scientist Theodore Lowi's argument for strong, inflexible rules to combat regulatory capture. They required strict standards for pollution control based on what was technologically possible, and they limited air pollution to levels that would provide "an ample margin of safety to protect the public health."[22] The policies were, by and large, effective, and pollution trended sharply downward in the years that followed.

This early-1970s wave of environmental legislation did not reflect much in the way of economic reasoning. Economists, who were also concerned about high levels of pollution, had a very different—yet internally coherent— way of thinking about the problem. From an economic perspective, pollution was an externality: a side effect of producing some good or service, whose cost was borne not by the consumer of that product, but by the breathers of air and drinkers of water. The solution to this market failure was to put a price on pollution, perhaps through a tax, so that consumers of polluting products, rather than members of the larger public, would bear their full cost.[23]

Economists were quite critical of the environmental approach taken by Congress in the early 1970s. From an economic perspective, the regulatory solutions it had settled on—rigid limits on how much pollution firms could emit and requirements that they adopt particular mitigating technologies— created problems of their own. They did not distinguish between changes that were inexpensive for firms to make and those that were very costly. They failed to acknowledge that the more pollution was reduced, the more expensive further reductions would likely be. And they did not account for the fact that, while pollution itself was unwanted, it generally accompanied some otherwise desirable activity, and limiting it would have costs.[24]

Economists were well-represented in the Nixon White House, but when it came to the environment, their views were largely ignored. Moreover, in an era of ascendant environmental politics, the idea of pollution taxes struck many policymakers as morally objectionable—"a purchased license to pollute."[25] One economist subtitled his retrospective analysis of the Clean Water Act, "Why No One Listened to the Economists."[26] But by the time Congress revisited the Clean Air Act two decades later, the situation had changed considerably. By 1990, the economic style had pervaded many more domains, including environmental regulation.

A centerpiece of the Clean Air Act Amendments of 1990 was the Acid Rain Program. In the 1980s, acid rain—a phenomenon created by power plants expelling sulfur dioxide from multi-hundred-foot-high smokestacks—became a major environmental concern.[27] Falling up to hundreds of miles from these sources, acid rain destroyed aquatic ecosystems, killed trees, eroded building materials, and harmed human hearts and lungs. The Acid Rain Program was a new and ambitious bipartisan attempt to solve this problem. But while earlier environmental legislation had made ecological references to "harmony" and "the interrelations of all components of the natural environment," Congress's new solution drew on the economic style.[28] Acid rain would be cut in half by "design[ing] mechanisms . . . which take advantage of the forces of the marketplace in our economy" to protect the environment in "economically efficient" ways.[29]

The Acid Rain Program proposed to do this by creating the first national cap-and-trade program in the United States. Rather than requiring power plants to install "scrubbers" that would remove sulfur dioxide, it limited how much of the pollutant they could emit and gave producers credits for reductions they made beyond that requirement. Companies could then sell these credits to other companies for whom reducing emissions was more expensive. Economists argued that a market in emissions credits would reduce the amount of sulfur dioxide in the atmosphere more efficiently than simply requiring all plants to limit their emissions by the same amount.[30]

Economists had been writing about the possibility of tradeable permits since the late 1960s and had strongly advocated for their incorporation into the Clean Air Act amendments.[31] They were delighted to see Congress incorporate an approach consonant with their own style of reasoning into policy thinking about pollution. In the thirty years since its passage, the Acid Rain Program has widely been viewed as a major success, contributing to an eventual 94 percent reduction in sulfur dioxide emissions, along with parallel improvements in the effects of acid rain on ecosystems and human health.[32] It has since served as a model for cap-and-trade programs around the world.[33]

The policy differences in approach between the Clean Air Act of 1970 and its 1990 amendments may seem subtle. Both laws passed with strong bipartisan support. Both represented serious attempts to ameliorate environmental problems. And both were successful at achieving meaningful pollution reductions. But the differences between the two laws represent a transformation in the logic of environmental policy.

Over the course of the 1970s and 1980s, environmental policy turned away from a moral framework that stigmatized polluters and toward the position that pollution was simply an externality to be priced. Instead of identifying acceptable levels of pollution, the policies began focusing on the most efficient means to achieve previously designated targets. Instead of promoting technologies of pollution reduction, it pushed technologies of market design. The top-down, one-size-fits-all regulatory approach of the 1970s was delegitimated in favor of more a flexible strategy that took costs into account—but that failed to take seriously some of the practical and political advantages of the original tactic, instead simply seeing it as economically illiterate.

This growing expectation that environmental claims should be made in economic terms, at least if they were to be upheld by federal agencies and the courts, changed the political space for making them. Ecological arguments, so integral to the passage of NEPA, rested on the idea that organisms and their environment depend on one another in complex, unpredictable ways; these ideas did not translate easily into economic equivalents. Instead, the 1990s saw ecology rethought in terms of "ecosystem services"—priceable contributions the environment made to human welfare—so that such services could be incorporated into cost-benefit calculations. Yet the ecosystem services concept failed to capture the deep interdependence of the living and nonliving elements in an ecological system. It also lacked the moral appeal ecological thinking had held for many.[34]

Similarly, when people of color organized in the 1980s to demand environmental justice in response to the disproportionate pollution of their communities, they drew on the language of civil rights, asserting "the right to participate [in environmental governance] as equal partners."[35] Yet when the EPA finally responded to these calls, it did so by turning demands for racial justice into an economic calculation of "the relative risk burden borne by low-income and racial minority communities."[36] Gone were their calls to end toxic waste production and references to the sacredness of Mother Earth.[37]

The power of economic reasoning rests partly in its ability to bring new concerns—whether with the value of pollinators or the siting of landfills in racialized communities—into its framework. But rethinking competing values in the language of economics often comes at the cost of some violence to the originals.

The implications of this shift toward economic reasoning in environmental policy continue to play out. The most important environmental issue of our time is climate change. But the language of moral imperative has been relegated to the margins of climate policy—perhaps something to be referenced in press releases, but not as a starting point for practical action. To be taken seriously by the Washington establishment, climate proposals must be consistent with the economic style—that is, they must understand greenhouse gas emissions as a particular kind of problem resolved by a particular kind of solution—one that fixes the market by pricing the externality. This requirement places significant constraints on the range of possibilities and types of approaches that policymakers define as reasonable. It is no wonder that more meaningful change has not taken place.

———

Environmental policy provides one illustration of how the economic style has changed the political conversation. But it is certainly not the only one. A wide range of policy domains adopted the language of economics between the 1960s and the 1980s. Analogous changes took place, to a greater or lesser degree, in social policy areas from poverty to healthcare to housing to education policy. Economics also gained influence in antitrust policy and in the governance of regulated industries like transportation, energy, and communications. And it affected not only environmental regulation, but regulation of public health and safety as well. In many of these arenas, economics was almost irrelevant to policy in the early 1960s; by the 1980s, its language shaped the terms of debate in domains once seen as well beyond its scope.

As was the case in environmental policy, the growing influence of the economic style went hand in hand with the declining legitimacy of competing frameworks for thinking about policy. Today, the economic style is so widespread as to be taken for granted. It was at the heart of the kinds of policies that were advocated by the Obama administration and that continue to be supported by centrist Democrats. In addition to its prevalence in climate policy, it can be seen in approaches to healthcare reform that emphasize choice and competition, means-testing, and the careful structuring of markets as a means to improve efficiency. It is reflected in an approach to antitrust that understands consumer welfare solely in terms of prices and defines issues like "too-big-to-fail" banks as beyond its scope. In each of these areas, competing frameworks for thinking about policy—ones that open up the possibility of more ambitious change—exist. But as long as such frameworks lack the legitimacy and institutionalized support that have been put into place for economic reasoning, they will struggle to gain ground.

The Spread of the Economic Style of Reasoning

Economists could be found in the federal government from the early twentieth century. They had real influence in particular policy areas—especially macroeconomic ones, like fiscal policy—in its middle decades. But the economic style of reasoning is a distinctively microeconomic approach. It brings the tools of economics to less obviously "economic" domains, like transportation governance and education policy. It only really began to take off in the 1960s, as two intellectual communities rooted in the economics discipline first brought their insights into policymaking.

One was a systems analytic group that came to Washington from the RAND Corporation at the dawn of the Kennedy administration. Kennedy's Secretary of Defense, Robert S. McNamara, introduced an initiative called the Planning-Programming-Budgeting System (PPBS) at the Department of Defense (DOD). The systems analysts—who mostly wanted to improve, not to shrink, government—thought that they could provide neutral, technocratic answers to the question, "How should government make decisions?" Their influence spread when, in 1965, President Johnson required nearly all executive agencies to adopt PPBS. Timed to coincide with the Great Society's dramatic expansion of social programs, PPBS introduced the economic style into welfare, health, housing, and education policy—domains where it was initially unfamiliar.

The systems analysts were joined by a second, looser network of industrial organization economists who had answers to the question, "How should we govern markets?" This network included both a liberal Harvard branch that was friendlier to government intervention and a conservative Chicago branch that was skeptical of it. Both groups, however, thought that the purpose of market governance was to promote allocative efficiency, and that the existing approach to regulation was making markets less efficient. By introducing economic reasoning to law schools, encouraging it at agencies like the Antitrust Division and the Federal Trade Commission (FTC), and building hubs in Washington—first at the Brookings Institution and later the American Enterprise Institute—industrial organization economists spread economic reasoning into areas like antitrust, transportation, energy, and communications policy.

As the territory of economic reasoning expanded, these two communities intersected and recombined in sometimes unexpected ways. Industrial organization's focus on eliminating economic regulation—that is, price and entry controls in various industries—would be married to the systems analysts' cost-benefit approach to produce "regulatory reform": cost-benefit analysis of environmental, health, and safety regulations. The systems analytic concern with policy efficiency would meet industrial organization's interest in market structure to promote ideas like emissions trading—as would be realized in the Acid Raid Program. While these networks were tied to different parts of the economics discipline, and focused on different policy problems, their underlying commitment to the economic style of reasoning—to the potential benefits of markets, and the value of efficiency— made them natural allies.

This book explores the arrival, institutionalization, and effects of the economic style of reasoning in the three key domains of social policy, market governance, and social regulation (that is, rules governing the environment, health, and safety). Each of these areas followed a pattern analogous to the one illustrated by environmental policy. Different ways of thinking, orthogonal to the economic style, dominated policymaking in the 1960s and into the early 1970s. But in each area, a competing approach grounded in economics was consolidating, and gradually gained influence, during this same time period. Over time, the economic style was institutionalized into the policymaking process in various ways, naturalizing it and making competing ways of thinking about policy seem less reasonable. In the chapters that follow, I demonstrate how this process unfurled in antipoverty policy, antitrust policy, environmental regulation, and various other domains.[38]

One major impetus for the growing influence of the economic style in the 1960s, at least in social policy and social regulatory domains, was the dramatic expansion of the federal government. With the War on Poverty and its associated Great Society programs, the Johnson administration raised the government's ambitions for antipoverty, healthcare, housing, and education policy. Another wave of growth, this one focused on social regulation, followed under Richard Nixon's watch: the Occupational Safety and Health Administration (OSHA), the National Highway Traffic Safety Administration (NHTSA), and the EPA were all created around 1970. In many policy domains, the spread of the economic style might best be understood as an attempt—mostly from the political center—to rationalize and temper this expansion of government.

In market governance, which saw less dramatic policy change during these years, the economic style spread via a different path. The United States' existing market governance regime had largely been put in place by the 1930s, primarily to ensure stability and access to markets at equitable prices. By the 1970s, many different actors, from consumer activists to populist politicians to Chicago economists, were coming to see this style of market governance as obsolete. The economic style, initially advanced by centrist Democrats, provided a compelling alternative framework and found influential allies on the populist left.

Critically, I argue that in contrast with accounts centered on the Chicago School, neoliberalism, and the Mont Pelerin Society, the most important advocates for the economic style in governance consistently came from the center-left. In none of these cases did the initial push for economic reasoning come from the political right. Over and over again, the economic style was introduced to policymaking by technocrats associated with the Democratic Party who wanted to use government to solve social problems. When Chicago School adherents did play a role in certain policy domains, particularly in the 1970s, they were decidedly more skeptical of the positive potential of government. But this is not, first and foremost, a story of right-wing economists pushing for smaller government and freer markets.

Yet whether they came from the left, right, or center, economists and other advocates of economic reasoning became increasingly active in various policy domains after 1965. As they did, the economic style was institutionalized to varying degrees through organizational change, legal frameworks, and administrative rules. Some parts of the federal bureaucracy created entirely new offices oriented toward economics; others expanded and upgraded the role of economics in existing offices. In the process, these offices sometimes reshaped how whole agencies thought about policy. Outside of government, law and policy schools hired economics PhDs and introduced economic reasoning into their curricula, while new funding streams fed the growth of economics-oriented policy research organizations that also helped set policy agendas. At the same time, economists helped to shrink or close government offices whose orientation directly conflicted with economic reasoning.

Evolving legal frameworks also helped institutionalize the economic style. At times, economists worked to tear down old frameworks that clashed with economic reasoning, as in their support for legislation dismantling the regulation of the airlines, rail, and trucking. At others, they built a constituency for new frameworks, as in their advocacy of an efficiency-centered vision of antitrust—a long-term project that was realized as the antitrust agencies, law schools, and eventually the Supreme Court came to agree with them. Administrative rules offered a third pathway through which the economic style was reproduced. Executive orders and agency rulings, for example, expanded the use of cost-benefit analysis in issuing environment, health, and safety regulation.

Institutionalizing the economic style through organizational change, legal frameworks, and administrative rules did more than increase the presence of economists, their allies, and their way of thinking in policymaking spaces. It also created a positive feedback loop. Institutionalizing economic reasoning in one location tended to generate more demand for it in another, as when Congress responded to the executive branch's growing analytic capacity by creating the Congressional Budget Office (CBO) to provide itself with such capacity. And hiring staff to meet one kind of analytic demand—for example, to conduct cost-benefit analysis—could also create a constituency of enthusiasts for the economic style who would promote its further expansion.

As the economic style of reasoning pervaded Washington, its previously unthinkable approaches to policy problems began to seem obvious, even intuitive. Deregulating railroads stopped seeming "heretical," as economist John Meyer declared the idea in 1959, and became the conventional wisdom.[39] Democratic members of Congress no longer saw the taxing of emissions and effluents as providing a "license to pollute," but as the most reasonable response to managing environmental quality—unless, even better, it might be possible to create a market for emissions credits. And bureaucrats increasingly made social policy decisions through a lens of cost-effectiveness, in which it seemed only sensible to limit access to public programs to those who could not afford to pay.

The economic style became a taken-for-granted approach to policy problems, one that was embedded in the state: in bureaucratic offices, in the ecosystem of policy organizations surrounding the federal government, and in the law and policy programs that trained the staff of both. Of course, politicians did not always use economic language, challenger groups continued to make other kinds of claims, and economists themselves remained frustrated at the sheer irrationality of much of the policy process. But within the technocratic communities of think tanks, regulators, bureaucrats, and professional schools—communities that played a critical role in setting the policy agenda and laying out political possibilities—"thinking like an economist" had become the new norm.

The Political Effects of the Economic Style

The economic style of reasoning provided an intellectual tool kit for thinking about policy problems. Many of its advocates saw it as value-neutral and were not themselves particularly partisan. Typically, they hoped economic reasoning would promote more rational decision-making in a process that was, most of the time, fundamentally illogical.

But the economic style was more than an approach to thinking about problems. Values were also built into economic reasoning—first and foremost, the value of efficiency. Indeed, Charles Schultze—Johnson's budget director, chair of Carter's Council of Economic Advisers, and archetype of the Democratic economist—famously argued that economists' most important job in Washington was to serve as "partisan efficiency advocates."[40] From welfare to health to housing policy, from regulatory to antitrust to environmental policy, the economic style made efficiency its cardinal virtue.

Efficiency, for economists, came in multiple varieties—productive, allocative, Kaldor-Hicks—the details of which we will save for later. Yet in each of our broad policy domains, economists saw some type of efficiency as a central guiding value. In social policy, the economic style typically valued policies that provided the most (measurable) bang for the buck—that is, that were cost-effective. In market governance, it valued the kind of efficiency produced by well-functioning markets not subject to failures like monopoly or unpriced externalities. And in social regulation, it valued policies that maximized societal benefits while minimizing societal cost.

While the virtues of these kinds of efficiency may seem self-evident, the pursuit of efficiency frequently conflicted with commitments to competing values. Advocates for national health insurance, for example, made their case by centering the right to medical care, equality of access, and universalism as important, whether for moral reasons or for political viability. If efficiency were the measure of good policy, however, the best healthcare program should be based on means-testing and cost-sharing, not universal full coverage, as it would provide the maximum amount of medical care at the minimal cost to government. Advocates of robust antitrust enforcement might rail about the political power of big business, or point to the role of small business in the fabric of local communities. These values conflicted with an economic vision that took no position on the desirability of small businesses or the danger of big ones, so long as prices remained at competitive levels. And advocates of strict environmental regulation might take that position because of concerns with the immeasurable ecological impacts of pollution, because of a belief that polluters should be punished, or because they thought rigid standards would make it harder for polluters to weaken environmental protections. Yet all these positions clashed with the economic idea that regulation should prioritize the maximization of measurable net benefits, while setting aside the morality of pollution and "political" questions like policies' practical viability or the issue of gained and who lost.

Economists, of course, were neither monolithic nor monomaniacally committed to efficiency. Many were deeply aware that the values inherent in the economic style conflicted with other values that they, themselves, might hold. Alice Rivlin, later founding director of the CBO, wrestled with these conflicts in 1960s memos to her colleagues as a young economist at the Department of Health, Education, and Welfare (HEW).[41] Kenneth Boulding, as president of the American Economics Association, addressed them in a 1968 lecture to the discipline titled "Economics as a Moral Science."[42] Arthur Okun, the chair of Johnson's Council of Economic Advisers, wrote *Equality or Efficiency: The Big Tradeoff* in 1975 to grapple with exactly these issues.[43] In the end, most decided that the benefits conferred by using the economic style—benefits that often had few advocates in the self-interested world of politics—outweighed the risk of squeezing out values less integral to economics.

Yet as the economic style was, in fact, institutionalized in various policy domains, and as considerations of efficiency were naturalized and sometimes legally required, it became harder for policymakers to make arguments based on these competing logics. How much harder depended on how fully the economic style was institutionalized, which varied across policy domains. Where the language of economics came to dominate, but its use was not built into formal rules, other arguments simply came to seem less legitimate. But where elements of the economic style were integrated into more formal decision-making processes, like legal frameworks, the barriers to challenging it rose. A series of Supreme Court decisions, for example, made consumer welfare—understood as allocative efficiency—the sole legitimate goal of antitrust policy.[44] This meant that advocates of alternative goals would not only have to convince others that their way of thinking was legitimate, but would actually have to change the law. This was a formidable task.

Many enthusiasts of the economic style wanted to use government to solve problems. They saw the style as an apolitical way to improve its effectiveness. But the collective effects of the economic style were less liberal than such advocates might have preferred. This, in turn, often placed Democratic economists into opposition with other members of the Democratic

Party. By the 1980s, for instance, Democratic advocates of the economic style typically preferred—on grounds of efficiency—housing programs that provided vouchers to low-income families instead of investing in public housing.[45] Democratic economists opposed universal health insurance, advocated against a universal family allowance, and thought tuition-free higher education was misguided. Centering efficiency repeatedly put Democratic advocates of the economic style into conflict with those they were otherwise politically aligned with.

The economic style could conflict with conservative values as well as liberal ones. For example, economists' focus on efficient solutions to poverty, like the negative income tax, left them relatively uninterested in the moral virtue of work, a central concern of conservative welfare reformers. And economists might advocate for public spending on health and education programs on the grounds that the payoffs in terms of human capital were likely to exceed the costs, while conservatives might prefer a smaller government role on philosophical, not economic, grounds.

On balance, though, the spread of economic reasoning was not as constraining for conservatives as it was for liberals for several reasons. First, value conflicts between the economic style and conservative positions were less frequent. Liberal economists of the 1970s, for example, typically supported less economic regulation and more limited antitrust enforcement, which aligned with conservatives' preferences as well. Second, the economic style prescribed government efficiency, but often implied no clear position on what government should or should not try to do. In practice, this meant that its advocates often argued against specific liberal programs—like the early 1970s push for a universal family allowance—on efficiency grounds, while supporting a more efficient alternative—like a negative income tax.[46] Yet when conservatives simply argued against using government to solve poverty, from either a moral or a practical perspective, advocates of the economic style had fewer compelling counterarguments.

More broadly, though, conservatives were better at using the economic style strategically, in pursuit of noneconomic objectives. This was true to some extent as early as the Nixon administration, which supported basic income experiments (favored by economists) in part because experiments defused activists' push for broader antipoverty programs. This phenomenon was particularly visible under Ronald Reagan, whose appointees used the economic style when convenient, and ignored it when not. The Reagan administration slashed support for economic analysis in social policy areas, where the president expected it to prop up the welfare state, while expanding it in areas like antitrust and environmental policy, where he thought it would support his preference for less regulation.

Ultimately, Republicans proved more willing than Democrats to simply ignore economic reasoning when it conflicted with other, more fundamental values or interests. The Carter administration, for example, substantially expanded cost-effectiveness analysis of regulation on efficiency grounds, even though the left wing of the Democratic Party opposed such moves. Reagan, though, shifted the focus to "regulatory relief"—simply removing regulations, regardless of whether their benefits outweighed their costs— out of commitment to small-government ideals and support for business interests. This difference set the stage for how Democrats and Republicans would continue to interact with the economic style over the next thirty years. In short, the economic style constrained Democrats, while Republicans used it strategically.

What Makes This Story Different

Many scholars have written about the political and economic transformation that began in the United States in the 1970s and continues to the present, sometimes subsumed under the term "neoliberalism." Economically, the nation saw a long, steady rise in inequality, as corporations became stronger, unions became weaker, median incomes flattened, and wealth began to concentrate.[47] Politically, it changed as well. Ronald Reagan promised to "bring our government back under control," and put it "on a diet."[48] But Democrats, too, became more business-friendly, more market-friendly, and reined in their expectations of what government could, and should, do.[49]

Multiple factors contributed to this transformation—global economic changes that were pressuring the United States in new ways, the fracturing of political coalitions and party realignment, collective action among the conservative grassroots and business elites.[50] On the ideological side, scholars have emphasized the limited-government, free-market ideology of the Chicago School and Mont Pelerin Society and the role of conservative think tanks and legal institutions.[51]

What the account presented here does is turn our attention in a new direction—toward an economic style of reasoning that is not associated with the right, that is not explicitly political (and indeed gets part of its power from its appearance of neutrality), and that has been advanced by Democrats even more than Republicans.

This substantially challenges our thinking both about what changed politically in the 1970s and about what the lasting consequences of those changes have been, particularly for the political left. I do not claim that the economic style of reasoning directly *caused* Democrats' rightward shift, which was driven by many factors. That is, I do not argue that, had economists been absent, Democrats would necessarily have remained committed to New Deal ideals, or ecological conceptions of the environment, or remained more "liberal" in any meaningful sense.

Instead, I make a subtler claim: that the economic style—and in particular its institutionalization through legal frameworks, administrative rules, and organizational change—was the channel through which such a shift was made durable. This shift made it much harder for competing claims, grounded in different values and ways of thinking, to gain political purchase. Centrist technocrats' efforts to advance the economic style reinforced the conservative turn in politics by undermining some of Democrats' most effective language—of universalism, rights, and equality—for challenging it. Understanding how this change occurred and why its effects have been so lasting is critical to understanding the larger political legacy of the 1970s.

This insight reorients the scholarly conversation, and particularly that part of it that focuses on how ideas have reshaped politics, in several ways. First, it points our attention toward the political center-left, and not the right. With rare exceptions—particularly sociologist Stephanie Mudge's impressive work on policy economists and the political left—accounts of the intellectual currents of this period have focused heavily on the rise of free-market economic ideology, with the implication that liberals were simply dragged toward a center that shifted rightward.[52] But technocratic centrism has its own underlying ideology that is just as important to understand. It should be seen as an independent force, not just a downstream effect.

Second, this account emphasizes the role of micro-, rather than macro-, economics. Again, while the occasional scholar—notably, historian Daniel Rodgers in *Age of Fracture*—has highlighted the importance of microeconomics as a distinctive way of seeing the world, the vast majority of scholarly attention has focused on macroeconomics, and particularly paradigm shifts from Keynesianism to monetarism or supply-side economics.[53] But while it is true that macroeconomics has long had influence in domains traditionally thought of as "economic policy" (fiscal policy, monetary policy), the spread of a distinctively microeconomic style of reasoning has dramatically extended the reach of the discipline by bringing all sorts of new policy domains, including those not obviously "economic," under its influence.

Third, this approach focuses on a diffuse *style of reasoning*, not economic policy advice. Most work has focused on the recommendations economists make to decisionmakers and whether they matter or not, or perhaps the position of economics in organizations like the Federal Reserve, where economists have decision-making authority.[54] But a close look at the more diffuse, but pervasive, style of reasoning about policy problems shows how the indirect influence of the economics discipline can be much greater than the direct influence of economists' policy advice. The economic style is not just advice from economics PhDs. It is a way of thinking that has become embedded in bureaucratic expertise and that is reproduced in the organizations and institutions in and around government.

Last, I draw our attention to how the economic style is embedded in the state itself, and not just advanced by overtly political actors. Most efforts to understand the political role of economics have emphasized the role of various groups, like business elites or conservative intellectuals, who have sought to leverage particular forms of economics to achieve specific political goals.[55] But the economic style of reasoning was not proposed as a self-consciously political project, and its power is partly a function of its perceived neutrality. The style's ongoing influence and its continued reproduction rests significantly on its embeddedness within government bureaucracy.

What It Means Today

This story is of more than historical or academic interest. It also has lessons for how we should think about the present political moment. The economic style of reasoning—anchored in the authority of the economics discipline, but extending well beyond it—is still dominant in and around many government organizations. It is dominant in places like the Congressional Budget Office, agency-level policy offices, and at most of the think tanks that produce policy options. It also remains dominant in public policy schools, and influential in law schools as well. This institutionalization means that a whole range of actors are constantly generating potential policies compatible with the economic style for the policy stream.[56] It also means that solutions grounded in other forms of reasoning are often rejected out of hand by those who populate such organizations (and others who look to them for cues) as objectionable, irrational, or inappropriate.

The institutionalization of the economic style, and the marginalization of alternatives, helps explain why the universe of options considered by the Obama administration seemed so impoverished to those on the left.

Democrats drew inspiration for their new policy options—from Obamacare to the Race to the Top program that encouraged states to compete for federal education dollars—from the economic style. When outside voices mentioned more ambitious possibilities—from Medicare for All to breaking up big tech—the policy establishment tended to dismiss them as unreasonable, by which they meant incompatible with the economic style. While these dynamics continue to evolve, their legacy has shaped the options available to the Biden administration.

A style of reasoning does not exist outside material interests. The economic style poses a barrier to more aggressive antitrust policy, but so, too, do the objections of powerful companies with deep pockets. A mutually advantageous relationship exists between those who benefit from the status quo and those whose way of thinking about the world tends to defend it. And when critics grow too loud, they may find powerful interests lining up against them. For example, when in 2017 the antitrust program at the New America Foundation, a prominent liberal think tank, became too vocally critical of the economics-dominated antitrust regime and its complacency about big tech, it ran afoul of Google, a major funder of the think tank, and found itself cut loose.[57] Similarly, while economists may question universal health insurance on efficiency grounds, it is the opposition of insurance companies, physician's associations, hospitals, and pharmaceutical companies whose profits it threatens that presents the most formidable barrier.

We know that strong public demand for a policy can overcome entrenched interests, particularly when it aligns with arguments made by intellectual elites.[58] If those elites dismiss such demands as unreasonable, though—that is, as inconsistent with the dominant style of reasoning—it will make the barriers to defeating those interests that much more formidable, even in the face of organized social movements. If policies with strong grassroots support, like Medicare for All, are dismissed as not sensible by think tanks reflecting the dominant approach (for example, Brookings) as well as by government organizations reflecting the economic style (for example, the Congressional Budget Office), the barriers will be high indeed. This is true not just for healthcare, but also in antitrust policy, climate policy, student debt policy, and many other areas.

This sort of constraint is much stronger for Democrats than Republicans. Although the economic style can certainly be found in conservative think tanks, the right has a much deeper bench of institutions grounded in other, noneconomic principles (for example, the Federalist Society, or the Cato Institute). The left wing of the Democratic Party has had some success in the past few years in getting its preferences on the policy agenda, mostly in areas where grassroots organizing has been accompanied by investment in an alternative intellectual infrastructure. Proposals for policies that have only recently moved inside the Overton window, like student debt cancellation, or breaking up big tech companies, or the Green New Deal, have been advanced by successful left-Democratic politicians (Bernie Sanders, Elizabeth Warren, Alexandria Ocasio-Cortez) working with a range of experts and activists, including economists not committed to the economic style.

More important than the advisors sought out by any single politician is the larger infrastructure that produces, and reproduces, particular ways of thinking about policy options. Smaller—but growing—think tanks like the Roosevelt Institute, Demos, and the Economic Policy Institute tend to be less attached to the economic style, and the economists they do rely on are often less central in disciplinary networks and more open to alternative approaches. Many of the ideas they advocate either emerged from, or have been taken up by, different intellectual networks on the edges of the economics discipline (for example, the baby bonds proposal to redress the racial wealth gap). Others come from legal circles developing alternatives to economic reasoning (the law and political economy movement), or from foundation spaces interested in promoting alternatives (the Hewlett Foundation's "Beyond Neoliberalism" initiative).[59]

New think tanks and research organizations have emerged in this space as well—the People's Policy Project, Data for Progress, the Open Markets Institute to name only a few—although they have a smaller donor base than their centrist counterparts. And as the grassroots left gains strength within the Democratic Party, the larger center-left think tanks find themselves more frequently inviting in experts whose policy positions are decidedly not grounded in an economistic, cost-benefit approach.

As of this writing, in the early days of the Biden administration, the political future of the United States is very much in flux. On the one hand, fascist and antidemocratic movements threaten to upend—and perhaps destroy—not only the current political order, but democracy itself. On the other, we have managed to successfully muddle our way through the presidential transition. The Biden administration is faced with the temptation to try to return to the past—to revive an Obama-era approach, which itself requires pretending that an Obama-era politics is even a possibility after the Trump years. But Biden came to office at a time when the progressive wing of the party was historically energized. The administration's early actions seem to signal a recognition that a third Obama administration is neither possible nor desirable.

The influence of this energized left wing will depend on two things. One is grassroots strength—from on-the-ground organizing, demographic change, and rejection of both Trumpism and the status quo that allowed it to emerge. But translating this into policy will require reckoning with the dominance of the economic style. This will mean either working to make it more open to alternative ways of thinking about policy, or—more likely—building intellectual frameworks, networks, and institutions that circumvent it and that can provide competing, and less limiting, ways of thinking about policy problems. For those sympathetic to such goals, when our political values align with those of economics, we should embrace the many useful tools it has to offer. But when they conflict, we must be willing to advocate, without apology, for alternatives—rather than allowing our values to be defined by the values of economics.

2

The Economic Style and Its Antecedents

This book follows the rise of a distinctive, microeconomic style of reasoning that took off in the world of policymaking in the 1960s. But the economists who gained policy influence during that decade were not the first to build ties between the academic discipline of economics and the power corridors of Washington. Such ties date back to the late nineteenth century—as long as economics has been its own field of study.[1] Indeed, as sociologist Marion Fourcade has argued, the discipline itself has always been co-constituted with the development of the state.[2]

The economists and fellow-travelers who arrived in the 1960s introduced a new way of thinking about how to make policy decisions and how to govern markets, which they would eventually institutionalize through new offices and organizations, as well as through laws and regulations. They were different from, and sometimes disdainful of, their predecessors in the discipline. Yet in their efforts to disseminate their own way of thinking and establish institutions that would help to reproduce it, these new economists built directly on earlier economists' efforts to create locations from which they could exercise policy influence.

To understand how the generation of economists who arrived in the 1960s eventually established so much influence, we must first give at least a little attention to the predecessors who laid the foundation that their successors would build upon. While parts of the U.S. government began interacting with the emerging academic discipline of economics during the Progressive Era and World War I, the most important antecedents for our story can be found in the decades that followed. In the 1920s and 1930s, both the administrative apparatus of the state and the role of experts in government more generally expanded.[3] As this took place, two successive waves of academic economists—one now largely forgotten, and the other still influential—began to build more lasting ties with Washington and shape the policymaking process.

The first wave, which started early in the twentieth century and crested in the 1930s, brought institutional economics. Institutional economists thought the workings of capitalism changed with the social, legal, and cultural institutions that governed it, rather than being ruled by unchanging laws of supply and demand. Historicist in method and progressive in politics, they had little interest in mathematical theory, but were avid gatherers of quantitative data.[4] By the 1930s, the decline of institutional economics within the academy had begun; by the 1950s, it had been relegated to the margins of the discipline.[5] Its influence in Washington lasted longer, though, and many government economics offices retained an institutionalist flavor into the 1950s and even beyond.

The second wave, of macroeconomics, emerged in the late 1930s and peaked in the early 1960s. Building on groundwork laid by the institutionalists, macroeconomists took the entire economy as their object of analysis, focusing on large-scale issues like employment levels, economic growth, inflation rates, and business cycles. Dominated at its peak by a Keynesian approach that saw recessions and depressions as a constant threat that government could avoid through careful management, macroeconomists reached their highest level of influence during the Kennedy administration. That influence declined somewhat after 1965, as the Keynesian consensus fractured and macroeconomists offered less clear guidance to policymakers. Unlike the institutional economists, though, macroeconomists' influence would plateau rather than plummet. They would remain influential in Washington.[6]

These two successive waves of policy-oriented economists created a lasting role for the economics discipline in Washington. They built an infrastructure for producing economic statistics, established organizational locations for conducting economic analysis, and routinized the giving of economic policy advice. Yet their influence was also, in many ways, limited. The institutionalists' approach to economics fell out of favor, while macroeconomists' impact was limited to a handful of policy domains. The perspective of macroeconomists remains important in organizations like the Federal Reserve, but their degree of influence has depended on the presence of a president interested in their advice.

By the 1960s, though, a new, *micro*economic style of reasoning was ascendant in Washington—one that would have both broader and deeper influence. Mathematical, quantitative, and organized around problems of constrained optimization, microeconomics fit a definition of economics offered by Lionel Robbins in 1932: "the science which studies human behaviour as a relationship between ends and scarce means which have alternative uses."[7] Having established a toehold in U.S. academia in the 1940s, by the 1950s this new economic style was becoming part of a recognizably modern "grand neoclassical synthesis" that would prove remarkably durable both in and beyond the discipline of economics.[8] This new economic style was distinct from previous waves of economics, but was indebted to connections that predecessors had made between the discipline of economics and the world of policy. Yet it would, in the end, transcend their influence by changing other academic fields as well, and by reaching policy domains in which economics had never before been understood as relevant.

The Rise and Fall of Institutional Economics

By today's standards, the institutional economists of the early twentieth century hardly look like economists at all. They preferred words to equations, had little interest in identifying general rules of economic behavior, were deeply interested in law and in history, and prioritized the collection of descriptive statistics. The mathematical economists who came to dominate the discipline after World War II would find little of value in institutionalism—dismissing it, in Tjalling Koopmans's well-known phrase, as "measurement without theory."[9] Yet institutionalists were completely in the mainstream of the economics discipline in the early twentieth century. They were the most influential economists in pre–World War II policy circles, and they started organizations that remain important links between government and academic economics even today.[10]

Although its origins date back to the late nineteenth century, institutionalism became a self-conscious intellectual movement in the years following World War I. Associated with such figures as Thorstein Veblen, John Commons, and Wesley Mitchell, American institutional economics emerged particularly in reaction to two separate developments: the rise of neoclassical economics, centered on a deductive, theoretical analysis of supply and demand; and a broader tendency in the emerging discipline toward pro-business, anti-government conservativism.[11]

Institutional economics had a distinctive methodological, theoretical, and political reaction to these currents. Methodologically, it was highly empirical. Institutionalism emphasized the collection of quantitative data, but with an inductive, historical approach in mind. Theoretically, it rejected neoclassical formalism in favor of a context-specific approach that assumed that humans were irrational, existing institutions shaped economic behavior, and economic laws evolved over time. Politically, it rejected a laissez-faire approach and tended to favor progressive-to-socialist reforms, with a strong role for the state.[12] While later generations of economists would portray institutionalism as less-than-scientific because of its lack of interest in formal, mathematical theory, institutionalists' respect for empirical evidence and consideration for findings in psychology, anthropology, and law led them to understand themselves as the most scientific of economists.[13]

Institutionalism was highly influential in economics during the pluralist period between the two world wars.[14] It was dominant at Columbia (where it centered around Wesley Mitchell) and Wisconsin (home to John Commons), two of the four major economics departments—and largest producers of PhDs—in the early twentieth century.[15] It was also highly influential in law schools, particularly through the legal realist movement of the interwar decades, which attempted to place legal scholarship on an empirical, social scientific basis. Indeed, law professor Herbert Hovenkamp has gone so far as to call legal realism "the lawyer branch of institutionalism."[16]

The impacts of institutional economics went well beyond the academy, though. Institutionalists were the first economists to exert a lasting influence on policymaking, through both direct and indirect channels. Although some of their efforts would prove more durable than others, collectively they laid the groundwork for future generations of economists who wanted to play a role in government. Their actions shaped the opportunities those future economists would have. Their impact took at least four different forms.

First, institutionalists played a major role in developing the economic indicators that the U.S. government would produce for the rest of the century. Here, their role began as early as World War I, during which Edwin Gay, a Harvard economist with institutionalist sympathies, led the effort of the wartime Central Bureau of Planning and Statistics to gather data on industry conditions to facilitate the government's exercise of administrative control. Elsewhere in the war administration, Columbia's Wesley Mitchell collected price data to assist with government price-fixing efforts.[17] After the war, Gay and Mitchell went on to found the National Bureau of Economic Research (NBER), "on the view that an increase in basic knowledge concerning the economy and its functioning was a prerequisite to improved economic policy and social control."[18]

NBER remained closely associated with the institutionalist movement in its early decades and pioneered the development of national income statistics in the 1930s.[19] Led by Simon Kuznets, a student of Mitchell, and conducted in partnership with the Department of Commerce, the effort to establish national accounts—a system for tracking all economic activity in the country—made it possible for the first time to talk about changes in "the economy."[20] While the history of the national accounts, and gross domestic product (GDP) in particular, is relatively well known, these were not the institutional economists' only important statistical contributions. They also shaped government decisions about how to measure the cost of living, the rate of unemployment, and industrial output, among other economic indicators.[21] The availability of these numbers made it possible for policymakers to think about the economic world in new ways, in much the same way that population censuses and survey data changed people's understanding of the social world.[22]

Second, institutionalist economists blazed a path in providing economic advice to policymakers. The decades after World War I saw the gradual expansion of both the administrative state itself and the importance of experts within it, and institutionalists were very visible in this expansion. When expert-led commissions like the Industrial Relations Commission and the U.S. Permanent Tariff Commission began to spread even before the end of World War I, they included institutionalists among their members.[23] In the 1920s and 1930s, presidents Herbert Hoover and Franklin D. Roosevelt turned more directly to economists—and particularly to institutionalists—in their efforts to manage the economy.

The institutionalists' affinity for expert-led governance and progressive social reform made them more obvious allies for some administrations than others. That said, even a conservative like Hoover, with his engineer's appreciation for statistics, could support their data-collection efforts and their interest in efficiency—although in his case, more directly while secretary of commerce than as president.[24] But FDR, whose political inclinations aligned closely with those of the institutionalists, drew heavily on "an informal president's council of economic advisors before there was such an institution," made up predominantly (although not entirely) of institutionalists.[25] While this type of economic advisory role would not be formalized until Congress created the Council of Economic Advisers (CEA) in 1946, this less formal pathway to influence set an important precedent.

Third, institutionalists helped establish a variety of new government offices in which economists would play significant roles. The Federal Trade Commission (FTC), for example, established an Economic Division two years after it was created, in 1915. Institutionalist in orientation, this office accounted for more than 25 percent of the FTC's budget in the 1920s and published a series of detailed industry reports running to as many as ninety-five volumes in length.[26] In 1922, the Department of Agriculture (USDA) created the institutionalist-influenced Bureau of Agricultural Econom-ics, which would become home to the largest collection of government economists before World War II and would find a place at "the vanguard of efforts to produce an economic knowledge that could be used for managerial manipulation."[27] The Department of Commerce saw its Bureau of Foreign and Domestic Commerce (a predecessor of the Bureau of Economic Analy-sis) grow to become a massive producer of new data on economic activity in the 1930s; its director was "allowed to increase its budget by a factor of six and its personnel by a factor of five."[28] And at the Department of Labor, a student of Thorstein Veblen turned the Bureau of Labor Statistics into an influential voice in national economic policy, similarly overseeing a qua-drupling of its budget and staff, before being followed by a student of John Commons.[29] While some neoclassical economists played a policy role in interwar Washington as well, theirs was not the dominant type.[30]

Last, institutionalists created important organizations at the interstices of academia and policy—organizations that would long outlast the institu-tionalists' own influence. NBER, for example, founded in 1920, was estab-lished "to conduct . . . exact and impartial investigations in the field of economic, social, and industrial science." Its board included representatives from academia, industry, and labor, and it worked closely with government agencies—particularly the Department of Commerce—to develop not only national income statistics but also studies of unemployment, immigration, and business cycles that would be used in policymaking.[31] The Brookings Institu-tion was similarly established by institutionalists in 1928 with the intent of bringing academic expertise to bear on government problems—particularly (but not exclusively) economic problems—and was led by institutionalist Harold Moulton for its first twenty-five years. Organizations like these linked academic economics with the world of policy in new and lasting ways.

But despite substantial organization-building, real development of new knowledge, and an initially promising trajectory, institutionalism did not maintain its place of prominence, either in departments of economics or in Washington. By the 1930s, marginalist economists were enjoying a resurgence in the discipline. The rise of Keynesianism—which attracted some of those interested in a critical challenge to the neoclassicals, and who in the past might have been drawn to institutionalism—soon followed: as economist Geoffrey Hodgson put it, "[a]s early as 1934 the writing for institutionalism was already on the wall" in academia.[32] Although institutionalist thought would continue to develop, particularly through the legal realist movement, it had already begun tipping into what would become a rapid decline in the economics discipline.

The influence of institutionalism in Washington, though, persisted substantially longer. Its pro-government orientation ensured that its adherents would be visible there even after its peak years. Institutionalist PhD-holders from the University of Wisconsin, for example, were overrepresented in government relative to PhDs from other economics departments in the mid-twentieth century.[33] The Council of Economic Advisers retained a notable institutionalist flavor even throughout the 1950s, as did offices like the FTC's Bureau of Economics.[34] The most powerful economist at the Federal Reserve in the 1950s received his PhD from the heavily institutionalist Brookings Institution (which had, for a time, its own graduate school).[35]

By the end of World War II, the influence of institutionalism was nevertheless clearly on the wane, even in Washington. Some of the institutionalist organizations, like NBER and Brookings, would gradually evolve along with the dominant frameworks in the economics discipline.[36] Others would simply decline in influence—a later director went so far as to call the 1950s Bureau of Economics "the graveyard of the FTC"—before their eventual reorganization and rejuvenation around new kinds of economics.[37] And some, like the USDA's Bureau of Agricultural Economics, would be shut down entirely, eventually to be replaced by new offices housing different kinds of economists.[38]

Later generations of economists often dismissed the work of the institutionalists as inconsequential. Ronald Coase, whose work would decades later inspire a more formal, neoclassically grounded "new institutionalist" movement, memorably argued that the old institutionalists "had nothing to pass on except a mass of descriptive material waiting for a theory, or a fire."[39] Yet, as sociologist Yuval Yonay notes, the reality is more complicated: the original institutionalists "had no theory *of the neoclassical type*. . . . This, though, does not mean they lacked theory in some other sense of the word."[40] And while their ninety-five-volume descriptive reports on utility corporations may have been easy for later economists to ridicule, the infrastructure for economic statistics that they produced would make much of those later economists' work possible.[41] Through their efforts to collect systematic economic data, their pioneering advisory roles, and their organizational footprints both within and around government, the institutionalists created a legacy that future economists in Washington would continue to rely upon—often unknowingly.

"Whispering into the Ears of Princes": Macroeconomics and Policy Advising

When political scientists write about the "political power of economic ideas," they typically mean macroeconomic ideas.[42] In these discussions, scholars debate the rise of Keynesianism or try to understand its displacement with monetarist and supply-side economics. Such conversations focus on a particular segment of the economics discipline, with particular relevance to a handful of policy domains—especially fiscal and monetary policy. This is the domain of macroeconomics.

Macroeconomics began its rise to policy influence after the 1930s, as institutionalism was passing its zenith. By the 1960s, it had become the dominant branch of economics in economic departments as well as Washington.[43] Modern macroeconomics is typically dated to the publication of Keynes's *General Theory of Employment, Interest, and Money* in 1936. Keynes argued that long-term underemployment, caused by inadequate aggregate demand, could become a self-reinforcing state owing to the "stickiness" of wages and prices. This condition, he claimed, was a common circumstance in which the rules of neoclassical economics no longer applied. Instead of limiting government spending and allowing wages to fall until the economy stabilized, Keynes argued that only government spending could reliably increase total demand and break this loop.[44]

Keynes's argument for deficit spending as a response to economic depression was not entirely new, having already been made by American institutionalists.[45] And while his larger framework was novel, the spread of Keynesianism in the United States was heavily shaped by the institutionalist legacy. It grew out of institutionalists' interest in business cycles—the periodic expansions and contractions of economic activity—that neoclassical economics could not explain, and the quantitative description of which was a prime focus of early NBER efforts.[46] Its development was heavily dependent on the existence of national income statistics and other macroeconomic data that the institutionalists had begun to collect.[47] And, like institutionalism,

Keynesian macroeconomics attracted those who were dissatisfied with the laissez-faire tendencies of academic economics and sought a justification for more government intervention. Keynes's American apostle, Harvard economist Alvin Hansen, had trained under institutionalists Richard Ely and John Commons; the approach would be disseminated in part through Hansen's many students, including luminaries like James Tobin and Paul Samuelson.[48] Indeed, many institutionalists saw Keynesians not as replacing them, but as their logical successors.

Yet over the next few decades, Keynesian economics would become a highly mathematized affair that distanced itself from the institutionalist approach, both at the theoretical level and as a framework for econometric modeling.[49] Although extremely generative within the discipline, the school was seen by some, in its early decades, as heretical owing to the major and explicit role it assigned to government in managing economic activity.[50] Indeed, the first Keynesian economics textbook, published in 1947, was subject to a coordinated attack instigated by Rose Wilder Lane, daughter of children's author Laura Ingalls Wilder and a libertarian activist, on political grounds.[51] Yet Keynesian macroeconomics would be integral to Samuelson's 1948 textbook, *Economics*—which he wrote "carefully and lawyer-like" to defend against such attacks. Its rise to dominance within the discipline would go hand in hand with the acceptance of Keynesianism in the political mainstream.[52]

This rise was facilitated by economists' important contributions to winning World War II. The war saw economists—working on questions ranging from "How do we hold down inflation?" to "How should we mix machine-gun ammunition?" to "How much harm can be inflicted upon the enemy per unit cost to us?"—mobilized to substantial effect.[53] Many of these economists—regardless of their academic background—found themselves dealing with microeconomic problems of resource allocation and rational decision-making, not with macroeconomic questions. But the experience of wartime also demonstrated the power of macroeconomic analysis. The rapid economic recovery that followed defense mobilization provided evidence for Keynes's argument that government spending could, indeed, end the Great Depression. World War II also helped demonstrate the practical value of national income accounts, as Kuznets and his colleagues at the War Production Board worked to assess how quickly the U.S. economy could grow and how rapidly it could ramp up munitions production.[54] As Samuelson himself wrote as the war was drawing to a close, "It has been said that the last war was the chemist's war and that this one is the physicist's. It might equally be said that this is an economist's war."[55]

But for economists and policymakers alike, the relief of the war's end was accompanied by widespread fears of a return to economic depression. In response, Congress passed the Employment Act of 1946, which for the first time tasked the federal government with "promot[ing] maximum employment, production, and purchasing power."[56] The Employment Act had deeply Keynesian origins, with its original language effectively requiring that the federal government spend enough funds to ward off unemployment.[57] Although this mandate was weakened considerably in the process of passage, the law nevertheless created an enduring framework for Keynesian countercyclical economic management.[58]

The Employment Act also created the Council of Economic Advisers, which for the first time gave social scientists a permanent presence in the White House. In its early days it was unclear how academic the CEA would be and what policy role it would play; as noted earlier, its early appointees tended toward institutionalism.[59] Relatively quickly, though, the CEA became defined by "growthmanship"—the pursuit of economic growth, often guided by a broadly Keynesian view of the economy—as an overarching political goal. While the Eisenhower administration adopted a more skeptical stance on Keynesianism than had Truman's, throughout the 1950s the CEA nevertheless continued to serve as a channel for Keynesian ideas, which were increasingly dominant in the profession.[60]

Macroeconomic issues—growth, inflation, productivity, income, unemployment—were of core concern to policy-oriented economists in the postwar years. In keeping with the Keynesian perspective, those economists tended to focus on fiscal rather than monetary policy. As economist and Federal Reserve historian Allan Meltzer notes, the Employment Act of 1946 neglected monetary policy because the conventional view among economists was "that fiscal policy was powerful and monetary policy was weak or impotent."[61] The Fed certainly employed economists, and the 1951 "Treasury-Fed Accord," which set the Fed on the path to greater independence from the Treasury Department, also gave it the potential to become more technocratic.[62] But at the time, its leadership was dominated by bankers and lawyers, with economists much less well-represented.[63] Moreover, the Fed in the 1950s was simply a much less powerful institution—not only in terms of independence, but also its perceived centrality to the nation's economic well-being—than it would later become.[64]

But while macroeconomists' influence on monetary policy was less than a contemporary reader might imagine, their advisory influence over the president would rise to new heights with the 1960 election of John F. Kennedy.

During the 1950s, the CEA had served as an on-and-off advocate for macro-economic fiscal policy, with neither its commitment to Keynesianism nor its influence in the White House terribly steady.[65] But Kennedy relied heavily on the advice of academic experts in general, and his trust in economists would prove no exception.[66] Keynesianism, through the channel of the CEA and its influential chair, Walter Heller, rose to new levels of political authority in the early 1960s. But this change mostly reflected Kennedy's personal interest in academic advice, rather than a lasting integration of economics into policymaking.

Kennedy's CEA was both an intellectual powerhouse and solidly Keynesian.[67] Heavily oriented toward economic growth, this "New Economics" of the Kennedy administration was confident—to the point of hubris—that economic "fine-tuning" was possible, and that the business cycle had finally come under (its) control.[68] Heller and his colleagues sought to reduce unemployment and stimulate the economy through tax cuts, and were largely responsible for persuading Kennedy to support such tax cuts in what became the Revenue Act of 1964.[69]

Growth, a macroeconomic issue, was a central concern of the Kennedy administration. Historian Robert Collins notes that the Commerce Department was festooned, in these years, with signs asking, "What have you done for Growth today?"[70] Yet Kennedy's CEA, while dominated by macroeconomics, was interested in much more than fiscal policy. Influenced by new arguments that human capital was itself an important source of economic growth, his advisors advocated for an expanded government role in education and health provision—arguments that anticipated the legislation of the Great Society and what would become Johnson's War on Poverty.[71]

Not long after, nagging inflation would begin to undermine the authority of the Keynesians. Macroeconomists' disagreement over how to respond would reduce their policy relevance in a lasting way. But while the fortunes of macroeconomics would indeed decline in Washington, it would experience nothing like the institutionalists' gradual slide into oblivion. Whether Keynesian or, later, monetarist or supply-side, macroeconomists would remain important voices and become more influential in the increasingly important Federal Reserve, even as they failed to recover a Kennedy-era level of influence over presidential decision-making.

Macroeconomists' influence as advisors in the early 1960s did set the stage for the entrance of yet another wave of economists. Yet in some ways, that influence was built on softer sand than the foundation laid by the institutionalists. Institutional economists had—perhaps unsurprisingly—built

THE ECONOMIC STYLE AND ITS ANTECEDENTS 35

new institutions: infrastructures for the production of statistics as well as lasting organizations both within and outside government. Even as the institutionalists themselves faded from the scene, many of their organizations would continue to link new kinds of academic economists with the world of policy. Their corridors would be filled with a new generation of economists willing and eager to speak to a range of policy domains much broader than the economists who came before.

A New Economic Style of Reasoning

The 1960s also saw a new type of economist, grounded in a distinctive style of reasoning, begin to arrive in Washington. These new economists were mostly trained in the more mathematical approach to economics that became dominant after World War II. They came from the growing part of the discipline that saw economics as the science of rational decision-making.[72] And their focus was largely on micro-, not macro-, economics.

While adherents of this new economic style worked on a variety of issues and had no single approach to either economics or policy, they shared a framework for thinking about problems that they would bring with them to the world of policy. Broadly neoclassical in orientation, their starting assumptions were that individuals (or firms) could be treated as rational actors who sought to maximize their utility (or profits). Decisionmaking—whether by individuals in a market or policymakers trying to implement programs—could be thought of as optimization within constraints. Analyses should focus on trade-offs at the margin—what the benefits of an additional unit would be relative to the cost, and what else those same resources might be used for.[73] Advocates of this new economic style typically favored formalization and quantification as a means to improve decisionmaking.

This framework was not new to the 1960s. Much of it was in place as early as the neoclassical era in economics, roughly 1870 to 1930, when economists like Alfred Marshall placed supply, demand, price, and the concept of marginal utility at the heart of the discipline. Throughout the early twentieth century, neoclassical economics was an important but by no means dominant approach to the discipline—one that coexisted with institutionalism. But while neoclassical economists were well-represented in academia, they were, with some exceptions, much less involved in policymaking than their institutionalist peers.[74]

Between 1930 and 1960, though, the discipline of economics changed in ways that would bring this broadly neoclassical style of reasoning to the center of economics and would lay the groundwork for its entry into policymaking as well. World War II, in particular, provided a stimulus to developments that would subsequently reorient the discipline. While macroeconomists were working on questions of how to mobilize the economy for war, microeconomists were developing a tool kit of techniques that could be used to answer specific, targeted queries on issues from minimizing losses as bombers were laying mines in Japanese waters to producing as much fuel as possible given existing raw materials.[75] Such techniques, often deployed under the umbrella of "operations research," played a critical wartime role and were highly valued by military and civilian leaders.[76]

The economists who engaged in these types of work operated within a highly interdisciplinary environment, in which they interacted with mathematicians, statisticians, physicists, operations researchers, and others. This intellectual ferment contributed to the increasing mathematization of economics after the war.[77] While the mathematical economics of the 1930s rarely looked beyond calculus, and even many proponents thought the use of mathematics had its limits, fresh methods and techniques now flourished. This new, more technical, version of the discipline was more often than not being deployed in new institutional locations as well.

Economist Paul Samuelson's *Foundations of Economic Analysis*, a book so technical that few economists were capable of reading it upon its 1947 publication, became the new foundation for graduate education in microeconomics.[78] Under the leadership of mathematician and economist Tjalling Koopmans, the Cowles Commission saw mathematical economists build on wartime inventions like linear programming to develop highly abstract economic theory—for example, the Arrow-Debreu model of general equilibrium—that would become central to the reorienting discipline.[79] New, mathematically centered economics departments were on the rise as well. MIT, under the leadership of Samuelson and others, notably transformed itself from a relative backwater in the 1940s to a position at the top of the national rankings by 1965.[80] This shift toward formalization and mathematization was happening in both macro- and microeconomics. By contrast, institutional economics—which might be quantitative but was not particularly mathematical—was increasingly shut out of the discipline.

While the 1950s saw the esoteric circle of top graduate departments fusing around a technically sophisticated, math-heavy core, the discipline was also disseminating a simpler, less technical version of itself through undergraduate textbooks. This would be particularly important as this new economic style began its move into policy. Samuelson himself helped to write this new story of the discipline in his undergraduate *Economics* textbook, first published in 1948 and updated every few years thereafter, which treated "microeconomic behavior as maximization under constraints."[81]

Although it has gradually evolved, the story set forth by Samuelson in *Economics* is still recognizable today. Historian of economics David Colander characterized the textbook's 1998 edition as presenting microeconomics as an "efficiency story," with one part describing the decision-making of rational individuals and a second the beneficial nature of markets in agglomerating those individual decisions: "The focus of this story is on rational choice; students are taught a variety of models—the profit-maximizing model of the firm, the utility maximizing model of the individual, and simple game theoretic models such as the prisoners' dilemma—that either reinforce the efficiency theme or have meaning in relation to it."[82]

The textbook did change over time, jettisoning descriptive material about economic institutions—about forms of business organization, the earnings distribution, the labor movement—while adding formal tools like game theory.[83] Yet even the earliest editions of Samuelson's textbooks fit Colander's description remarkably well. Samuelson's sixty-year best seller established a basic account of individuals, markets, and the relationship between them that became the standard way novices were introduced to the discipline. This account would reach many who would not go on to study economics in great depth, but who would retain some of its lessons.[84]

It would take time for these changes to reach all corners of the discipline. Historian of economics Roger Backhouse reminds us that, as measured through the contents of three major economics journals, "the mathematization of the subject . . . was far from complete," even by 1960.[85] But the cutting edge of the discipline had, in the 1950s, moved rapidly in that direction, and its students, whether at the undergraduate or graduate level, were increasingly being exposed to a newly crystallized microeconomic style of reasoning.[86]

———

This newly consolidated microeconomic story is what I refer to throughout this book as the "economic style of reasoning." In both its introductory and its more advanced versions, the economic style had implications beyond individual decisionmaking and the private sector. It also had clear ramifications for how one should approach policymaking: in thinking about how government should make decisions, and about what rules should govern markets. In both cases, the story implied that efficiency was the appropriate lens through which to look.

But economists brought multiple types of efficiency to bear on policy questions, depending on the nature of the problem at hand. To identify the best policy for reaching a democratically determined end goal, the economic style prescribed productive efficiency: seeking to achieve that goal at minimum cost. If one's object was to defend the United States against a Soviet missile attack, for instance, one should compare the relative costs and benefits of alternative programs for reaching this goal and choose the most cost-effective option. While it might be difficult to do, putting a dollar value, however tentative, on these cost and benefits was the best way to make seemingly incomparable options commensurate.

But the economic style could also be applied to decide what government should try to accomplish in the first place. Here, Kaldor-Hicks efficiency was the objective. The Kaldor-Hicks criterion stated that government decisions were net improvements if all those who benefited could, in theory, compensate all those who lost, and still be better off—regardless of whether such compensation actually took place.[87] For example, one might want government to "protect the environment." But how much protection should it try to achieve? The correct strategy involved measuring the costs and benefits of achieving a particular level of protection, then choosing the level that maximized net benefits.

In addition to providing guidance for government decision-making, the economic style provided a framework for thinking about how policymakers should govern markets. Well-functioning, competitive markets resulted in a third type of efficiency, allocative efficiency. That is, they would produce goods to the point where the marginal cost of producing an additional unit equaled the marginal benefit to the consumer. Yet economists recognized that market failure was relatively common. Monopoly might lead to inefficiently high prices and low levels of production; negative externalities like pollution might impose costs on third parties and keep prices inefficiently low.[88] The role of government, then, was to provide a legal framework that would keep markets competitive—by preventing monopoly, for example, or taxing pollution—thereby promoting allocative efficiency.[89]

The economists who advocated for this new economic style saw it as a neutral, technocratic framework for decision-making. They saw its goals—various forms of efficiency—as inherently unobjectionable, and its methods as objective and apolitical. Part of its power was that it could flexibly be applied to a wide range of policy domains, including many that had not previously been seen as "economic." And from a present-day perspective, in which the economic style is pervasive, this approach may not seem especially controversial.

Yet as the economic style was consolidating in the 1950s, and as it started to become influential in policy circles in the 1960s, it did in fact seem both novel and controversial to the uninitiated. This new economic style was unrepentantly utilitarian and consequentialist. Policies were not good because they were well-intentioned, or because they reflected important moral values. Instead, a decision was a good decision if it had the effect of maximizing economic well-being, defined in a particular way.

But this approach conflicted with common ways of thinking about policy, among both policymakers and the public, in at least three different ways. First, it clashed with widely held deontological views—that is, moral values that were considered ends in themselves, rather than good because of their consequences. "Human life is sacred," for example, is a deontological rule. If one subscribed to this rule, one could not ethically assign a dollar value to human life, as economists proposed, in order to weigh the costs and benefits of a government decision. Indeed, the very concept was so controversial in the 1950s that when the RAND Corporation reported to the Air Force on how best to achieve military objectives, it sidestepped putting a value on pilots' lives entirely, in the process opening its economists up to a different sort of criticism.[90] Similarly, if one saw pollution as morally objectionable, and something companies should not do simply because it was unethical, then allowing companies to compensate for their bad behavior by paying pollution taxes seemed wrong on principle.

Second, even in the absence of a pointed moral conflict, others might object to the economic style because they prioritized goals other than efficiency. While economists sought a legal framework that would promote efficiency within markets, for example, many policymakers—with the Great Depression still in memory—ranked stability as even more important. Other politicians wanted to protect small business because of its role in the civic fabric of small-town America, even if this produced market inefficiencies. In both cases, the resistance was not based on any moral objection to economic reasoning, but on having different priorities.

Last, even when others shared a goal with economists, they might reject the economic style in favor of a competing framework for thinking about how to reach that goal. During the War on Poverty, economists and advocates of community action both sought to improve the lives of poor Americans. But while most economists favored a negative income tax as an efficient way of reducing poverty, community action advocates thought that increasing democratic participation was a critical step to ending it. If one subscribed to the latter framework, a negative income tax would never be a sufficient response, however efficient it might be. Similarly, many policymakers and economists shared a desire to reduce pollution. But if one believed that Congress should set strict environmental standards because corporations would inevitably capture regulatory agencies, then designing procedures so those agencies could carefully weigh the costs and benefits of different regulatory standards was fundamentally misguided, because it would be politically ineffective.

The foreignness of the new economic style meant that its spread into policy circles was neither frictionless nor inevitable. Yet the consolidation of its academic version in the 1950s set the stage for that expansion in the 1960s and 1970s. During this period, economists working in the knowledge-producing esoteric circle of the discipline would continue to develop the economic style in new ways. They would apply its basic framework to novel areas, like discrimination and crime.[91] They would flesh out its methods, developing new techniques for valuing intangibles like outdoor recreation or human life.[92] And, increasingly, they would export the textbook version of economics into other professional schools—first law schools, then policy schools as well.[93]

These academic developments went hand in hand with the expansion of the economic style into new policy domains—initially, in defense, but soon in social policy and market governance. Here, advocates of the economic style would build on the networks and organizations established by the institutionalists and by Keynesian macroeconomists—but they would achieve a deeper, more pervasive influence. By first stabilizing a style of reasoning within the economics discipline, and then disseminating a basic version of that style both to professional schools and to organizational locations in and around government, economists in the esoteric circle nurtured a broader exoteric circle of advocates for the economic style—while retaining the centrality of core PhD departments as the ultimate arbiters of high-status economic knowledge.

The economics discipline itself would continue to develop and evolve. While it became ever more technical, it also gradually became more eclectic. Over the next several decades, the cutting edge of economics research would move further and further from the simple neoclassical model reflected in the economic style.[94] But the textbook version of the economic style—the one that had become standard in the 1950s—remained almost every student's introduction to economics. At some level, even more sophisticated students of economics internalized its lessons, and turned to it when navigating the difficult terrain of policy, in which attention to efficiency was typically in short supply.

The process of introducing the economic style of reasoning to the world of policy was a long, slow one: of building networks, building institutions, and building knowledge. Much of this work was undertaken by two intellectual communities—a group of "systems analysts" from the RAND Corporation and a looser network of industrial organization economists, initially centered at Harvard. Both groups were grounded in the newly dominant microeconomic framework, but each focused on a different aspect of policymaking: the systems analysts on how government should make policy decisions, and the industrial organization economists on how it should govern markets. The next two chapters will show how these communities began to build ties with Washington, and how the changes they initiated would start to reshape not only government, but law and policy schools as well.

3

How to Make Government Decisions

The economic style of reasoning solidifying in the 1950s was rooted in academic departments at Harvard, MIT, Chicago, and other elite institutions—departments that produced the discipline's PhDs and decided what kinds of knowledge would authoritatively count as economics. But the intellectual community that would play the most critical role in bringing that style to Washington developed not in an academic institution, but rather at the RAND Corporation, a few blocks from the beach in sunny Santa Monica. This community did so by bringing its basic conceptual tool kit to problems that were well-suited to its rapidly developing mathematical techniques, particularly systems analysis.

RAND (short for Research ANd Development) was a highly interdisciplinary organization, but one in which economists played a dominant role. Established by the Air Force in 1948 as a contract research center to continue scientific research begun by the military during the war, RAND's mathematically oriented economists were tightly networked with the emerging elite of the changing discipline.[1] Over the course of the 1950s—just as the economic style was consolidating in the discipline—RAND's economists would develop systems analysis as an answer to the question, "How should government make decisions?" Systems analysis—originally short for "weapon systems analysis"—was a general approach to decision-making that started with questions like, "Here is the mission that some weapon must accomplish: what kind of equipment, having what sort of characteristics, would be best for the job?"[2] According to the experts at RAND, such "problem[s] of choice" could be answered through "systematic examination . . . in which each step of the analysis is made explicit wherever possible," in contrast with "a manner of reaching decisions that is largely intuitive." Its proponents described systems analysis as "quantitative common sense."[3]

Although economics was present at RAND from its outset, the organization was not initially centered on economics. Systems analysis began as a project of RAND's mathematicians and engineers. But RAND's early systems analyses were met with disfavor by the Air Force, and it was only when economists became involved that the organization identified workable solutions to decision-making problems that had stumped the mathematicians. Over the course of the 1950s, RAND's economists used their techniques to advance both answers to the Air Force's questions and their own influence within RAND.[4]

The economists' systems analyses were better received than the mathematicians', yet they nevertheless felt underappreciated by their patrons in the military. As they experimented with applying their tools to nonmilitary problems, their ambitions began to grow. In 1960, they hitched their wagon to John F. Kennedy's presidential campaign. When Kennedy won the hotly contested election, RAND's systems analysts soon found themselves in prominent positions in the Department of Defense (DOD), where they became Secretary Robert S. McNamara's "whiz kids."[5]

Led by Charles Hitch, former head of RAND's Economics Division and now comptroller of defense, the RANDites at DOD threw their energies into transforming systems analysis into a new approach to government decision-making called the Planning-Programming-Budgeting System (PPBS). PPBS began by specifying the broad goals of an agency or office; identifying the various programs that might be used to achieve those goals; quantifying, to the extent possible, the cost-effectiveness of those alternative programs; and then using that information as a guide to budgeting.[6] Although PPBS's fast rollout at the Pentagon was met with some resistance, within its first few years it had been widely credited with improving decision-making throughout the DOD. In 1965, President Lyndon B. Johnson announced that he would be implementing PPBS across the entire executive branch.[7]

Over the next two years, PPBS made a huge splash in Washington. According to one observer, it "probably caused as noisy a disturbance . . . as any administrative idea since performance budgeting twenty years earlier."[8] As it spread, it propagated the economic style of reasoning it was based on and created new locations for its reproduction—first, in new analytic offices across the executive branch, then through the establishment of graduate programs in public policy, and last through the expansion of policy analysis in Congress. These offices were typically led by economics PhDs, which both linked them to the academic discipline and provided an employment pipeline for young researchers graduating from the new masters of public policy programs.

The spread of PPBS, and the economic style it carried with it, did not occur without conflict. The systematic, quantitative approach to decision-making that it embraced was deeply unfamiliar to most people in government. Agencies were not used to thinking of their activities either in terms of measurable goals or cost-effective means of achieving those non-existent goals—and often had no real desire to do so. Others criticized PPBS for its focus on what could be quantified and its tendency to disregard the rest, regardless of the relative importance of the unquantifiable. And last, while PPBS professed to be a neutral, apolitical decision-making tool, in practice it tended to centralize power within agencies while also providing window dressing for traditional behind-the-scenes politicking.

Within a few years, it was becoming clear that PPBS, as well as systems analysis more generally, could not deliver on its lofty promises. Rationalizing government decision-making, it turned out, was even harder than anticipated. The shine began to fade, and in 1970, President Richard Nixon quietly reversed LBJ's order. Yet the organizational changes precipitated by PPBS would long outlast the technique itself. The analytic offices created to implement it, and the graduate programs developed to staff them, live on to the present. While PPBS was, as a management tool, mostly a failure, it linked the economics discipline to the world of policy in lasting ways and created permanent homes in Washington for the new economic style of reasoning.

Inventing Systems Analysis at RAND

The RAND Corporation's exotic place in the Cold War imagination was captured most evocatively in the 1964 movie *Dr. Strangelove*, in which the title character reports on a study of a "doomsday machine" commissioned from the "Bland Corporation." The organization itself was an odd hybrid of laid-back California openness (a 1959 feature in *Life* noted, "Staff members like to lunch in the patios") and Cold War security (the same feature also emphasized that "many of the rooms are barricaded against even RAND employees who do not have the proper clearance").[9] Its initial mission, though, was to

FIGURE 1. The caption of this image, from the May 11, 1959, issue of *Life* magazine, reads: "After-hours workers from RAND meet in home of Albert Wohlstetter (*foreground*), leader of RAND's general war studies. They are economists gathered to discuss study involving economic recovery of U.S. after an all-out war." Leonard McCombe / The LIFE Picture Collection via Getty Images.

conduct research in service of the Air Force, although the organization had a considerable degree of freedom in how it chose to go about doing that.[10]

Most of RAND's earliest work focused on hardware (airborne vehicles, rockets, electronics, nuclear physics), but one of RAND's original five sections, "Evaluation of Military Worth," tackled problems of decision-making: "to what extent is it possible to have useful quantitative indices for a gadget, a tactic or a strategy, so that one can compare it with available alternatives and guide decisions by analysis."[11] RAND initially conceived of the work of the Evaluation Section as applied mathematics, and as such, it was led by the brilliant and charismatic mathematician, John Williams.[12] Williams was interested in bringing social science to bear on these problems as well, though, and the Evaluation Section was soon split into three divisions: Mathematics, Social Science, and Economics.[13]

RAND proposed to answer the Air Force's questions about strategic decisions through an approach it called systems analysis. While systems analysis drew on the mathematical tools of operations research that had rapidly developed during the war, systems analysis was more open-ended and "future-oriented."[14] Economist Malcolm Hoag called the difference between operations research and systems analysis "less a matter of substance than degree":

> Consider, for example, the purchase of a house. . . . One aspect of that decision may be the choice of a refrigerator, and we may find that a space only 30 inches wide exists in the kitchen for a refrigerator, that the house is wired only for 115-volt current, and that no gas lines are available. Consequently our choice of refrigerators is very constricted, and for that reason the problem of choice may be fairly easy. On the other hand, if we are buying a new house, one yet to be designed, our choice of a refrigerator is quite a different problem. If we sit at the drawing board with an imaginative architect, the kind of house we can have, including a refrigerator, is wide-open. We are no longer constrained to think the refrigerator must be no more than 30 inches wide, and we can consider the alternative of a gas rather than an electric refrigerator, or even an electric refrigerator that will utilize 220-volt current rather than 115-volt if that alternative is relevant. Under these circumstances, our range of choice is far broader and the number of alternatives that are relevant is consequently far greater.[15]

RAND conceptualized systems analysis as the less constrained, more imaginative of these two types of decision-making.

Economists would soon become integral to systems analysis and to RAND, but they had not been central to the development of wartime operations research, its most direct antecedent. And the Economics Division did not play a leadership role in RAND's first attempt at systems analysis, headed by mathematician Edwin Paxson.[16] Completed in 1950 after three years of work, the Strategic Bombing Study sought to identify for the Air Force "the most efficient way for the United States to deliver nuclear weapons to Soviet territory."[17] Massive in scope, its core recommendation was that the United States should seek to saturate Soviet targets. In an era when atomic weapons could only be dropped from the air, the Air Force's best strategy would be to build a larger number of slow, relatively inexpensive turboprop planes, rather than fewer expensive jet bombers.[18]

Despite the Paxson study's technical sophistication, the Air Force rejected it. In seeking to understand the project's failure, RAND's leaders identified two primary issues. First, the Strategic Bombing Study sought to provide a single, mathematically defensible answer to a complex and evolving strategic problem. Doing so required the analysts to make fixed and unrealistic assumptions about a one-strike campaign using existing equipment. Second, the study struggled with what RAND called the "criteria problem": on what criteria would the "best" solution be determined? The Strategic Bombing Study chose to maximize damage inflicted per dollars spent, a criterion that ignored pilots' lives entirely. But pilots also disliked the alternative criterion proposed—aircrews lost per damage inflicted—for callously quantifying the value of their lives.[19]

RAND was initially somewhat complacent about its ability to handle these problems. But, as political scientist Charles Lindblom reported after an early-1950s visit, "[h]aving spent the summer tearing my finger nails on the rhinoceros hide of the criteria problem," it "is surely as tough as it is ever said to be at RAND and much tougher than could be inferred from the relative ease with which it is disposed of in systems analysis."[20] Soon, RAND's analysts became intensely immersed in an internal debate over systems analysis in general, and the criteria problem in particular.[21]

Finding a workable solution to these problems was what propelled the Economics Division to a central position within the organization. Division head Charles Hitch described what made economists' approach different:

If you post a military problem—say, the defense of the United States against nuclear attack—to a group of physical scientists and to a group of economists, my experience is that the two groups will set about solving it in strikingly different manners. The physical scientists will start almost immediately with the characteristics of the hardware systems alleged to be available, and with the design of analytic models (e.g., of possible air battles) to reflect and predict the empirical world. The economists, by contrast, will usually begin by asking what we really want to do; what our national objectives are; what broad alternative means there are to achieve them; what test or criterion we can use to select the best or a good one in the light of national objectives.[22]

The problem with RAND's system analysts, in other words, was that they were thinking like physicists, or engineers. To truly accomplish their mission, they needed to think like economists.

Hitch and his economist colleagues proposed a three-part solution to the problems encountered by the Strategic Bombing Study. The first involved looking for a handful of strategies robust to a range of possible conditions, rather than seeking one optimal decision under a specific set of constraints. The second was to embrace suboptimizing. A family trying simply to optimize its spending in all areas was bound to fail: "We could not write down the family's general utility function because the family could not tell us what it was, and we could not conceivably derive it from any other source."[23] But an economist might be more successful at tackling the smaller problem of optimizing the family's spending for an upcoming trip to New York, subject to certain constraints. Problems of military strategy must be broken down similarly.[24] The third, and most important, part of the solution made cost-effectiveness the ultimate criterion for comparing options. If the criterion of aircrews lost per damage inflicted had felt callous to Air Force pilots, putting a dollar value on their lives seemed even more so. But, argued the economists, only by making lives, equipment costs, and damage inflicted commensurable could one make a rational choice among alternative options.[25]

RAND's mathematicians and engineers recognized that, on this point, economists had a certain comparative advantage. Mathematician Edward Quade later recalled his work on a systems analysis conducted in 1951, just after the Paxson study, that also lacked an economist. When briefed on the study, the economists called it "naïve." "We didn't understand these things at all," Paxson said, so that the economists "were able to catch us in errors, show us where we were wrong, and make us look ridiculous."[26] Soon after, RAND produced its first systems analysis led and mostly staffed by the Economics Division. The Strategic Air Bases Study advised the Air Force on where it should locate the numerous bases it was expecting to build to stage its atomic strike force. While the Air Force had originally prioritized

minimizing costs, the study pointed out that the least expensive option—
building a small number of large overseas bases—would leave the Air Force
at greater risk of catastrophic failure if the Soviets struck without warning.
Using cost-effectiveness as the decision criterion, RAND argued that bas-
ing the strike force in the United States and placing refueling bases overseas
would best balance costs, strike capacity, and vulnerability to attack under
a variety of conditions.[27] The study created a different kind of tension with
the Air Force, not over its methodological choices but over its recommendations, which dissented from the branch's existing plans.[28] But within RAND
itself, the Air Bases Study, and the economic approach it took, were seen
as quite successful.[29]

The Economics Division's workable solution to the challenges of systems
analysis moved it to RAND's intellectual center. In the process, it expanded
dramatically. What began as RAND's smallest division in 1949, with fourteen
staff members, expanded to fifty in the following decade, even as two entirely
new departments (Cost Analysis and Logistics) were spun off from it.[30] Its
intellectually high-powered staff included, among others, Armen Alchian,
Harry Markowitz, Burton Klein, William H. Meckling, Alain Enthoven,
Richard Nelson, Thomas Schelling, Daniel Ellsberg, and Robert Summers.[31]

RAND was not primarily an academic organization, but its Economics
Division was tightly networked with the academic elite. Its lengthy list of
consultants, who often spent time in residence at Santa Monica, included
luminaries like Kenneth Arrow, Robert Dorfman, Carl Kaysen, Albert
Hirschman, Tjalling Koopmans, Wassily Leontief, Paul Samuelson, Theodore Schultz, Herbert Simon, and Robert Solow.[32] Indeed, RAND itself was
a place "to see and be seen," in Simon's words, in the "postwar quantitative
social sciences."[33] And within RAND, by the early 1960s, the Economics
Department (as it was renamed in 1960) "viewed itself, rightly or wrongly, as
the leader."[34] Hitch, who oversaw this growth, later recalled, "No one fore-
saw just how important the economists and social scientists would be. . . .
If they had, they might not have let us in."[35]

As some of RAND's economists came to see themselves as having solved
the major limitations of systems analysis, they developed ambitions to make
the techniques behind it applicable to a broader range of problems. Systems
analysis had been developed for military purposes, but, as RAND economist
Roland McKean noted, it was "closely related" to both operations research
and cost-benefit analysis. He described all of these techniques as tools for
resolving "problems of choice": "[I]n all such research an attempt is made
to trace out significant consequences of alternative policies that might be
chosen." As typically used, operations research compared alternatives for

business contexts, systems analysis for weapons systems, and cost-benefit analysis—which at this point had primarily been used to make decisions about the building of dams—for water-resource projects.[36] In the 1950s, RAND's economists, including McKean, began to see these categories of analysis as increasingly permeable.

As generally practiced up until this time, cost-benefit analysis was the domain of engineers and bureaucrats, who typically applied it to compare the ratio of benefits to costs for a given set of water-management options. When RAND's economists began to dip their toes into the realm of water resources, they brought the economic style with them and again, began to pick logical holes in the accepted methods of doing things. McKean argued that benefit-cost ratios were the wrong approach, because they put large projects at a disadvantage even if their payoff might be high. Instead, water resource analysis should maximize the net present value of benefits—the total value of benefits minus costs, adjusted to account for how far in the future the benefits would be received—a criterion that would eventually become accepted as standard.[37] In 1958, McKean published *Efficiency in Government through Systems Analysis: With Emphasis on Water Resource Development*, which later became "a sort of Bible for cost-effectiveness calculators."[38]

As Hitch later noted, "water is a good subject matter for such studies, because there's a lot of money involved and a lot of things you can measure."[39] But for McKean, and for RAND more generally, "water" came on the right side of the colon: it was interesting primarily as a place to apply systems analysis. Nor did RAND's interest in applying systems analysis to civilian governance end with water. By the late 1950s, McKean was collaborating with his Economics Division colleague Joseph Kershaw to extend systems analysis to the domain of education, where, unlike water resources, there was no antecedent for quantitative decision-making. Over the next few years, McKean and Kershaw wrote several papers on "the possibilities of making quantitative comparisons of education systems," and argued "for more work to be done toward estimating the 'input-output relationships' in education."[40] Increasingly, RAND's ambitions were becoming broader than the canvas with which the Air Force provided it to work.

To the Pentagon and Beyond: Bringing Systems Analysis to Washington

At the time that RAND's economists had begun to explore the application of systems analysis to water resources and education, the vast majority of the think tank's work focused on problems of immediate interest to the Air

Force, its major patron.[41] Internally, RAND saw its weapon systems analyses, led by the Economics Division, as a great intellectual success that demonstrated the power and flexibility of their marquee technique. But trouble was on the horizon: RAND's findings had begun to challenge Air Force priorities and doctrine—in particular, the viability of President Eisenhower's commitment to massive nuclear retaliation. RAND's economists were pointing out unpleasant truths—for example, that the entire U.S. capacity for retaliation could be wiped out with twenty well-placed Soviet warheads.[42]

The resultant tensions between RAND and the Air Force came at a time when RAND's systems analysts "continued to believe, indeed with increasing urgency, that their methods and ideas deserved elevated influence in the national policy structure."[43] Alain Enthoven, the young star economist who had written the report about U.S. vulnerability to attack, got "fed up" and left for a position in the Pentagon in early 1960.[44] Enthoven was not, though, the only person at RAND looking for new opportunities. Around the same time, Daniel Ellsberg—then a young RAND economist freshly arrived from Harvard, but later best known as the source of the *Pentagon Papers*—put his new colleagues in touch with the presidential campaign of Senator John F. Kennedy.[45] Seeing an opportunity to bring their ideas to a larger stage, a key group of RANDites began to advise the Kennedy presidential campaign without the knowledge of their Air Force patrons.[46]

This was a dangerous move for the systems analysts. RAND's relationship with the Air Force was already tense; if news of RAND's partisan loyalties got out and Kennedy lost the election, RAND might soon find itself without a sponsor. But Kennedy, more so than any president since Hoover, had an affection for expertise. As early as 1958, he had established an informal group of academic advisors in Cambridge, including a number of economists.[47] And the systems analysts' style—a form of Cold War liberalism that envisioned a strong role for government but embraced the idea that hardheaded, rational decision-making could improve it—was uniquely well-suited to Kennedy's politics. Signing on with the Kennedy campaign was, as much as anything, a calculated bet.

The bet paid off. When Kennedy was elected president in November 1960, he quickly asked Robert McNamara to serve as his secretary of defense. McNamara had just been appointed president of the Ford Motor Company in recognition of his use of scientific management to revolutionize the firm's operations.[48] During the war, McNamara had worked in operations research himself; these were the techniques he had applied so successfully at Ford.[49] He was primed to appreciate the potential contribution of RAND's systems analysis to Pentagon operations. And the Pentagon's exploding budget was a growing concern in the late 1950s, as Eisenhower's farewell address—which noted that "We annually spend on military security alone more than the net income of all United States corporations"—emphasized.[50] By the time Kennedy came into office, getting this spending under control was a top priority.

During the 1950s, RAND had worked to integrate the principles of systems analysis into the Air Force's budgeting process as well as more general types of decision-making. In 1954, David Novick, an original member of RAND's Economics Division, proposed that the Air Force use a "program budget," which would begin not with categories of expenditure (for example, installations, aircraft, personnel, petroleum), but would rather work backward from goals.[51] The budgetary needs of a program like the Strategic Air Command, whose goals could be specified, might be broken down into the types of planes that contributed to those goals (for example, medium bombers, heavy bombers, reconnaissance, fighters), with specific costs then worked out within those areas.[52] The general idea of program budgeting— starting with program areas rather than procurement categories—was not new. But the idea of starting with policy goals, using systems analysis to compare the cost-effectiveness of different methods of reaching them, and then working backward from there to make budgeting decisions based on the most cost-effective way of achieving those goals, was.[53]

The Air Force ignored Novick's recommendations. Within RAND, though, enthusiasm for program budgeting remained. For the next several years, Charles Hitch and Roland McKean worked on a book that would provide a clear, accessible argument for RAND-style "quantitative common sense" as applied to national defense. When published in 1960, *The Economics of Defense in the Nuclear Age* incorporated contributions from a number of RAND economists.[54] The book explicitly made the case for non-economists to adopt the economic style, both in military problems and in government decision-making, more generally. The authors explained, "Economics is concerned with allocating resources—choosing doctrines, equipment, techniques, and so on—so as to get the most out of available resources. To economize in this sense may imply spending less on some things and more on others. But economizing always means trying to make the most efficient use of the resources available."[55] *The Economics of Defense* emphasized "program" thinking (in Novick's sense), efficiency, opportunity costs, choosing the right criteria, the challenges of incommensurables (for example, comparing lives with dollars), the problem of uncertainties, and the importance of discount rates (an issue that water resource policy had long been concerned with). In other words, the volume synthesized the best that RAND, and the economics discipline, had to offer.[56]

When Robert McNamara read *The Economics of Defense*, its rational, quantitative approach resonated. McNamara almost immediately offered Hitch the job of assistant secretary of defense—comptroller.[57] As Enthoven later said of Hitch and McNamara's initial meeting, "I'm told it was love at first sight."[58] Hitch, eager for an opportunity to put his methods into action, accepted. His charge as comptroller was to design a centralized, program-based budgeting system for use throughout the Pentagon—a massive task that McNamara wanted ready to go in six months.[59] Building and launching this system would mean synthesizing Hitch and McKean's economic approach to defense decision-making with Novick's budgeting techniques.

To accomplish this ambitious goal, Hitch called upon his RAND colleagues. Alain Enthoven quickly transferred into the Comptroller's Office, where he would lead a new Office of Systems Analysis.[60] Henry Rowen, an author of the Air Bases Study that had helped make economics central to systems analysis, became deputy assistant secretary for international security affairs.[61] And RAND's Economics and Cost Analysis Departments (the former now under the leadership of Joseph Kershaw, and the latter still headed by David Novick) established a satellite office in suburban Maryland, staffed with old RAND hands and new recruits.[62] Other RANDites were "loaned" from RAND to DOD; as Kershaw wrote later that year, owing to such loans "perhaps a dozen RAND people have had a hand, and an important one, in many of the most important national security matters before the nation."[63] Reinforcements were brought in from academia as well; Merton "Joe" Peck, a Harvard economics PhD then teaching at the business school, soon became assistant deputy comptroller for systems analysis under Enthoven.[64]

Over the next couple of years, the RANDites worked overtime to integrate systems analysis into defense budgeting practice through what came to be known as PPBS, the Planning-Programming-Budgeting System. PPBS started by "planning" the military's broad goals. It then compared the cost-effectiveness of different packages of "programs" that might be combined to reach them. Program packages were, in turn, broken down into program elements, "outputs such as B-52 bombers, POLARIS systems, or Army airborne divisions," which in turn consisted of "a bundle of integrated inputs . . . 'a combination of equipment, men, facilities, and supplies—whose effectiveness can, in some way, be related to national security policy objectives.'"[65] Last, one "budgeted" for these basic elements in ways that would allow the broad policy goals to be achieved in the most cost-effective manner possible. Ultimately, this would produce a Five-Year Defense Plan intended to efficiently use the nation's resources in pursuit of its military objectives.[66] It reflected Hitch's, and RAND's, underlying belief that "only by using the economist's complex tools of analysis to judge the cost and efficiency of each alternative course can military commanders choose the best solution."[67]

PPBS encountered substantial resistance from career officers, especially given the perceived "arrogance" of the "young professors" in charge of executing it.[68] As one senior officer put it, "I am profoundly apprehensive of the pipe-smoking, tree-full-of-owls type of so-called professional 'defense intellectuals' who have been brought into this nation's capital."[69] PPBS also centralized budget decisions in McNamara's office, forcing military branches to compete against each other on cost-effectiveness, thereby reducing their strategic autonomy.[70] Military brass criticized the system for the limitations of its methods, their opacity, their disconnection from realities on the ground, and their potential for hiding political decisions behind neutral-sounding numbers.[71] Many in Congress also saw PPBS as a threatening power grab by the executive branch.[72]

Yet McNamara stood firm behind Hitch and PPBS, and the general perception in Washington—at least in its initial years—was that the program was a great success. Its implementers and fans wrote enthusiastic accounts in venues from the *American Economic Review* to the *Saturday Evening Post*.[73] It did not take long for others to begin looking with interest at these new, rational methods that claimed to improve budgeting and policy decision-making while also increasing control. Even in 1954, David Novick had emphasized to the Air Force that "[t]he military [was] selected solely for purposes of illustration" of his ideas: "The systems analysis methodology is applicable to other areas of governmental operations."[74] By 1962, he confidently— and accurately—predicted that "[v]ariants of PPBS may be expected to be adopted by other Government agencies," adding, "As a matter of fact, some agencies have already indicated more than a cursory interest."[75]

From DOD to BOB: Promulgating PPBS

John F. Kennedy was the president friendliest to expertise in several decades, and particularly to the advice given by economists. Under his administration, the Council of Economic Advisers (CEA) played an unprecedented role in policymaking, and he was the first to appoint economists to lead the Bureau of the Budget (BOB, the predecessor to today's Office of Management and Budget).[76] Lyndon Johnson was much more skeptical of academic expertise than Kennedy had been, yet it would be under his presidency that the economic style of reasoning—as distinct from the advisory influence of economists—expanded most rapidly.[77] PPBS was the means through which this expansion took place.

Kennedy's Budget Bureau knew about PPBS, of course. Economist David Bell, BOB's director from 1961 to 1962, worked closely with McNamara to implement the system at the Defense Department. His successor, economist Kermit Gordon, later emphasized that PPBS had influenced the Bureau "very much, very much!" even before it was rolled out more broadly. As early as 1963, Gordon had begun "an effort to press the agencies into a more systematic and rigorous approach to the evaluation of the programs they were running and an examination of the alternative strategies which were available to them."[78] But it was not until 1965, when Charles Schultze had replaced Gordon as budget director (making him the third economist in a row to lead the office), that BOB officials made the case to Johnson for a broader rollout of PPBS.

By that point, RAND economists had themselves become well-represented among BOB leadership. William Capron, who had spent five years at RAND and collaborated with Hitch before joining Kennedy's CEA staff, was appointed assistant director in 1964.[79] Henry Rowen, coauthor of the Air Bases Study, moved from Defense to take the other assistant director position in January 1965.[80] And when Capron followed Gordon to the Brookings Institution that summer, Schultze replaced him with yet another RAND economist, Charles Zwick, to serve in what Zwick later said had become "almost a RAND chair."[81] Thus by 1965, three of the top four positions at the Budget Bureau were held by economists, two of whom were alumni of RAND.[82]

When Johnson tapped Joseph Califano, then a young lawyer serving as McNamara's special assistant at Defense, to serve as his top domestic advisor, it provided the perfect opportunity to move things forward. As Califano described it, "[t]here was a happy coincidence of people. Harry Rowen, who had been a PPBS man in the Pentagon, was an assistant budget director. . . . Charlie Schultze had just begun as budget director; he and I started within a few weeks of each other with the same idea" about expanding the use of PPBS.[83]

By the summer of 1965, when the decision took place, Johnson's Great Society was well under way. Antipoverty and civil rights legislation had been passed the previous year, the Elementary and Secondary Education Act a few months before, Medicare and Medicare were created that summer, and the Higher Education Act was in the pipeline. At the same time, the political mood was just beginning to shift. Republicans' nomination of conservative Barry Goldwater as their 1964 presidential candidate suggested a new interest in limiting, not expanding, government—at least in some quarters. And with spending on Vietnam starting to ramp up, some Democrats were starting to feel the tension between guns and butter as well.

The leaders of the Budget Bureau were appointed by a Democratic president. They were not, in principle, anti-government. They believed government could and should be used to solve social problems. But, by virtue of their institutional location as holders of the purse strings, they were also concerned with cost and efficiency. In the case of the economists, their professional training also inclined them in this direction. Although Schultze did not come from RAND—he earned a 1960 PhD from the University of Maryland and had spent most of his career to date in government—he believed that promoting efficiency in government was, in fact, economists' comparative advantage.[84] While systems analysis may have come from RAND, it resonated with Schultze—as it would with other trained economists—who intuitively saw it as a better way of making government decisions.

When Schultze and Rowen pitched PPBS to President Johnson, it was with several purposes in mind—certainly rationalization of budgetary decisions, but also centralization of budgetary control (as BOB unsurprisingly favored) and as a counterweight to the more expansionary tendencies of the War on Poverty. They recommended each department develop a five-year plan with specific goals, and Califano strongly endorsed the recommendation.[85] On August 25, 1965, at a cabinet meeting followed by a press conference, President Johnson ordered nearly all of the executive branch to adopt PPBS, saying, "This system will improve our ability to control our programs and our budgets rather than having them control us."[86]

As it had four years earlier at the Defense Department, PPBS caused quite a stir in the Washington bureaucracy. It created, for example, an unlikely best seller out of David Novick's new book *Program Budgeting*, with federal agencies alone ordering 5,000 copies in the month after PPBS was announced.[87] As one observer noted, "There were training courses galore to convert budgeteers (and many others) into PPBSers, a plethora of new monographs, case studies, and texts, and many new university courses and programs in pursuit of the new light."[88] By the middle of 1968, the General Accounting Office (GAO) identified about 1,000 full-time equivalent employees outside the Defense Department who were devoted to the implementation and management of PPBS.[89]

Yet while PPBS created a great deal of activity around its implementation, its use in most agencies remained superficial. The rational quantitative comparison of the most effective means to achieve well-specified policy goals never became a guiding force for agency decision-making, for several reasons. First, most agencies saw it as the BOB power grab it was and responded with successful foot-dragging rather than a sincere effort at implementation. Just as military brass recognized that PPBS transferred authority to McNamara's office, the executive agencies perceived PPBS as existing largely for the benefit of the Budget Bureau. But while the bureaucratic hierarchy of the Defense Department limited internal efforts to resist PPBS, BOB's authority over the executive agencies was much more restricted. Indeed, a 1968 study of the implementation of PPBS found that the agencies that agreed most strongly with the statement that PPBS was implemented primarily to serve BOB's needs, rather than the agencies', were among those that made the least progress in adopting the method.[90]

Second, systems analytic thinking was in many ways even harder for non-Defense agencies, with their ambiguous goals and lack of economic expertise, to adopt than it was for the military. The experience of the U.S. Geological Survey was a common one: it found itself lacking in "well-defined objectives which could readily be translated into plans amenable to Planning-Programming analysis."[91] Its staff possessed expertise in geology and other fields of the earth sciences, rather than in economics or quantitative analysis. The Geological Survey particularly struggled with identifying its "output" and the value of that "output" to its users.[92] Many agencies never quite got the hang of it; those that did often succeeded by hiring former RAND staffers to show them the ropes.

Third, it quickly became clear to many agencies that, despite the reams of analyses they were dutifully producing and sending to BOB, PPBS was often window dressing for a more political budgeting process going on behind the scenes. The White House might propose a budget, but Congress enacted it, and the political process on Capitol Hill created a back channel for challenging the decisions produced using PPBS. This phenomenon further undermined agencies' sense that the exercise was useful or meaningful.[93]

Last, observers like political scientist Aaron Wildavsky criticized PPBS for promising rational, neutral decision-making that it could never achieve. In addition to highlighting its political effects, which the agencies were well aware of, such critics emphasized the important things—perhaps the *most* important things—that couldn't be measured, and thus were ignored in cost-effectiveness calculations. And they emphasized that far from being value-free, systems analysis valued a particular sort of efficiency, one that treated the marketplace was the correct arbiter of worth, and the existing distribution of income as appropriate.[94] Agencies, too, were reluctant to accept that the only contributions that mattered were those that could be counted in dollars, and that cost-effectiveness was the best criterion for evaluating what they did.

When BOB and the GAO independently surveyed agencies about their implementation of PPBS in 1969, "[t]he scorecard was dismal."[95] While twenty of twenty-one agencies examined had developed *some* kind of PPBS framework as Johnson had required, only three had made "substantial progress" toward implementation.[96] The long-term impacts of PPBS would be large, but they would take place through the introduction of new offices and types of personnel, not the budgeting system itself. In 1971, President Richard Nixon quietly eliminated the requirement for PPBS. With the exception of the Defense Department, it quickly fell out of use across the government.[97]

On its own terms, PPBS was largely a failure. Although elements of its approach would be integrated into later fads like zero-based budgeting and management by objectives, it was never a real driver of budget decisions. It certainly did not rationalize the budgeting process so that policymakers were choosing the most efficient means to achieve well-specified ends. Yet the effort to implement PPBS had enormous indirect impact in disseminating the economic style of reasoning throughout the federal government. This took place through two distinct pathways: organizational change that created beachheads for economic reasoning, first in the executive agencies and eventually in Congress; and the creation of a new academic discipline of public policy that would train a future generation of policymakers in the basic logic of economics.

A Beachhead for the Economic Style in the Executive Branch

When Johnson announced the widespread rollout of PPBS, he also told his cabinet heads, "[E]ach of you will need a Central Staff for Program and Policy Planning accountable directly to you."[98] In the months that followed, departments scrambled to find staff who could fill such a role and help implement the new and largely unfamiliar budgeting system.

A few agencies—NASA, the National Science Foundation, the Department of Labor—did this without changing their organizational structure.

Most, though, created some kind of new office analogous to the Office of Systems Analysis that Hitch and Enthoven had established at DOD—often reporting, as Johnson had implied, directly to a department secretary.[99] These offices had a variety of names, and were frequently renamed over the years. Often, though, they contained words like "policy," "planning," "program," or—especially a few years later—"evaluation."[100] Collectively, I will call them policy planning offices (PPOs).

Few people already working in the executive branch had the relevant skills for implementing PPBS, so department heads looked elsewhere for the new offices' leadership. One popular option was to turn directly to RAND. The Department of Health, Education, and Welfare (HEW), for example, tapped William Gorham, who had spent nine years as an economist in RAND's Cost Analysis Department before moving to Defense in 1962 as head of its new policy planning office.[101] At the new Office of Economic Opportunity (OEO), which was leading the War on Poverty, Joseph Kershaw, chair of RAND's Economics Department, was chosen for the analogous position.[102] When Kershaw moved to Washington, he brought economist Robert Levine, an "old friend" and former RAND colleague, along as his deputy.[103] As Charles Zwick, former RANDite and soon-to-be BOB director, noted, "you can see we had a certain amount of incest going on here at this point in RAND."[104]

Agencies that did not have the good fortune to hire a systems analyst trained at RAND typically turned to the next best thing: someone with graduate education in economics. The new Department of Housing and Urban Development (HUD), for example, hired William B. Ross, who held a graduate degree in economics from Princeton.[105] The USDA, which had a long tradition of economic analysis, appointed its own Howard Hjort, who also had graduate economics training.[106] While these economists may not have been the "whiz kids" of RAND, they shared an educational background that made the cost-effectiveness, choice-among-alternatives approach of PPBS seem natural. They also possessed the skill set conducive to making such comparisons.

The new offices varied in size, organizational location, degree of support from agency leadership—and effectiveness. A handful, mostly in social policy, "ma[d]e substantial progress toward implementing systematic planning and analysis" and had "staffs headed by individuals with acknowledged analytic and managerial skills."[107] In others, as a BOB study observed in 1969, "analysis . . . played a small role in agency decision making because systematic planning efforts [were] fragmented by relatively strong bureaus and other disintegrative factors."[108] Where they were functional, though, they introduced RAND's systems analytic approach to policy to environments where such thinking was quite foreign.

At HEW, for example, Gorham hired three Harvard economics PhDs— including Alice Rivlin, who would go on to run the Congressional Budget Office and the Office of Management and Budget—and a political science PhD. Collectively, the office began working "to create a tradition of, if you will, scientific decision-making, which hadn't been there at all." As Gorham later recalled,

> I interviewed in my office every single manager of every program of HEW. And I had a series of very simple questions like, "What is your program trying to do?" And it was amazing how few people had thought in those very simple ways. And after he answered that question, I said, "Well, what is it that you keep track of?" One of my memories: adult basic education, which was basically teaching people to read; it was literacy training. He'd say, "Yes, we're trying to train people to reach at least the sixth-grade level." That's a clear objective. "Well, what is it that you measure?" "We measure attendance." Well, attendance isn't measuring; I mean, that just says somebody's there. But that's the kind of conversation it would be.[109]

By producing program analyses of specific areas, like "disease control," Gorham's office tried to determine how best to spend additional funds to "show the highest payoff in terms of lives saved and disability prevented per dollar spent."[110] This was a radically different way for the department to think about its activities, and Gorham's office used the approach to advocate for particular programs: "Look . . . you've got a screening program for uterine cancer. For every dollar you spend you save this many lives. You also have a tuberculin program, in which you're not saving lives any more; you're far past the point where you're saving lives. This is a much better way to spend money."[111]

At a handful of agencies—the damning 1969 report on PPBS specifically pointed to HEW, USDA, and the OEO as exceptions to the rule—the new policy planning offices substantively shaped agency decision-making.[112] At the USDA, this success was assisted by the agency's long history with economics. Its Bureau of Agricultural Economics had, before the war, been "the most active and experienced agency in applying social science in government planning." The bureau was broken up in the early 1950s, but economists continued to be represented in very significant numbers at the agency.[113]

Howard Hjort, who led its PPBS effort, benefited from the strong support of Secretary Orville Freeman, and even the USDA's budget office—often the group most threatened by the implementation of PPBS—saw the new office as serving a useful function. As one budget official explained, "I have never seen a bureau which did not tend to defend its programs. Without an independent evaluation at the Secretary's office, no changes can be made."[114]

At OEO, the implementation of PPBS was similarly effective but less smoothly achieved. As a new agency, the OEO had no entrenched culture to overcome, but most of its initial staff came from activist backgrounds or had ties to disciplines like sociology and social work, which placed a higher premium on empowering poor people than on efficiency. Yet, as we will return to in chapter 5, the agency's PPO nevertheless became increasingly influential within the agency. As it did, it effectively reoriented OEO's focus away from community action and toward the goals and programs that made sense from a systems analytic lens, while also linking the agency more closely with academic economics.[115]

At other agencies, new PPOs were much less effective at their explicit purpose of introducing systems analysis into agency budgeting processes. But they nevertheless often created a foothold for economic reasoning in new locations—a foothold that typically long outlasted PPBS itself. The Department of Labor, for example, established a PPO that did not report to a high-level appointee and was initially ineffectual.[116] But when economist George Shultz became secretary of labor in 1969, he created the Office of the Assistant Secretary for Policy, Evaluation, and Research (ASPER) and prioritized increasing the department's analytic capacity.[117] During the early 1970s, academic economists Orley Ashenfelter, George Johnson, Frank Stafford, Alan Gustman, and Daniel Hamermesh all served in leadership roles at ASPER. The office became a leading player in intragovernmental debates about the effects of welfare policy.[118]

PPOs at other agencies served similar roles in seeding the economic style of reasoning in ways that had limited short-term impact but long-term payoffs.[119] The Federal Communications Commission's PPO, for example, would successfully advocate for auctions of the telecommunications spectrum in the 1980s.[120] The Environmental Protection Agency's PPO, created in the waning days of PPBS, would promote cost-benefit analysis of environmental regulation and develop the prototype for emissions trading.[121]

Even as PPOs failed to change budgeting practices within federal agencies, they changed how those agencies understood their problems. As economist Robert Nelson, a director of the Department of Interior's PPO, later wrote, the office "has been an advocate not so much of specific solutions as of a broader way of thinking and an overall outlook on the world. . . . This outlook, derived in significant part from economics, is often at odds with other ways of thinking that are well represented in the DOI policy-making process."[122] By "creati[ng] an analytical staff at the department level," in Alice Rivlin's words, and bringing in "a group of people who were trained to think analytically and whose job it was to improve the process of decision making," PPBS created lasting homes for the economic style—and tied those homes not only to RAND and its systems analysts, but to the discipline of economics more broadly.[123]

From PPBS to Public Policy Programs

The rollout of PPBS across the executive branch quickly made it clear that the skills required to implement it were in short supply. While President Johnson told his cabinet members they would need a program planning staff, he couldn't provide staffers who knew how to conduct a systems analysis or were comfortable with cost-effectiveness thinking. It quickly became clear to the Budget Bureau, which was in charge of PPBS's implementation, that ordinary government employees with no particular background in economics, operations research, or systems analysis would need to be brought up to speed.

BOB's Program Evaluation Staff, who were supervising the rollout, began making plans for how to train these neophytes almost immediately. Within five months, they had begun planning a range of courses, ranging from two-day seminars for these who merely needed familiarity with basic PPBS concepts, to a nine-month residential program for midcareer staffers who wanted serious training in policy analysis.[124] Within a year, 2,000 government managers had taken the short class, and another 300 had undergone a three-week training at the University of Maryland, Harvard Business School, or the Naval Postgraduate School. Some eighty agency employees were also beginning an academic-year program at one of seven universities across the country.[125]

While the two-day seminars were necessarily superficial, the three-week course had slightly more ambitious goals. In addition to introducing PPBS, the course would "provide the student with a grasp of the underlying economic base of program budgeting" and "introduce the student to quantitative approaches to management planning and control, and improve his ability to communicate intelligently with quantitative analysts."[126] By mid-1968, nearly 1,100 people had enrolled.[127] Many reported that learning "economic concepts" had been the "greatest professional benefit" of the course, and large majorities of those who completed the training agreed those economic concepts had influenced their thinking about government programs in terms of outputs, cost, objectives, and, especially, alternatives.[128]

But while it reached the fewest people, it was the academic-year program that had the greatest long-run impact: less because of who it trained than what it led to. The "Mid-Career Educational Program in Systematic Analysis" (EPSA) was initially offered at Carnegie Tech (soon to become Carnegie Mellon), Chicago, Harvard, Maryland, Princeton, Stanford, and Wisconsin.[129] While each university proposed its own course of study, the programs shared a similar core: "mathematics (either as a prerequisite or as part of the curriculum), macroeconomics, microeconomics, public expenditure theory, and a workshop in benefit-cost and systems analysis."[130]

EPSA was not especially successful as a program for teaching government employees to become systems analysts. The executive agencies (who had to pay for employees to attend) had to be strong-armed into participating.[131] For their part, some universities were disappointed with the quality of students.[132] Several of the students, meanwhile, reported feeling like an afterthought at universities focused on other priorities.[133] A BOB-commissioned report by public administration scholar Allen Schick was critical of what students actually learned: "At most of the participating schools, EPSA is Masters-level education in Economics, with a heavy dosage of econometrics," but "excessive reliance on economic skills robs PPB[S] of its utility for public decision makers."[134] But the shortcomings of the EPSA program did little to deter the BOB's desire for a new curriculum centered on program budgeting. Schick's report declared: "We must coin a new discipline."[135] In this new discipline, "economics must have the leading position," but "[m]any other disciplines must be brought to bear."[136]

There was, of course, an applied discipline of government already in existence: public administration. The first public administration programs had been founded in the nineteenth century, and the field's professional association was established in 1939.[137] Yet public administration, while well-established, taught a very different set of skills than PPBS required. Focused on management, such programs intentionally avoided questions of what policy should be, or of its efficacy, in favor of "training neutrally competent personnel."[138]

Advocates of systems analysis tended to be critical of public administration for lacking a "clear conceptual identity" or even a coherent curriculum.

A mid-1970s survey found "little consistency in core course requirements and (that) several programs have no core requirement at all."[139] Fans of RAND-style policy analysis called public administration "low in quality and academic prestige," and found its "courses short on sophistication, lacking theory of any power, devoid of quantitative analysis or, indeed, rigorous analysis of any kind, generally unconcerned about costs and rarely weighing them against benefits, and always fearful of dealing with policy."[140] As RAND economist Burton Klein told the field's professional association in 1967, "of one thing I am fairly certain. If public administration is ever to get to grips with the problem, it will have to be by . . . substituting an entirely new line of thinking essentially based on the insights that lawyers and economists have gained."[141]

The implementation of PPBS shook up the field of public administration. As Joel Fleishman, a founder of Duke's program, put it, PPBS "was instantly perceived by alert academics in key institutions as a potential market for universities to supply with graduates, a market likely to grow even larger. Moreover, it was a market for a fairly well-defined product—persons trained to do analyses like those done at RAND!"[142] Between 1967 and 1972, about a dozen new academic programs were rolled out, primarily at elite institutions, to meet this perceived need—not in the suspect discipline of public administration, but in an entirely new field: public policy.[143]

The emergence of these new programs was not the result of an organized project. As one founder said, their creation "all seemed to happen at once, apparently without any prearranged effort."[144] There was, though, "some exchange of ideas among the principals . . . [p]artly through various associations with the RAND Corporation."[145] Indeed, a proposal for what would become the University of Michigan's school of public policy was first published as a RAND discussion paper in 1968.[146]

Some of the new programs were at institutions (Harvard, Michigan, Minnesota) that already had schools of public administration, while others (Berkeley, Carnegie Mellon, Duke) did not. A couple (Harvard, Carnegie Mellon) had also been EPSA participants, but most were not. One (the RAND Graduate Institute for Policy Studies, founded by Henry Rowen shortly after he left BOB) was an entirely new school.[147] Despite their institutional diversity, these programs shared an intellectual sensibility and a fairly unified curriculum, "emphasiz[ing] analytical/statistical techniques and macro/micro economics," that overlapped heavily with the mix of courses included in the nine-month EPSA program.[148] One dean described the programs as combining microeconomics, macroeconomics, statistics ("packaged as 'quantitative analysis'"), and elements of operations research and decision analysis.[149] In other words, the new public policy programs were producing "RAND lite." Some early promoters even pointed to RAND's Air Bases Study "as the implicit model of the kind of analysis graduates should be capable of doing and, perhaps, as a model of the process of policy making and implementation desirable for government."[150]

During the 1970s, the new discipline would achieve maturity, establishing its own journals and professional associations.[151] By 1976, more than 100 universities offered degrees in "policy studies," and in the 1980s the Association for Public Policy Analysis and Management found that 150 schools had moved at least to labeling their programs as "public policy."[152] By 1990, about a thousand new masters of public policy (MPPs) were being produced each year—roughly the same number as economics PhDs.[153] These public policy programs were producing a new breed of analyst: not economists, but comfortable with an economic style of reasoning; focused on choice among alternatives, cost-effectiveness, and quantitative analysis. These holders of the new MPP degree had "little difficulty finding places in the governmental system."[154] "It turns out," a Stanford professor noted in 1975, "that demand for these skills [analysis, evaluation, and assessment] exists disproportionately in the 'central analytical staffs' of the federal government: the Defense Department, the Office of Management and Budget, and HEW"—that is, the offices where systems analysis had taken off.[155]

The new public policy schools not only trained RAND-style policy analysts, but they also promoted the use of policy analysis to maintain demand for their graduates. Graham Allison, dean of the Harvard's Kennedy School of Government from 1977 to 1989, noted the schools' importance in "champion[ing] the role of powerful staff offices in government agencies which hired individuals who could perform these tasks [of systematic analysis of public policies], and would allow them to become influential in public policy making and implementation."[156] By 1990, holders of the MPP had become "legion" in "the various policy analysis and program evaluation sections" (that is, the PPOs), as well as in the Office of Management and Budget (formerly BOB). They were also common elsewhere in the executive branch and Congress.[157]

While the new policy analysts might not do work recognizable as economics to faculty in economics departments, their approach nevertheless reflected the economic style. The concentration of economics PhDs within policy school faculty moreover ensured that the two fields would remain closely linked. As policy schools themselves became institutionalized, the indirect ties between academic economics and the world of Washington were, once again, strengthened.

Analysis Begets Analysis: From the Executive to the Legislative

The executive agencies created PPOs to meet the demands of PPBS, and universities created public policy programs to produce graduates with the training to staff them. When the Nixon administration abandoned PPBS, the PPOs and the policy analysts remained. Indeed, many agencies soon realized that the numbers PPOs produced could be used as a tool for self-defense.[158] The competitive dynamic that resulted, in which offices expanded their capacity for policy analysis in order to defend themselves from other offices wielding competing numbers, contributed to the further growth and spread of analytic offices over the next decade, not only within the executive branch but in Congress as well. While this did not rationalize decision-making, as the architects of PPBS had once hoped, it did allow the economic style of reasoning to take root in new locations.

This competition unfolded in multiple ways. At times, the battle of the analysts took place within a single government agency. HEW, for example, had a main PPO located within the Office of the Assistant Secretary for Planning and Evaluation (ASPE), as well as an Office of Program Planning and Evaluation, located in the Office of Education. The two offices had conflicting interests: ASPE wanted to gather information that might drive changes in federal or local educational policies, but the Office of Education's PPO sought data to defend the programs it administered.[159] ASPE wanted to take a cost-effectiveness approach to evaluating Title I (of the Elementary and Secondary Education Act (ESEA), which funded schools with many low-income students), but struggled to identify inputs, outputs, and even the right population to study; the Office of Education began by trying to measure test scores, but when that proved difficult, turned to case studies of exemplary projects—a less analytical approach it took "over [assistant secretary for planning and evaluation] Alice Rivlin's dead body."[160] By 1972, HEW had spent more than $50 million evaluating Title I, but as one Office of Education evaluator confessed, evaluation had been "prostituted to such an extent now that it can't possibly have an impact . . . because everyone knows it is just fun and games."[161]

More commonly, the analytic arms race took place across agencies, not within them. A few years later, during the Carter-era debate over welfare

reform, ASPE found itself in a similar competition with ASPER, its counterpart at the Department of Labor. While HEW favored a negative income
tax approach to welfare policy, Labor preferred a jobs program.[162] Because
ASPE had been developing computer models to simulate the effects of welfare policy changes since the 1960s, the office had considerable capacity to
analyze the potential effects of reform proposals.[163] Lacking such capacity,
ASPER now beefed up its resources and began to develop its own microsimulation model as a way to counter ASPE's position.[164] Unsurprisingly,
while ASPE's model suggested that a jobs program would cost more than
cash assistance, ASPER's said just the reverse.[165] The competition failed to
provide decisive knowledge about the effects of policy decisions, but did
support the growth of policy analysis at Labor.

But the expansion of analysis was not only a phenomenon of the executive branch. Analysis begat analysis within the legislative branch as well.
Indeed, by the end of the Reagan era, which saw cutbacks in the analytic
capacity of the executive branch, Congress had arguably become the branch
with the greatest analytic resources.

Congress initially resisted analysis. Senators and representatives (accurately) saw McNamara's introduction of PPBS as an attempt to increase his
influence over budget decisions at the expense of their own. Their anger
was intensified when McNamara declined to share key reports of the DOD's
Office of Systems Analysis with Congress, arguing that they were privileged
recommendations for the president alone.[166] By 1967, the Senate Subcommittee on Security and International Operations had launched a series of
hearings challenging DOD's use of PPBS.[167]

Apart from conducting hearings, Congress attempted to reassert its control by limiting funding for executive-branch analysis. At the same time, the
legislative branch began—very slowly at first—to develop its own analytic
capacity.[168] The General Accounting Office, a Congressional office established in 1921, was the first site of this shift. In the decades after World War II,
the GAO was, as its name suggested, actually an office of accountants, who
audited the books of government agencies and consulted on their accounting
needs.[169] This changed in 1966, when President Johnson appointed Elmer B.
Staats, who as deputy director of the Budget Bureau had helped Schultze
implement PPBS, to the fifteen-year term of comptroller general, head of
the GAO.[170] Although Staats held a PhD in political economy, not economics proper, he favored the use of systems-analytic techniques to help "top
decisionmakers to visualize the full implications of alternative courses of
action."[171]

Under Staats's leadership, Congress began to turn to the GAO as an in-house source of policy analysis and evaluation, first through a major study of the poverty program.[172] In 1970, Congress authorized the GAO to conduct cost-benefit studies of government programs, and further expanded its analytic responsibilities in 1974.[173] This shift brought with it a diversification of expertise. In 1968, nearly all (96 percent) of GAO's professional staff were accountants, with the rest lawyers. That year, the organization hired its first professionals from other fields: eleven management analysts, nine mathematicians, six economists, two statisticians, and one engineer.[174] By 1977, only 64 percent of GAO professionals were accountants or lawyers.[175]

Neither economists nor the economic style of reasoning ever dominated the GAO. But the agency did become friendlier to the approach, particularly in its new focus on cost-effectiveness. While the old guard was accounting-driven, investigative, and fact-focused, the newcomers were "social scientists educated in public administration or economics and trained as policy specialists."[176] As one GAO accountant reflected, "When I worked with an economist, I found that we thought on different wavelengths."[177]

Nor was the GAO the only Congressional office to move in an analytic direction in this period. The Legislative Research Service, which conducted research for individual members of Congress, was in 1970 renamed the Congressional Research Service (CRS) and given "new responsibility to provide policy analysis." In 1972, Congress also created the Office of Technology Assessment (OTA), meant to analyze the effects of technological change.[178] Neither CRS nor the OTA had a particular orientation toward economics. But the Congressional Budget Office (CBO), established in 1974, would become a key site for institutionalizing the economic style in Congress, as well as for linking academic economics with the world of policy.

The CBO was a product of intense budget conflicts between Congress and President Nixon in the early 1970s. To restrict or even eliminate programs he did not like, Nixon impounded (that is, refused to disperse) funds authorized by Congress for the executive agencies—which Congress saw as a clear infringement on its power of the purse.[179] Among other responses to this interference with its authority, Congress created the CBO as an attempt to reassert control over the budget.[180] The exact responsibilities of the new organization were, though, left quite vague. While the House of Representatives saw the CBO as an organization that would simply produce cost estimates of proposed legislation, the Senate imagined something with a broader approach and more analytic capacity.[181] These different visions played out in a protracted debate over who would be appointed as the organization's first director.[182] The House's candidate was Phillip "Sam" Hughes, a "public administration type" whose professional background emphasized budgeting and accounting over economic analysis.[183] The Senate, in contrast, wanted economist Alice Rivlin, former head of HEW's ASPE, who had written a whole book on systems analysis.[184]

The Senate won. Under Rivlin's leadership, the CBO became an organization that not only provided cost estimates of legislation but that also had the autonomy to conduct economic analysis of the likely effects of policy options not currently on the table.[185] To carry out this mission, Rivlin hired four PhD economists into key positions, one a RAND alum and two with PPO experience.[186] Within six months, CBO had grown from two employees to 193, led largely by economists.[187] In addition to producing "scores" (cost estimates) of legislation, the office launched the annual volume *Budget Options*, which presented Congress with, as one veteran of the office put it, "various options to reduce the deficit . . . rang[ing] from the relatively small effects of replacing the dollar bill with a dollar coin to major proposals to means-test entitlement programs such as social security."[188]

In the late 1970s, the organization staked a claim to an expansive interpretation of its mandate when, on its own initiative, it analyzed President Jimmy Carter's energy plan, even in the absence of proposed legislation that needed to be scored. CBO's critical analysis established its broad role as an independent source of information willing to challenge the numbers being put out by the administration in power.[189] By producing such analyses, CBO not only demonstrated its own autonomy and professionalism but also defined the range of options it considered legitimate.

As the CBO settled into its lasting form, economics became firmly established as its orienting discipline. The ten permanent directors who have followed Rivlin have, with one exception, all held PhDs in economics.[190] Not only was the CBO "centered on the economist," it was directly tied to the academic discipline.[191] Rivlin established a bipartisan Panel of Economic Advisers to the organization, and appointed highly visible economists like Joe Pechman, Alan Greenspan, Barbara Bergman, Paul Samuelson, Lawrence Klein, Walter Heller, James Tobin, Albert Rees, Herbert Stein, and Robert Solow.[192] This helped both with recruiting employees who had the appropriate training in economics and with maintaining an ongoing connection between current staff and the economics discipline.[193]

These close linkages produced an organization whose allegiance was to profession over politics—in part because staffers did not typically come from Congressional offices, but had careers in research organizations, whether in government, think tanks, or universities.[194] The CBO gave economics a voice in the halls of power with no real equivalent in other disciplines, one that would shape policy conversations in lasting ways.

The Success of Failure: PPBS and the Creation of an Analytic Infrastructure

The systems analytic movement, and the Planning-Programming-Budgeting System it championed, was a powerful channel for moving an economic style of reasoning into Washington. Its new approach to answering a very old question—"How should we make government decisions?"—encouraged policymakers to clearly quantify the goals of policy and systematically compare potential pathways to reaching them in terms of their relative cost-effectiveness. As economist Robert Haveman wrote in 1976, "In effect, [PPBS] was the vehicle chosen by the executive branch to bring economic analysis into the budgetary and other allocative decisions with which it was confronted."[195]

PPBS was a failure at its stated goal of rationalizing the budget process around forward-looking, systematic comparison of alternative means to achieve well-defined ends. Most agencies never fully implemented it, it was never a real driver of budget decisions, and no agency besides the Defense Department continued to use it as a budgeting method much past 1970. Even so, its long-term effects in spreading the economic style—calculative, efficiency-focused, choice-within-constraints-oriented—were considerable. PPBS created new and lasting organizational footholds for economic reasoning, most immediately through policy planning offices, but indirectly in Congress as well. And it directly led to the invention of the academic discipline of public policy, grounded in microeconomics, which would train future generations of policy analysts to think, at least a little, like economists. It did this in the face of considerable resistance, both from those who found its approach unfamiliar, and from those critical of its intended and unintended effects.

The systems analytic movement was not identical with, or limited to, economics. Yet its success durably linked the world of policy with the economics discipline and enabled the movement of both people and ideas between the two. Its advocates were not anti-government or strongly laissez-faire. On the contrary, they were brought in by a Democratic administration and were generally optimistic about the capacity of government to solve social problems. As they saw it, PPBS, and systems analysis more generally, were tools for improving government decision-making, not a rejection of its necessity.

But it was not only through systems analysts that the economic style made forward strides in policymaking, although their efforts would provide a scaffold for others to build upon. Another group of economists would also come to Washington in these years, bringing their own answers to a different question, "How should we govern markets?" Although the two groups occasionally overlapped, and in the years that followed their paths frequently crossed, they came from different intellectual locations and entered through distinct sets of pathways. It is to this second community, the industrial organization economists, that we turn next.

4

How to Govern Markets

As RAND's systems analysts were developing their techniques for using economics to improve government decisions, another intellectual community was beginning to ask itself, "How should we govern markets?" This group championed industrial organization (I/O), the subfield of economics that studies the relationship between firms, industries, and markets.

Just as systems analysts brought a distinctive approach to thinking about government decision-making to policy debates, I/O economists had their own way of thinking about how the world worked—one with definite implications for governance. Politicians, in the 1950s, thought about the business world primarily in terms of industries—the automobile industry, the textile industry—with economic aspects, but also political and social ones, that governance must take into account.

But economists were coming to think about these industries first and foremost as *markets*—places where the production and consumption of goods and services was coordinated through exchange and the price mechanism. Well-functioning markets, they believed, would distribute resources in optimal ways. Firms would compete with one another to offer more desirable products and to lower costs, and the fluctuation of prices would encourage more production where there was greater demand, and less production where demand was less. This would, in turn, produce "allocative efficiency": the nation's resources would go into producing the goods and services that consumers valued most highly, at the lowest sustainable prices.

The industrial organization framework focused on trying to understand the conditions under which markets strayed from perfect, or at least "workable," competition, and failed to produce these desirable outcomes.[1] The framework implied that allocative efficiency was a socially desirable outcome, and that government's role was to create the legal rules that would promote it. This might mean preventing mergers that would lead to monopoly, or regulating prices in a "natural monopoly"—that is, a business like electricity transmission in which having multiple producers would be inefficient—so that firms did not abuse their market power by raising prices above a competitive level.

But a corollary of the I/O framework was that government rules promoting goals for markets other than allocative efficiency were inappropriate. Such rules might pursue particular social outcomes, as when politicians sought to protect small business because of its role in the civic fabric of small-town life. Or they might be political in nature, as when lawmakers advocated for breaking up large firms because they represented a dangerous concentration of power.

Industrial organization economics began to emerge in the 1930s and 40s at Harvard and was consolidating in the 1950s—just as the discipline of economics was taking its modern form, and as systems analysis was developing at RAND. But while Harvard was an important site for the field's development, industrial organization did not emerge from the hothouse environment of a single institution like RAND. Instead, it comprised a looser, more diffuse network, centered in economics departments but gradually becoming tied to both law schools and, eventually, Washington.

Even as Harvard's economics department remained a lodestar for I/O economics into the 1950s, a competing outpost was developing at the University of Chicago. The two schools shared some fundamental beliefs about the nature of markets. In particular, they understood achieving allocative efficiency as the main purpose of market governance. But the two groups took away somewhat different lessons for policy from their study of economics: while Harvard believed relatively high levels of government intervention were needed to ensure well-functioning markets (at least by present-day standards), Chicago prescribed a laissez-faire approach.

But despite their differences, their focus on efficiency meant that I/O economists from both traditions sought to move away from governing industries with attention to their social and political effects, as well their economic ones. And these economists would increasingly bring their distinctive ways of thinking about markets from the halls of academia to the halls of power in the 1960s and 1970s. First, they introduced economics into law schools, initially to the legal fields of antitrust and regulated industries. Increasingly, lawyers began to have some basic exposure to an economic style of reasoning—exposure they took with them into jobs in government and elsewhere. Next, members of this community increased the role of economics in two important regulatory agencies—the Antitrust Division of the Department of Justice and the Federal Trade Commission (FTC) of the Department of Commerce. Last, they established a network of I/O economists (and fellow-travelers) in Washington who would eventually come to play important roles in other government bodies that regulated industry, like the Department of Transportation, the Civil Aeronautics Board, and the Interstate Commerce Commission, as well as in the White House and Congress.

Initially, the Washington network of I/O economists was centered at the Brookings Institution, which was itself closely tied to the Harvard pole of industrial organization. By the early 1970s, though, the insurgent Chicago School of I/O was rapidly displacing Harvard as the dominant approach within the subfield. By the mid-1970s, the Washington network's center of gravity was shifting—from the center-left Brookings to the conservative American Enterprise Institute (AEI). But the liberal and conservative I/O networks overlapped considerably, with their shared prioritization of efficiency, and both favored deregulation of transportation and other industries.

The shift toward thinking about industries as markets took time to achieve. Most policymakers took for granted that the regulation of business required attention to social and political, as well as economic, factors. They were concerned, like Eisenhower, about the "unfettered power of concentrated wealth," and had some sympathy for the Jeffersonian idealization of small business.[2] They understood government restrictions on prices and competition, which were in place in a whole list of industries, as necessary in many cases to maintain stability and ensure fairness. Indeed, when a group of Harvard economists recommended removing such controls on the transportation industry in 1959, they acknowledged that this "depart[ed] sufficiently from the emphasis of the solutions usually suggested as to be heretical."[3]

Yet by the 1970s, advocates of the economic style were growing more influential. With their approach increasingly taught to lawyers, key offices staffed with PhD economists, and a durable network linking academia, think tanks, and government offices, economists' distinctive way of thinking about market governance became increasingly mainstream. In the decades that followed, particular schools of thought would rise and fall within industrial organization economics, but the broad influence of economic reasoning in market governance—and the locations and networks that helped to reproduce it—would remain. Through industrial organization, the discipline of economics would become durably tied to the world of policy along a second axis.

Industrial Organization at Harvard and Chicago

Mid-century industrial organization economists were, more than some of their colleagues, focused on practical questions—questions that would be helpful in thinking about the real, on-the-ground world of business. Their central interest was in understanding what made markets competitive and under what conditions they strayed from competition, allowing firms to raise prices and produce suboptimal outcomes. They tended toward topics that can only be called unglamorous—studies of economies of scale across twenty industries, for instance, or the decline of monopoly in the metal container industry.[4]

In marked contrast to the economists at RAND, who directly sought to shape defense policy, most I/O economists were oriented toward academic conversations. Nevertheless, the industrial organization community was certainly aware of the policy relevance of its work—particularly so in the period following World War II, when it was taken for granted that government would play a major role in governing industrial activity. In fact, far from idealizing free markets, the I/O community associated with Harvard in the 1950s took for granted that markets ordinarily operated under conditions of oligopoly—control of a market by a handful of firms—and imperfect competition. While its members were interested in understanding the causes and consequences of this at an intellectual level, at a practical level they wanted to know what actions could be taken to make markets work better. They often assumed that these actions would take the form of government interventions.

The Harvard School of industrial organization originated in the 1930s. It was developed in Harvard's economics department by Edward Chamberlin and Edward Mason, who, along with a generation of their graduate students, would go on to define it as a subfield.[5] Chamberlin, whose 1933 book *The Theory of Monopolistic Competition* took a marginalist, microeconomic approach to thinking about the conditions under which monopolistic behavior would emerge, provided the theoretical framework; Mason, whose leanings were more institutional and policy-focused, contributed his considerable administrative talents.[6]

Over the next two decades, their students would combine the two approaches, producing dozens of "industry studies" examining the competitive workings of particular industries, ranging from petroleum to tobacco to rayon to aluminum.[7] From today's perspective, these industry studies look almost institutionalist, with their extensive, detailed empirical descriptions of the costs of moving a ton of goods a mile on different types of transportation, or how pricing decisions were made by the "big three" cigarette companies.[8] They also still paid attention to non-economic factors that shaped the functioning of markets, like historical patterns with lasting effects and the beliefs of businessmen about how their industry worked.[9]

Yet these economists understood their work as departing from institutionalism in important ways. They saw their own approach as more theoretical than that of the institutionalists, with, as one observer noted, a "recognizable line of descent from neoclassical partial equilibrium theory."[10] And they were increasingly moving toward a more abstract conceptualization of industries, focused not on their historical specificities or the details of pricing decisions, but on the fundamental characteristics—numbers of competitors, or the extent of economies of scale—that allowed them to operate efficiently as markets.

The Harvard School's works collected loosely around what would come to be called the "structure-conduct-performance" (SCP) framework. The SCP framework began with the assumption that market structure (for example, the number of competitors) determined firm conduct (for example, whether firms raised prices above the competitive level), which in turn determined industry performance (for example, whether firms consistently earned "excess profits," which implied inefficiency).[11] Much of this work focused on the emergence of monopoly and oligopoly, but often within the context of practical issues around how market governance could encourage competition.[12]

The Harvard approach to industrial organization produced a pragmatic approach to policy questions that was in step with the highly regulated nature of the U.S. economy in the 1950s. At the time, antitrust enforcement was at historically high levels. Antitrust law dated back to 1890, when the Sherman Antitrust Act banned monopolization and the attempt to monopolize.[13] Since 1914, the Clayton Antitrust Act had outlawed companies from buying another company's stock if "the effect of such acquisition may be to substantially limit competition."[14] The 1950 Celler-Kefauver Act had extended this restriction by also prohibiting firms from acquiring rivals' assets under such conditions, chilling the climate for mergers considerably.[15] The government additionally exercised significant control over major industries, including rail, trucking, airlines, communications, banking, natural gas, and electricity. In many cases, government entities had the authority to determine whether firms could enter into markets and the prices that they could charge.

For the most part, Harvard School economists took this reality for granted; they assumed government would play a substantial role in regulating markets. At the same time, though, they also believed that competition produced economically beneficial outcomes by promoting efficiency, keeping prices low, and encouraging innovation.[16] They also believed that efforts to use regulation to achieve non-economic goals, as had historically been the norm, were largely misguided. Thus, their approach was not completely out of line with Washington's expectations that markets would be highly regulated. But these economists tended to favor less regulation than the status quo, and they strongly opposed regulation that pursued other goals—like protecting small business, or ensuring "fair" prices—that might come at the expense of efficiency.

Two important books published by Harvard economists in 1959 illustrate what the Harvard I/O perspective on market governance looked like; five of their six authors would go on to play important policy roles in the following decade. *Antitrust Policy: An Economic and Legal Analysis* was written by Carl Kaysen, a Harvard economics professor, and Donald F. Turner, a Harvard law professor (and economics PhD). It was the culminating product of an influential Harvard antitrust seminar, led by Edward Mason throughout the 1950s, and applied the SCP framework in a way meant to influence attorneys and policymakers.[17]

Antitrust Policy sought to use economics as a practical framework for making antitrust decisions. It carefully weighed several possible goals for antitrust policy, including social and political ones like ensuring "fair dealing" and limiting the broad social power of big business.[18] It then proposed that antitrust should instead focus on promoting competition in the broader service of efficiency. It would do this by limiting "market power"—the ability of a firm to "behave persistently in a manner different from the behavior that a competitive market would enforce on a firm facing otherwise similar cost and demand conditions."[19] The volume argued that decisions about whether market power existed should be made within an SCP framework, in which market structure determined firm conduct, which in turn affected market performance.[20] Building on this framework, Kaysen and Turner advocated for policies that were broadly in line with the high-enforcement antitrust regime that dominated in the 1950s. They proposed, for example, that mergers between firms that would constitute 20 percent of a market be made prima facie illegal—a standard that today seems surprisingly strict. Efficiency, though, was still the overarching criterion—Kaysen and Turner recommended exceptions be made if such a size would produce significant economies of scale.[21]

But while *Antitrust Policy* received favorable reviews from both economists and legal scholars, its reception was cooler outside the academy than within it.[22] Big business found Kaysen and Turner's recommendations to limit potential mergers threatening, with *Fortune* magazine calling *Antitrust Policy* "a disturbing new book."[23] The reception by antitrust lawyers in government was no more friendly. Here, the conflict was not over the degree of enforcement, but between a legalistic approach that saw the purpose of antitrust policy as fully enforcing the letter of the law, and an economic one that sought to identify what enforcement actions would help achieve market efficiency.[24] Many lawyers simply found the economic approach illegitimate, in conflict with the basic purpose of rule-based law, producing an environment "where economists were considered to be dangerous people."[25]

As Kaysen and Turner were writing *Antitrust Policy*, four of their colleagues—John R. Meyer, Joe Peck, John Stenason, and Charles Zwick—were working on another book that applied Harvard I/O to policy questions: *The Economics of Competition in the Transportation Industries*. Meyer was a recent Harvard economics PhD who had subsequently joined the faculty; Peck, Stenason, and Zwick were graduate students and instructors in the department.[26]

At the time, the railroad and trucking industries were heavily regulated at the federal level, with the Interstate Commerce Commission limiting entry into the market and setting the prices that could be charged on different routes. *The Economics of Competition* drew on detailed data from those industries to hypothesize, on the basis of industry costs and consumer demand, what the market structure would look like in the absence of federal regulation. Starting with the assumption that "an efficient allocation of resources" is the goal of regulatory policy, Meyer and his colleagues argued that, given the current state of technology, the market structure of transportation industries would be relatively competitive.[27] Indeed, they recommended a regime in which "[r]egulation in the strict sense would be retained mainly over rates in those very limited areas of transportation in which monopolies continue to exist," such as oil pipelines.[28]

While the authors clearly asserted that competition was preferable to government regulation where possible, they also accepted its need in situations where "workable competition" could not be achieved—for instance, in the case of pipelines.[29] Yet they also recognized that their proposition to mostly deregulate transportation was so out of step with political reality as to be "heretical."[30] The heresy was partly because deregulation conflicted with the interests of the regulated industries, which liked the stability it provided. But it was also because Meyer and his colleagues approached transportation policy with the same economic style that antitrust lawyers found so alarming in Kaysen and Turner's work. They focused on what they saw as a tractable goal—that is, the efficient use of resources—and they used economics to propose governance rules that would allow that goal to be achieved. But the regulatory system itself had been built around complex and conflicting goals that included not just efficiency but also a desire for stability and an interest in fair access to shipping routes—aims that *The Economics of Competition* considered but dismissed relatively quickly. As was the case in antitrust policy, the economic style would encounter resistance not only because of its policy implications, but because of the very way economists approached policy problems.

———

The Harvard approach to industrial organization was clearly dominant in both academia and policy circles by the 1960s, but a competing approach was developing at the University of Chicago. Both schools saw themselves as building on the neoclassical tradition, and conceptualized the world in terms of markets, more than industries. But Chicago I/O took its work in another direction, coming to different conclusions both about the nature of market competition and how it should be encouraged.

Even before World War II, the Chicago School of economics was known for classical liberalism and skepticism of government intervention. Yet in that era, it exhibited wariness toward big business. For example, Professor Henry Simons's 1934 pamphlet, *A Positive Program for Laissez Faire*, opposed business concentration almost as much as it opposed collectivism.[31] With the arrival of economist Aaron Director—a contemporary of Harvard's Chamberlin and Mason and devotee of Simons—at the law school, Chicago economics dropped that caveat. Director, a one-time socialist who had converted to a laissez-faire position as a Chicago graduate student, led a series of working groups: first the Free Market Study Project (1946–52), and then the Antitrust Project (1953–57).[32] While Director began this period with some ambivalence about the dangers of business concentration, he gradually worked out a different stance over the next decade. Stimulated by the studies of his students, Director gradually embraced the position that competition would tend to undermine monopoly, that barriers to entry were of little importance, and that high levels of market concentration typically reflected business efficiency, not exploitation of market power.[33]

During the 1950s, the Chicago group collectively worked out an alternative to Harvard's structure-conduct-performance paradigm, one with a different set of implications for market governance.[34] PhD student G. Warren Nutter, for example, wrote a dissertation that empirically challenged the common assumption that monopoly had been increasing in the United States since 1900.[35] John McGee, then an instructor, found that Standard Oil had not been engaging in predatory pricing at the time it was widely assumed to have been doing so.[36] More generally, Chicago I/O shared a neoclassical starting point with Harvard, but dismissed the Harvard belief that there was a meaningful (if not yet theoretically grounded) relationship between market structure, firm conduct, and market performance. Chicago's divergence on this point implied little need for strong government enforcement of antitrust law.[37]

Although the Antitrust Project itself would end in 1957, the intellectual momentum of these efforts continued to build. Director founded the *Journal of Law and Economics*, which became an important outlet for I/O research, in 1958. That same year, future Nobel Laureate George Stigler, who published extensively in industrial organization, was recruited to join the economics department.[38] Director's Antitrust Project students, moreover, were beginning to take positions at other universities; some ended up in economics departments, while others—including Robert Bork—went to law schools.[39]

At the same time, the broad Chicago approach to I/O—centering price theory, not market structure—was becoming more influential beyond the institution itself. In part, this took place through the building of ties between Chicago and other institutions. Yale Law School, for example, hired Director students Ward Bowman and Robert Bork in the 1960s. Chicago scholars were also increasingly networked with institutions whose economists had similarly free-market inclinations, including the University of Virginia, UCLA, and Rochester. And beyond academia, Chicago scholars played an integral role in the Mont Pelerin Society, an international network devoted to advancing classical liberal ideas against collectivism, and of which Director and Stigler, along with Chicago colleagues Friedrich Hayek and Milton Friedman, were founding members.[40]

Throughout the 1960s, the Chicago position remained a minority school of thought in industrial organization and the legal scholarship that was informed by it. A review of two major antitrust law journals from 1965 to 1970, for example, found ten economists or economics-focused legal scholars among the fifteen most-cited authors; seven of these were Harvard-type structuralists (Turner and Joe Bain, another Mason student, held spots one and two on the list; Kaysen occupied the fourth), while only two were associated with Chicago (Stigler, at number five, and Bork, at eleven).[41] Although its time would come, at this point Chicago's arguments about antitrust and regulatory policy were even further removed from decisions taking in place in Washington than Harvard's.

Eventually, the Chicago approach to industrial organization—with its strong laissez-faire implications for market governance—would come head to head with Harvard's approach, with its interventionist tendencies and its emphasis on concentration as an indicator of market power. But while the schools had different understandings of how economics applied to real-world markets and what policy lessons should be learned from that analysis, what they shared was as important as what they did not. For Harvard, as well as Chicago, market competition was fundamentally beneficial, and allocative efficiency its socially desirable outcome. Government should create a legal framework that would promote well-functioning markets, and not use its regulatory power to try to achieve potentially conflicting social and political goals. While Harvard and Chicago I/O economists might disagree on what sort of government rules would produce such efficient markets, they agreed that this goal was the appropriate one for policymakers to center, and that economics provided useful tools for thinking about how to reach it.

Bringing the Economic Style into Law Schools

Industrial organization economics, like systems analysis, would extend its influence via professional schools. But while systems analysis traveled first from RAND to Washington, and only then into public policy programs created specifically to meet the new demand for systems analysts, industrial organization moved from economics departments into law schools even before its major policy impacts began.

The separate fields of law and economics had a long and complex history by the 1960s. While some branches of law had virtually no interaction with economics, others—particularly those that governed economic institutions—had long traveled hand in hand with the economics discipline.

The story of law and economics in the second half of the twentieth century, then, is not about the initial introduction of economics to law, but about the introduction of the microeconomic style of reasoning more specifically, and about its spread to a much broader scope of legal scholarship and teaching.

The 1930s had seen an alliance between institutional economics and the "legal realist" school of law.[42] Legal realism argued that judges did not interpret the law using a handful of universal principles, as the previously dominant school believed, but instead that judges' decisions did, and should, reflect the empirical context in which decisions were made, as well as the effects of those decisions on the real world.[43] This perspective implied an important role for the social sciences in law. And so, during this period, the boundaries between (primarily institutional) economics and law were relatively fluid, with trained economists like Walton Hamilton and Robert Hale teaching in law schools.[44]

But as legal realism was entering its period of peak influence in the 1930s, institutionalism was already beginning to be eclipsed by neoclassicism within the discipline of economics. Neoclassical economics, with its abstract principles and—at the time—relative lack of empiricism, did not offer legal realists the kinds of tools they were looking for to help make decisions in real-world contexts.[45] Moreover, by the 1950s, legal realism was itself being displaced by the legal process school. This approach saw legal rules as being justified not on the basis of their empirical consequences, but on having been created "through a legitimate set of procedures by legitimate institutions keeping within their proper roles."[46] Legal process theory had little use for economics, whether institutional or neoclassical in character. The 1950s, then, marked a low point for interactions between law and economics.[47] Connections still existed, but they were fairly limited, largely institutionalist, and mostly in decline.

Yet it was just during this period of ebb that industrial organization began to build a new set of connections between departments of economics and law schools. Both Mason's antitrust seminar at Harvard, and Director's, at Chicago, used neoclassical tools to think about legal questions; both were located at the intersection of the two fields, drawing representatives from each discipline. Industrial organization, and antitrust, would be the entry point through which the modern economic style would first be introduced into law. Over the next two decades, economics would move from the margins of the law to its very center, coming to play at least some role (and sometimes a very significant one) not only in antitrust, but in almost every part of law.

As of 1960, Turner's and Director's positions as law school faculty with qualifications in economics were anomalous. They, along with Director student Ward Bowman at Yale, were the only trained economists with faculty appointments in the four most elite law schools of Harvard, Yale, Chicago, and Stanford.[48] All focused on antitrust. But at Harvard, Turner would soon have company. Already, his colleague Derek Bok had authored an important piece on "the merging of law and economics" with regard to the Clayton Act.[49] Now, in 1961, Turner was joined by Phillip Areeda, whose antitrust casebook took, in Turner's words, "[t]he explicit and recurrent resort to economic analysis [that was] vital to rational treatment of antitrust issues."[50] In 1967, the faculty would add future Supreme Court justice Stephen Breyer, who had just finished a turn as Turner's special assistant at the Antitrust Division, and who would also take an economic approach to antitrust, and law more generally.[51]

Economics' impact on law at Chicago was even greater. Partly, this was because the *Journal of Law and Economics* (*JLE*)—a publication which had no equivalent at Harvard—consolidated an intellectual community beyond Chicago's boundaries. But it was also because Chicago economists more rapidly applied economics to legal fields beyond antitrust. Although he was then still at the University of Virginia, Ronald Coase's 1960 publication of "The Problem of Social Cost" in the third volume of the *JLE* opened the door for scholars to apply economics to new areas of law.[52] Today the most-cited legal article of all time, the piece argued that, in the absence of transaction costs, private individuals in conflict over how to negotiate over externalities (for example, a confectioner whose noisy machinery disturbed the practice of a doctor next door) would bargain to the most efficient outcome, regardless of the initial distribution of property rights.[53] Coase's work, which until then had focused on standard I/O topics like the organization of firms, monopoly, and regulated industries, opened the door for economics to influence a wide range of legal issues, from contract law and torts to regulation more generally.

In 1964, Chicago Law hired Coase, who upon his arrival became editor of the *JLE*. This move marked the beginning of a rapid expansion of research at the intersection of law and economics at the university.[54] By the late 1960s, Chicagoans had applied economic analysis to corporate law, employment law, and even criminal law.[55] Economists like Gary Becker and William Landes were doing law-and-economics from the economics department.[56] And Richard Posner, who would go on to become not only the dominant figure in law and economics but the most-cited legal scholar of all time, had joined the law school faculty as well.[57]

Harvard and Chicago industrial organization were not the only points of origin for the law and economics movement. Yale's Guido Calabresi published a landmark article introducing economic analysis to tort law in 1961 that started a separate, fruitful line of intellectual exploration.[58] But the example I/O economists set led to the rapid expansion of the economic style into other legal fields. By the end of the 1960s, economics had become pervasive in elite legal scholarship at law schools across the country. A survey of articles published in the Harvard, Yale, Chicago, and Stanford law reviews found that the percentage that could be classified as "law and economics" increased from 6 percent in 1960 and 7 percent in 1965 to a full 28 percent in 1970.[59] The number of formally trained economists on the faculty of top-four law schools increased from three (of 134) in 1960 to eight (of 163) in 1970.[60] A substantially larger number of legal scholars saw themselves as doing law and economics, and that number was growing.[61]

Perhaps even more important for imbuing aspiring attorneys with a broad sense of how to "think like an economist," however, was the spread of economic theory classes in law schools. While in the late 1960s only four schools offered such a class, by 1973, fifteen of the twenty-two national schools taught one.[62] These classes, which might be titled something like "economic analysis and the law," focused on issues familiar to students of microeconomics: marginal utility, consumer choice, supply and demand, competitive markets, and market failures. They nodded, as well, to systems analysis and cost-benefit analysis.[63]

Law and economics would experience a second wave of development after 1973 with the publication of Posner's *Economic Analysis of Law*. This work not only applied economic concepts to a wider range of legal fields but argued that legal institutions themselves have, and should, evolve to increase efficiency and reduce transaction costs.[64] Its influence would continue to expand into the early 1980s.[65] But by the time Posner launched this new wave, much of the initial introduction of economics into law had already taken place. Students at leading law schools, and particularly those focusing on the laws governing industries—or, as they were increasingly being conceptualized, markets—were already being exposed to a broadly economic style of reasoning as important for thinking through legal questions. They would take this exposure with them as they moved out into the world, and some of them would bring the economic style with them to Washington.

Bringing the Economic Style into Antitrust Policy

As modern economics was beginning its move into law, the industrial organization community was also advancing the economic style in the government's
antitrust agencies. By virtue of their disciplinary training, I/O economists,
regardless of their lineage, believed that the purpose of antitrust policy was
to promote efficient markets by ensuring that firms could not exercise market power—that is, set prices above a competitive level. The two dominant
schools disagreed on how common it was for firms to be able to acquire and
use market power, how difficult it was for new competitors to challenge
them, and what government should do as a result. But they were in solid
consensus that the social and political goals of antitrust, which included
limiting the political power of big business and protecting less-efficient small
businesses, were bad policy and bad law.

Economists had been studying monopolistic behavior for decades. But
in the early 1960s, their influence on antitrust policy, and particularly the
Department of Justice's Antitrust Division and the Federal Trade Commission, the two agencies charged with enforcing antitrust law, was quite
limited. Instead, these agencies were dominated by lawyers who had no
systematic exposure to the modern economic style of reasoning. Antitrust
lawyers were not generally interested in evaluating whether existing law
was bad, or whether a particular merger would increase productive efficiency or reduce allocative efficiency. They were interested in winning cases:
prosecuting as many violations as the law would allow in order to gain litigation experience.[66] And, as employees of the executive branch, they set
the enforcement agenda for the Antitrust Division and the FTC within the
bounds of what their presidents would support.

Economists did have some presence at both agencies, but they were
economists from an earlier era. The FTC's Bureau of Economics had existed
in some form since the agency's inception in 1914, and the Antitrust Division hired its first economists in 1936. As of 1962, the latter had an "Economic Section" that employed twenty-six "professional economists."[67] These
offices, though, were established during the period in which institutionalism dominated government economics; furthermore, their staff was neither
highly trained nor highly ambitious. Instead, consistent with the institutionalist style, they were expert compilers of data. The main function of the
Bureau of Economics was to produce "painstakingly detailed descriptions of
the structure and business practices of a particular firm or industry"; such
reports could run to dozens of volumes.[68]

As the status of institutionalism had declined in economics, and the relationship between law and economics weakened, the status of economics declined within the lawyer-dominated antitrust agencies as well. In 1953, the FTC moved its economists out of the economics bureau, placing them under the direct supervision of lawyers, many of whom "saw little value in economic analysis." The Bureau of Economics subsequently became "the graveyard of the FTC."[69] Similarly, when Harvard's Carl Kaysen and a colleague were asked to report on the role of economists in the Antitrust Division in the mid-1950s, they found that "[t]hey really had relatively low stature": "[T]he lawyers thought of the economists pretty much as statistical clerks. . . . Because of the shortage of space, they even were housed separately, twenty minutes across town, so they had to come to work on a bus."[70] Even the directors of the economics offices themselves, in the early 1960s, emphasized economists' "support" role at the agency, calling them "assistants to the legal staff."[71] The type of economist that Kennedy was bringing to Washington—the whiz kids of the Defense Department—had not yet made it to the antitrust agencies.

The economic style would only be institutionalized in the antitrust agencies through organizational change. In 1965, Lyndon Johnson appointed Donald Turner as assistant attorney general of the Antitrust Division of the Department of Justice. He would be the first economics PhD to hold the position. Turner, by then forty-four years old, came to the job with a strong sense that the division, and antitrust policy more generally, should focus on pursuing cases that had a clear economic rationale. That meant moving away from the presumption that "bigness is badness," as those focused on social and political antitrust goals often presumed. It also meant that Turner did not encourage his staff to prosecute "every case he kn[ew] he could win," a position with which some in the Division "deeply disagree[d]."[72] Turner expanded the agency's policy planning office and asked it to review proposed cases to make sure they were economically, as well as legally, justifiable.[73] He also created a rotating "special economic assistant" position to bring in highly qualified young economists to advise him; future Nobel Laureate Oliver Williamson was one of Turner's special assistants.[74]

Turner lasted until 1969; his replacement, Richard McLaren, undid some of his efforts.[75] But when Nixon in turn replaced McLaren with University of Michigan law professor Thomas Kauper, more lasting changes began. Kauper was not closely associated with either Harvard or Chicago, but he held an undergraduate degree in economics and had also made the case for emphasizing economic goals in antitrust.[76] When the longtime director of the old-school Economic Section retired, Kauper replaced the Section with a new Economic Policy Office (EPO), and put his special economic assistant, George Hay, in charge.[77]

Hay, a young I/O economist on leave from Yale, turned out to be a talented administrator. For the rest of the decade, he would oversee the steady upgrading of economics at the Antitrust Division.[78] Although the EPO inherited many less-sophisticated analysts from the old Economic Section, Hay prioritized hiring of young economists with PhDs from elite institutions.[79] EPO also worked to introduce the division's lawyers to economics, both by bringing in outside economists to lecture and eventually through "a mandatory course taught by George Hay."[80] As this office gradually gained strength over the course of the decade, it became an important advocate for economic reasoning about antitrust policy, as well as an important employer of I/O economists.

As these changes were taking place at the Antitrust Division, economics was being substantially upgraded at the FTC as well. In 1969, a new round of critical reports of the largely ineffectual FTC led to a period of major reform, which saw the replacement of most top-level staff along with "nearly a third" of other FTC employees.[81] Critics from a variety of backgrounds agreed that the agency needed more, and better-trained, economists. A reorganization in 1970 established a new economic advisor position similar to the one that brought Oliver Williamson and George Hay to the Antitrust Division; it also created a policy planning office.[82] The FTC's old Bureau of Economics, now headed by well-established I/O economists, was also steadily expanded and professionalized over the course of the 1970s. H. Michael Mann—one of Turner's special economic assistants—was the first to lead the reorganized Bureau; he was followed by Frederic M. Scherer, a Harvard PhD and student of Joe Peck.[83] During the decade that followed its staff would double, from forty to eighty economists, and their educational credentials would improve substantially. In 1970, only a fifth of the staff held PhDs, whereas ten years later a majority held such degrees—increasingly at prestigious universities. The rest were doctoral candidates.[84]

By 1970, then, the status of economic analysis had begun to be upgraded in both the Antitrust Division and the FTC. This change would prove durable. Economists, along with lawyers committed to economic reasoning, would eventually manage to legally redefine the purpose of antitrust as promoting the efficient working of markets. They placed discussions of the political power of big business, or the protection of small business, outside its bounds. Liberals and moderates, not Chicago School conservatives, were at the vanguard of this shift. Initially led by Harvard's Donald Turner, these advocates of economics held no antipathy toward the government's involvement in markets. While Chicago School antitrust would become much more influential over the course of the 1970s, industrial organization had by that point already introduced the economic style to antitrust policy.

Bringing the Economic Style into Regulatory Policy

Industrial organization economics spoke to questions of market governance beyond antitrust. In the late 1950s and early 1960s, I/O economists began to argue that the government controls on certain industries—on who could enter the market, the prices they could charge, and the conditions under which they could offer service—might have negative effects. Accordingly, I/O economists began to build networks in Washington that would advance an economic style of reasoning about market regulation instead. That style, which centered allocative efficiency as the core purpose of market governance, implied that governments should remove price and entry restrictions in transportation and several other closely regulated industries.

Industry-specific regulation, like antitrust enforcement, was at a historical high point at this time. While the legislation that had created bodies like the Interstate Commerce Commission, the Civil Aeronautics Board, and the Federal Power Commission dated from decades earlier, such agencies had become increasingly important in the 1950s and 1960s with the rapid expansion of interstate transport and commercial airline travel.[85] That legislation, and the regulatory regime it produced, had sought to achieve social and political goals, not market efficiency. Each of the agencies had been created in times of severe economic turmoil and was intended to stabilize its respective industries and limit the consequences of "ruinous competition." The agencies had also been meant to ensure reasonably equitable access to what were seen as necessary services, like rail transport and electricity.

Price and entry regulation in these industries, as carried out by the federal agencies, had more-or-less successfully achieved the purposes it was designed to fulfill. But by the 1960s, policymakers' concerns with stability and equity no longer felt so pressing. Now, industrial organization economists argued that government action should center efficiency as the primary goal of regulating markets. Their analyses, which typically set questions of stability and equity to the side, increasingly showed that deregulating a number of industries—initially rail, trucking, and airlines, but soon natural gas, electricity, and telecommunications as well—would produce more efficient outcomes.

Advocacy for deregulation is often associated with a Chicago School, free-market approach.[86] But while Chicago School economists were indeed supporters of deregulation, industrial organization economists from Harvard and elsewhere were more directly involved in advocating for their approach in Washington in the 1960s. Liberal and conservative economists shared the view that industry-specific regulation—certainly of transportation, and increasingly of other industries as well—produced a net harm by limiting competition and keeping prices too high.[87]

On this point, the economists had good timing. In contrast with broad public support for antitrust enforcement, scholars from several disciplines were growing increasingly critical of industry-specific regulation in the 1960s. Political scientists and legal scholars like Samuel Huntington, Marver Bernstein, and Louis Jaffe began arguing in the early 1950s that regulatory agencies were often "captured" by the industries they were charged with overseeing.[88] They were joined, over the following decade, by both public choice theorists who provided formal arguments to explain why regulators might not act in the public interest and radical historians who saw government itself as largely subservient to the needs of business.[89]

Yet economists' way of thinking about regulation—as problematic because it interfered with competition and the price mechanism that would produce efficient market outcomes—was distinctive and, at least through the 1960s, relatively unfamiliar to policymakers. During that decade, though, I/O economists—particularly those associated with Harvard—would introduce their approach into Washington along two different paths. First, economists would come to play a growing role in transportation policy, just as new offices like the Department of Transportation were being created. And second, they would build a new Washington-oriented network, centered at the Brookings Institution, that would eventually become integral to a larger deregulatory movement.

———

Harvard industrial organization was well-positioned to make such inroads during the Kennedy and Johnson administrations. Edward Mason, the "grandfather" of American I/O, had particularly deep connections in Washington.[90] Mason had led the Research and Analysis Branch of the Office of Strategic Services during World War II, a position that put him in charge of fifty of the country's most highly regarded economists, including at least one future Nobel Laureate.[91] After the war, he had turned down an offer to serve as chair of the Council of Economic Advisers.[92] Instead, he returned to Harvard but retained his networks. His student Joe Peck later recalled Mason declining to be interrupted by a call from the president of the United States until class had finished.[93]

Thus, when John F. Kennedy, Harvard man and fan of expertise, became president, it is not surprising that many of Mason's students and colleagues found themselves tapped for trips to Washington. Unlike Mason, they tended to take the calls.[94] The requests did not always involve their capacity as scholars of industrial organization; Carl Kaysen, for example, served as Kennedy's Deputy National Security Adviser.[95] On other occasions, though, the Kennedy administration consulted with the Harvard I/O economists specifically for their disciplinary insights. Kermit Gordon, the member of Kennedy's Council of Economic Advisers (CEA) with responsibility for industrial organization and transportation matters, played an important role in bringing in this particular intellectual community.[96] He turned to Harvard's John Meyer and Richard Caves, another Mason student who had worked on the Meyer transportation study, to serve as consultants.[97] As a result, the 1963 *Economic Report of the President*—the annual volume produced by the CEA—advocated, unusually for the time, for "diminished regulation" of transportation.[98]

Gordon continued to bring industrial organization economists into policymaking when he became director of the Budget Bureau at the end of 1962. He ensured that Johnson's 1964 Task Force on Transportation was made up entirely of economists, and that Harvard I/O was prominently represented. While Mason, whom he suggested as chair, did not ultimately serve in that role, Meyer and three other Harvard economics PhDs were among the task force's nine members.[99] Its report, which emphasized "efficient accomplishment of the primary mission of the transport system," again recommended broad deregulation of the sector, as well as the creation of a Department of Transportation to oversee it.[100]

Nor would Gordon be the only Budget Bureau economist who wanted more I/O in transportation policy. In 1965, after Gordon had departed to take a leadership role at Brookings, new Budget director Charles Schultze brought in Charles Zwick as assistant director. Zwick, a coauthor of *The Economics of Competition in the Transportation Industries*, had gone to RAND after receiving his Harvard PhD, where he became head of the logistics department before moving to Washington.[101] Zwick saw the existing system of transportation regulation as "hidebound." He also supported a new Department of Transportation on the grounds that "it would supply a very useful function of shaking up the existing structure."[102]

As the Johnson administration moved toward creating a Department of Transportation, Zwick played a key role, heading a new task force on the new department's mandate and helping to draft the legislation that created it in 1966.[103] Unlike the existing regulatory agencies, the new Department of Transportation (DOT) included an institutionalized role for economists. Harvard PhD James R. Nelson became the first director of its Office of Economics, and DOT established an economic research advisory committee on which both Meyer and Joe Peck served.[104] The DOT would become an ongoing advocate for transportation deregulation during the 1970s; Peck also personally advanced deregulatory arguments as a member of LBJ's Council of Economic Advisers.[105]

Bringing industrial organization economists into the government offices that shaped transportation policy was important, but building Washington networks outside of government offices was also critical. In 1967, Kermit Gordon became president of the Brookings Institution. That same year, with a major grant from the Ford Foundation, Brookings also began a new program on government regulation of economic activity.[106] Initially led by Peck, the program was intended to "evaluate the impact of government regulation upon the industries affected" and to "recommend changes in policies, institutions, and procedures in the interest of promoting the national welfare and improving economic efficiency."[107]

In practice, much of the Brookings program's efforts were devoted to building a community of academic economists studying government regulation through their particular lens.[108] Over the next eight years, it commissioned books, supported research, and brought scholars—mostly economists, but also legal scholars oriented toward economics—and policymakers together. It also funded workshops and graduate students in industrial organization at seven different universities, including ones led by Caves at Harvard, Coase at Chicago, and Peck after he returned to his academic position at Yale.[109] While much of the program's early work focused on the transportation industries, it was soon publishing volumes on regulation and technological change, communications, sports, and energy as well.[110] During its tenure, the program supported dozens of books, dissertations and journal articles, while stimulating new interest by economists in the study of regulation.[111]

The Brookings program had particularly close ties to the Harvard branch of I/O economics. Of the twenty-three members of the advisory committee, five were current or recent Harvard faculty and an additional nine held Harvard PhDs.[112] The makeup of the advisory committee also highlights the close ties between the emerging economics of regulation community with antitrust scholarship, with several representatives working primarily in that area.[113] And while the committee included a couple of outspoken conservatives, including Chicago's George Stigler, its membership largely reflected Brookings's close association with the Democratic Party.[114]

The economists and legal scholars brought together by Brookings's program on government regulation would go on to play major roles in the deregulatory movement of the 1970s, working with both Democrats and Republicans.[115] Even by 1970, Brookings-connected supporters of regulatory reform had already spread out enough in Washington to constitute something of a community.[116] Nearly all of these reformers were thinking about regulation using the economic style: focusing on the governance of markets, and centering the goal of efficiency.

This is not to suggest that Brookings's economists were the only ones critiquing regulation of transportation and other industries in the 1960s and 1970s. Ralph Nader and his followers were making antiregulatory arguments from further left.[117] They too thought that regulation mostly served the interests of incumbents at the expense of consumers, although they approached the topic with a focus on power and equity, rather than market efficiency. Meanwhile, Chicago School economists were making them from the right. Stigler's "Theory of Economic Regulation," which stated that "[s]o many economists . . . have denounced the [Interstate Commerce Commission] for its pro-railroad policies that this has become a cliché of the literature," was published in 1971.[118] Still, by far the best-organized and most systematic critique at the time was coming from the center-left and was also firmly grounded in economics. This pragmatic, reformist approach argued that deregulation would produce more competition, lower prices, and more efficient markets. Ultimately, these newly developed networks for bringing economic expertise to Washington would prove important not only in regulatory debates to come, but also in domains quite far afield from transportation or energy policy.

The Rise of Chicago in Academia and Washington

During the same years that Harvard I/O was making its way to Washington, economists and legal scholars at the University of Chicago were building and strengthening their own distinctive approach to industrial organization, laying the groundwork for greater policy influence in the following decade. Both schools thought the purpose of government regulation should be to promote market efficiency. But while the Harvard economists concluded that this meant reining in antitrust enforcement somewhat and deregulating a handful of industries, the Chicago economists advocated that government should take a much larger step back.

The divergence in the two schools' policy preferences was tied to the approach each took to economics. Harvard's structure-conduct-performance framework assumed that in markets with high levels of concentration, firms would be able to raise prices above the competitive level, producing inefficient outcomes. This implied the need for government to limit market concentration through antitrust policy. Chicago turned this assumption on its head. Rather than assuming concentrated markets were probably inefficient markets, Chicago believed large firms got that way because they were *more* efficient than others. And if they tried to raise prices above the competitive level, they would attract new competitors—from outside the industry, if competition was limited within it. Chicago's approach suggested that government rarely needed to intervene, even in concentrated markets.

During the 1960s, the Chicago approach to industrial organization—and indeed, to economics more generally—was on the rise. Initially, this took place mostly in the economics discipline, but by the mid-1970s the change was visible in Washington as well. Multiple factors contributed to Chicago's climb. Some were intellectual. By the early 1970s, Harvard's structuralist approach was hitting a wall. The evidence that market concentration did consistently predict high prices was not strong, and Chicago's argument about the efficiency of big firms was convincing. Chicago's framework also had an elegance that many found compelling; some of its most prominent supporters, like future judge Richard Posner, converted because of its appeal.[119]

But Chicago scholars were also successful proselytizers. Henry Manne, for example, was a Chicago-trained lawyer who had been part of Director's antitrust workshop as a student, and who applied economic concepts to corporate law in the mid-1960s.[120] Around 1971, he set up an annual summer school for law professors at the University of Rochester—by then, becoming a Chicago outpost—which would teach them the basics of economics, Chicago-style.[121] Over the next few years, these professors formed an informal network of law-and-economics-friendly faculty across elite and less-elite institutions; while they were not all Chicago-oriented themselves, their exposure to economics had a Chicago flavor.[122]

Chicago also benefited from an elective affinity with the interests of the increasingly organized business community. The school had always received some financial support from conservative foundations who approved of its free-market stance. But during the 1960s, big business felt increasingly threatened, both by antitrust enforcement in particular and by anti-business sentiment in general. As a result, organized business, which had not been closely associated with a particular school of economics, became more interested in Chicago ideas.[123] Manne, for example, found that between 1968 and 1971 it became much easier to raise money from large corporations for his "summer camp." As he later told political scientist Steven Teles, "At this point, the [corporate] world knew that Chicago economics was the only thing that could possibly save them from an antitrust debacle, and I related it strongly to that. . . . Well, of the eleven [major corporations] I wrote to, within a few weeks I had $10,000 from ten of them, and the last $10,000 came in a few weeks later."[124]

Soon, Chicago I/O was strengthening its ties with Washington, as well. Some signs could be seen by the end of the 1960s, when Nixon commissioned a "Stigler Report" on antitrust policy. The Stigler Report sharply reversed the recommendations of a similar (Harvard-inflected) task force appointed by President Johnson, instead reflecting the low-enforcement consensus of a group that counted Chicagoans Posner, Coase, and Ward Bowman (along with the eponymous Stigler) among its members.[125] But its influence was becoming more visible by the mid-1970s, when Chicago I/O scholars began to displace Harvard-oriented economists at some of the new sites where they were located in Washington.

The Antitrust Division's Economic Policy Office and the FTC's Bureau of Economics, for example, were rapidly expanding, and the new PhDs they hired tended to be influenced by Chicago. Assistant Attorney General Thomas Kauper later reported that by the time he left the Antitrust Division in 1976, "our own economists disagreed, both with each other and with many outside the Division."[126] At the FTC, political scientist Robert Katzmann observed that, by 1978, "[m]ost of the staff [of the Bureau of Economics] attended institutions that are generally described as satellites of the U. of Chicago"—a statement that would not have been true five years earlier.[127] The FTC's Office of Policy Planning and Evaluation also took a sharp turn toward Chicago with the 1974 appointment of Wesley J. Liebeler, a UCLA law professor and Director student, to run it.[128] Under his leadership, the press characterized the office Liebeler ran as "an Olympian observer loosing bursts of thunderbolts on the most obnoxious mortals down below. At least once a year, at budget time, Olympus would erupt, raining rhetorical destruction left and right (but mostly left)."[129]

The turn taking place in the antitrust agencies could also be seen in the think tank world. In the early 1970s, Republicans had no equivalent to the

Brookings Institution, a valuable resource for Democrats.[130] But now, the American Enterprise Institute (AEI)—a several-decades-old, but politically marginal organization—emerged as "a conservative Brookings."[131] AEI began to invest in economic experts of its own, particularly free-market advocates in the Chicago tradition. At first, the organization focused on establishing its intellectual respectability, which meant publishing fairly academic monographs by scholars like Stigler, Posner, and their colleagues.[132] In very short order, though, the AEI embraced a faster, more responsive, more media friendly, and more combative identity.[133]

In 1975, AEI created a new Center for the Study of Government Regulation.[134] Despite the monographs, AEI was not yet a center of influence on regulatory policy.[135] But as it built its fundraising capacity, the think tank was able to secure grants from the Sloan Foundation, the Lilly Endowment, the Richardson Foundation, and the Glenmede Trust, all aimed at supporting the economic analysis of regulation.[136] The Center, led by economists Marvin Kosters (a Chicago PhD) and James C. Miller III (whose PhD was from the closely aligned University of Virginia), quickly launched an accessible policy journal, *Regulation*, coedited by conservative economist Murray Weidenbaum and then-Chicago-law-professor Antonin Scalia.[137] The intellectual center of gravity for deregulatory conversations moved sharply toward AEI.

By the latter part of the decade, then, the I/O community had introduced an economic style of reasoning to a number of new locations in Washington, and the policy views of the modal industrial organization economist had changed. As Chicago became the dominant approach within the subfield, economists increasingly answered the question of "How should we govern markets?" with, "less." Less antitrust enforcement, less regulation of price and entry in transportation and other industries, and soon, less regulation of business in general. Substantial diversity remained in terms of just what economists thought government should do and what was the right amount of intervention for specific situations. But the days of governing industries with attention to their social and political, as much as economic, impacts were long gone. There was increasing agreement that efficiency was the appropriate criterion for judging how, exactly, government should regulate markets.

Industrial Organization and the Spread of Economic Reasoning

Unlike their colleagues the systems analysts, industrial organization economists did not come to Washington with a single clear project in mind. Yet while their points of entry into policymaking were more diffuse, I/O economists, and the economics-friendly legal scholars they associated with, became much more influential in the 1960s and 1970s. Starting with a focus on antitrust, and soon expanding their concern to transportation and other regulated industries, they brought a disciplinary perspective to the question, "How should we govern markets?" While the industrial organization community included a range of perspectives on just how much governance of markets there should be, its members agreed that the purpose of such governance was to promote the efficient allocation of resources, and that a neoclassical framework was useful for thinking about how to achieve it.

While the systems analysts clustered politically around the center-left and the Democratic Party, the industrial organization community included both a center-left, Democratic strand (associated with Harvard) and a conservative-libertarian, Republican strand (associated with Chicago). The shared language of economics and common commitment to efficiency, though, meant that the two groups were often on the same page when it came to questions of market governance. Although the latter strand would come to dominate both discipline and policy circles by the end of the 1970s, it was the former group that first began to build links between academia and Washington, starting in the Kennedy and Johnson administrations.

These efforts bore little direct fruit in the 1960s, and even in the first half of the 1970s. But the networks and institutions they established left I/O economists in place when the political winds began to change in the 1970s. Industrial organization economists built the law-and-economics movement, and they introduced the basics of the economic style of reasoning into the standard legal curriculum. They modernized the economics offices at the antitrust agencies and made them more influential. And they built networks of economists—initially centered at the Brookings Institution, and later AEI—interested in regulation and supportive of regulatory reform. These networks would go on to play a major role in the nascent deregulatory movement. All of these efforts went against prevailing winds, which did not yet see market governance through a lens of efficiency.

While the I/O economists were a distinct group from the systems analysts, economics was a small discipline, and there was plenty of cross-pollination between the two communities. Joe Peck, a coauthor of *The Economics of Competition in the Transportation Industries* and advocate of deregulation in Johnson's CEA, also served as Alain Enthoven's deputy in the Defense Department's Office of Systems Analysis.[138] Frederic M. Scherer got his start collaborating with Peck on a systems-analytic study of the weapons acquisition process, but would go on to lead the FTC's Bureau of Economics in the mid-1970s.[139] Charles Zwick, another coauthor of the transportation book, became head of RAND's department of logistics before helping create the Department of Transportation from his position at the Budget Bureau.[140] As economists began to apply cost-benefit analysis to regulatory questions in the 1970s, those networks would intersect in new ways.

By the time that intersection took place, the microeconomic style of reasoning that these two communities introduced into Washington had already begun to change how policymakers thought about the work of government. In the next three chapters, we will look at how the economic style was institutionalized in three broad policy domains: social policy, especially poverty and health; market governance, especially antitrust and transportation; and social regulation, especially environmental policy. The values embedded in the economic style prescribed certain types of policy solutions, while rejecting others, setting up conflicts between advocates of the economic style and other approaches to policymaking.

5

The Economic Style
and Social Policy

The systems analysts and I/O economists who brought the economic style to Washington typically saw it as neutral and technocratic. But its core values— particularly, its commitment to efficiency—led its advocates to distinctive types of policy solutions. Often, those solutions came into conflict with competing approaches to policy problems, particularly those represented by the liberal wing of the Democratic Party. As the economic style became partially institutionalized in federal policymaking, these conflicts became more visible.

In the case of social policy, the spread of the economic style was a second-order consequence of the major expansion of government that began in the mid-1960s. The Great Society, starting with the War on Poverty and continuing with Medicare and Medicaid, the Higher Education and Elementary and Secondary Education Acts, and a number of pieces of urban and housing legislation, massively scaled up the size and ambition of government. But Great Society legislation was not grounded in the economic reasoning of efficiency and cost-effectiveness. Instead, it prioritized other types of arguments that Lyndon Johnson and a substantial fraction of Democrats found compelling, including those based on universalism, equality, and rights.

These arguments came from a number of different places and interacted in complex ways. Some of them, dating back to the Progressive Era, were grounded in the logic of social insurance—that is, the idea that universal government programs could be used to protect people against risks associated with old age, unemployment, and sickness or disability. Others, more recent in origin, emphasized democratic participation or the establishment of new rights, including the right to income, to housing, and to medical care. Still others, emerging from the civil rights movement, sought to ensure racial and gender equality. These values imbued the laws that established a wide range of Great Society programs, even as they ran into resistance from politicians who subscribed to competing American political ideals.

The economic style of reasoning was not integral to Great Society legislation. Indeed, it often conflicted with the values that motivated Great Society programs. Nevertheless, the Great Society would facilitate the rapid spread of the economic style throughout the U.S. federal government. The dramatic expansion of domestic policy programs began at just the moment that Johnson required the executive agencies to put PPBS into place to identify "the least costly and most effective means of attaining [national] goals."[1] The policy planning offices created to implement PPBS grew rapidly alongside social policy spending, and they were staffed by the new kinds of experts who embraced the economic style, particularly economists and policy analysts from the new schools of public policy. As the Great Society produced a massive new stream of funds for research and evaluation of social policy, these experts would find homes in a whole ecosystem of policy research organizations both old (like RAND) and new (like the Urban Institute) that were exploding in size and number.

These experts tended toward the politically liberal, but they saw themselves as neutral. They typically accepted the values inherent in economics while understanding their approach as scientific and value-free. Their influence would prove uneven—significant in antipoverty policy, expanding in health and housing policy, and initially stymied in education policy. Where they became influential, though, they changed the terms of policy debate. Proposals to politically empower poor Americans, to provide a family allowance to all households with children (as did the U.K. and Canada), or to establish national health insurance started to seem inefficient or irrelevant, while proposals that emphasized cost-sharing, means-testing, and "institution-building for competition" increasingly seemed natural.[2] The commitments to universality, rights, and equality had been sidelined by an emphasis on efficiency, incentives, and choice.

PPBS Meets the Great Society

The Economic Opportunity Act of 1964, initiated by Kennedy but signed by Johnson after Kennedy's assassination, was the first of many pieces of legislation that would, collectively, transform U.S. social policy. This centerpiece of the so-called War on Poverty created a whole range of antipoverty programs, from the Job Corps to college work-study programs to Volunteers in Service to America (VISTA).[3] But at the White House's new Office of Economic Opportunity (OEO), most of the energy focused on one element of this ambitious, multipart initiative: the Community Action Program (CAP).[4]

Community action sought to empower impoverished rural and urban communities to initiate projects that would give residents a political voice while simultaneously providing access to social services.[5] The legislation's references to the "maximum feasible participation" of the poor were grounded in a sociological—and fairly radical—view of poverty that saw poor people as structurally excluded from political and economic participation. To end poverty, then, would require giving poor communities political power.[6] At first, White House economists endorsed CAP, which they conceptualized as a practical means of service delivery, not a tool for redistributing political power.[7] Relatively quickly, they realized the community action approach conflicted with their economic worldview, which saw poverty as an income problem to be solved through investment in human capital through education and healthcare.[8]

Kennedy's Council of Economic Advisers, which nurtured concern with poverty throughout his administration, had provided much of the impetus for the Economic Opportunity Act, even if its members did not foresee how central community action would become to it. Economists would play a smaller role in shaping legislation for the other policy areas the Johnson administration tackled—health, education, housing, and urban problems— than they did in creating the OEO. The Great Society programs consistently reflected Democratic policymakers' conceptualization of problems, not that of most economists.

Indeed, much Great Society legislation centered decidedly noneconomic values. The 1965 creation of Medicare, for example, was inspired by the Progressive Era movement for social insurance, which saw universal health insurance as a logical means of protecting Americans from potentially catastrophic risk.[9] The Elementary and Secondary Education Act and the Higher Education Act, both passed in 1965, focused on ensuring the rights of all children to an education and improving equity and access to that right.[10] And the urban and housing bills that passed in the late 1960s—the Housing Acts of 1965 and 1968, the Demonstration Cities and Metropolitan Development Act of 1966, and the Fair Housing Act of 1968—combined a New Deal commitment to "strong public institutions" with community action ideals and civil rights concerns.[11] None of these laws emphasized cost-effectiveness or the economic payoffs to these programs.

Although they were passed into law with little input from economists, systems analysts, or economic reasoning, the Great Society programs would be implemented through PPBS. With its emphasis on identifying clear goals and then systematically comparing the cost-effectiveness of competing means to reach them, PPBS was one manifestation of a broader economic style of reasoning that centered incentives, choice, and competition. When President Johnson, pleased with how RAND's systems analysts had implemented PPBS in the Defense Department, announced in August 1965 that PPBS would be rolled out in most government agencies, he set the stage not only for expanding economic reasoning in social policy, but also for reining in the Great Society.[12]

In the second half of the 1960s, advocates of the economic style—mostly liberals who saw themselves as supporting the Great Society's general aims—used PPBS to manage this dramatic expansion of social programs. PPBS allowed the economists to push for their own way of thinking about the means and ends of social policy—a conceptualization that was quite different from that of the policymakers and bureaucrats who launched the programs. Where they were successful, the economic style of reasoning took hold, and efficiency became a more central goal of social policy. To the extent that it became dominant, the economic style displaced the competing, incompatible logics behind Great Society programs.

The Budget Bureau economists who advocated for PPBS's use beyond the Defense Department found it appealing for just that reason.[13] Programs like community action were threatening because they decentralized decision-making authority, putting it into the hands of people—implicitly, people who were poor, Black, or both—who might not share the Budget Bureau's perspective on the appropriate response to poverty, and whose actions were likely to create political problems for the administration. PPBS, as its DOD rollout suggested, was a powerful tool for the central consolidation of decision-making.[14] So it is perhaps unsurprising that the agencies most affected by Great Society legislation—the OEO and the Department of Health, Education, and Welfare (HEW)—found themselves with two of the most influential PPBS offices, led by high-powered economists who had firsthand experience at RAND.[15]

Expanding Policy Planning Offices

As the Great Society moved from legislation to reality, the policy planning offices at OEO and HEW became particularly important advocates for economic reasoning in social policy. Newly created in 1965, the Office of Research, Plans, Programs and Evaluation (RPP&E) at OEO and the Office of the Assistant Secretary of Planning and Evaluation (ASPE) at HEW gave economists access to top decisionmakers, linked the economics discipline to the policymaking process in new ways, and promoted policy continuity across presidential administrations. They also nurtured the careers of economists like William Gorham, Alice Rivlin, and Robert Levine, who would subsequently advance the economic style at not-yet-created organizations like the Urban Institute and the Congressional Budget Office.

While policymakers found the idea of PPBS appealing for a number of reasons, its potential for consolidating authority over unwieldy and intransigent programs ranked high on the list. Although Kennedy's economists had supported making community action a key part of the War on Poverty, they did not expect it to become the heart of the Economic Opportunity Act. But the political compromises behind the legislation's passage made the Community Action Program more central to the War on Poverty than even its proponents had expected.[16] And when Sargent Shriver, Kennedy's brother-in-law, was installed as head of the new Office of Economic Opportunity after the August 1964 passage of the act, he needed to quickly demonstrate what this new office could do.

The result was the rapid deployment of community action funds to grassroots organizations, with relatively limited oversight. In the next five months, OEO committed more than $200 million in local grants, including community action grants to nearly thirty states, cities, rural areas, and Indian reservations.[17] This support went to a wide range of organizations, most of which were focused on the coordination of social services or collaboration with low-income Americans to identify and meet their needs. A relative handful championed the more radical goal of mobilizing the political voice of poor people.[18]

The members of Johnson's administration who advocated for the broad rollout of PPBS—Budget Bureau director Charles Schultze and assistant director Henry Rowen, both economists, and LBJ advisor and former McNamara assistant Joseph Califano—were skeptical of this decentralized approach to the War on Poverty even in its earliest stages, before CAP had become a highly politicized and racialized program.[19] Indeed, just months after the passage of the Economic Opportunity Act, and nearly a year before

PPBS was fully rolled out, the Budget Bureau noted that the advantages of the consolidated decision-making it afforded made it "obvious that OEO needs a [Charles] Hitch-type operation"—that is, one of the sort that RAND had brought to the Defense Department.[20] By virtue of both their institutional position and their intellectual commitments, the economists of the Budget Bureau favored a centralized, systematic approach to goal-setting and program planning over the bottom-up model of community action.

But these leanings were amplified as CAP *did* become politicized and as the War on Poverty quickly fractured along the fault line of race. Although most community action agencies were not focused on political mobilization of poor people, the ones that were rapidly began challenging city governments and urban political machines, provoking unhappiness in local power structures. In cases where local community action agencies represented Black people or other racialized groups, and city politics was white-dominated, this dynamic became explosive.[21] By the summer of 1965, LBJ found himself facing a full-on "mayors' revolt"—by the local Democratic leaders who were supposed to be his supporters.[22]

What made the BOB economists increasingly anxious about community action was the political implications for Johnson of this threat to white supremacy in local Democratic politics. As Schultze wrote to the president a few months later, while recommending $35 million in budget cuts for the program, "[CAP] is setting up a *competing political organization* in [the mayors'] backyards. . . . [W]e ought not to be in the business of organizing the poor politically."[23] Schultze's solution, which Johnson approved with his initials, was not to eliminate CAP but to reorient community action agencies toward providing services to the poor, rather than empowering them.

It was in this context that BOB announced the broad rollout of PPBS in August 1965. That same month, Los Angeles saw the Watts revolt—partly a response to the War on Poverty's failure to reach the Black community in Los Angeles—galvanize national attention and usher in an even more intense period of racial conflict.[24] Shortly thereafter, RPP&E was established to oversee the implementation of PPBS at OEO. Almost immediately, the office became a beachhead for recapturing control over the War on Poverty from community action advocates.

More generally, RPP&E was committed not only to systems analysis specifically, but to a broader economic style of reasoning about poverty.[25] With its emphasis on increasing political participation, CAP operated on the assumption that poverty was, at least in part, a cultural problem. In contrast, the economists at RPP&E understood poverty as a problem of income, and therefore set about finding better ways to measure it.[26] RPP&E's staff was deeply invested in the War on Poverty's larger aim of ending poverty in the United States, but they saw that goal primarily in economic terms. If the goal was to bring all Americans above the income-based poverty line, what was the most efficient means to do so?[27] And while, as one RPP&E economist later reflected, systems analysis might seem highly sophisticated, "the truth was that the practitioners were seldom using much more than sound microeconomic principles out of Paul Samuelson's elementary economics textbook."[28]

This commitment to efficient solutions quickly led the RPP&E to the idea of a negative income tax (NIT). As the name suggests, a negative income tax would simply provide additional money to households with earnings below the poverty line or some other specified amount. Popularized by libertarian economist Milton Friedman, the concept had also intrigued Kennedy's Council of Economic Advisers.[29] Its obvious efficiency endeared it to RPP&E as well—the concept certainly seemed more compatible with the systems analysis framework than the scattershot, loosely defined, hard-to-evaluate programs that made up Community Action.[30] When RPP&E released its first five-year plan for OEO, in the fall of 1965, the office proposed that the majority of the agency's spending take the form of a substantial new negative income tax. CAP would be relegated to a service coordination role.[31]

OEO director Sargent Shriver, who ran hot-and-cold on community action from the beginning of his involvement in the War on Poverty, was already inclined to take RPP&E's recommendations seriously. But the timing of RPP&E's plan, shortly after Watts amplified the administration's concern with white backlash against community action, increased Shriver's receptivity to the office's technocratic approach.[32] This put RPP&E in a position to displace CAP at the center of OEO.

Even as RPP&E sought to limit and deradicalize the Community Action Program, its ambitions for the War on Poverty remained bold. In fact, it proposed a budget of $9 billion for the OEO budget in 1967, more than quintuple what the agency expected to receive in 1966.[33] Here, though, its timing was less fortuitous. August 1965 also saw President Johnson announce that he would be sending substantial numbers of new troops to Vietnam—a decision that introduced competing budget priorities that would constrain OEO's future even as it provided a new, less welcome kind of political opening for RPP&E.[34] By the time RPP&E carried out its next annual round of planning, budget constraints had come to dominate decision-making. OEO's $9 billion budget request had, by the end of 1965, garnered a $1.5 billion counterproposal from BOB.[35]

This dramatic reining-in was crushing to the ambitious poverty warriors at the OEO, including those at RPP&E. According to one colleague, upon receiving BOB's counterproposal, director Kershaw "indicated right then and there he wanted to resign."[36] Yet it was in this new context of budget limitations that RPP&E proved its value to OEO, both practically and politically. When there was an expectation of massive spending increases, the OEO felt little pressure to rigorously evaluate the cost-effectiveness of its activities: the priority was growth. But now, with expectations slashed, OEO had to decide not only what to do in the War on Poverty, but more importantly, what not to do. Here, RPP&E's numbers proved useful both in defending the agency's requests and in guiding reductions within OEO itself.[37]

The lower-than-expected budgets also opened a door for experimentation. Suddenly, research—rigorous, well-designed research of the sort favored by the systems analytic community—and small-scale demonstration seemed a much more appealing, or at least realistic, course of action in the War on Poverty than widescale, community-directed programming. The RPP&E expanded its research efforts dramatically, with consequences that would play out far beyond OEO itself.[38]

By the time LBJ left office in early 1969, the War on Poverty had lost much of its steam. OEO had narrowly avoided being disbanded by Congress in 1967, and director Shriver had departed in 1968.[39] The more radical flank of poverty warriors, with their commitment to political participation of poor people, had been almost entirely supplanted by the systems analytic approach.[40] With its commitment to quantitative evaluation of the most efficient ways to reach well-defined goals, and its economic conception of poverty as an individual problem defined by lack of income, systems analysis had proved its value both in making policy decisions and reining in radicals. OEO's policy planning office would initially thrive under President Nixon, as would the economic approach to poverty more generally. By the time Nixon closed the Office of Economic Opportunity entirely, in 1973, much of the work of disseminating economic reasoning about poverty was complete—not only within OEO, but, as we shall see, to organizations well beyond it.

————

While the War on Poverty was the opening salvo of the Great Society, the wave of legislation that followed the Economic Opportunity Act expanded the aims of social policy well beyond antipoverty efforts. In these other arenas, HEW's ASPE would prove instrumental in advancing the economic style of reasoning. ASPE had a different set of challenges than RPP&E, and would not become so dominant within its agency. In the long run, though, it would have an even greater impact across a range of social policy domains.

Like RPP&E, ASPE was created in response to Johnson's 1965 requirement that executive agencies implement PPBS. But while OEO was a brand-new office, free of existing fiefdoms and bureaucratic routines, the Department of Health, Education, and Welfare (HEW) was an established institution, having been formed in 1953 from a number of already-existing agencies. Charged in 1965 with overseeing the new Medicare and Medicaid programs, as well as expanding support for primary, secondary, and higher education, HEW experienced dramatic growth in the 1960s. Its budget more than doubled between 1963 and 1969, from $20 billion to over $50 billion, by which point it accounted for nearly a quarter of all federal expenditures.[41]

William Gorham, an economist with experience at both RAND and the Defense Department, was given the job of using PPBS to tame this behemoth.[42] Gorham brought in the usual suspects to staff his new office: three Harvard economics PhDs—Robert Grosse, who Gorham had known at RAND; Alice Rivlin, whom Gorham hired away from the Brookings Institution; and C. Worth Bateman, who also came from Defense—as well as Samuel Halperin, a legislative specialist who held a PhD in political science.[43] Gorham faced a challenging task: applying PPBS to a massive agency that possessed a well-entrenched bureaucratic apparatus with no clear hierarchy. While expanding budgets made hiring possible, ASPE was nevertheless small. Gorham inherited about ten employees and hired a dozen more.[44] Initially, the office lacked any funding to conduct research of its own.[45]

With limited staff, oversight of a budget in the tens of billions, and very little existing program data on which to base analytic recommendations, ASPE was forced to focus its efforts to, in Gorham's words, "sharpen . . . the knife that cuts the public pie."[46] Gorham began by requesting analyses of five important program areas: Disease Control, Human Investment, Child Health, Income Maintenance, and Financing Higher Education. In keeping with the systems analytic approach, each study attempted to promote better government decisions by applying cost-effectiveness criteria linking agency programs to policy goals. While this approach was standard for the systems analysts, it was a radically different way for most HEW employees to conceptualize their activities. Most program managers at the time did not think of their programs in terms of measurable indicators.[47]

As was the case at RPP&E, the economists and policy analysts at ASPE understood the purpose of social policy differently from many of their HEW colleagues, not to mention those outside the agency who were affected by its programs. ASPE, for example, saw health and education as "human investment programs . . . designed to increase the income earning capacity and improve the functioning of individuals and families."[48] They saw them, in other words, in terms of human capital: investments in individuals that would improve their economic productivity, and therefore (they assumed) their wages as well. Yet, as Rivlin noted in an internal memo, "rightly or wrongly, doctors and teachers and social workers do not think in economic terms and will resent our efforts if we seem to stress the economic aspects of their activities."[49]

This tension at HEW between advocates of the economic style and those who took a more holistic view of the value of health and education inevitably produced conflict. And it produced resistance to the use of PPBS, which many experienced agency hands viewed as "either a nuisance or a threat."[50] As was the case in other agencies, much of the existing HEW bureaucracy reacted to PPBS with "foot dragging."[51] Yet Gorham regarded the ASPE's analyses as effective in at least some instances. Looking back on his time at the office, he noted that ASPE "force[d] . . . the reallocation of money" toward more cost-effective programs—for example, from a tuberculin program to one screening for uterine cancer.[52]

As the office increased its influence over program priorities within HEW, ASPE also began to push the Johnson administration to think differently about its larger political agenda for health, education, and welfare—for example, on higher education funding. With college enrollments expanding rapidly, there was a broad policy consensus within government that higher education required more federal support.[53] Within that consensus, policymakers debated whether that support should take the form of institutional aid—aid going directly to colleges—or individual aid to students in the form of grants or loans.[54]

In the wake of the passage of the access-oriented Higher Education Act in 1965, the administration favored more institutional aid.[55] This was how K–12 education was funded, and served as the basis for the public university model. But ASPE, reflecting a minority position, strongly favored individual aid. From an economic perspective, it made sense for students to bear the cost of higher education, because human capital theory implied students would personally benefit: education would increase their economic productivity, which would in turn raise their wages. The economists at ASPE favored student loans, which were not heavily used at the time. The office did support grants for lower-income students, but they saw funding colleges directly as regressive, because much of that money would effectively flow to well-off students—students who would receive financial benefits from their degree, yet could have afforded to pay their own way. ASPE economists also liked the market pressure that individual aid would bring to bear on colleges that would have to compete for students.[56] Reflecting this perspective, Gorham argued that "a 'program of general stringless institutional support' would be 'a serious error.'"[57]

ASPE's advocacy led the Johnson administration to shift its priorities. Instead of drafting legislation that would have created such a program of institutional support, LBJ turned his higher education funding initiative over to Alice Rivlin—who in 1968 replaced Gorham as director of ASPE— for further study.[58] The 1969 Rivlin Report, released just as Johnson was leaving office, recommended support centered on student aid, including a substantial loan component. Institutional aid would come primarily in the form of a cost-of-education allowance tied to individual students, which would still promote competition.[59] The Rivlin Report remained a key reference point under the Nixon administration, its imprint clearly visible in the Higher Education Act Reauthorization of 1972, which prioritized individual aid over institutional support.[60]

ASPE's priorities produced similar continuities between the Johnson and Nixon administration in other policy areas. As was the case for RPP&E, ASPE thrived in periods of retrenchment. Administrators at the HEW found the office's numbers and analysis useful in deciding how to spend shrinking resource pools. The office would grow in both size and influence during the Nixon presidency, becoming the administration's "locus of power" in health affairs and playing a critical role in welfare reform efforts.[61] And its influence would be felt well beyond HEW, as the office's alumni and the funding streams it came to control nurtured a new generation of economic thinkers about social policy.

———

Policy planning offices, and the economic style of reasoning that went with them, did not have as much influence in every social-policy-focused agency as they did at OEO and HEW. As we have seen in chapter 3, many federal agencies resisted the PPBS process; some agencies did not develop strong, economically oriented PPOs in the 1960s at all. Yet even in places where they did not initially take off, such offices were created, expanded, and upgraded in the 1970s—after PPBS itself was abandoned—as the perceived value of policy analysis increased.

The Department of Labor, for example, oversaw "manpower" programs—job training efforts and the like—yet initially lacked any serious implementation of PPBS.[62] Only under the Nixon administration, when the executive branch was moving away from the use of PPBS itself, would Labor create its Office of the Assistant Secretary for Policy, Evaluation, and Research (ASPER)—partly to rein in those very programs.[63] But while ASPER's creation came relatively late, in the 1970s the office would be led by a series of high-powered labor economists. Like the rest of Labor, ASPER continued to advocate for jobs programs. Unlike the rest of the department, it pushed for a "net impact" approach that would use either experimental methods or econometric models to estimate the treatment effects of such programs. The more rigorous methods also made it harder to demonstrate program effectiveness, a key reason George Shultz, Nixon's labor secretary, supported the office.[64] By the end of the decade, ASPER was a serious analytic competitor to ASPE, and well-positioned to marshal data of its own to argue for its preferred programs.[65]

Similarly, the Department of Housing and Urban Development (HUD), created the month after PPBS was rolled out, was in charge of a substantial portion of the Great Society agenda.[66] The agency was even led by an economist—Robert C. Weaver, the first Black Harvard economics PhD as well as the nation's first Black cabinet member.[67] But Weaver, who was fairly alienated from the economics profession, was uninterested in PPBS, and a 1969 study rated HUD one of the least effective agencies at implementing it.[68] It was not until Nixon's second term that a new Office of Policy Development and Research, reporting directly to the secretary and led by economist Michael H. Moskow, was created.[69] Already Nixon had shifted HUD's focus away from public housing and toward a focus on low-cost building technologies.[70] Now, with Moskow's appointment, HUD's attention shifted again: toward the Experimental Housing Allowance Program (EHAP), which would test the effectiveness of giving low-income families vouchers to reduce the cost of housing, as an alternative to politically unpopular public housing projects.[71] This would signal a new direction in housing policy, and one in which economic analysis would play a much larger role.

The influence of policy planning offices during the PPBS era, then, was significant but uneven. But as the economic style became more pervasive in social policy, these offices continued to develop. Their importance was not limited to the Great Society period itself. Indeed, in most cases their influence actually increased during the Nixon years, as they continued to disseminate economic reasoning not only within their agencies but—particularly through the research and evaluation they supported—well beyond.

From Policy Planning Offices to Policy Research Organizations

Policy planning offices advocated for an economic approach to thinking about decision-making in their own agencies and their own policy domains. At the same time, they also helped disseminate an economic style of reasoning to a much broader policymaking space. Conducting systematic analysis required good, quantitative information about what a given agency's programs were doing and how successful they were at achieving their stated goals. Yet such information was typically difficult, if not impossible, to come by.

In seeking to fill this gap, policy planning offices became major supporters of both applied research—research that could be used to promote better government decision-making—and policy evaluation. The Great Society programs funneled unprecedented sums of money into research and evaluation. Although only a fraction of this was spent by the policy planning offices directly, their staff bore the primary responsibility for determining which grantees and contractors this money would go to. As these funding streams grew dramatically, they came to support a new and growing ecosystem of policy research organizations, oriented toward a broadly economic style of reasoning, that would ultimately dwarf the policy planning offices themselves. Eventually, this new world of policy research organizations, sustained by government research and evaluation contracts, would themselves help to shape the terms of social policy debate.

The initial steps of PPOs to support outside research were tentative and met with mixed success. At OEO, RPP&E quickly realized its need for an "academic RAND" that would produce knowledge useful for conducting the War on Poverty. It began by funding the new Institute for Research on Poverty (IRP) at the University of Wisconsin, hailed by *Business Week* as "a think tank that thinks for the poor." Although IRP was generously supported by OEO and attracted "top-notch" economists, the different work cultures of Wisconsin's academics and Washington's policymakers produced immediate tension. The academics expected to set their own research agenda and focus on long-range questions, while the bureaucrats had hoped IRP would respond to their short-term policy problems.[72] It soon became clear that a purely academic institution would not be able to meet all of OEO's needs for policy research.

ASPE, too, sought to commission outside research to improve the cost-effectiveness of HEW programs, in its case, by leveraging evaluation requirements that were being written into Great Society legislation. Senator Robert Kennedy had ensured that the Elementary and Secondary Education Act (ESEA) required that schools report on their results and "projects be regularly assessed for effectiveness."[73] Kennedy's concern was not with efficiency, but with the possibility that the resources provided by the bill might not actually reach low-income, and especially Black, children.[74] As Samuel Halperin, who helped shepherd ESEA through Congress as an Office of Education appointee, observed, Kennedy's "notion of evaluation was that poor people should have made available the numbers and figures on how their kids are doing." They deserved access to information that could help them demand accountability from both local leaders and Washington—a stance aligned with the idea of "maximum feasible participation."[75]

Kennedy recognized that Southern states, especially, would resist allowing federal funds to go to Black students. So, to ensure equitable access to promised resources, he added in an evaluation requirement that applied to a billion dollars per year of Title I funds directed to disadvantaged children. But to the economists at ASPE, the point of conducting an evaluation was to assess the cost-effectiveness of HEW's investments in education. In Gorham's words, the evaluation funds presented the opportunity for "a vast experiment designed to find effective ways of reaching disadvantaged children."[76]

From Gorham's perspective, education was a production function. The game was to identify the relationship between inputs—money, teachers, classrooms—and outputs—gains in academic achievement. Through careful measurement and estimation, the analyst could "help the decision-maker realize that an extra dollar spent in one way may involve greater welfare gain than a dollar spent in another way."[77]

The evaluation program got off to a rocky start. ASPE's early contracts with outside research organizations to conduct preliminary cost-effectiveness analyses of Title I produced mostly frustration. An initial effort, for example, asked TEMPO—a division of General Electric—to identify the features of Title I projects that were effective at compensating for educational disadvantage. Yet "[e]ven within a universe of supposedly 'successful' programs, TEMPO analysts were able to identify neither a Title I population, nor a Title I program, nor significant achievement gains that could be attributed to Title I funds."[78] The way funds were spent in the real world simply did not map onto a systems analytic conception of government.

The next round of research and evaluation partnerships between RPP&E, ASPE, and outside organizations produced more satisfying results. At OEO, the turning point was the New Jersey Income Maintenance Experiment, which took the then-novel approach of randomly assigning some poor families to receive a negative income tax, and others not.[79] While Wisconsin's IRP played a role in running the experiment and contributed academic legitimacy to the project, a then-small consulting group called Mathematica carried out much of the day-to-day work.[80]

Mathematica had been founded in the late 1950s by a group of Princeton faculty—economists and mathematicians—to apply "abstract mathematical research in problems of marketing and management."[81] By the mid-1960s, it had diversified into policy studies, although its total budget was still under $1 million.[82] The company's breakthrough moment came in 1966, when Princeton economists William Baumol and Albert Rees proposed to OEO that they, on behalf of Mathematica, should lead its NIT experiment.[83] Over the next few years, the New Jersey Income Maintenance Experiment channeled $4.4 million to the firm—more than was actually distributed to recipients of the experimental NIT.[84] As Great Society research contracts became Mathematica's new bread and butter, the company grew rapidly, reporting over $2 million in contracts by 1969 and $7 million by 1972.[85]

Like RPP&E itself, both IRP and Mathematica reflected an economic style of thought. Economists made up a plurality of Mathematica's principal staff in the mid-1960s. A 1970 National Academy of Sciences panel noted that "while not entirely of the economics discipline, [IRP] is disciplined by economics."[86] Although sociologists and social psychologists also worked on the NIT experiment, and the psychologists, at least, had more experience with experimental design than the economists, a follow-up study reported that "economists dominated the design process."[87] On the one hand, the centrality of economists made sense, given that the experiment was intended to estimate the effects of an NIT on labor force participation. But their dominance meant that recipients' feelings of anomie and alienation, which the sociologists thought were important, were dismissed because the economists "regarded [them] as bordering on the ridiculous."[88]

In the years that followed, the New Jersey Income Maintenance Experiment would serve as a model for several other major social policy experiments. These studies would provide additional resources to contract research organizations—what historian Alice O'Connor has called the "poverty research industry," although its attention was directed well beyond poverty—in years to come.[89] This money would flow primarily to organizations oriented toward an economic style of reasoning, expanding its sphere of influence within social policy.

Back at ASPE, William Gorham remained optimistic about the possibilities of evaluation, despite the office's initial frustrations with Title I programs. When another Great Society bill—this time, the Child Health Act of 1967—crossed his desk for comment, he seized the opportunity to secure a new flow of resources that could be used to expand and improve evaluation efforts in the future.[90] As he later recalled in multiple accounts, "I'd been terribly troubled by this fact that evaluation wasn't going to get anywhere unless it had some money."[91] And so, he proposed that 1 percent of all money appropriated for the bill be used for evaluation. After BOB director Charles Schultze signed off on the plan for the Child Health Act, it became standard practice to set aside 1 percent of social policy funding for evaluation. Between 1967 and 1973, twenty-seven new laws affecting poverty, health, education, and more included the set-aside language.[92] In 1969 the government had spent a total of $17 million on evaluation efforts; just three years later, that had increased to roughly $100 million, most of which went through HEW and ended up in the hands of various contract research organizations.[93] More than $50 million was spent evaluating Title I alone.[94]

———

OEO and HEW were not the sole sources of support for the new and expanding policy research organizations. The growing attention to urban problems led, for example, to the establishment of an important new think tank, the Urban Institute, that would similarly reflect the economic style. The creation of HUD in September 1965 gave housing and urban problems an official administrative home. But no "urban RAND" existed to conduct research that would inform the new agency's decision-making.[95]

In the second half of 1966, economist Henry Rowen—then implementing PPBS from the Budget Bureau, but having just been selected as RAND's next president—began advocating for "a Great Society policy research center [to] be established at RAND." The idea was to create an "Urban Institute" that would be financially supported by the new HUD, but independent of it.[96] After some internal politicking, though, President Johnson decided to establish an entirely new organization instead. In December 1967, Johnson announced the formation of the Urban Institute, calling its relationship with HUD "analogous to the relationship of Rand [*sic*] to the Air Force."[97]

The analogy with RAND was indeed appropriate. The Urban Institute would be led, for the next thirty years, by William Gorham, who left his position as assistant secretary at HEW to take on its presidency.[98] Urban's earliest reports were "ground[ed] . . . in the methods of cost-benefit analysis"; it even "shared a building" with RAND's Washington outpost.[99] In its first two years, Urban's budget came mostly from government, including $6 million from HUD and $1 million from the Department of Transportation. It received an additional $1 million from the Ford Foundation.[100] Like Mathematica, the organization expanded rapidly during the late 1960s thanks to research and evaluation dollars. By 1972, its budget had grown to about $10 million a year.[101]

RAND lost the opportunity to house the Urban Institute itself, but it nevertheless found a way to insert itself into the rapidly growing social policy research space. As president, Rowen actively pursued the diversification of RAND's almost entirely defense-centered research portfolio. By the end of his first year, RAND had secured contracts from OEO, the new Department of Transportation, the National Institutes of Health (part of HEW), and HUD, as well as from several foundations and the city of New York.[102] Over the next few years, RAND would expand these efforts in several different directions. It began working on education "on a substantial scale" in 1969. By 1972, it was conducting some fifteen education-related projects, including a study of the effectiveness of private companies at improving test scores in public schools (sponsored by ASPE) and an evaluation of a school voucher experiment (sponsored by OEO).[103]

While many of the government contracts that supported Urban, RAND, and other policy research organizations were relatively modest in size, the political success of the New Jersey Income Maintenance Experiment produced a wave of social policy experiments in the early 1970s that would provide resources on a larger scale. RPP&E and its successors would support the Rural Income Maintenance Experiment (1969 to 1973), which focused on families in rural, rather than urban, locations; the Gary (Indiana) Income Maintenance Experiment (1971 to 1974), which focused on Black households, many led by single women; and the Seattle/Denver Income Maintenance Experiment (SIME/DIME, 1971 to 1982), which offered a larger income and, for some recipients, a longer time period.[104] The income maintenance experiments alone produced tens of millions of dollars for the outside organizations that conducted the studies and analyzed their results.

The social experiment trend did not end with income maintenance. The 1970s also saw HUD sponsor the Experimental Housing Allowance Program (EHAP) to test the effectiveness of a "housing allowance" that low-income recipients could use where they chose.[105] In terms of participants, length, expense, and organizational complexity, EHAP was the largest of all the social experiments of this era.[106] Over the decade it channeled $175 million—close to three-quarters of a billion today—through the Urban Institute, RAND, the Stanford Research Institute, and Abt Associates and trained a generation of economics-oriented researchers on housing issues.[107] The decade also saw RAND conduct its OEO- and ASPE-funded Health Insurance Experiment (HIE), which examined the effects of a variety of cost-sharing agreements on consumption of medical care and on health outcomes.[108] And the Department of Labor tested its new Supported Work program, which provided transitional work for the "hard-core" unemployed. The program in turn committed $80 million to an entirely new organization, the Manpower Demonstration Research Corporation (later MDRC), to carry out an experiment of its own.[109] Economists were heavily represented among MDRC's leadership, and MDRC, too, would grow rapidly during these years.[110]

Between the major social policy experiments and the new federal set-aside for evaluation, hundreds of millions of dollars flowed into the coffers of policy research organizations in the 1970s. Evaluation was proliferating so rapidly in the early 1970s that one of the Urban Institute's first major projects was an evaluation of evaluations—a review of those conducted at HUD, OEO, HEW, and the Department of Labor—led by Joseph Wholey, formerly Alice Rivlin's assistant at ASPE.[111] While evaluation research would ultimately develop in different directions, some of which were qualitative and fairly distant from economics, a substantial portion of evaluation money supported organizations and studies that relied upon econometric methods and reproduced the economic style.[112]

The research and evaluation money that grew out of Great Society legislation produced massive growth among policy research organizations in the 1970s. By 1974, Mathematica was involved in federal studies on health insurance, housing assistance, income maintenance, "Black Perceptions," welfare reform, and childcare. Its revenues that year were $12 million.[113] By 1980, Urban's budget would approach $20 million and RAND's $50 million, about half of which was being spent on social policy research.[114]

The omnipresence of these organizations gave them a disproportionate voice in social policy conversations, particularly in setting the terms of debate: pushing antipoverty policy, for example, to focus on the effects of income on individual work and family decisions, or encouraging health policy to center the issue of moral hazard—whether insured people used more healthcare than they needed, because they did not directly pay for it—above all other policy questions. The terms of policy debate that were accepted by this community became the terms of debate that policymakers centered more generally. And ultimately, these new terms of debate would shape the kinds of policy positions that were seen as legitimate to take.

Competing Conceptions of Social Policy

The Economic Opportunity Act, Medicare and Medicaid, the Elementary and Secondary Education Act, and other Great Society laws and programs focused on equality, universalism, rights, and democratic participation. In contrast, economic reasoning focused on efficiency and cost-effectiveness, which typically meant means-testing and measurable outcomes. As economic reasoning expanded into these new domains, it became a way for first the Johnson administration and even more so Nixon's to contain some of the effects of Great Society legislation that they found politically inconvenient. The policymakers who sought out advice based on economic reasoning were receptive to advocates' claims of value neutrality. This neutral epistemic authority, which proponents claimed gave them the ability to make rational decisions about what social programs would be most efficient and effective, delegitimated value-based arguments grounded in competing worldviews.

The economic perspective rejected the idea that poor people's lives would only be improved through increased political participation. Instead, its advocates argued that antipoverty efforts should be evaluated through scientific tests, ideally experimental, of measurable effects of specific government interventions. The economic perspective could not justify universal healthcare on the grounds that social insurance programs were more politically resilient than welfare programs, or that medical care was a human right. Instead, it pointed out that it was inefficient for government to insure those who could pay for private insurance, and that people who did not have to pay for healthcare would likely use more of it. While some adherents to the economic worldview acknowledged what the perspective necessarily overlooked, the more typical response was simply to discount these alternative ways of thinking about social policy.

This dynamic played out in multiple policy domains that were central to the Great Society. In antipoverty, health, housing, and education policy, economic reasoning reached deep into government, but encountered resistance from other types of political claims. Where the economic style gained influence, it visibly changed the space of political debate, making it harder to defend claims grounded in political values that conflicted with economic reasoning.

THE NEGATIVE INCOME TAX VERSUS SOCIAL INSURANCE

Nowhere were these tensions more evident than in debates over how to solve poverty. Here, the economic style conflicted not only with proponents of community action, who centered political participation, but also with advocates of social insurance, who preferred universal programs to those aimed specifically at the low-income. Within the OEO, RPP&E was the primary channel through which the economic style counterbalanced and eventually came to displace the Community Action Program. But economists in the Council of Economic Advisers, which had encouraged Kennedy to tackle poverty in the first place, also worked to advance economic reasoning by pushing back against the universalism of social insurance advocates within the administration.

While the community action proponents were newcomers to Washington, the social insurance approach had a much longer history. Social insurance programs focus on protecting citizens from risk through universal coverage—for example, through national health, unemployment, or old age insurance. Everyone eligible is required to contribute, and the receipt of benefits is tied simply to participation, not to the amount contributed. In the United States, the social insurance concept gained influence in the New Deal, with its principles reflected in both the Social Security Program, established in 1935, and Medicare, created in 1965. The 1960s also saw social insurance proponents advocating for family allowances, which had been implemented in Canada and the U.K., and which provided a cash benefit to all households with children as a protection against child poverty.[115]

Advocates of social insurance liked universal programs in part because of their political durability. As Wilbur Cohen, an architect of Social Security and Medicare, famously argued, "[a] program for the poor will most likely be a poor program."[116] Yet liberal economists viewed social insurance programs with relative skepticism, prioritizing program efficiency over Cohen's goal of ensuring broad-based political support. Social insurance programs benefited—unnecessarily, in the economists' view—the well-off as well as the needy, making the programs both less progressive and more expensive. Economists much preferred the negative income tax as a solution to poverty, as it efficiently targeted the neediest Americans.[117]

Between 1965 and 1972, economists made the case for an NIT in a range of outlets, typically over the objections of advocates of universal programs. For example, in 1966 *The Public Interest*, then a new magazine aimed at dispassionate analysis of social policy, published an extended exchange between James Tobin, a Kennedy CEA member and NIT advocate, and Alvin Schorr, a former social worker who held posts in OEO and HEW and was a strong advocate of family allowances.[118] Schorr criticized Tobin's NIT proposal on multiple grounds, arguing instead for what he called "income-by-right"—universal programs like social security and family allowance. Tobin, by contrast, dismissed the desirability of family allowance based on its inefficiency as an antipoverty program.[119]

Even if an NIT was not on the table, advocates of the economic style still favored means-tested assistance over universal social insurance, again on efficiency grounds. When Cohen, also known as "Mr. Social Security," became secretary of HEW in 1968, he urged the Johnson administration to use its final months to pursue an across-the-board increase in Social Security benefits. He strongly opposed the idea of expanding programs targeting solely the poor.[120] This put him at odds with CEA member Joe Peck, who was instead pushing for a modest expansion of welfare (Aid to Families with Dependent Children) in conjunction with the introduction of means-testing into Social Security.[121] This proposition—means-testing Social Security!—was abhorrent to Cohen, yet Peck was reportedly "furious when the White House summarily rejected his plan and chose Cohen's."[122] Neither of these proposals became policy at the time. Yet as economic reasoning became more entrenched in the policymaking process, the barriers to advancing social insurance proposals that conflicted with the efficiency mandate would grow higher.

Advocates of the economic style continued to push for an NIT into the Nixon administration. President Nixon was no poverty warrior, but discontent from the states about the uneven distribution of welfare, plus the fresh memory of urban revolts, meant that welfare reform of some sort was high on the agenda.[123] When John Veneman, a liberal California Republican and undersecretary at HEW, was placed in charge of fleshing out the details of Nixon's reform plan, he turned to analysts left over from the Johnson administration as the best available sources of welfare program expertise.[124] At his request, Worth Bateman, one of Gorham's initial hires at ASPE, and James Lyday, an economic analyst at OEO, developed and advocated for an NIT-based proposal.[125]

The conservative wing of the Nixon administration opposed welfare reform based on an NIT, instead preferring more modest changes that would even out state-to-state variation without centralizing federal control. But command of the numbers worked in Bateman and Lyday's favor. While both wings purported to be grounding their recommendations in systems analysis, only the actual analysts had access to the computerized database from which a systems analysis could be built. Thus, both sides were dependent on the HEW/OEO analysts to provide numbers to back their policy recommendations—and those analysts had an agenda.[126] Ultimately, Nixon signed on to the NIT proposal, not least because of Bateman and Lyday's ability to present convincing numbers.[127]

The Bateman and Lyday proposal—written by liberal economists— became the basis of Nixon's Family Assistance Plan, which guaranteed a minimum income, required recipients to seek work or job training, and gradually phased out assistance with increased income so as to incentivize work. Indeed, as Alice Rivlin recalled of the transition to the new administration, "I couldn't believe that I was sitting there talking to a Republican administration that seemed eager for this new solution [NIT] that six months before I hadn't been able to convince Wilbur Cohen was the right thing to do."[128] While the Family Assistance Plan died in Congress—the closest the United States has ever come to a guaranteed income—the fact that it became the administration's plan at all shows how economic reasoning was changing the terms of debate.[129]

COST-SHARING AND COMPETITION VERSUS NATIONAL HEALTH INSURANCE

Economic reasoning was even less visible in first round of Great Society healthcare legislation than it was in the Economic Opportunity Act. The CEA economists who helped to spark the War on Poverty had little involvement in the passage of the Social Security Amendments that established Medicare and Medicaid in 1965.[130] That legislation, the product of a decade of debate and negotiations, joined multiple logics to justify an expanded federal role in healthcare through a grand political compromise.[131] Medicare Part A paid for hospital care for all Americans over sixty-five; the optional Medicare Part B allowed older Americans to purchase heavily subsidized insurance to cover the costs of physicians' services; and Medicaid expanded the 1960 Kerr-Mills Act that had begun to provide medical coverage for the low-income.[132]

The debates leading up to the establishment of Medicare and Medicaid were driven partly by the logic of social insurance. Medicare Part A, in particular, involved compulsory contributions leading to universal access for those who reached the age of eligibility.[133] Both programs were also shaped by demands for civil rights—hospitals in the South were still racially segregated in 1965, and the public benefits system built into federal health-care legislation forced that to change.[134] In addition, a growing public sense that medical care was not just a privilege, but a right, undergirded the entire debate.[135]

From the beginning, leaders in Congress had expressed concerns about limiting the potential costs of the program. Wilbur Mills, the powerful chair of the U.S. House Ways & Means Committee, played a particularly important role in cutting the final deal.[136] Yet no one carried out anything resembling a systems analysis of the proposed legislation—there was no scoring of its cost akin to what the not-yet-created Congressional Budget Office would later do—nor was the debate conducted in the language of efficiency and cost-effectiveness. While legislators were concerned about the potential price tag of Medicare and Medicaid, those bills nevertheless became law untouched by the analytical framework of economics.

Even after the passage of these landmark bills, when PPBS was bringing the economic style into antipoverty policy, economic reasoning still had a limited impact on health policy. Nor had healthcare attracted much attention within the academic discipline of economics until the 1960s.[137] Future Nobelist Kenneth Arrow had published an important paper on the fundamental role of uncertainty in the healthcare market in 1963, and Victor Fuchs, a Columbia PhD, established health economics programs at both the Ford Foundation and the National Bureau of Economic Research in the mid-1960s.[138] At that point, though, "health economics" did not yet exist as a separate subfield within economics.

This would change overnight with the creation of Medicare and Medicaid. Rising costs became an issue almost as soon as government got into the healthcare business in a serious way. In August 1966, Johnson requested HEW "study the reasons behind the rapid rise in price of medical care" and "offer recommendations for moderating the rise."[139] In response, ASPE published the "Gorham Report," prepared under Alice Rivlin's supervision, which analyzed healthcare as a market—at the time, an unconventional approach—and centered heavily on finding ways to promote efficiency.[140] Its recommendations led to a National Conference on Medical Costs in 1967 and the creation of the National Center for Health Services Research and Development a year later. The latter would become an important funder of health economics research.[141]

These efforts—and more generally the funding that accompanied this new government interest in understanding and controlling medical costs—would help support health economics as an emerging field. But during the Johnson administration, these ideas still occupied the fringes of health policy. It was not until Nixon's presidency that the PPBS infrastructure created by Johnson's liberal economists would meaningfully affect health policy, and the conflict between the economic style and the logics of social insurance, universalism, and rights would become clear.

The Nixon administration was more attuned to questions of cost control and healthcare inflation than Johnson's had been, and these concerns continued to shape health policy debates. Yet Nixon was also forced to respond to a new sortie coming from the left wing of the Democratic Party. In 1968, the United Auto Workers organized the Committee for National Health Insurance, which included among its more prominent members Senator Edward (Ted) Kennedy.[142] The committee drafted a model bill called Health Security, which would fold Medicare and Medicaid into a new, federally run health insurance program. The program would be universally available to U.S. citizens and permanent residents, without age or income restrictions, and require no cost-sharing on the part of the insured. It would be fully national health insurance.[143]

Not wanting to be preempted by Kennedy, yet having no clear alternative to offer, Nixon spent a good part of his first term looking for a competing plan of his own. His administration's response was shaped by the legacy of PPBS in two important ways. First, it solicited a proposal from RAND for a massive Health Insurance Experiment (HIE).[144] In 1968, economist Mark Pauly, a new PhD at the time, had published "The Economics of Moral Hazard" in the *American Economic Review*.[145] Pauly's paper made an argument familiar to insurers, but then new to economists: that individuals who are insured against all health costs will seek out more care than those who are not fully insured, implying that insurance that includes no deductible or cost-sharing will result in "overuse" of care.[146] The work attracted immediate attention in the discipline, as well as stimulating policy interest.[147]

The RAND HIE, initiated by OEO's policy planning office, was effectively a large-scale experimental test of the effects of moral hazard: households were provided with access to health insurance providing different levels of coverage, and researchers followed both their use of medical care and their health outcomes. It was organized around the assumption that the appropriate policy question was not whether consumers should pay part of the cost of medical care directly, but what the appropriate level of cost-sharing was. Indeed, from the RAND perspective, "comprehensive [national health insurance] was a problem, not a solution."[148]

Like all the large-scale social policy experiments, the HIE took a long time to produce results, and it had no immediate effect on policy debate.[149] Supported first by OEO and then ASPE, and carried out in partnership with Mathematica, the HIE lasted fifteen years and eventually cost $80 million, the equivalent of roughly $400 million today.[150] Yet its size meant that the experiment trained a whole generation of researchers who accepted its foundational assumptions and who would go on to make other contributions to the healthcare debate.[151] As economist John Nyman argued in 2007, this early work on moral hazard "provided the intellectual justification for transforming the healthcare delivery system of the 1960s and 1970s into the one we have today."[152]

More immediate than the impact of RAND's HIE, though, was ASPE's role in helping Nixon develop a health policy direction. With few strong preexisting commitments in healthcare, Nixon turned to his relatively liberal HEW appointees for ideas, who in turn looked to the similarly liberal technocrats at ASPE.[153] Neither Nixon's appointees nor the career analysts opposed the idea of national health insurance; indeed, Lewis Butler, Nixon's first assistant secretary for planning and evaluation, wrote in 1969 that "ultimately some kind of national health insurance system should be enacted."[154] "But," he continued—and here the career analysts generally agreed—"the immediate problem is to ... get ... into more efficient systems."[155]

This priority made ASPE quick to embrace the concept of health maintenance organizations (HMOs), a new spin on prepaid group practice that physician Paul Ellwood advocated as a path to cost control by promoting competition and efficiency. As political scientist Lawrence Brown later wrote, the HMO strategy reflected the emerging "notion that the proper manipulation of incentives, markets, competition, reorganization, and the like can improve on present arrangements."[156] Distinct from the systems analysts' focus on comparing the cost-effectiveness of government programs, this type of "institution-building for competition" was nevertheless very much of a piece with the economic style.[157] HMOs became an early and central part of the Nixon healthcare strategy. A watered-down version of HEW's proposal would become the Health Maintenance Act of 1973, Nixon's first attempt at healthcare reform.[158]

But with Ted Kennedy and Wilbur Mills introducing a new national health insurance bill that same year, and with the threat of Watergate looming over Nixon, the president now charged HEW with producing a bill of its own.[159] Stuart Altman, the deputy assistant secretary of planning and evaluation for health who ended up writing most of it, was himself a product of the PPBS community. A labor economist who was once a "junior whiz kid" under Gorham in the McNamara Defense Department, Altman was a self-proclaimed "believer" in markets. He did not consider himself particularly political.[160] Working closely with OMB economist Peter D. Fox, Altman led the development of Nixon's second attempt at healthcare reform at a moment when national health insurance seemed so close to becoming reality that Rivlin called it "virtually certain."[161]

Altman's plan, embraced by Nixon, included a mandate for employers to provide comprehensive health insurance to employees and a government-funded program run by private insurance companies to insure those not covered by employers or Medicare. The plan would be free for people with low incomes, with assistance phased out at higher incomes.[162] While the plan included "substantial cost sharing," it was, as Altman and David Shachtman wrote in 2011, "a plan that many health policy advocates in the Obama administration would be happy to support."[163]

From today's perspective, the ideas proposed by Nixon's ASPE seem liberal. They were not in fact so distant from what would eventually become Obamacare.[164] Yet the focus on cost-sharing for everyone and means-testing for those not covered by employers or Medicare reflected the economic style of reasoning and its prioritization of cost-effectiveness. By contrast, Nixon's plan conflicted with the social insurance approach, which emphasized universal access and had animated Medicare. At that time, many Democrats hoped to simply extend Medicare's coverage to the whole population. Nixon's plan also conflicted with arguments about the right to medical care, which by the late 1960s were being endorsed by civil rights leaders, the feminist movement, the emerging welfare rights movement, and the public health community.[165] Indeed, Ted Kennedy's 1971 Health Security bill began by stating that "adequate health care for all of our people must now be recognized as a right."[166]

Yet from the economic perspective, support for universal free access and absolute rights to care made little sense, given its commitment to efficiency and cost-effectiveness. The Health Security bill required consumers to pay nothing for care; cost-sharing was a frequent target of criticism from the left.[167] But for economists—including liberal economists—and their analytical allies, cost-sharing seemed like the only reasonable approach, even before the RAND experiment provided convincing evidence that healthcare, too, followed the laws of supply and demand.[168] Indeed, Rivlin, writing in the *New York Times*, blamed organized labor for continuing to maintain the position that national health insurance should "provide free care for everyone without any cost-sharing" and was relatively approving of the Nixon plan.[169] The more economic reasoning became a necessary means to justify new policy proposals, the harder it became for more liberal Democrats to advance arguments about universalism and rights.

BEYOND POVERTY AND HEALTH

Across a whole range of social policy domains, similar conflicts between the logic of efficiency and the logics of equality, rights, and universalism continued to play out. Over time, the organizations and networks put into place by PPBS gradually changed the terms of debate. The institutionalization of the economic style was uneven, but where it took hold, its effects were significant.

In housing policy, for example, Great Society legislation reflected a (tempered) commitment to the idea of public housing, along with a civil-rights-based commitment to ending racial segregation.[170] Liberal economists, though, typically preferred housing allowances, or vouchers, as a more efficient means of assisting low-income families. They tended to skirt the question of race entirely—a pairing of positions that set them up for a productive alliance with Nixon.[171] While Nixon was leery of housing policy that promoted desegregation, he also sought to make his mark as a "conservative domestic innovator." With his hopes for passing a Family Assistance Plan disappearing, Nixon increasingly saw housing allowances as a way to achieve something similar. What was more, the approach hewed to conservative principles of limited government and individual responsibility by paying support directly to recipients and not requiring government ownership or complicated programs.[172]

Nixon's position proved fortuitous for advocates of the economic style. The first half of the 1970s saw a dramatic expansion of economic analysis at HUD. The massive Experimental Housing Allowance Program, discussed earlier, was grounded in the idea that aid to individuals that could be used in the open market might be a more effective form of assistance than public housing. In 1974, HUD introduced the Section 8 voucher program, which would become the backbone of federal housing policy.[173] Housing vouchers brought together moderate Republicans with liberal economists. More efficient than either public housing or subsidies for builders, they also expanded choice for renters and competition among landlords. From Nixon's perspective, vouchers also offered the benefit of sidestepping racial politics by moving assistance from the level of housing projects, where it produced visible conflict, to individuals, where discrimination would be hidden.[174] With its embrace of vouchers, Nixon's HUD used economic logic to move sharply away from the New Deal commitment to "strong public institutions" in housing as well as the civil rights commitments of Great Society housing legislation.[175]

A similar conflict between the economic style and logics of equality played out in education policy, but—at least in the short term—produced different results. Great Society education legislation was motivated by ideals of access and equity for poor students, Black students, and other disadvantaged groups.[176] Liberal economists typically shared these goals, but they focused on the question of how to achieve them in a cost-effective manner.[177] In addition to promoting a shift toward individual, rather than institution-level, support for higher education, they aimed to make schools more efficient at turning inputs (for example, teachers, buildings) into outputs (higher test scores). They were also increasingly intrigued by the idea of expanding choice and competition in education.[178]

In 1972, Congress created the new National Institute of Education (NIE) within HEW, which was imagined as a National Science Foundation for education research.[179] The NIE was closely tied to the analytic community, with ASPE among its strongest advocates. Economist Thomas K. Glennan, its first director, was an alumnus of both RAND and OEO's policy planning office. Such supporters hoped the NIE would serve as a "sparkling gem of rationality" within what they saw as a muddled and ineffective education establishment, and with its creation, economic reasoning looked poised to fully take hold in education policy.[180]

But bad timing (budgets were not as generous in 1972 as they had been in 1965), political missteps (Glennan was a sharper analyst than he was a political actor), and the competing presence of "educationists" (practitioner-focused researchers trained in schools of education, not at all oriented toward economics) led to a rapid loss of congressional support for NIE. When Congress created the new, standalone Department of Education in 1979, NIE was downsized and downgraded, before being eliminated entirely.[181] By the time the National Academy of Sciences conducted an in-depth survey of the fields influencing education research in 1992—cognitive sciences, psychology, sociology, among several others—economics did not even merit a mention.[182]

The language of efficiency, competition, and choice would eventually rise again in education policy, the second time stronger than before. But the reversals of the 1970s meant that the spread of the economic style into education policy was more halting than in other domains of social policy. Yet even in this domain of more limited influence, the institutional resources produced by the Great Society kept economic reasoning alive in educational policy, and in the 1990s it made a resurgence. By the early years of the twenty-first century, the economic style had become the governing logic of federal educational policy as well.[183]

Institutionalizing the Economic Style in Social Policy

Lyndon Johnson's Great Society legislation transformed a wide range of social policy domains. This historic wave of legislation would never have come to pass without a varied set of political developments, from postwar economic expansion to the Civil Rights Movement to John F. Kennedy's assassination. Still, advocates' arguments on its behalf consistently centered a handful of ways of thinking about the legislation's purpose that focused on universalism, equality, and rights.

One of these was a logic of social insurance, which advocated for compulsory, universal government programs to insure Americans from unavoidable risk—of reaching old age, of sickness, of unemployment. Another, newer to the 1960s, was a logic of political participation. This emphasized the importance of citizens having a meaningful voice in government programs meant to assist them. A third was a logic of equality, especially racial equality, but also equality of opportunity for lower-income Americans. And a fourth, newly resurgent in the 1960s but also echoing Franklin Roosevelt's Second Bill of Rights, was a logic of rights, in which Americans had not only civil rights, but a right to welfare if needed, to decent housing, to medical care, to a good education.

The logics behind the Great Society legislation conflicted in many ways with economic reasoning, which emphasized efficiency and cost-effectiveness over rights, universalism, and equality. Yet the Great Society programs themselves, launched simultaneously with the rollout of PPBS, inadvertently boosted the role of economic reasoning in multiple policy domains. Policy planning offices advocated for an economic way of thinking about policy problems, while new streams of research and evaluation funding supported a growing ecosystem of economics-oriented policy research organizations. Across a range of domains, a broadly economic approach to policy problems began to flourish.

Policy analysis in the economic style was originally introduced to make social programs work as well as possible, if "success" was defined as getting the most bang for the taxpayer's buck. This definition already moved the goalposts from the original aims of program advocates. But the economic style of policy analysis had an epistemic authority those advocates lacked. It proved surprisingly useful for political purposes as well. The Johnson administration found it a valuable tool for regaining control over the War on Poverty, as community action started to become a political liability for the Democratic Party. Its importance as a means for deciding how best to spend government money only increased as the budgetary mood began to turn from expansionary to contractionary in 1966.

The election of Richard Nixon in the fall of 1968 might, at first glance, have seemed to spell the end of an era for Johnson's liberal policy analysts. The leadership of various policy planning offices changed hands, and the conservative wing of the Nixon administration attempted to undo the government expansion of the Great Society. Yet the analytic community found an unexpected ally in Nixon, whose first term focused more on transforming the Great Society than on repealing it. The analysts' organizational base in the executive bureaucracy allowed them to advocate for a range of policy ideas that still reflected a belief that government had a major role to play in these policy domains. Even so, their economic approach conflicted with the commitment to universalism, equality, and rights that had motivated the Great Society. Just as Johnson's economists had, Nixon's economists circumvented the explosive issue of race by finding ways to address social problems while ignoring their racial dimension, in a way that liberal programs like community action or public housing could not. Indeed, while the economics-oriented analytic community experienced some setbacks under Nixon, on balance the Nixon years were a time of substantial growth for it.

The economic style of reasoning meanwhile continued to spread across the nominally nonpartisan space of policy conversation both in and out of government—through policy planning offices and policy research organizations, through the training of public policy students and lawyers in the basics of economics, and eventually through the creation of the Congressional Budget Office. Within this space, economic reasoning came to be seen as the appropriate stance for thinking about social policy problems. From this perspective, even if one believed in using government to improve people's lives, the Great Society's orientation toward universalism, equality, and rights was misguided. One might achieve the same goals more efficiently through targeted programs, the argument went, and absolute rights to health or education might come at too high a cost. A handful of groups—labor unions advocating for universal health insurance, educationists prioritizing equity for underserved students, and civil rights leaders skeptical that housing vouchers would work as well for Black Americans as for white Americans—continued to center competing arguments. But their perspectives were becoming more marginal even within the Democratic Party, which was increasingly taking its cues from advocates of the economic style.

The economic style advanced unevenly across social policy domains. Its influence was always subject to pushback. Yet by the time Democrats returned to the White House under Carter, it had come to play a much more visible role in shaping liberal policy proposals. Increasingly, arguments about social policy reform were arguments about choice, incentives, and cost-effectiveness. Arguments focused on universalism, rights and equality were moving out of the mainstream of policy debate. With the analytic community a critical source of new policy proposals, competing approaches had become increasingly easy to dismiss.

6

The Economic Style and Market Governance

The late 1960s and early 1970s saw systems analysts and their heirs disseminating an economic style of reasoning in social policy: evaluating government programs on their cost-effectiveness and promoting the use of incentives, choice, and competition. But they were not the only group advocating for the use of economic reasoning in Washington. It was during this same era that industrial organization (I/O) economists began encouraging policymakers to govern markets through the lens of efficiency.

Market governance policy domains include all those that set the rules for market competition, either across the economy broadly (for instance, antitrust or intellectual property policy), or in specific sectors that are seen as requiring special rules (transportation, energy, finance, communications, healthcare).[1] At the time that I/O economists were making their way to Washington, antitrust policy as well as many of the industry-specific policy domains were governed by legal frameworks put into place decades before, between the Gilded Age and the New Deal. When first implemented in the late nineteenth century, antitrust policy and railroad regulation were motivated by logics that would continue to resonate as regulation was extended to both existing (electricity, natural gas) and emerging (trucking, airlines, telecommunications) industries in the 1930s. These included a concern with limiting corporate power; demands for a rough equity in access to, and pricing of, services; and a desire to bring stability in the face of "ruinous competition." While these goals were often contested, and legislative battles to achieve them hard-fought, by the end of the 1930s a regulatory regime had been put into place that largely reflected them.

By the 1960s, though, the frameworks that had proved compelling thirty or sixty years before were starting to show their age. The trusts were a thing of the past, and with the Great Depression increasingly distant, policymakers had lost their fear of market instability. With the proliferation of options in transportation and shipping, officials no longer regarded equitable access to markets and pricing as such pressing concerns. And observers on both left and right were increasingly concerned that regulation often seemed to serve the interests of the regulated over those of the general public.

This changing political-economic context set the stage for advocates of the economic style—industrial organization economists and similarly inclined lawyers, for the most part—to challenge the existing regime of market governance. From an economic perspective that valued markets for their efficient allocation of resources—keeping prices competitive and giving as many people as much of what they were willing to pay for as possible—it seemed only logical that market governance should focus on promoting such efficiency.

This position, by the 1960s already a consensus one within the economics profession, was often at odds with the values that had historically motivated U.S. antitrust and regulatory policy. Yet as I/O economists and those who adopted their framework moved into positions of influence across all three branches of government as well as in policy think tanks, they advocated for this way of thinking about market governance.[2] In antitrust, this meant moving away from simply limiting size and toward evaluating policy on the basis of whether it promoted competition and efficiency. In regulatory policy, it meant pushing for the end of price controls and barriers to entry—particularly in transportation industries, but also in energy, communications, and elsewhere. And it eventually reached policy arenas, like healthcare policy, that had not always been seen as markets to be governed at all.

Early on, proponents of the economic approach to market governance tended to be liberal and associated with the Democratic Party; as the 1970s progressed, Chicago School conservatives and libertarians became more prominent voices. What both camps shared, though, was a commitment to efficiency. And as they found themselves in positions of increasing influence, the older legal frameworks of market governance—intended to limit corporate power, ensure equity, and promote stability—were gradually dismantled, and new ones—centered on efficiency, choice, and competition—were put in their place.

The Slower Spread of the Economic
Style in Market Governance

The spread of an economic style of reasoning was slower and more piecemeal in market governance than it was for social policy. In part, this reflected the relatively diffuse networks of industrial organization, the subfield of economics most immediately relevant to thinking about how government should regulate markets. Unlike the systems analysts who developed their approach in the hothouse environment of RAND, advocates of the economic style in market governance were scattered across economics departments and law schools, although important clusters could be found at Harvard and Chicago. Those who occupied positions within the policy realm in the late 1960s, like Donald Turner at the Antitrust Division of the Department of Justice or Joe Peck at the Council of Economic Advisors, tended to work as individual advocates rather than heads of well-resourced policy planning offices. When it came to market governance, there was no single precipitating event like the PPBS rollout to rapidly advance economic reasoning.

Turner, Peck, and their like-minded colleagues encountered another challenge that the systems analysts working in social policy sometimes avoided: entrenched bureaucracy. As new government offices, the fundamental orientation and day-to-day administrative practices of entities like the OEO and HUD were still up for grabs. In these and other new offices established as part of the Great Society, the economic style had only to displace relatively novel approaches, like community action programs, that were not yet fully rooted in the bureaucracy or in law. In market governance, by contrast, advocates of the economic style encountered a body of legislation passed as early as 1887 and largely completed by the end of the 1930s, decades of case law, and the organizational culture of the Antitrust Division and longstanding independent regulatory agencies like the Interstate Commerce Commission. Instead of displacing weakly institutionalized alternative logics advanced through recent legislation, advocates of the economic style had to tear down a very durable legal and organizational framework—one grounded in a fundamentally different way of thinking about the purpose of government—that had been put into place decades before.

Centering efficiency, choice, and competition in market governance required advocates of the economic style to change decision-making processes in those long-established agencies, sometimes through the introduction of new leadership and sometimes through the expansion of economics offices within them. It required replacing legislation that propped up the old order, particularly through bills deregulating specific industries like airlines, railroads, and trucking. And in antitrust, where the courts played a major role in determining policy, it required new case law that rejected older frameworks that balanced a set of competing policy goals and instead embraced the promotion of efficiency as the sole purpose of antitrust.

A final challenge of introducing the economic style into market governance concerned its orientation toward governance itself. In social policy, even those policymakers who advanced the economic style worked from the underlying assumption that government *should* act in the realm of social policy—the question was what kind of actions it should take. But in market governance, advancing the economic style did, in many cases, mean limiting government intervention. This was not always the case; sometimes, as in healthcare policy, advocates argued for a government role in building an infrastructure for competition.[3] In domains like railroad, trucking, and airline regulation, though, advocates of the economic style saw their primary task as dismantling existing systems for setting prices and controlling entry into the relevant markets. In effect, they proposed to regulate by deregulating.

As all this was accomplished, the older ways of thinking about market governance as a way to limit corporate power, ensure equity, and promote stability mostly faded away. This was not only because the economic style had come to dominate the space of policy debate, as in social policy, although it increasingly did. With the ascent of the economic style, the underlying priorities associated with it—of efficiency as a central goal of policy, with choice and competition as its corollaries—were also incorporated into legal frameworks.

Establishing the Consumer Welfare Standard in Antitrust

Since its origins with the Sherman Act of 1890, the very purpose of antitrust policy has been persistently contested. The original antitrust movement, motivated by fears about Standard Oil and other trusts that had effectively monopolized entire industries, reflected a broad set of concerns about the growing power of big business over farmers, labor, and government. The Sherman Act itself declared contracts, trust combinations, and conspiracies in restraint of trade or in attempt to monopolize illegal.[4] But at less than a thousand words in length, it left much to the imagination. Scholars—and the courts—have repeatedly reinterpreted it, arguing at different times not only that it was meant to limit economic power broadly defined, but also that its main intent was to protect competition, increase consumer welfare (often defined specifically as allocative efficiency), protect small business, or even redistribute wealth.[5]

The most politically salient aspect of these concerns would vary tremendously over the next seventy-five years. In the 1930s, many Americans feared that the rise of chain grocery stores—particularly the rapidly growing A&P supermarket—would devastate local businesses and undermine the economic fabric of small-town life. The Jeffersonian impulse to protect small businesses drove Congress to pass the Robinson-Patman Act in 1936, which limited manufacturers' ability to give discounts to big chains, and very nearly led to legislation that would have taxed chains out of existence.[6] But the 1930s also saw "the consumer" emerge as a stand-in for the public interest more generally, with policymakers expressing a growing concern for protecting consumers from high prices.[7] This consumer protection impulse was recognized in court decisions like *Apex Hosiery v. Leader* (1940), which interpreted the Sherman Act as barring practices that "restrict production, raise prices, or otherwise control the market to the detriment of purchasers or consumers of goods and services."[8] This impulse sat in tension with the desire to protect small businesses, which frequently had to charge higher prices than their larger, more efficient competitors.

As these examples suggest, Congress and the courts shared responsibility for, and sometimes sparred over, setting the priorities for antitrust policy. With the Sherman Act and other antitrust laws so open to interpretation, the courts played an outsized role in determining the actual contents of antitrust policy. Between 1962 and 1967, the Warren Court upheld a series of government challenges to mergers that by present standards seem quite modest.[9] For example, in the landmark *Brown Shoe Co. v. the United States* decision (1962), the Court invalidated a merger that would have given the firm in question a 5 percent share of the market, because of what it saw as a general tendency toward consolidation in the shoe industry.[10]

Into the 1960s, the Supreme Court accompanied appeals to Jeffersonian democracy with a stated commitment to limiting corporate power and protecting consumers, to the point of invoking inconsistent judicial reasoning. The court consistently asserted its desire to protect competition and, at least through the 1960s, issued decisions that limited mergers and restricted corporate behavior. In *Brown Shoe*, it noted that the Congressional debate around the Celler-Kefauver Act of 1950 reflected Congress's "fear of what was considered to be a rising tide of economic concentration in the American economy. . . . Other considerations . . . were the desirability

of retaining 'local control' over industry and the protection of small businesses." Here, competition meant "the protection of viable, small, locally
owned businesses," even if it meant "occasional higher costs and prices."[11]
At other times, the court emphasized that "the test of a competitive market
is . . . whether the consumers are well served," not only through low prices
but also through freedom of choice. But because prevailing economic theory
suggested that market concentration would lead firms to raise prices, a judicial approach that prioritized the well-being of consumers also led to court
decisions that limited mergers.[12]

The courts had long acknowledged that big businesses might be able to
produce at lower cost than smaller businesses, potentially keeping prices
lower as well. Yet regardless of whether the Supreme Court centered small
business or consumers in its decisions, efficiency—whether in its productive
sense of resulting in the most output with the fewest inputs, or its allocative
sense of producing the collectively most-valued goods and services—had not
been a central theme of the court's antitrust decisions. In the early 1960s,
though, the Supreme Court began to cite economics more frequently—if
erratically—in antitrust cases. For example, *United States v. Philadelphia
National Bank*, a 1963 Supreme Court case that prohibited the merger of two
banks that would have controlled 30 percent of the regional market, cited
several economists, including Turner, Carl Kaysen, and George Stigler.[13] The
opinion itself was written by Richard Posner, then a recent Harvard Law
grad and a clerk for Supreme Court Justice William Brennan, in one of his
first encounters with the economics literature.[14] It required mergers leading
to control of an "undue" percentage of the market to show they would not
have anticompetitive effects.[15]

Industrial organization economists, of course, had already begun to
articulate an efficiency-centered vision of antitrust by this time. Turner, the
Harvard School economist who would be appointed chief of the Antitrust
Division in 1965, was particularly concerned that, in its effort to protect
small businesses, the courts were preventing mergers that would increase
efficiency and thereby benefit consumers. Turner called this position "not
only bad economics but bad law."[16] However, as an adherent to the structure-
conduct-performance (SCP) framework, Turner also believed that high levels of market concentration tended to produce anticompetitive conduct—
including the ability to raise prices—which in turn would reduce allocative
efficiency. Posner's opinion in *Philadelphia National Bank* was grounded in
this framework, although Posner would, upon converting to the Chicago

School a few years later, come to reject the position.[17] Thus, Turner endorsed the idea of a sweet spot for antitrust policy: allowing mergers might promote efficiency, but too much concentration was likely to reduce it.

Robert Bork and Ward Bowman, representing the insurgent Chicago School, similarly centered efficiency as the ultimate purpose of antitrust. But from their perspective, the protection of small businesses was misguided. They rejected the SCP framework and assumed that both size and concentration typically reflected efficiency. As they noted in 1965, "the existence of the trend [toward concentration] is prima facie evidence that greater concentration is socially desirable. The trend indicates that there are emerging efficiencies or economies of scale . . . which make larger size more efficient."[18] Their statement not only endorsed efficiency as the proper lens for evaluating policy but also assumed that if markets were concentrated, it was for good reason.

In the mid-1960s, representatives of the I/O community—both economists and sympathetic legal scholars, like Bork—moved into positions of policy influence. As they did so, they worked to advance, and ultimately institutionalize, their efficiency-centered view of the purpose of antitrust. And as Chicago came to replace Harvard as the dominant school of thought in industrial organization during the 1970s, the policy implications of economic reasoning would change significantly. By the 1980s, this process would be complete: antitrust policy would be based on the value of efficiency rather than a commitment to limiting political power or encouraging small business.

This change was gradual, and took place along two pathways. The first was through the integration of economic reasoning into the executive branch, specifically the Antitrust Division of the Department of Justice and the Federal Trade Commission at the Department of Commerce. As I/O economists gradually filled the ranks of these bureaucracies, these agencies began pursuing different kinds of cases. The second change took place through the courts, which gradually came to accept a new, efficiency-centered conception of consumer welfare as the primary purpose of antitrust law. As the courts changed their approach to these cases, a feedback loop developed: as the courts interpreted antitrust more narrowly, the agencies became less likely to bring cases that they once might have considered, and as the agencies narrowed their own criteria for thinking about antitrust, the courts pointed to those changes to justify their own decision-making. Soon enough, antitrust policy in the United States was locked into the economic style.

ADVANCING EFFICIENCY THROUGH
ORGANIZATIONAL CHANGE

At the time Donald Turner was appointed Assistant Attorney General in 1965, staff at both of the antitrust agencies saw their role primarily through an enforcement lens. Dominated by attorneys whose careers advanced through litigation experience, and little influenced by economists, the agencies focused not on evaluating the larger purpose of antitrust policy or the economic rationale behind a particular legal challenge, but on prosecuting as many winnable cases as they could.[19] Replacing this perspective with an efficiency lens, in which the agencies would only challenge mergers or corporate behaviors that reduced allocative efficiency, required significant organizational change. Not only would the agencies need to create modern economics offices, but they also had to revise their decision-making processes to incorporate economic reasoning in case selection.

In much the same way that the Johnson administration's political calculations about the perceived radicalism of the OEO propelled systems analysts into positions of power, the arrival of I/O economists in the antitrust agencies responded to a political problem. Lyndon Johnson appointed Turner in part to appease the business community, which was increasingly anxious about the impact of decisions like *Brown Shoe* on their corporate strategies.[20] Economic boom times led corporate America to seek expansion through mergers, and the mid-1960s saw the largest merger wave in forty years.[21] The Celler-Kefauver Act had made it harder for firms to sidestep the Clayton Act prohibition on mergers that "substantially limit[ed] competition," however, and, as the *Wall Street Journal* observed, "Many a company, faced with the prospect of long and costly litigation, has decided not to go ahead with a merger, even though it might actually enhance competition."[22]

As assistant attorney general of the Antitrust Division, Turner set the course for the Department of Justice's antitrust policy, and he particularly pushed the use of the economic style. Upon his arrival, he created a policy planning office and a special economic assistant position. He also initiated the division's first published merger guidelines, issued in 1968, which were particularly important in signaling a shift in the purpose of antitrust policy. The guidelines made no reference to broad economic power or the virtues of small business, instead emphasizing that "the primary role of Section 7 [of the Clayton Act] enforcement is to preserve and promote market structures conducive to competition"—a structuralist, but recognizably economic, interpretation.[23] While it was initially unclear whether the courts would defer to the new guidelines, it turned out that they were taken seriously.[24]

Turner's efforts encountered opposition from the litigation-minded attorneys of the division. As political scientist Suzanne Weaver observed, "[S]omeone had, in the lawyers' eyes, changed the criteria of review, adding standards alien to the lawyers and repugnant to their notions of good prosecution. One did not turn down a case involving a clear, predatory violation of the law simply because it had little economic impact."[25] When President Nixon replaced Turner with the more enforcement-oriented Richard McLaren, many of the division's attorneys experienced a sense of relief.[26]

McLaren, though, proved politically problematic for Nixon. While Turner had been friendly to the conglomerate mergers that were the dominant form in the 1960s, McLaren was not.[27] He filed multiple suits challenging conglomerate mergers pursued by International Telephone and Telegraph (ITT), a major Nixon backer.[28] Nixon intervened, telling attorney general Richard Kleindienst to "stay the hell out of [the ITT mergers]," or "McLaren's ass is to be out within one hour."[29] When McLaren did not oblige, Nixon disposed of him by appointing him to serve as a federal judge.[30] The subsequent scandal, exposed by *Washington Post* columnist Jack Anderson, was the first in a series of escalating events that eventually culminated in Watergate.[31]

McLaren's replacement, Michigan law professor Thomas Kauper, was friendlier both to conglomerate mergers and to economics.[32] Although not a strict Chicago School adherent, Kauper was influenced by Richard Posner's recent work, which argued that economic efficiency should be the only consideration of antitrust policy.[33] Working in close collaboration with economist George Hay, who oversaw the creation and expansion of a new Economic Policy Office (EPO), Kauper integrated economic reasoning into the process of developing cases while minimizing the ire it raised from litigators. One strategy involved bringing economists into the case selection process early, rather than having them review cases that attorneys had already sunk time into developing. Indeed, Kauper and Hay found ways to make the EPO *generate* economically rational cases that the lawyers might otherwise overlook—thus countering economists' in-house reputation as "case-killers."[34] And, of course, they began teaching basic economics to the lawyers.[35] The 1976 passage of the Hart-Scott-Rodino Antitrust Improvements Act, which encouraged the division to analyze mergers before their consummation, rather than litigate them after, facilitated their efforts.[36]

Although the project was not without its challenges, and conflict within the agency continued, over time efficiency become a much more central lens through which the Antitrust Division selected cases.[37]

A similar process was under way at the FTC, where the Bureau of Economics was likewise substantially upgraded during the 1970s.[38] At the FTC, the policy planning office, created in the agency's 1970 reorganization, also played a significant role in advancing economic reasoning—particularly, its Chicago variant. Initially, the Office of Policy Planning and Evaluation undertook PPBS-inspired activities like "develop[ing] a formal econometric model to determine where enforcement efforts would reap the greatest benefits."[39] But with the 1974 appointment of Wesley J. Liebeler, a UCLA law professor and one-time student of Aaron Director, the office took on greater importance and a different approach.[40] This new office would play a significant role in advancing economic reasoning at the agency as the decade progressed.[41]

Liebeler dramatically increased the policy planning office's role in budgetary review and pushed for the agency to reallocate resources toward what he took to be the agency's mission. As he described the purpose of antitrust law, "[T]he basic objective of these laws is to maximize consumer welfare [that is, allocative efficiency]. . . . We are not aware of any other operationally viable objective available to the Commission in setting priorities." He explained that the FTC should base its programming and decisions "on the basis of their expected economic impact on the consumer in dollars-and-cents terms."[42] This meant ignoring behavior that was, on its face, illegal, but that could not be directly demonstrated to reduce market efficiency. The litigating bureaus pushed back against what they saw as Liebeler's overreach, and some of his recommendations—like an effort to give the Bureau of Economics and the policy planning office veto power over the conduct of preliminary investigations—were not realized. But Liebeler nevertheless succeeded in centering efficiency as the main criterion for agency decision-making.[43]

By the time of the Carter administration, economics and efficiency had become much more integrated into antitrust decision-making—to the point where it was difficult for new agency leadership to even try to pursue an enforcement agenda motivated by other goals. In one telling example, Assistant Attorney General John Shenefield expressed "almost evangelical" support for a Ted Kennedy bill that would have put strict size tests on mergers, and "acknowledged he was going after bigness as such."[44] Yet after promising to bring a "shared monopolies" case within half a year, Shenefield was forced to recant "'because we didn't know and do not know' the outcome of a lengthy staff investigation."[45] While antitrust appointees could try to set their own policy directions, they relied on career staff to do the legwork that would make action possible. If career professionals saw a particular direction as fundamentally in conflict with the agency's mission, they might drag their feet.

Similarly, Shenefield's successor, Sanford Litvack, oversaw limited enforcement, even as he voiced a traditional view of antitrust. Reflecting on his term as assistant attorney general, he observed that the Antitrust Division "appears to be backing away from this law enforcement obligation. . . . [M]uch more emphasis is now placed on economic theory, study, and research, while less emphasis is given to investigation, prosecution, and the nuts and bolts of effective litigation."[46]

Even when Carter's appointees did convince their agencies to pursue antitrust enforcement, they increasingly encountered resistance in the courts. At the FTC, Carter appointed as chair consumer activist Michael Pertschuk, who made his concern with "the dispersal of economic and political power" explicit.[47] Pertschuk, who replaced Liebeler with the liberal Robert Reich, was able to leverage the support of sympathetic structuralist leadership in the Bureau of Economics to pursue a fairly aggressive agenda, if one couched in economic language.[48] But despite this, the FTC's success rate in the courts fell in half, from 88 percent in 1976 to only 43 percent in 1981.[49] The courts, as well as the antitrust agencies, were also coming to accept an efficiency-centered framework—and, specifically, one grounded in Chicago School reasoning—for interpreting the antitrust laws.

ADVANCING EFFICIENCY THROUGH SUPREME COURT DECISIONS

As decision-making processes were changing in the antitrust agencies, the courts were undergoing an evolution of their own. As late as 1967, the Supreme Court had explicitly articulated concern with the protection of small business as a factor it considered in its decisions—in three different cases, no less.[50] But, as in the *Philadelphia National Bank* case, it was increasingly mixing these non-economic considerations with ones based on structuralist economics.[51] Over the next decade, the Supreme Court moved toward centering efficiency as its sole lens for making decisions about antitrust cases, to the exclusion of competing concerns about small business or corporate power. Moreover, when it drew on economic reasoning, it would increasingly rely on a Chicago School approach, rather than Harvard structuralism.

This shift did not, of course, take place outside the context of politics. Between 1969 and 1971, Nixon appointed four Supreme Court justices, ending the Warren era and ushering in the Burger Court. At the same time, the big business community was becoming better organized, and antitrust was one of its major areas of concern. The exact relationship between the changing composition of the Supreme Court, organized business's increasingly vocal displeasure with the state of antitrust, and the rise of Chicago I/O, each of which contributed to the shift, is difficult to disentangle.

Regardless of the mix of factors that contributed to it, over the course of the 1970s the Supreme Court came to thoroughly reject noneconomic conceptions of antitrust policy. In no case issued after 1967 did the court invoke small business protection as a goal of antitrust. Each of several significant antitrust decisions issued in the first half of the 1970s gradually increased the standard of evidence required to restrict corporate behavior, and each invoked economic reasoning.[52] *Brunswick Corp. v. Pueblo Bowl-O-Mat* (1977) placed the final nail in the coffin for the protection of small business as a legitimate goal of antitrust. Citing *Brown Shoe* to new purpose, the unanimous opinion emphasized that "[t]he antitrust laws . . . were enacted for 'the protection of *competition*, not *competitors*,'" and that private antitrust litigants could not challenge a merger on the likelihood that it might drive smaller competitors out of business.[53] This decision effectively marked the end of noneconomic concerns being addressed, even erratically, by antitrust policy.

At the same time, the Supreme Court was increasingly enshrining efficiency as the specific purpose of antitrust policy, and a Chicago approach as the correct one for thinking about how to promote it. That same year, the court decided *Continental Television, Inc. v. GTE Sylvania, Inc.*, which has been called "the most important [in antitrust] since World War II," and which drew heavily on the work of Chicagoans Robert Bork and Richard Posner. The majority opinion declared that resale restrictions it had found per se illegal in 1967 were in fact not illegal, because they could potentially increase efficiency.[54] In a concurring opinion, Justice Byron White criticized the majority reasoning for "summarily rejecting" concern with "the autonomy of independent businessmen," arguing that "this principle is without question more deeply embedded in our cases than the notions of 'free rider' effects and distributional efficiencies borrowed by the majority from the "new economics of vertical relationships."[55] And yet, this was a concurrence, not a dissent.

By 1979, the Court had fully accepted Robert Bork's argument, laid out in his landmark 1978 book, *The Antitrust Paradox*, that consumer welfare should be defined as allocative efficiency.[56] In *Reiter v. Sonotone Corp.*, Chief Justice

Burger—in something of an aside to the main argument—quoted Bork, writing, "Congress designed the Sherman Act as a 'consumer welfare prescription.'"[57] Since then, the courts have accepted consumer welfare, generally understood narrowly as economic efficiency, as the sole legitimate purpose of antitrust (although debate continues over exactly how it should be defined).[58]

Over the course of fifteen years, the purpose of antitrust policy narrowed from a complex mix of goals, including the promotion of broad consumer interests, the protection of small business, and the limiting of corporate power, to a single, efficiency-centered conception of consumer welfare. The change took place because both the federal antitrust agencies and the U.S. Supreme Court embraced the economic style, at a time when the business community was organizing and advocating for less aggressive antitrust enforcement. The "Reagan Revolution" has sometimes been seen as the start of a new era in antitrust, but for the most part, economic reasoning was already institutionalized by the time Reagan's appointees arrived at their desks. As political scientist Marc Eisner wrote in his analysis of the antitrust agencies, "this revolution in antitrust was at most a coup."[59]

Deregulating Transportation Markets

Centering efficiency in antitrust policy involved positive change: institutionalizing a new style of reasoning in the antitrust agencies, and a new goal for antitrust—consumer welfare—in the courts. As this took place, older, competing purposes were gradually delegitimized. In transportation policy, by contrast, the spread of economic reasoning involved a more active tearing down of an existing regulatory regime. By the 1970s, the United States maintained an extensive system of market regulations in the transportation industry that regulated prices and controlled entry into the rail, trucking, and airline industries. This system was designed not to promote efficiency, but rather to create stability and preserve a rough equity across consumers in different locations.

Economists across the political spectrum believed that easing these restrictions was desirable because it would improve efficiency. Doing so would require dismantling nearly a century's worth of regulatory measures and agencies. This took place through the passage of legislation that deregulated each of these industries, as well as the elimination of the organizational locations (the Interstate Commerce Commission [ICC] and the Civil Aeronautics Board [CAB]) that propped up the old regime. A view of efficiency as the purpose of transportation regulation became hegemonic in the world of think tanks and policy advisors, yet it was never institutionalized through the law.

———

Federal regulation of transportation began with the railroads, sparked by the same late-nineteenth-century social upheavals that produced the antitrust movement. The Interstate Commerce Act of 1887 resulted from an uneasy alliance between a variety of groups with conflicting interests (farmers, shippers, merchants), but who shared an opposition to the monopolistic power of the railroads.[60] Nearly fifty years later, New Deal legislation prioritized stability and access in the trucking and airline industries in the face of cutthroat competition.[61] Carriers assented to price regulation and a commitment to ensuring broad access to service (including on unprofitable routes) at equitable prices, in return for which they would receive considerable protection from competition.

These principles remained solidly established into the 1960s. The regulated industries supported the existing governance regime, which faced little organized opposition. But by now, economists had begun to articulate a competing vision of market governance—one that applied not only to transportation industries, but to a variety of markets (energy, communications) where government set prices and limited entry. In this vision, the main goal of policy was to promote allocative efficiency.

In the 1960s, the economists gained a somewhat unexpected ally: liberal Democrats. A generation earlier, New Deal Democrats had supported transportation regulation out of a desire to achieve stability and equity. Starting in the 1950s, though, liberal political scientists—who began with the Interstate Commerce Commission and then moved on to agencies like the Civil Aeronautics Board, Federal Communications Commission, and Federal Power Commission—started to argue that government regulation tended to serve the interests of industry, which "captured" the agencies that governed it.[62] By the 1960s, radical historians were amplifying the critique, claiming that the entire Progressive-era regulatory movement had effectively subsumed the public interest to the interests of business.[63] Meanwhile, a growing consumer movement led by Ralph Nader portrayed transportation regulation as a technique to keep prices artificially high.[64] Both the academic and popular critiques of economic regulation were more interested in market fairness than market efficiency, but they nevertheless produced liberal Democratic allies for economists' deregulatory arguments.

Even so, the economists' position remained a hard sell throughout the Kennedy and Johnson administrations. Both the strength of pro-regulatory interests and a strong conventional wisdom favoring transportation regulation favored the status quo. Johnson notably did display some curiosity toward deregulation by, for example, calling for "heavier reliance on competition in transportation" in his 1965 State of the Union address, but showed little follow-through.[65] While Kennedy and Johnson paid lip service to the deregulatory arguments of their economists, the issue failed to gain momentum during their years in the White House.

Richard Nixon, surrounded with his bevy of Chicago School economists, moved transportation policy a step closer to deregulation. He created a committee, led by Harvard economist and CEA member Hendrik Houthakker, to review the possibility of "decontrol" of trucking and railways, a prospect Nixon thought might allow him to bring in the consumer movement as allies. When the massive Penn Central Railroad filed for bankruptcy in mid-1970, Nixon hoped that a deregulatory coalition might be put together that could overcome the almost certain opposition of truckers and other beneficiaries of regulation.[66] But when his Department of Transportation drafted a bill proposing partial deregulation of the two industries in mid-1971, the administration abandoned it, declining to lobby on its behalf.[67] Staff at the CEA and Antitrust Division continued to support the bill, but thought the administration's lack of support was weakening its prospects.[68]

Houthakker continued to advocate for deregulation after returning to Harvard in 1971, to no immediate avail. The administration prepared another bill to deregulate railways in mid-1973, but by this point Nixon was becoming mired in Watergate, and no further progress was made.[69] As CEA member Gary Seevers described them, the Nixon-era deregulatory efforts were "the story of a few brave but lonely economists stubbornly attacking the American economy's largest legal cartel."[70]

———

It was not until Gerald Ford took office in August 1974 that the deregulatory tide began to turn. By that point, the bipartisan, Brookings-centered network of I/O economists had expanded. Not only had the group supported an outpouring of academic work on the economics of regulation, but it had established ties with the CEA, the Antitrust Division, the Department of Transportation, and the Senate Judiciary Committee, among other locations in Washington. As future Supreme Court justice Stephen Breyer, a linchpin of this network, later recalled, by this point "[t]hey were all over the place, this group of people interested in deregulation, or lessened regulation."[71]

Growing concern with inflation—which by mid-1974 had reached a record rate of almost 10 percent—also created an unexpected opportunity for economists to push deregulation up the political agenda.[72] Upon ascending to the presidency, Ford immediately convened a "summit conference" on inflation that brought together a wide-ranging group of economists, both liberal (Kermit Gordon, Walter Heller, John Kenneth Galbraith) and conservative (Milton Friedman, Herbert Stein).[73] The economists admitted they did not know how to stop inflation, but nearly all agreed that removing price and entry restrictions in regulated industries would be good policy. When Thomas Moore, a senior staffer in Nixon's CEA and the author of a monograph on freight regulation, presented the group with a list of deregulatory goals, he found widespread support.[74] All but two of the twenty-three economists present—including nearly all the liberals—signed off on the program.[75] Although even Moore admitted that the link between economic deregulation and inflation was somewhat tenuous, he argued—and his colleagues apparently agreed—"I do think that it will help move things in the right direction . . . it is a desirable thing to achieve."[76]

This growing advocacy among economists might not have mattered had Ford himself not been a strong personal advocate of deregulation. A month after the economists' conference, Ford gave his "Whip Inflation Now" speech, which proposed deregulating the natural gas industry, establishing a National Commission on Regulatory Reform to overhaul the independent regulatory agencies, and reviewing the inflationary impact of all major executive regulations.[77] Over the next two years, Ford repeatedly used his platform to advocate for deregulation, particularly, although not exclusively, of the transportation industries.[78] Indeed, proponents of deregulation within his administration were pleasantly surprised, and his political strategists a bit dismayed, by just how committed to the project Ford turned out to be.[79]

Ford's efforts were facilitated by a counterpart on the other side of the political aisle. Ted Kennedy, who saw himself as a consumer advocate, had become a champion of airline deregulation thanks to the efforts of Stephen Breyer. In the years since leaving his position as special assistant to Turner at the Antitrust Division, Breyer had honed his arguments for energy deregulation in a Brookings volume coauthored with Yale economist and Ford CEA member Paul MacAvoy.[80] In 1974, he became special counsel for a Senate Judiciary subcommittee chaired by Senator Kennedy. From that post, Breyer advocated for airline deregulation—the industry where the strongest deregulatory case could be made.[81] Kennedy picked up the issue and, in early 1975, orchestrated major hearings on airline deregulation that turned out to be "an outstanding dramatic success."[82] The substantially lower cost of intrastate flights in California and Texas, which were not subject to the same federal regulations governing interstate travel, proved to be a media hook that put a public face on the issue: "[W]hy can I fly from Los Angeles to San Francisco for $18, but to go from Washington to Boston is $45?"[83] To Breyer's surprise, not only did the hearings get media coverage, "it was front page of the *New York Times*. . . . Page one! We didn't think it would be page one."[84]

Indeed, between Ford's repeated advocacy and the Kennedy hearings, media coverage of regulation increased dramatically in the mid-1970s, as evidenced, for example, by headlines in the *New York Times*. This growing public attention proved helpful when Ford sought to leverage a crisis in the railroad industry into a new political opportunity. By mid-1974, no fewer than eight railroads had filed for bankruptcy protection, an opportunity Ford sought to leverage by asking Congress to make railroad loans conditional on deregulation. After difficult negotiations, he managed to get the Railroad Revitalization and Regulatory Reform Act, which gave railroads more freedom to set their own rates, through Congress in February 1976.[85] Upon its signing, Ford noted with satisfaction that removing these regulations would help "our railroads to operate efficiently and competitively."[86]

By 1976, Ford had also begun to move the needle on airline deregulation. He appointed John Robson, a strong supporter of deregulation, as chair of the Civil Aeronautics Board (CAB), which set fares and routes for the airline industry.[87] Robson used his position to advocate for a deregulatory agenda within and beyond the agency—for example, in its communications with Congress.[88] And John Snow, an economist serving as a senior official at the Department of Transportation, was put in charge of assembling a bipartisan coalition. Snow organized a major push to identify likely supporters in Congress, and talked to some seventy-two members himself. Inspired by the arguments that I/O economists had been developing for a decade but facing a more favorable environment for action in the wake of Kennedy's airline hearings, Ford's appointees continued to build support for airline deregulation. Yet momentum on the issue disappeared as the presidential campaign got fully under way, and Ford would not be the one to see the issue through.[89]

President Jimmy Carter ultimately became the unlikely champion of transportation regulation. While the issue did not feature prominently in his campaign, as president, Carter oversaw deregulation of all three major modes of commercial transportation: air, trucking, and rail.[90] While Carter became a strong advocate of deregulation, the rising tide of Congressional support and his staff's commitment to the issue, along with decreasing industry opposition in the face of de facto deregulation by CAB and the changing public mood, were more important than his advocacy. As political scientists Martha Quirk and Paul Derthick put it, "it was a ripe issue to which he conveniently fell heir."[91] But other developments were more important to deregulation's success than Carter's personal support.

First, Congressional leaders from both sides of the aisle continued to advocate for transportation deregulation. Kennedy's commitment to airline deregulation persisted; in 1978 he also held hearings on trucking deregulation.[92] Fellow Democrat Howard Cannon, chair of the Senate subcommittee on aviation, became an advocate as well.[93] And Mary Schuman, who helped write an early Kennedy-Cannon airline deregulation bill from her staff position at the Senate Commerce Committee, became Carter's main staffer in charge of deregulatory legislation.[94] Republicans, too, supported the effort; both James B. Pearson, the ranking minority member of the Senate aviation subcommittee, and Gene Snyder, his House counterpart, were proponents of airline deregulation.[95]

Second, Carter's economists, like Ford's, were basically unanimous in their support of transportation deregulation.[96] Charles Schultze—onetime champion of PPBS as director of LBJ's Budget Bureau—chaired Carter's CEA. During a recent stint at Brookings, he had written *The Public Use of Private Interest* (published in 1977), which advocated for the use of markets and incentives, rather than rules, to achieve regulatory goals.[97] Both of the economists who filled the CEA's microeconomics slot (first William Nordhaus then George Eads) were strong supporters of deregulation.[98] And the Council on Wage and Price Stability, an economics office established by Ford to combat inflation that Carter continued, saw deregulation as an important component of its project.[99]

Yet while the economists' take on transportation deregulation was now bipartisan and widely held, industry interests in maintaining the regulatory regime were still too entrenched to permit immediate legislative change. Across the transportation industries, the incumbent players appreciated the stability of government regulation, the protection it offered from competition, and the market it ensured. They had significant influence in shaping the form regulation took, even if they did not always like being confined by it. While smaller participants—regional airlines, independent truck owner-operators—might chafe at being restricted from some markets, the support of the biggest regulated companies for the existing regulatory regime was a significant barrier to its removal.

The critical step in overcoming that block was Carter's appointment of an avid deregulator to chair the CAB, a decision that indirectly pushed the Interstate Commerce Commission, which oversaw the rail and trucking industries, in a deregulatory direction as well. Through administrative means alone, the regulatory agencies began to dismantle the regulatory process, destabilizing the environment and thus removing one of the major benefits of regulation for the dominant industry players. Eventually, this reached a point where some industry leaders began demanding congressional action—which would at least restore predictability—as preferable to continued uncertainty.

The most important actor in this process was Cornell I/O economist Alfred Kahn, who Carter appointed to lead the Civil Aeronautics Board in the summer of 1977.[100] Kahn began his career as an institutional economist with a strong pro-regulatory bent, but in the 1960s he underwent a road-to-Damascus conversion to neoclassical economics.[101] His politics remained liberal, and his two-volume 1971 classic, *The Economics of Regulation*, continued to reflect an institutionalist attention to real-world detail, but Kahn nevertheless adopted the deregulatory position that had become standard among modern economists.[102] In the mid-1970s, as chairman of the New York Public Service Commission, he led a major reform of electricity and telephone regulation in New York State that launched his national reputation as a policymaker as well as an economist.[103]

It is not surprising, then, that Kahn was Carter's pick. Indeed, Stephen Breyer later recalled that "[t]he object [upon Carter's election] was to get Fred Kahn appointed [c]hairman of the CAB. . . . Everybody [in the deregulatory network] is working for that."[104] Upon arriving in Washington, Kahn quickly got to work. He garnered headlines with his mediagenic personality (he once quipped to airline executives, "I really don't know one plane from the other. To me they are all marginal costs with wings"), but he made substantive changes behind the scenes, including in staffing the board.[105] Kahn immediately appointed new leadership at the CAB more in line with his own views, including Philip Bakes (an attorney who had worked on Kennedy's airline hearings) and Michael E. Levine (a law-and-economics professor best known for a 1965 article on the airline industry titled "Is Regulation Necessary?").[106] Then he created a new Office of Economic Analysis and placed economist Darius Gaskins, most recently director of the FTC's Bureau of Economics, in charge.[107] Kahn also benefited from the strong support of fellow Carter CAB appointee (and I/O economist) Elizabeth E. Bailey, who Kahn later called "the most ardent deregulator on the board."[108]

With committed proponents now in key positions, CAB began deregulating unilaterally.[109] The agency began giving airlines a greater ability to discount fares, by as much as 50 percent, from the CAB-approved rates.[110] It authorized applicants to fly out of new airports, like Chicago Midway, to promote competition. By mid-1978, half of coach tickets were being sold for less than the official rate set by CAB. Kahn and his allies on the board were highly satisfied with the changes they had made to CAB's procedures.[111] And those changes not only increased economic efficiency, to Kahn's satisfaction, but were popular with consumer advocates like Nader, who did not particularly value efficiency for its own sake.

With Kahn making headlines at the CAB, other regulators paid attention. At the Interstate Commerce Commission (ICC), A. Daniel O'Neal, an attorney who had been appointed to the commission by Nixon and made chair by Carter, was not a particular supporter of deregulation at the time he was elevated into the position. But in response to the prevailing political winds, O'Neal hired an economist to head a new policy planning office within the ICC.[112] Armed with economic insights from his new analysts, O'Neal began dismantling the regulatory framework that governed freight transport. These efforts only intensified when Carter appointed Darius Gaskins, head of CAB's Office of Economic Analysis, to replace O'Neal as ICC chair in 1980.[113]

The 1976 Railroad Revitalization and Regulatory Reform Act had already stripped the ICC of most of its authority over rail transport. By the time Carter took office, the ICC's responsibilities primarily focused on trucking. The measures that first O'Neal, and later Gaskins, implemented in the trucking industry paralleled the changes that Kahn set in motion in the airline industry. Just as CAB had, on its own volition, allowed airlines to sell tickets for less than the government-approved rate and encouraged competition on new routes, the ICC also increased truckers' flexibility in setting rates and started approving new entrants much more freely. By encouraging competition and allowing the market, not the government, to set prices, supporters hoped these industries would become more efficient, with benefits for producers and consumers alike.[114]

On their own, CAB and the ICC could not simply repeal transportation regulation. But they had considerable discretion in their actions. Congress had asked them to set rates for the transportation industries, and gave them authority to limit who could offer service on particular routes. But the agencies could carry out their mission so in ways that were more or less promoting of price competition, reflecting their own view of their purpose. Their leadership could also change the agencies' internal structure and staffing, so that adherents to the economic style were better represented. This would encourage the agencies to carry out their work in ways that favored, instead of limiting, competition.

These sorts of unilateral changes also had a political ripple effect, in that they disrupted the status quo and made the regulatory regime look increasingly undesirable to regulated industries, which favored it in part because of its predictability. By changing the politics of the situation, the leadership of the regulatory agencies created the space for Congress to act. The airlines withdrew their opposition to a deregulatory bill, and the trucking industry came to actively support one.[115] Congress forged ahead with the passage of the Airline Deregulation Act in 1978, followed in 1980 by the Motor Carrier Act and the Staggers Rail Act, which further loosened rules already relaxed by the 1976 railroad deregulation legislation.[116] Significantly, these laws not only removed price and entry restrictions in transportation industries, but also put the regulatory commissions themselves on a path to disappearance. The Airline Deregulation Act set CAB to sunset in 1984, and the trucking and rail laws limited the ICC's scope. The latter would be abolished entirely at the end of 1995.[117]

In transportation policy, the advance of the economic style meant tearing down an existing regime instead of restructuring it. By helping to pass legislation that ended price setting and entry restrictions in transportation markets, and by eliminating entirely the commissions that had, for decades, used a stability-and-equity lens to administer those restrictions, advocates of the economic style changed the rules of market governance so that they centered efficiency in fact, if not in law.

Beyond Antitrust and Transportation

While the influence of the economic style in antitrust policy and transportation regulation is particularly striking, economic reasoning also became more important to other types of market governance. In a number of actively regulated markets, the logic of efficiency became increasingly visible in the 1970s. As I/O economists and likeminded thinkers changed the terms of debate, their approach came into conflict with other prominent logics, including fair prices, equitable access, reasonable returns, and professional privileges. The institutionalization of the economic style was not always as thorough in these other domains as it was in antitrust, nor were economists' recommendations as fully implemented as they were in transportation policy—but to the extent that institutionalization occurred, it produced visible effects on policy.

In policy domains governed by a New Deal stability-and-equity regime, including energy, telecommunications, and banking, an embrace of the economic style generally meant making efficiency a central goal. It could, though, also involve attention to other concerns, like innovation, that made sense within an economic framework. Economists working in these policy domains typically advocated for deregulation—that is, removing restrictions on competition and allowing the market, not government, to determine prices—but they favored it less uniformly in areas beyond transportation, in which the economic evidence was understood to be quite strong. Regardless of the extent to which they thought a given industry should be deregulated, though, advocates of the economic style usually viewed allocative efficiency as the goal that market governance should be striving toward.

Telecommunications, for example, was governed by regulatory arrangements that were solidified with the creation of the Federal Communications Commission (FCC) in 1934. Like transportation, the telecommunications regime sought to ensure nondiscriminatory, "fair and equitable" access to telephone services at "just and reasonable" prices.[118] Decades later, some industrial organization economists still believed that natural monopolies existed, that telephone service might be such a monopoly, and that government regulation of a natural monopoly might produce a better outcome than leaving the monopoly unregulated. But they viewed the question of whether the government should be regulating prices and entry through the lens of maximizing total surplus rather than fairness or equity.[119]

For most of the twentieth century, long-distance telephone service was monopolized by AT&T, a conglomerate whose regional subsidiaries also controlled local phone service in most of the United States. The FCC regulated the rates AT&T could charge for long distance and the services it could offer, largely with the company's approval. The FCC began taking baby steps toward promoting competition as early as 1968 in response to congressional criticism that it was too lax in its oversight of "Ma Bell," and the monopoly's inability to keep up with demand for certain specialized services.[120] These changes were meant as tweaks to the existing regulatory paradigm, rather than being motivated by the economic style. But with the deregulatory movement gaining influence in the 1970s, Charles Ferris, Carter's FCC chair, began staffing his agency with the same sorts of economists who were driving change in antitrust and transportation policy. He expanded the commission's Office of Plans and Policy, placed it under the direction of economists, and "more than doubled the total number of economists in the agency, "to about 100."[121] In the following years, the FCC increasingly discussed the purpose of telecommunications governance in economic terms, rather than in its older language—a shift that would affect, for example, its management of the electromagnetic spectrum.[122] And while each regulatory domain unfolded along its own path, similar patterns could be seen in the governance of energy markets (oil, natural gas, electricity) and in banking.[123]

Not all less-than-perfect markets, though, were governed by a stability-and-equity regime. Healthcare, for instance, had not generally been thought of as an industry prior to the 1970s, and indeed the very notion would have been rather odd. This meant that medicine was not subject to the same kind of government rate-setting and direct control over entry seen in telephone service or the airline industry. For most of the twentieth century, the federal government left medicine mostly to the states, which treated it as a profession, granting a monopoly to physicians in exchange for ensuring the qualifications of practitioners and a nominal commitment to an ethical code. But as Washington stepped in with the creation of Medicare and Medicaid in the 1960s, medical care moved closer to becoming another federally regulated industry in which government set prices and controlled the entry of providers. Policymakers justified this shift with concerns about equity and the idea of a right to medical care.[124]

Over the next decade, advocates of the economic style—including a RAND-aligned group committed to efficiency in government spending and a Chicago-aligned group committed to efficiency through market forces— came to articulate a competing vision for healthcare.[125] They championed "institution-building for competition," with the goal of harnessing market forces to promote efficiency, over either professional monopoly or government regulation of prices and entry.[126] The view culminated in Alain Enthoven's late-1970s proposals for what would come to be called managed competition.[127] As economists became more influential at agencies like the Department of Health, Education, and Welfare and the FTC, they were increasingly able to advocate for this market-centered view of healthcare.[128]

In contrast with markets governed by New Deal stability-and-equity regimes, advancing the economic style in healthcare did not require tearing down existing frameworks, beyond overturning case law that limited competition among medical professionals. Instead, it meant preventing a somewhat laissez-faire governance regime from being replaced with command-and-control-style regulation—a project advanced in part by creating regulatory frameworks that would support new forms of competition between insurers and among healthcare providers. While it would take some time for this economic conception of healthcare governance to come to full fruition, by the end of the 1970s it was already beginning to gain ground.[129]

Institutionalizing the Economic Style of Market Governance

Between the late nineteenth century and the New Deal era, the United States established a legal and organizational framework for governing both market competition in general (antitrust policy), and a range of specific markets that showed tendencies toward monopoly or where stability and broad access were concerns (for example, transportation, energy, and banking). Introduced while the country was adapting to massive technological and economic change, and cemented during a period of economic collapse, this framework centered several ways of thinking about the purpose served by market governance. Although the exact motivations for regulating varied, none focused on the promotion of efficiency.

In antitrust, these purposes included limiting concentrated political and economic power, as had been embodied by Standard Oil and other late-nineteenth-century trusts. It also meant protecting the existence of small businesses, which policymakers (and many members of the public) saw as integral to civic life. In the transportation, energy, and financial industries, it meant ensuring stability and protecting those industries from "ruinous competition." And in areas where markets on their own might not provide service to all, like electricity and telephones, regulatory policy aimed to ensure equitable access, even when services could not be delivered at a profit.

The economic style of reasoning, which centered the promotion of allocative efficiency and the expansion of economic surplus as the purpose of market governance, had not yet consolidated when this framework was being put into place. Yet by the 1960s, as the economic style was coming to dominance in academic circles, the social, political, and technological circumstances that had produced the original framework for market regulation had changed considerably. Technologies had evolved and industries developed in ways that restructured markets, making some of them potentially more competitive. In the boom decades after World War II, economic stability seemed like an increasingly distant concern. And meanwhile, a range of observers both inside and outside the academy were becoming concerned that regulation was serving the interests of the regulated, not those of the larger public.

These changes opened the door to economists' efficiency-centered critique of the older market governance regime—of an antitrust regime that was anti-bigness, even if that meant being anti-efficiency, and of regulation that prevented competition and kept prices artificially high. During the 1960s and 1970s, this critique steadily gained ground—championed first by Harvard School structuralists who were typically liberal and often served under Democratic administrations, then, increasingly, by more government-skeptical adherents of the Chicago School. These two groups of scholars differed in their broad political orientations and in their faith in the beneficial potential of government. Yet their shared commitment to the economic style helped them to find common ground and to advocate for policies that challenged the status quo and sought to promote efficiency.

Over the course of the 1970s, this economic approach to market governance gained ground. Economics offices became larger, more professionalized, and more influential in a range of regulatory agencies. In transportation policy, administrative decisions destabilized the old regime, setting in motion of series of legislative actions that ultimately undid their authority. These decisions established market competition, with efficiency as the de facto policy goal. In antitrust policy, a feedback loop between enforcement actions and court decisions institutionalized economic reasoning as the only legitimate lens through which policy could be pursued. As these changes took place, the older goals that had motivated the original market governance regime—limiting concentrated power, protecting small business, promoting stability, and ensuring equity—became increasingly marginal.

As was the case in social policy, the economic style was not uniformly influential across the various domains of market governance. Yet by the end of the Carter administration, it had come to play a substantial role in redefining the goals of policy in a number of important areas. In antitrust, in transportation regulation, and increasingly in areas like telecommunications policy and even healthcare, debates over the future of policy were beginning to take place in economic terms, with other concerns shunted aside. But the influence of economic reasoning would not be limited to questions of market pricing and entry alone.

7

The Economic Style and Social Regulation

Between 1966 and 1973, policymakers in Washington unleashed a massive wave of social regulation that transformed the role of the federal government. Implemented at a moment of historic optimism about how government could improve the lives of ordinary Americans, the surge of legislation and administrative rules transformed Americans' relationships to work, safety, and the very environment in which they lived. These years saw the creation of the Environmental Protection Agency (EPA), the Occupational Safety and Health Administration (OSHA), and the National Highway Traffic Safety Administration (NHTSA), among other new agencies, as well as the passage of laws like the National Environmental Policy Act (NEPA) and the Clean Air and Clean Water Acts.

The laws expanding social regulation, like those creating the institutions of the Great Society, did not reflect the economic style of reasoning. Instead, they were grounded in different ways of thinking about policy, including ideas about rights to clean air and water and a logic of good governance tied to theories about how strong, inflexible, technology-based regulatory standards might avoid regulatory capture. Almost immediately, though, industry groups began demanding that policymakers incorporate cost-benefit analysis into proposed regulations. While industry groups mostly wanted cost-benefit analysis because they expected it to limit regulation, liberal economists—who typically supported government's role in ensuring the public's health and safety—liked it for a different reason: its promotion of efficiency.

The authors of the initial wave of 1960s social regulation anticipated this response. They therefore insisted that rules designed to protect the public's welfare set high standards while excluding, wherever possible, consideration of costs. Coming in the age of the moon shot, the initial regulatory salvo also incorporated a marked optimism about the power of technology to solve problems. In response to concerns about regulatory capture, they built ambitious and relatively rigid rules—like simply banning water pollution unless the "best available technology" for pollution control was used—because they saw inflexibility as a tool for preventing capture.[1] The new social regulation limited administrative agencies from weighing costs and benefits, and it did not seek efficient outcomes, focus on incentives, or systematically consider trade-offs, as the economic style might prescribe.

The backlash was predictable and immediate. Over the course of the 1970s, industry groups allied with economists from across the political spectrum who believed that social regulation could be made more efficient. The economists who took up their standard spanned both the systems analytic and industrial organization communities and worked in both Republican and Democratic presidential administrations. Whatever their professional or political background, they shared a desire to center efficiency and cost-effectiveness as policymakers made decisions about how to govern markets.

As had been the case with the Great Society, the ascendance of the economic style in social regulation conflicted with the values of the environmental and consumer movements that had produced the new social regulation in the first place. The economic style, for example, dismissed an ecological approach that saw the value of individual species as impossible to disentangle from those species' role in sustaining larger ecosystems. The economic style saw arguments for fundamental rights to clean air or a safe and healthy workplace as unreasonably rigid, as such arguments failed to consider the economic trade-offs of ensuring those rights. The economic style was moreover unmoved by environmentalists' arguments that environmental protections would erode under cost-benefit analysis because a flexible rulemaking process would inevitably fall prey to regulatory capture.

Together, advocates of the economic style established administrative rules that placed cost-benefit analysis at the heart of social regulation and made efficiency the main criterion for determining its quality. In the process, they further institutionalized the use of economic reasoning in a variety of regulatory domains and built capacity for economic reasoning within the executive branch. This, in turn, set the stage for the introduction of other approaches to regulation—emissions trading, for example—that were more compatible with the economic style than what economists and then a wider range of critics came to call, somewhat derogatorily, "command-and-control" regulation.

As usual, the economic style had more impact in some areas than others—more, for example, in environmental policy than occupational safety. Yet to the extent that the economic style was successfully institutionalized, efficiency became a more central lens for evaluating what made for good policy in the arena of social regulation. Competing frameworks—whether grounded in the idea of sacrosanct rights, the unpredictability of ecological interactions, or a distinct theory of good governance—moved to the sidelines of political debate.

The Noneconomic Roots of Social Regulation

By the late 1960s, the side effects of increasing consumer affluence in the United States were becoming more and more apparent. Even in the 1950s, widespread pollution of the air and water was becoming visible not only to neighbors of contaminant-spewing factories, but to a more politically influential swath of white, middle-class Americans whose leisure activities it was beginning to impact. The 1962 publication of Rachel Carson's *Silent Spring*, which described the deadly effects of the widely used insecticide DDT on other parts of the food chain, raised the public's awareness of other, less directly visible, ways that human actions were harming the natural environment.[2]

The growing salience of environmental concerns was matched by increased discussion of other issues that a well-off society could afford to pay more attention to than it had in earlier stages of industrialization, like public health and safety. In 1965, Ralph Nader's *Unsafe at Any Speed* drew national attention to the safety risks of automobiles, causing a public uproar.[3] And in 1967, the news of the cancer deaths of a large number of uranium miners, emblematic of a broader increase in industrial accidents and occupational health risks, helped give workplace safety a more prominent place on the political agenda.[4]

Public demands that the government protect the environment and address workplace safety coalesced into a movement that brought together environmental activists and consumer movements, public health professionals, and organized labor. And with an activist Congress in office, Washington was ready and willing to respond their demands. Increasingly, Democrats embraced regulation as a strategy to solve these kinds of problems, as regulation promised to address such issues without requiring the same budgetary commitment as new government programs.[5] Indeed, in many ways the dramatic expansion of social regulation that began in the late 1960s can be seen as a second wave of the Great Society—taking place after guns had begun to squeeze out butter, but before cynicism about government's capacity to solve problems had fully set in.

During the 1960s and 1970s, but especially between 1966 and 1973, Congress passed a series of bipartisan laws that created new regulatory agencies and set ambitious new environmental, health, and safety standards. All in all, thirty-six new agencies were established during these two decades. Both the number of federal regulators and their budgets grew fivefold.[6]

These agencies ranged from the National Highway Traffic Safety Administration (NHTSA, created in 1966) to the Occupational Safety and Health Administration (OSHA, 1970) to the Environmental Protection Agency (EPA, 1970) to the Consumer Product Safety Commission (CPSC, 1972)—among many others.[7] The laws establishing these agencies were complemented by other historic pieces of legislation, like the Clean Air Act of 1970 and the Clean Water Act of 1972, that set out bold new goals for the country to achieve. This dramatic expansion of the role of government began under Lyndon Johnson, but much of it was achieved with the active, if sometimes reluctant, cooperation of Richard Nixon.[8]

A variety of movements and interest groups advocated for this expansion of social regulation, and it had no single organizing principle. Yet much of its foundational legislation was built on a handful of ways of thinking about government—about what it should try to accomplish, and about how to ensure the success of those attempts.

One prominent theme, for example, was a logic of rights. As legal scholars Jerry Mashaw and David Harfst note, during the 1960s, "[i]n programs ranging from housing to legal services to medical care, Congress was busily creating whole new bundles of need-based 'rights.'"[9] The environmental and consumer movements drew inspiration from the success of the civil rights movement, and activists increasingly positioned health, safety, and access to clean air and water as part of a larger egalitarian framework of rights. The Occupational Safety and Health Act, for example, "created a universal and substantive right to safety and health."[10] If health, safety, and a clean environment were *rights*, it implied that achieving them was worth almost any cost.

These laws also reflected a deep desire within government agencies at the time to harness national progress to scientific achievement. The space program, in particular, reflected a moment of technological optimism. Many of the new regulations incorporated the idea of "technology forcing"—that government could set high standards as a means of pushing industry to develop and adopt the new technologies that would help to meet them.[11] Within environmental law, to an extent that can be surprising from the present, the regulatory framework also depended on an ecological mind-set that emphasized the interconnectedness of the natural world.[12] If the loss of a single species or the contamination of a specific stream could have unpredictable effects on the larger ecosystem, this implied a need for greater protection than if the consequences of environmental damage were more linear.

Last, this wave of legislation was shaped by ideas about good governance, and particularly by a specific theory of regulatory politics. Recent experience had shown legislators the difficulty of producing environmental legislation that would live up to its intent. In 1965 and 1967, for example, Congress had passed Water and Air Quality Acts that offered states a great deal of flexibility, but turned out to be relatively feeble—an outcome that encouraged lawmakers to move toward less flexibility in future attempts at environmental improvement.[13] More generally, as we have already seen in the case of market governance, lawmakers were increasingly convinced of the need to protect agencies from regulatory capture. Some of this reaction was prompted by Ralph Nader's emerging consumer movement, which attacked government agencies for being far too receptive to the concerns of the industries they oversaw.[14] But legislators were also significantly influenced by arguments from academics.[15] In particular, they listened to political scientist Theodore Lowi, whose influential 1969 book, *The End of Liberalism*, argued that executive agencies were particularly susceptible to industry capture when they were given too much leeway by Congress.[16]

Congress responded to these pressures by writing legislation that insulated regulatory agencies from weakness and capture. These laws created executive-branch offices led by political appointees, rather than independent ones governed by fixed-term commissioners, under the theory that more direct accountability to the president would curb regulatory agencies' responsiveness to industry. New agencies oversaw particular issues, like workplace safety or the environment, rather than specific industries, like airlines or banking. And, critically, legislation set high, inflexible standards that limited the consideration of cost in regulatory decisions.[17] The Occupational Safety and Health Act, for example, assured no "material impairment of health or functional capacity even if such employee has regular exposure to the hazard dealt with . . . for the period of his working life"—an undeniably high standard.[18] The Clean Water Act required that "the discharge of pollutants into the navigable waters be eliminated by 1985"; the Clean Air Act set air quality standards at the level "requisite to protect the public welfare from any known or anticipated adverse effects associated with the presence of such air pollutant[s]."[19] Indeed, as political scientist George Hoberg later wrote of the Clean Air Act of 1970, it "reads as if it were written by Theodore Lowi himself."[20]

This initial wave of legislation and administrative rulemaking was notably devoid of economic reasoning. The economic style, with its emphasis on trade-offs and efficiency, never would have prescribed rules that did not take cost into account. From a cost-benefit perspective, the optimal level of air pollution, worker illness, or car accidents might be lower than its current rate, but it was probably not zero. It was irrational and misguided to simply legislate a certain level of worker health or traffic safety without evaluating the costs of achieving that goal.[21]

It was not that economists lacked things to say about these policy domains. As early as 1965, the Council of Economic Advisers suggested "a system of fees for the discharge of effluent"—a proposal very much out of sync with the contemporary policy environment—and it continued to make such suggestions in both Democratic and Republican administrations.[22] But economists were not yet significant players in this particular arena. Only one economist—employed by the AFL-CIO, and trained in the institutionalist era—was called to testify in the protracted series of hearings leading to the Clean Air Act, for example.[23] The ultimate result of this lack of influence was legislation that "economists generally condemned."[24] As economist Marc Roberts wrote with frustration of the Clean Water Act, "There is to be no case-by-case balancing of costs and benefits, no attempt at 'fine tuning' the process of resource allocation. All state/local discretion on how clean different streams are to be is effectively eliminated. Technology alone will be the constraint."[25]

Yet while economic reasoning did not, for the most part, directly make its way into this wave of environmental, health, and safety legislation, systems analysis was nevertheless still in the air and had some effects on the form that one major new law took. While the immediate impact of the systems analytic approach was relatively modest, its limited introduction nevertheless opened the door to a subsequent expansion of economic reasoning into social regulation—an expansion that in the long run would prove significant and consequential.

NEPA and an Opening for the Economic Style

The National Environmental Policy Act (NEPA) provided the crack in the social regulation door through which economic reasoning slipped. Passed in 1969, NEPA required executive agencies to issue Environmental Impact Statements on their proposed activities as a means to force them, for the first time, to pay attention to those impacts. It also created the Council on Environmental Quality (CEQ)—a new White House office—to oversee NEPA, analyze the state of the environment, and produce an annual Environmental Quality Report. Strongly inspired by ecological ideas about the interconnectedness of all living things, the bill's stated purpose was "[t]o declare a national policy which will encourage productive and enjoyable harmony between man and his environment." Its text referred to the "biosphere" and "ecological systems."[26]

Yet NEPA also exhibited systems analytic thinking in its discussion of "relevant alternatives and analysis of all consequences."[27] Environmental Impact Statements required agencies to tabulate the environmental costs of their activities, much as they did for economic costs. The CEQ was modeled after the Council of Economic Advisers (CEA) and shared with it a broadly economic style of economic reasoning.[28] Senator Henry Jackson, NEPA's "chief architect," argued that the law would serve as a basis "for applying to environmental management the methods of systems analysis that have demonstrated their value in universities, private enterprise, and in some areas of government."[29] Legal scholar Colin Diver later pointed to it as part of the "triumph of comprehensive rationality," in which "Congress endorsed the idea of comprehensive analysis for a broad class of administrative decisions."[30]

Although systems analysis was in the air, NEPA's use of the cost-benefit approach drew on traditions beyond RAND and its network of policy analysts. Cost-benefit analysis had a long and independent (but intersecting) tradition in water resource policy, where it was used to evaluate projects like building dams.[31] Originally developed by engineers and practitioners, the practice found its way into welfare economics in the late 1950s, through work conducted by RAND and Resources for the Future (RFF), a small Washington think tank closely networked with RAND that conducted economic research on natural resource issues.[32] The history of cost-benefit analysis in water resource policy, and the prominence of RFF within this community, meant that policymakers working on environmental legislation were likely to be exposed to this style of thinking through multiple channels—not just the Planning-Programming-Budgeting System (PPBS).

The way such thinking was actually incorporated into NEPA, though, was relatively informal. NEPA simply sought to "insure that presently unquantified environmental amenities and values may be given appropriate consideration in decision-making along with economic and technical considerations." The law required all agencies to accompany their recommendations and reports with statements on (1) environmental impacts of the proposed action, (2) unavoidable adverse environmental effects, (3) alternatives to the action, (4) the relationship between short-term and long-term effects, and (5) any irreversible resource commitments involved.[33] Nothing in the enabling legislation required formal cost-benefit analysis, or even that environmental protection be weighted as heavily as other goals.[34]

It was the judicial branch that interpreted NEPA as a mandate for cost-benefit analysis. Beginning with *Calvert Cliffs' Coordinating Committee, Inc. v. AEC*, a landmark 1971 decision, the courts insisted on a "rigorous balancing of costs and benefits" in environmental protections. In that case, the D.C. Court of Appeals found that the Atomic Energy Commission, which had historically shown limited concern with the environmental impacts of nuclear weapons and energy, had neglected to sufficiently consider the potential environmental costs of a nuclear power plant being constructed on Chesapeake Bay.[35] The commission responded by including a formal cost-benefit analysis as part of its Environmental Impact Statement. Encouraged by reaffirming court decisions, other agencies soon followed suit.[36]

This interpretation of NEPA opened the door to much more expansive requirements for cost-benefit analysis across the federal government, just as the introduction of PPBS at DOD had led to its rollout in other agencies.[37] The court's decision also made the actual techniques used for such analysis potentially subject to judicial review.[38] At the beginning, the focus was on evaluating the (environmental) costs of government *projects*, not the costs (environmental or otherwise) of government *regulations*. Yet the precedent of *Calvert Cliffs'* shifted expectations and left open the possibility that government regulations, as well as projects, might eventually be subject to such tests.[39]

Advancing Cost-Benefit Analysis of Social Regulation

Regulatory skeptics saw in cost-benefit analysis a tool for controlling government agencies in much the same way that centrists within the Johnson administration deployed PPBS as a tool to tame the radical edges of Great Society programs. The analytical technique had long played this role within federal water policy: the history of cost-benefit analysis was essentially an ongoing series of battles between the Army Corps of Engineers and the Bureau of Reclamation, both of which wished to build large dams, and the Bureau of the Budget, which wanted to rein them in.[40] The logical pathway from using cost-benefit analysis to control government spending, to using it to control government rulemaking, was not a long one.

An early indication of how the politics of cost-benefit analysis would play out came in the debate over the 1966 Motor Vehicle Safety Act. The auto industry called for the law—one of the first in this wave of social regulation—to include language which would require "a balancing of costs versus benefits" in the demands it made.[41] Over the next few years, the auto industry would continue this strategy, with carmakers arguing first to the NHTSA and then the courts that new regulations should be subject to cost-benefit tests.[42]

Not long after, the same idea was proposed in a different context by Allan Schmid, a Michigan State University agricultural economist on leave at the Army's Systems Analysis Group. The Systems Analysis Group—a legacy of the introduction of PPBS to the Defense Department—oversaw the Army Corps of Engineers, among other groups, and was initially tasked with reviewing Corps projects.[43] Schmid suggested "that cost-benefit analysis should be applied not just to the evaluation of public expenditures, such as flood control projects, but to regulatory rulemaking as well."[44] "Both public spending and rulemaking decisions," he wrote in a 1969 paper presented to Congress's Joint Economic Committee, "produce benefits and have opportunity costs, and thus can be compared and ranked together as alternatives in a PPB system."[45] Following his lead, the Systems Analysis Group began conducting such reviews on regulations proposed by the Corps, "including those related to the zoning of flood plains and controlling the water levels in dams for the competing uses of flood protection, water supply, power, and recreation."[46] Although the scope of their efforts was narrow, the staff who developed techniques to carry out this work would later take their experience with them—and subsequently apply it to much broader regulatory domains.

————

While automakers were advocating for cost-benefit analysis of social regulation as early as the mid-1960s, a broader swath of industry began to pick up this strategy in the early 1970s as new environmental laws were passed. Nixon was begrudgingly forced by public opinion into protection of the environment. But he also established the National Industrial Pollution Control Council (NIPCC), a White House advisory body, in 1970 to represent industry interests.[47] The NIPCC, which counted not only automakers but companies like DuPont, Exxon, and U.S. Steel among its members, achieved what one participant described as "a broad corporate consensus on environmental policy" that centered on cost-benefit balancing as the working principle of environmental regulation.[48]

The NIPCC initially faced an uphill battle. While the Chamber of Commerce had advocated for cost-benefit weighing in hearings leading up to the Clean Air Act, the legislation that passed intentionally excluded language that would account for the cost of cleaning the air.[49] And the new EPA, also established in 1970, took a surprisingly aggressive approach to enforcement. Under the leadership of administrator William Ruckelshaus, the new agency dived headfirst into action, in a scramble Ruckelshaus liked to refer to as "running the 100-yard dash and taking your own appendix out at the same time."[50] The EPA brought under one roof scientists from a hodgepodge of preexisting offices with backgrounds ranging from civil engineering to entomology, but it was dominated by lawyers. Like their legal colleagues at the antitrust agencies, the EPA's lawyers gravitated toward a "culture of enforcement" that interpreted success through the lens of winnable cases.[51] Neither the scientists nor the lawyers operated within an economic framework.

While advocates of the economic style were thin on the ground at EPA, they did have one small foothold from which they could grow their power. The agency quickly established a PPBS-style Office of Planning and Management (OPM), led by economist Robert Sansom, and within it an Economic Analysis Division employing eight staff researchers.[52] Consistent with the systems analytic tradition, Sansom envisioned economic analysis as a tool for administrative decision-making.[53] And while the early EPA was dominated by a legal enforcement approach to environmental problems, Administrator Ruckelshaus understood the political power of economic analysis in protecting the agency from critique, both in and out of government.[54]

Yet in keeping with the statutory requirements of the Clean Air Act, the EPA did not consider costs in setting air quality standards. This was a matter of great concern to the corporate polluters represented by the NIPCC, which began spelling out its position in increasing detail. The group began collecting a litany of member complaints castigating the costs of environmental regulation as a burden on American industry. In what soon become a theme in industry pushback to environmental regulation, their studies consistently invoked economic reasoning.[55]

In response to this corporate pressure, the Nixon administration organized an agency oversight process called the Quality of Life Review.[56] An attempt to exert some form of centralized control over the new social regulation, Quality of Life Review sought to "insure that the action agencies make suitable analyses of benefits and costs and that outside viewpoints are taken into account." The review moreover recommended agencies produce "Economic Impact Statements" for new regulations, just as NEPA required Environmental Impact Statements.[57] It required that agencies submit proposed "significant" rules, including cost-benefit comparisons of the proposal and alternatives, to the new Office of Management and Budget (OMB, formerly the Budget Bureau) for review.[58]

Within the OMB, the office put in charge of this process was led by Jim Tozzi, an economics and business administration PhD who had most recently led the Army Systems Analysis Group that had pioneered cost-benefit analysis of regulation.[59] Now, he and other former staffers adapted the techniques they had developed overseeing the Army Corps of Engineers to new contexts.[60] In theory, Quality of Life Review applied to all environmental, health, and safety programs. But in practice, the office effectively targeted the EPA.[61]

Members of Congress objected to a process that they described—accurately—as giving industry a back door into regulatory decision-making that Congress had not intended.[62] Yet the Quality of Life Review could exert only informal pressure; it did not give OMB authority to reject EPA's regulatory decisions. Nevertheless, the review process put pressure on the EPA to be, as one anonymous EPA official put it, "more reserved, more scientifically aggressive, less environmentally aggressive" than it might otherwise have been.[63] The review also led to an important change in the EPA's procedures, with the agency increasingly seeking input from the parties subject to regulation before issuing their decisions.[64]

Quality of Life Review also pushed EPA to develop a capacity for economic analysis that it otherwise still lacked. Industry representatives were happy to provide OMB with their own estimates of the cost of environmental regulations. Responsibility for countering those numbers, as well as for providing estimates of benefits, fell to EPA's policy planning office.[65] The office's work developing new methods of calculating costs and benefits helped the agency protect itself from what a later administrator called the Quality of Life "hit squad."[66] Yet while Quality of Life Review initially applied only to EPA regulations, soon other agencies would also be pressured to account for costs in regulatory decisionmaking.

———

Under the Ford administration, economists, attracted to the idea of promoting the efficiency of government action, picked up the call for cost-benefit analysis. Surprisingly, these initial voices came not from the systems analytic community, but rather from industrial organization economists focused on economic regulation—price and entry restrictions in transportation and other industries. And again, as in transportation deregulation, inflation created a political opening.

Early in his administration, Ford—plagued by hard-to-control inflation—created a White House Council on Wage and Price Stability (CWPS) to limit labor wage demands and industry price increases.[67] CWPS was not created to oversee regulatory policy. It nevertheless included a small office focused on government contributions to inflation, led first by George Eads, an I/O economist best known for his work on airline deregulation, and then Jim Miller, a transportation economist who had served on the staff of the CEA and at the Department of Transportation.[68] These economists argued that one obvious potential contributor to inflation was government regulations that required industry to spend more on pollution controls. Considering such possibilities led CWPS' Government Operations and Research Office to become an unexpected champion of cost-benefit analysis as a means to rationalize social regulation.

While the Quality of Life Review developed by Nixon continued under the Ford administration, it lost momentum over Ford's two-and-a-half years in office.[69] But by now, cost-benefit analysis had other institutional champions in the White House. Within months of the creation of CWPS, the NHTSA requested that the Government Operations and Research Office review NHTSA's cost-benefit analysis of "a proposed regulation concerning the performance of truck air-braking systems." CWPS disagreed with the analysis and filed a public comment on it, which began a more general practice of reviewing and filing comments on proposed regulations.[70] By the end of the Ford administration, CWPS had filed comments on the economic effects of about 125 regulations distributed across a range of departments and agencies.[71]

Eads and Miller both had closer ties to the I/O network than the systems analytic community. Both had published books in the Brookings Institution's series on economic regulation, for example.[72] But thinking about social regulation in cost-benefit terms—as a question of trade-offs, opportunity costs, and efficiency—was a natural extension of the economic style. As Eads wrote to an EPA administrator about the regulation of aircraft noise, "we reject the notion that annoyance must be reduced at all costs." He elaborated on the idea that protecting the public's welfare nevertheless involves trade-offs: "The reduction of this annoyance imposes costs in a world of limited resources that reduces the health and welfare society derives from other goods, services, and amenities that must be sacrificed to produce the reduction in noise.[73] More generally, Miller argued that "[t]he evidence we do have on the effects of social regulation suggests that the costs are enormous and in many cases overwhelm any reasonable estimate of benefits."[74]

While the Quality of Life Review specifically targeted environmental regulation, the regulatory commenting process initiated by CWPS was not aimed primarily at the EPA. In addition to issuing comments on proposed EPA regulations, CWPS also commented frequently on actions at NHTSA, OSHA, the CPSC, and the Food and Drug Administration, as well as agencies concerned with industry-specific rather than broader social regulation, like the Civil Aeronautics Board and the Interstate Commerce Commission.[75]

CWPS's efforts pushed incremental, rather than dramatic, change in how agencies wrote social regulation. At one end of the spectrum, OSHA enforced legislation that strictly limited economic considerations.[76] OSHA resisted any accounting of costs and benefits and employed no full-time economists in this period.[77] In the middle, the EPA responded by continuing to develop its capacity for cost analysis, which expanded moderately during the Ford years.[78] And at the other end of the spectrum, I/O economist (and transportation deregulator) John Snow was appointed administrator of the NHTSA in 1976.[79] With Snow in charge and CWPS "raising hell over NHTSA's treatment of costs and benefits in rulemaking," the engineer-dominated NHTSA began to defer to the agency's policy planning office, which had a capacity to respond to CWPS criticism that the engineers did not.[80]

———

While Ford's economists tended to be relatively skeptical of government, the Carter administration brought appointees who believed in using government to solve problems. Yet Carter's technocratic style and commitment to efficiency also led him to favor advisors who embraced economic reasoning. Despite holding liberal political values, such advisors tended to ally with industry in advocating for the expansion of cost-benefit analysis. Ultimately, Carter oversaw the most significant expansion of economic reasoning in social regulation to date.[81] Charles Schultze, the chair of Carter's Council of Economic Advisers (CEA), was determined to create a new review process to regain control of social regulation—by rationalizing it through economic analysis.

Schultze was familiar with using such techniques as a means of administrative control, having overseen the implementation of PPBS a decade before as director of Johnson's Budget Bureau.[82] More recently, Schultze had written books from his perch at the Brookings Institution that advocated for replacing environmental regulations with pollution taxes and for creating incentive-based systems to achieve regulatory goals.[83] Schultze saw social regulation through the same lens that he and the systems analysts had seen budgeting: as requiring rigorous, apolitical analysis of the costs and benefits of competing alternatives.

Rather than asking OMB to lead the new regulatory review process, Schultze built on what had been done at CWPS under Ford. He developed a new system in which CWPS would staff regulatory analyses and the CEA would coordinate the process. Schultze himself would lead a new inter-agency committee, the Regulatory Analysis Review Group (RARG), in conducting the reviews.[84] In March 1978, Carter established this new process through executive order.[85]

RARG was tasked with analyzing major regulations—the ten to twenty a year expected to have an impact of $100 million or more. Agencies were to conduct their analysis on the basis of cost-effectiveness, rather than cost-benefit—that is, they were not expected to ask if the benefits of the regulation outweighed the cost, but merely the least costly way to reach a specified goal.[86] If RARG identified alternatives that were significantly more cost-effective than agency proposals, it would negotiate with the regulating agency to try to resolve the difference. If a resolution could not be achieved, the president would decide.[87]

Carter's review process went beyond Nixon's and Ford's. It was not limited to environmental regulation; of the "big five" regulations that RARG initially targeted, only two originated with the EPA, while the others came from Interior, Transportation, and OSHA.[88] And while the Ford administration had provided only after-the-fact comments, the Carter procedure allowed RARG to intervene earlier in the regulatory process. The approach echoed that of PPBS, which required systematic comparison of the cost of competing programs for achieving a particular policy goal. The new review process also benefited from the support of the increasingly strong community of I/O economists in the White House.[89]

The agencies themselves loathed the RARG process, which they saw as intruding on their prerogatives and introducing cost considerations counter to their statutory missions. Indeed, as legal scholars Jerry Mashaw and David Harfst put it, the agencies made it a verb: "To be 'rarged' was to be subjected to the incessant demands for information and reanalysis by RARG's band of beady-eyed economists."[90] As one anonymous CEA staffer said, "The first time an agency is 'RARGed,' it is like a cold shower. . . . Many have never done cost-benefit analysis and OSHA, for example, had at most only one economist in the whole agency."[91]

RARG could not actually force regulatory revisions. An early fight with OSHA over cotton dust regulation, for example, resulted in a trip to the Oval Office in which RARG was overruled by the president, an upset that put White House analysts on the defensive.[92] Yet RARG also had real consequences—limited in terms of immediate regulatory outcomes, but greater in terms of expanding analytic capacity at the agencies.[93] As Schultze wrote to the president, "Ultimately, we want them to improve *their own* economic analysis."[94] And the agencies responded accordingly by increasing support for their policy planning offices. EPA's Office of Policy Management, for example, received a substantial boost in influence during this period.[95] At NHTSA, the power of the policy planning office continued to increase relative to that of the once-dominant engineers.[96] OSHA, still resistant to weighing costs, finally brought an economist in-house in 1979.[97] As had been the case when PPBS was implemented, analysis begat analysis.

The Carter administration got far from everything it wanted when it came to the expansion of regulatory analysis. Carter failed to pass the regulatory reform bill he had hoped to, and RARG was challenged by environmental groups who argued that the review process "violate[d] the spirit of open and accountable agency deliberations based on a public record."[98] Yet more than ever before, agencies were pushed to consider the economic effects of their rules, and they began to rely more heavily on economic reasoning. While regulated industries had been the first to advocate for such a change, cost-benefit analysis became entrenched in government because Democratic economists saw it as a rational approach to decision-making.

Competing Conceptions of Social Regulation

The environmental, health, and safety laws of the late 1960s and early 1970s reflected a broader expansion of legal rights, a moment of technological optimism, and new ideas about ecological interdependence. Collectively, they embodied a political theory that saw strong, inflexible standards as the best way to achieve regulatory goals while avoiding capture. The economic style, by contrast, centered efficiency and cost-effectiveness as the measure of good regulation. Ironically, given that regulatory capture is now a concern often associated with economics, advocates of the economic style paid less attention to capture, instead assuming that rational decision-making processes would produce objectively better regulations.

Despite the fact that the initial pushback to these rights-based regulations came almost entirely from industry, advocates of the economic style understood their own position not as political but neutral and almost self-evident. How could one defend regulations that cost more than their expected benefits, or choose one regulatory path when another was more cost-effective? The economic style discounted the idea that some rights—like the right of those with disabilities to access public facilities—might be invaluable, and thus that cost-benefit analysis was morally inappropriate.[99] It downplayed the unpredictability of ecological effects, which might warrant extra caution when it came to environmental protection. And it set aside the possibility that a rigid regulatory strategy might be politically wise, or that cost-benefit analysis might create its own opportunities for regulatory capture. While some economists took such issues seriously, more typically such concerns were dismissed as irrational.

This pattern can be seen across the range of policy domains in which social regulation was enacted. The impact of economic reasoning was greater in some areas than in others, and mattered most where it become institutionalized into administrative rules and agency decision-making. But to the extent that the economic style gained influence, it changed the criteria for thinking about what made for good regulation and made it harder to defend regulatory strategies that were grounded in other logics.

REVISING THE OZONE STANDARD

These conflicts were particularly visible in a 1978 fight over the safe level of ozone in the air. The Clean Air Act of 1970 required National Ambient Air Quality Standards (NAAQS) to be established for five atmospheric pollutants.[100] It reflected ideas about the importance of rights (in this case, to health), the promise of technology, and the danger of regulatory capture. It was also specifically written to exclude economic reasoning, on the grounds that allowing consideration of costs would open the door to delay and foot-dragging. As Senator Edmund Muskie, architect of the Clean Air Act, said in debate leading up to its passage, "the concept of this bill as it relates to national ambient air quality standards . . . is not keyed to any condition that the Secretary [of Health and Human Services] finds technically and economically feasible. The concept is of public health, and the standards are uncompromisable in that connection."[101] The air standards, therefore, were simply to be set at a level that would "protect the public health" with "an adequate margin of safety."[102]

Ozone (O_3), which affects people with asthma and other respiratory conditions, was one of the five substances initially regulated by the Clean Air Act. The legislation gave regulators only 120 days to set initial standards, so the EPA's initial limit of 0.08 parts per million (ppm), published in 1971, was selected hastily, with limited technical justification. As the law prescribed, the limit did not take costs into account. The 0.08 ppm cutoff turned out to be difficult to meet, and the EPA's efforts to enforce the standard threatened petroleum refiners and the auto industry. In response to a formal petition from the American Petroleum Institute—which later suggested a standard of 0.23 to 0.28 ppm—EPA announced in late 1976 that it would be revisiting the ozone standard.[103]

After a thorough internal review of the complex and often contradictory scientific evidence on the health effects of ozone, Douglas Costle, Carter's EPA administrator, proposed raising the standard—but only to 0.10 ppm. Again, the fossil fuel industry protested. When John Hahn, a lawyer whose firm represented the American Petroleum Industry, heard a RARG economist give a speech on regulatory reform, he took the opportunity to plead the refining industry's case. In one telling, Hahn told the RARG staffer that "the proposed ozone standard was by far the most costly regulation the administration had ever devised." The economist brought the complaint to CEA chair Charles Schultze, who asked RARG to investigate.[104]

The battle was on. RARG, with its economist's focus on cost-effectiveness, took issue with EPA's proposal. Lacking a clear threshold at which the health impacts of ozone jumped significantly, the EPA had chosen, somewhat arbitrarily, to protect people at the ninety-ninth percentile of ozone sensitivity. RARG argued that, in the absence of a well-defined health threshold, economic reasoning should be used to set the target. An RARG memo suggested that the EPA consider instead the "marginal cost of reducing the aggregate amount of exposure above some given level (in person hours). At some point," the memo continued, "the marginal cost per reduced person-hour of unhealthy exposure would begin to increase sharply." This "elbow" was the point at which the standard should be set: around 0.16 ppm.[105]

The more enforcement-oriented staff at EPA strongly disagreed with this interpretation. Some within the EPA did not want to raise the standard at all. David Hawkins, head of the air office, argued that the 0.08 ppm standard should be retained. More to the point, EPA staffers pointed out that economic criteria were legally impermissible. As Walter Barber, another air official, argued, "Nowhere does the [Clean Air] Act authorize such balancing of costs and benefits. . . . The Act does not authorize the administrator to abandon air pollution control simply because the marginal cost is less for a comparable health unit in another public health or safety program."[106]

The partial exception was the EPA's Office of Planning and Management, with its economic orientation. William Drayton, the office's head, recommended a standard of 0.15 ppm, a number closer to RARG's 0.16 ppm than to Hawkins's 0.08 or even Costle's 0.10. Drayton angered Hawkins by sending OMB a letter mentioning the billion dollars that could be saved by raising the standard. Such a letter could create problems for the agency, if the EPA was indeed legally constrained from considering costs. Here, RARG had to concede the EPA's point.[107]

Each office sought support from White House science advisors to resolve the impasse. Perhaps reluctant to decide the debate itself, the science office punted, suggesting that a standard in the 0.10 to 0.16 ppm range would be appropriate. After a two-day meeting with all the major EPA players, Costle, with whom the decision ultimately rested, chose 0.12 ppm as the new standard. As he later noted, "It was a political loser no matter what you did. . . . The minute you picked a number . . . everybody can argue that it can't be that number, or it could just as easily be another number. . . . [It] was a value judgment." Schultze, furious, pushed back, but President Carter let Costle's decision stand.[108]

RARG, led by Carter-appointed Schultze, was not an obvious ally of the petroleum industry. Yet the office's commitment to the economic style, which meant balancing the health effects of ozone against the increasing marginal cost of ozone reductions, produced these strange bedfellows. From the economic perspective, the EPA's desire to set standards without taking cost into account simply made no sense. After the standard was issued, Senator Muskie hauled Costle, Schultze, and Alfred Kahn, head of CWPS, before the Senate Environment Subcommittee to call them to task for considering costs. As Muskie pointed out, "The statute clearly prohibits the use of economic considerations in the setting of health standards. . . . [I]t is the heart of the Clean Air Act."[109] But while the absolute standard written into the Clean Air Act still had its supporters in 1977, it was, in fact, already being eroded.

FROM COST-BENEFIT ANALYSIS TO EMISSIONS TRADING

Cost-benefit analysis was not the only technique for regulatory decision-making that flowed out of the economic style of reasoning. As economic reasoning continued to gain ground in environmental policy, its advocates pointed to another kind of policy solution that would eventually create a new set of conflicts—the creation of markets in pollution rights. According to microeconomic theory, a market-based approach to regulation could achieve regulatory goals more efficiently than command-based regulation. While the development of what came to be called "emissions trading"—today more commonly known as cap-and-trade—was still in its early phases in the 1970s, its conflicts with older ways of thinking about environmental policy were already clear.

In addition to establishing NAAQS, the Clean Air Act of 1970 created New Source Performance Standards (NSPS): levels of pollution that would be permitted for new industrial activities, like a freshly built factory. The NSPS were aggressive, requiring the EPA to prevent entirely the creation of new sources that would emit any air pollutant at a level that that could "cause, or contribute to, an increase in mortality or an increase in serious irreversible, or incapacitating reversible, illness."[110] This approach to regulation drew inspiration from the idea of "technology forcing": that setting high, even seemingly unrealistic, standards based on technology that was in the pipeline but not yet widely available, could drive rapid improvements.[111] Like the NAAQS, the NSPS were grounded in the idea that the public had a right to healthy air, regardless of cost, as well as an implicit belief that pollution was morally wrong and therefore punishable. Both standards were shaped by the theory that strict, inflexible standards would limit industry delay and capture.

The ambition of the NSPS produced a strong reaction from the industries most affected by them, particularly the steel industry. As early as 1972, the industry was petitioning the EPA to change its interpretation of a "stationary" source. Rather than defining "source" as a particular point from which pollution was emitted—a smokestack, for example—smelters wanted to be judged on their overall emissions, so that an unusually dirty smokestack could be "offset" by a particularly clean one.[112]

In 1975, EPA agreed to do this by creating what it called a "bubble": an imaginary construct that covered all of a company's emissions sources. Introducing this concept would permit "the trading off of emission increases from one facility . . . with emissions reductions from another facility, in order to achieve no net increase in the amount of any air pollutant" overall.[113] The D.C. Circuit Court quickly struck down this form of "netting," which evaluated only the net change in emissions under the imaginary "bubble," rather than the emissions of any point source of pollution.[114] EPA was sent back to the drawing board.

By now, economists had joined industry groups in criticizing what Charles Schultze named "command-and-control" regulation, which simply set a regulatory standard and required firms to meet it, arguing in favor of market-based approaches that used incentives to achieve the same ends.[115] While cost-effectiveness analysis allowed agencies to compare the efficiency of various regulatory alternatives, economists pointed out that even more efficiency would be achieved by replacing flat restrictions on what firms were allowed to do with prices on the behavior government hoped to reduce. From an economic perspective, pollution was a negative externality, whose cost fell not on its producers, but on the larger public. The most efficient solution would not simply require firms to pollute less, because this approach would be cheap for some firms and very expensive for others. Rather, regulations should internalize the externality—that is, make sure those third-party costs were somehow incorporated into prices.

One obvious solution was to tax pollution, an idea that dated back to the 1910s.[116] Pollution taxes were briefly debated in Congress in the early 1970s, and by 1975 Schultze had become a vocal and high-profile advocate of the approach.[117] But a newer idea was percolating as well, one that was at the time much further from the political mainstream. As early as 1966, economists had proposed the idea of a market in pollution rights—the policy instrument now known as cap-and-trade.[118] The ability to emit pollution could be transformed into a property right that could be bought and sold. Firms that could inexpensively pollute less would do so and would sell the rest of their pollution rights to companies for whom pollution reduction was more expensive. Like taxes, pollution markets were, from an efficiency standpoint, preferable to one-size-fits-all regulation.

The 1977 Clean Air Act Amendments inadvertently opened the door in this direction. The original 1970 Act had included a punishment for geographic areas not attaining the NAAQS by their deadline: a growth ban. The measure prohibited these areas from adding new sources of any pollutant they were still emitting too much of. As it became clear that many industrial cities would not meet the deadline, this raised the politically problematic prospect of banning new factories in polluted, but economically struggling, cities. The 1977 amendments sought to solve this problem by creating "offsets" of its own. With offsets, companies could still build new pollution-emitting facilities in noncompliance areas. But when they did, total emissions produced across old and new facilities in that area had to decline.[119] This legal change reopened the possibility that EPA could create a "bubble" as part of the New Source Performance Standards.

Legislators added offsets to the Clean Air Act for political reasons, not reasons of efficiency. But by allowing companies, and cities, to focus on the reductions that were easiest and least expensive to make, they created an opportunity for others to make the efficiency argument. And it was on efficiency grounds that the EPA's Office of Planning and Management, under the leadership of Bill Drayton, would become a new champion of the bubble idea.[120]

Drayton was an attorney, not an economist, but he had studied economics as a postgraduate at Oxford and worked as a McKinsey consultant for most of a decade.[121] In that role, he had led the implementation of a program in Connecticut that brought the economic style to environmental law enforcement. As he described the program, it "recapture[d] the gains realized from noncompliance by charging violators an amount just sufficient to make compliance as economically attractive as profitable commercial expenditures."[122] By all accounts an unusually successful manager, as well as a fan of using market mechanisms to improve government action, Drayton supported cost-benefit analysis of environmental regulation.[123]

But the bubble was Drayton's real baby. As one colleague said, "[W]hat was driving Bill was pure intellectual conviction that this was a truly elegant approach—The Right Approach, with a capital 'T' and a capital 'R.'" Drayton believed that instituting a market-based approach to regulation would not only increase efficiency relative to command-and-control regulation, but would also sidestep the latter's tendencies to produce endless litigation. Instead, the bubble would usher in "a Golden Age where we could get totally beyond the confrontational relationship between environmental advocates and industry."[124]

After passage of the 1977 amendments, Drayton took charge of an agencywide bubble task force and increased the number of staff working on offsets. The aim was to allow each firm to place all its point sources of pollution under one umbrella. The EPA would still decide the maximum amount of pollution a company could produce, but the company could make those reductions by focusing on the point sources it could clean up most affordably, rather than requiring all point sources to achieve the same result. Working closely with Armco, a "good actor" from the steel industry, Drayton negotiated the myriad of practical details that had to be worked out before EPA could issue an official "bubble policy." Could open-dust reductions—particulates coming off unpaved roads and storage piles—be offset against smokestack emissions, whose smaller particles had greater health impacts? Could the bubble "float"—that is, could the company change the mix of emissions within a bubble over time, so long as the total emissions didn't rise? Could companies that were already out of compliance participate?[125]

EPA staff who saw their job through the lens of enforcement regarded the bubble concept with skepticism. The whole reason the Clean Air Act had been written with such detailed requirements was to avoid regulatory capture. Wasn't this just another opportunity for industry to evade compliance? David Hawkins, head of the air office, feared it might be: "I have this nagging image of a political cartoon which shows a steel plant in the distance with soot billowing out big, black clouds while in the foreground a citizen's group is screaming for action and an EPA administrator is trying to quiet them by saying, 'But they're watering the roads!'" Even proponents recognized the reality of "gross defects in air quality management" that bubble schemes had the potential to compound.[126]

EPA nevertheless did issue a bubble proposal at the beginning of 1979. Hawkins's own legacy was to strategically introduce a great many restrictions into the policy—so many as to make it practically unusable.[127] Still, as one EPA advocate noted, what was important "was the fact that the agency had made the proposal public and committed itself to further publicity" for the bubble concept. Moreover, this proposal used phrases like "greater economic efficiency" as if that were something the EPA should and would seek as a regulatory goal.[128]

The bubble project also further embedded economists into the power structure at the EPA. Drayton established a small Regulatory Reform Staff (RRS) within the policy office to oversee implementation of the bubble and related economic incentive activities. For example, OPM began to interpret the Clean Air Act amendments to allow "banking" of emissions, essentially allowing offsets across time, rather than space. Under the leadership of attorney Michael Levin, these new activities were brought under the purview of the RRS, which grouped the regulatory concepts EPA had been developing independently of one another—bubbles, banking, netting, offsets, credits—and tied them together with a single name: controlled trading.[129]

Levin worked to strengthen the RRS, but ultimately realized that the policy office alone lacked the power to institute controlled trading as national environmental policy. The rest of the EPA would have to believe in it, too. "Institutionalization," Levin wrote, "means the reform becomes a normal part of program office thinking. . . . If the reform continues to be seen as a foreign body, a planning staff creature, over the long run it will wither and fail."[130] To move in this direction, he worked to place trading advocates into state and local program offices. Over time, people with an allegiance to the economic style, or at least one policy representing it, became seeded in more and more locations throughout EPA.[131]

Critics of the bubble policy, and emissions trading more generally, remained. In addition to fears that it would make it easier for industry to keep polluting, some pointed to the likelihood that offsetting would concentrate pollutants in the most disadvantaged communities—a concern that would later be labeled as "environmental justice." Others noted the political difficulty of requiring further reductions, once complicated bubble compliance plans were put into place. Still others pointed out that offsets would in fact tend to increase total pollution, because firms would no longer need to build in a margin of error so that emissions from individual point sources never went above permissible levels.[132]

But from the economic perspective, these concerns were easy to dismiss. With efficiency as the guiding value, emissions trading looked like a winning strategy. Neutral and technocratic, it appeared to be a way to achieve policy goals while sidestepping politics. Emissions trading reconceptualized regulatory compliance in a way that built efficiency in.

BEYOND ENVIRONMENTAL POLICY

The spread of the economic style, and the conflicts it produced, was particularly visible in environmental policy. But those conflicts were present in other social regulatory domains as well. Although economic reasoning advanced unevenly, where it did, efficiency became increasingly important as a lens for decision-making.

In transportation safety, for example, the NHTSA was created "at the intersection of the civil rights movement and the space program," reflecting an "egalitarian logic" about equal protection, as well as technological optimism about how to achieve it.[133] The 1966 law which created it had prescribed technology-forcing standards that were "reasonable, practicable and appropriate," with no mention made of cost, and the agency's approach reflected an engineering logic that focused on rulemaking.[134]

But economists saw highway safety regulation through a cost-benefit lens. The combination of the political power of the auto industry and economist John Snow's appointment as NHTSA administrator shifted the balance of power within the agency away from the engineers. NHTSA began to issue more vehicle recalls—whose costs were not visible and which were not subject to regulatory review—rather than regulations, and Snow gave the Office of Plans and Programs more influence in the rulemaking process. As the Carter administration intensified review through the RARG process, it encouraged the agency's new and increasing tendency to evaluate its own rules through the economic lens that it knew RARG would take. By the end of the Carter administration, this external pressure had led NHTSA to take a cost-benefit approach to its regulations in practice, even if the letter of the law said it could not.[135]

The 1968 legislation that established the Occupational Safe and Health Administration had, like the EPA's enabling legislation, emphasized a rights-based approach with its declaration of a "universal and substantive right to safety and health." Pushed by an alliance of health and safety advocates, the labor movement, public health, consumer, and environmental groups, the Occupational Safety and Health Act required a standard that would assure no "material impairment of health or functional capacity," even if a worker was exposed for their whole working life.[136] In the 1970s, economists at CWPS and RARG supported cost-benefit analysis of OSHA regulations, but the courts' interpretation of OSHA's statutory language left little wiggle room. While a 1974 decision by the D.C. Circuit Court noted that OSHA was required to consider "economic feasibility," it found that a regulation was infeasible only if it threatened an entire industry, not simply because it was financially burdensome—or even life-threatening—to individual firms.[137]

Carter's OSHA administrator, Eula Bingham, was a strong defender of the original language.[138] Yet even Bingham was pushed by external demands for economic reasoning, halting OSHA's first economist. Soon OSHA was playing the same game as other regulatory agencies, using economic arguments to rebut industry's claims about the costs of compliance. Despite the rights-based language written into its founding statute, the White House effort to center efficiency in workplace health regulations pulled OSHA away from its commitment to protecting every worker, regardless of cost, in favor of a more cost-effective approach that simply accepted that some workplaces would remain unsafe.[139]

In all of these cases, the expansion of economic reasoning was shaped by changes to the letter of the law and the courts' interpretations as well as the arrival of economists. In the 1970s, new social regulatory legislation began to move modestly and unevenly toward a greater consideration of costs, a shift that can be seen, for example, in the Federal Insecticide, Fungicide and Rodenticide Act (1972) and the Toxic Substances Control Act (1976).[140] Even so, for most of the 1970s the courts largely interpreted legislation that did not *specify* cost considerations as preventing such considerations from being required. This interpretation is evident not only in the D.C. Circuit's "economic feasibility" decision on OSHA, but also in court decisions regarding efforts to require the weighing of costs in New Source Performance

Standards, endangered species protection, and cotton dust regulations.[141] Yet while economic reasoning was not fully institutionalized by the end of the Carter administration, new administrative rules and organizational changes had made it much more central to social regulation.

Institutionalizing the Economic Style in Social Regulation

The wave of environmental, health, and safety legislation that passed in the late 1960s and early 1970s dramatically expanded the role of government in ensuring Americans' rights to health and safety—whether on the roads, in the workplace, or in the natural environment. The result of overlapping social movements advocating for consumers and the environment, as well as activist groups of health and safety advocates, it reflected a particular set of ways of thinking about these problems and the role of government in preventing them.

One was a logic of rights. Inspired by the success of the civil rights movement, and expanding on a growing list of human rights, egalitarian ideas about the right to health and safety shaped these debates. Another was optimism about the capacity of technology to solve such problems, and of government to promote the development and adoption of such technologies. In environmental policy in particular, ecological ideas about the interdependence of life played an important role. And an underlying political theory, that the best way for government to act without being captured by private interests was by establishing ambitious, inflexible standards, shaped the form these laws took.

Economic reasoning played very little role in the legislation that launched this wave of social regulation, which intentionally set ambitious policy goals regardless of cost, an approach that actively conflicted with the economic style. But by the late 1960s, that style was already becoming well-established in Washington. Its broader presence meant that there were plenty of people in the policymaking community who were inclined to evaluate "good" regulation through a different lens, even if they were sympathetic to the goals of using government to improve health, safety, and environmental quality.

The ambition of these new laws unsurprisingly produced a reaction among those affected by them. While big business was not particularly well organized when this regulatory wave began, by the early 1970s it was developing an increasingly unified political voice. And one of the loudest calls it made with that voice was for formally weighing the costs of regulatory compliance, which it argued were extremely high, against its benefits.

Industry's push for cost-benefit analysis and economists' advocacy of it as a more rational way to make regulatory decisions reinforced each other over the course of the 1970s. Through a series of incremental steps—executive orders and new review procedures—the White House pushed regulatory agencies to increase their use of cost-benefit and cost-effectiveness analysis, first of environmental but eventually of all major social regulations. These demands also led agencies to make their analytic offices, themselves a legacy of PPBS, larger and stronger in order to meet them.

As this took place, the policy offices themselves tended to gain a greater voice in agency decision-making, and increasingly shaped the internal terms of debate. The economists and policy analysts within them, including many who identified as liberals or Democrats, called for efficiency as a primary goal of regulation. By the second half of the 1970s, such proponents of the economic style had also begun to advocate for new regulatory modes that used incentives and market mechanisms to produce such outcomes—developments that would continue in decades to come. While these efforts began under Nixon and Ford, they were particularly successful during the Carter administration, when liberal economists allied with regulated industries to push EPA and other agencies to focus more centrally on cost-effectiveness.

This process was not complete by the end of the Carter administration, but it was well on its way. And as economic reasoning became increasingly naturalized as the appropriate way of thinking about social regulation, the competing logics that had motivated it in the first place—of commitment to rights, of technological optimism, of concern with ecology, of avoidance of capture—became more and more marginal to the conversation. What had successfully been dubbed the "command-and-control" approach to protecting the environment, health, and safety was coming to seem inappropriately rigid, inefficient, and unrealistic. Neutral, technocratic efficiency was there to replace it.

8

How the Economic Style
Replaced the Democratic Left

By the end of the Carter administration, the economic style of reasoning had become institutionalized in Washington. Fifteen years earlier, policymakers rarely thought of social policy, market governance, or environmental, health, and safety regulations through the lens of efficiency, incentives, or competition. Indeed, politicians' approaches to many policy questions—particularly among those who wanted to see a more activist government—often openly conflicted with such values. Yet while economic reasoning might not always *win* policy debates, by 1980 it was nearly always present. From its expansion into law and policy schools, to its representation in policy planning offices and the new Congressional Budget Office (CBO), to its dominance in the rapidly growing space of think tanks and policy research organizations, to its incorporation into administrative rules and case law, the footprint of the economic style had grown large.

Advocates for the economic style counted both liberals and conservatives among their members. Both groups helped expand its foothold in Washington. Yet it was the liberals, who shared a belief in the power of government to do good and wanted to improve its functioning, who played the more important role in advancing it. They wanted more cost-effective federal programs, lower prices for consumers, and better environmental protections, and they perceived a role for the government in achieving these goals. Certainly, there existed an active community of economists who preferred free markets and limited government, and their political influence was increasing during the 1970s. But they did not drive the expansion of economic reasoning in policy circles.

And yet, a peculiar thing happened. Repeatedly, the liberal analytic establishment—which saw its techniques as apolitical and value-neutral—found itself allying with moderate Republicans, and against liberal Democrats, in its policy arguments. Its prioritization of efficiency led its members to favor cost-sharing and means-testing in social programs over less efficient universal options. Its belief that economic regulation—government control over prices and market entry—was inefficient helped produce bipartisan support to deregulate first transportation and then other industries. And its emphasis on cost-effectiveness in government regulation led adherents to form alliances with conservatives and industry in support of cost-benefit analysis.

Liberal advocates of the economic style often found that their embrace of efficiency as a core virtue of policy put them in direct conflict with liberal Democratic policy positions, including support for implementing universal health insurance, limiting industry concentration, and establishing strong and inflexible environmental standards. Such positions rested on a competing set of coherent logics: a belief in the principle of social insurance and in medical care as a right; a concern with the risks of concentrated economic power in a democracy; a view of pollution as a moral wrong best contained by strict standards.

From the economic perspective, these positions focused on the wrong things. Many of these Democratic policy stances were based on arguments about rights, universalism, or equality. These arguments tended to dismiss efficiency, and were not always interested in a consequentialist analysis of the effects of a particular policy choice. Other liberal positions relied on a theory of politics that prioritized controlling powerful interests and maintaining a broad base of support for programs one believed in. Advocates of the economic style, by contrast, did not always have much of a theory of politics, instead seeing their approach as neutral and able to operate outside of politics. From this technocratic perspective, choosing less-efficient policies because of their moral implications or political consequences was clearly misguided.

When the economic style first began to spread in Washington in the mid-1960s, this efficiency-centered approach faced an uphill battle. Its way of thinking was deeply unfamiliar to most policymakers, many of whom dismissed it as disconnected from reality. Some even mocked it. Yet as it spread and became at least partially institutionalized, Democrats making the kinds of noneconomic arguments that had been successful in the Kennedy and Johnson administrations found themselves increasingly on the defensive. The tables had turned. Now it was liberal advocates of rights, equality, and universalism who found themselves having to defend the logic of their positions against the seemingly unassailable rationality of the economic style.

The Fall of National Health Insurance and the Rise of Competition

The fate of national health insurance illustrates how this realignment worked in social policy. The structure of Medicare and Medicaid, created in 1965, reflected a grand compromise between the desire to provide the widest possible access to medical care and the desire to protect physicians' interests in a private system, all without triggering Americans' generalized fear of "socializing medicine." Medicaid insured the poor, and Medicare covered the elderly, but most Americans remained in the employer-based private system—which worked for some, but not all.[1] For liberal Democrats, who saw healthcare as a right and believed in social insurance as a means to achieve it, the obvious next step was to expand Medicare and Medicaid into a form of universal national health insurance.

When, in 1970, Senator Ted Kennedy introduced his Health Security bill on Capitol Hill, it reflected this vision. He proposed a national insurance plan, available to all Americans, that established a right to healthcare and required no cost-sharing by those who used it.[2] The early 1970s saw widespread support for Kennedy's and similar bills. As the *New York Times* noted in 1971, "Subtly but unmistakably, Americans from all strata of society and all economic classes are swinging over to the idea that good health care, like a good education, ought to be a fundamental right of citizenship."[3]

Advocates of the economic style—even politically liberal ones—were less enamored of such an approach. Concerned with the cost-effectiveness of government programs, they expressed skepticism about the expense and necessity of paying for all Americans' insurance with tax dollars. The emergence of a new academic literature on moral hazard moreover gave them a new argument for cost-sharing as a means to discourage overconsumption of medical care.[4]

Thanks to the lasting effects of the Planning-Programming-Budgeting System (PPBS), by 1970 nearly every federal agency housed advocates for the economic style. Indeed, when Nixon began looking for a healthcare plan of his own to counter the threat of Kennedy's Health Security proposal, he turned to the Office of the Assistant Secretary of Planning and Evaluation (ASPE) at the Department of Health, Education, and Welfare (HEW)—created to implement PPBS, and led by economists—to give him options.[5] Although ASPE's staff consisted of civil servants, rather than political appointees, its members had largely been hired by Johnson's assistant secretaries, William Gorham and Alice Rivlin. Stuart Altman, the deputy assistant secretary who led the development of Nixon's health plan, was a Nixon appointee, but he had previously worked for Gorham and was not particularly conservative.[6]

The Comprehensive Health Insurance Plan that ASPE proposed, and Nixon adopted as his own, combined an economic perspective with a substantial expansion of government capacity. It required employers to provide health insurance to their employees and created a means-tested, government-funded insurance program with significant cost-sharing for those who still remained uncovered.[7]

The conservative wing of Nixon's administration regarded this healthcare plan as government overreach, a product of the liberal analytic community put into place by Johnson's PPBS.[8] From the perspective of many members of that liberal analytic community, it was insufficiently generous. But for those who were committed to the economic style, the efficiency-centered approach of the Nixon plan placed it within the space of reasonable debate. By contrast, members of this community tended to see Kennedy's Health Security plan as not only politically unrealistic, but as promoting overuse of healthcare and costing too much because it covered those who could have afforded their own insurance.[9] As Brookings economist Karen Davis noted at the time, plans like the Health Security Act "have such extensive insurance coverage even for families reasonably able to meet their medical expenses directly as to invalidate any automatic market incentives for efficiency or cost constraint."[10]

The negotiations that ensued over some combination of Kennedy's proposal and the Nixon healthcare plan brought the United States the closest it had ever come to national health insurance. Kennedy and Nixon, though, failed to strike a deal before the Watergate scandal forced the president's resignation.[11] The healthcare reform agenda foundered under Ford, who, faced with a significant recession, announced that he would veto any health insurance legislation for budgetary reasons. And while Jimmy Carter announced support for comprehensive national health insurance on the campaign trail, once in office he sidelined the issue in favor of an attempt at welfare reform.[12]

Carter picked up the mantle of universal health insurance again only when faced with a potential primary challenge from Senator Kennedy in early 1978. Like Nixon before him, he turned to HEW for advice.[13] ASPE had new leadership, of course, but the office continued to reflect the economic style of reasoning. Karen Davis, now in the post of deputy assistant secretary of planning and evaluation for health, was a strong advocate for expanding health insurance coverage, but she was also concerned with limiting costs. She remained wary of the moral hazard implicit in plans like the Health Security Act: "The absence of any consumer payments . . . greatly increases the cost of the plan to the federal government . . . [and] may well cause greater utilization of medical care services by high-income people."[14] After considerable delay, HEW produced four proposals for Carter to consider.[15]

With inflation and cost containment the administration's highest priority, and the same office in charge of policy proposals, perhaps it is not surprising that Carter's plan resembled a warmed over version of Nixon's. It contained a familiar mix of employer mandates, Medicare and Medicaid expansion, and new private options for the middle-income, working-age uninsured.[16] Senator Kennedy continued to push competing alternatives from the left. But by this point, the economists' arguments against national health insurance— about its wastefulness and encouragement of overconsumption—were becoming conventional wisdom in Washington, even among Democrats. Both the vision of collectively financed social insurance and the idea of healthcare as a right were beginning to fall by the wayside.

Conservative economists, meanwhile, had set upon another path: expanding access to healthcare by improving the function of the healthcare market. The Chicago School had long been critical of the professional monopoly of physicians, arguing that it kept doctors' incomes high at the expense of patients.[17] But "market" was, as one close observer noted, "a word that had rarely, if ever, turned up in bibliographies concerning health care."[18]

In the United States, medicine was traditionally regulated as a profession, governed by rules that limited competition in exchange for special obligations (for example, to meet licensing standards and uphold professional ethics) on practitioners. Now, with national health insurance on the horizon, medicine was on the verge of becoming what one commentator referred to as "the next great 'regulated industry.'"[19] But another possibility existed. Conservative economists argued that healthcare might be understood, and governed, as a *market*—one in which competition and choice would produce collectively beneficial results.

The early 1970s saw the flowering of a community of economists and fellow-travelers who were devoted to pursuing this possibility. Much of this interest was nurtured by Clark Havighurst, a Duke University law professor who arrived at the framework of healthcare-as-market through his exposure to the new idea of health maintenance organizations (HMOs). As originally proposed by physician Paul Ellwood in 1970, HMOs would provide a suite of health services for a fixed annual fee.[20] Conservative economists soon embraced the concept as a way to promote efficiency through choice and competition.[21] Encouraged to develop this perspective by a stint at Henry Manne's law-and-economics summer camp, Havighurst began to organize publications and conferences that brought together Chicago types with more liberal economists to discuss issues of competition in healthcare.[22]

Within a few years, Havighurst's arguments about promoting competition in healthcare were being picked up by the Federal Trade Commission (FTC), where Wesley J. Liebeler, the Chicagoan leading its policy planning office, was pushing for attention to occupational licensing as an antitrust issue. Following a 1975 Supreme Court decision that limited the historic exemption of the "learned professions" from antitrust enforcement, the FTC launched a full investigation of the healthcare industry, including physicians' control of Blue Cross/Blue Shield, HMO restrictions, limits on advertising and solicitation, and price fixing.[23] The agency also filed suit against the American Medical Association, arguing that "'ethical' proscriptions . . . against advertising and other forms of 'soliciting' patients . . . deprive consumers of valuable information," thereby limiting competition and potentially worsening healthcare costs.[24] More broadly, the FTC was helping to build an economics-centered community that understood healthcare as a market. In 1977, its Bureau of Economics organized a conference on "Competition in the Health Care Sector" that attracted 600 attendees.[25] Speakers included a wide range of prominent health economists and others active in policy circles, ranging from Havighurst and Altman to RAND's Joseph Newhouse and Kennedy CEA staffer Burton Weisbrod.[26]

While this effort was led by conservatives, liberal economists' shared commitment to the economic style meant that they were receptive to the goal of improving competition in healthcare. Liberals might note the need to consider distributional effects, in addition to allocative efficiency, in the process. Or they might point to the limited information available to consumers when making healthcare decisions.[27] But they were very comfortable with the market framework itself. The pro-competition message—particularly its more populist aspects, like tackling the privileges of physicians—appealed not only to liberal economists but to consumer allies like Kennedy and Carter FTC chair Michael Pertschuk.[28]

It was in this context of burgeoning interest in promoting healthcare competition that Joseph Califano, Carter's HEW chair (and Johnson-era advocate of PPBS), turned to Alain Enthoven (a father of PPBS) for health reform advice in 1977.[29] Enthoven presented a plan that drew from both the systems analytic and industrial organization strands of the economic style. Indeed, he himself saw it "as the 'working out' in the health care economy of an example of [Charles] Schultze's general propositions" on how to move beyond command-and-control regulation through use of market-like incentives, which Schultze had recently introduced in *The Public Use of Private Interest*.[30] Seeking "informed choice among competing alternatives" while arguing that "direct economic regulation will not make things better," Enthoven advocated for what he called a "consumer-choice health plan"—"a system of competing health plans in which physicians and consumers can benefit from using resources wisely."[31]

Enthoven's plan featured universal health insurance funded through a combination of tax credits and vouchers for the low-income. It centered on regulated private health plans from which individuals could choose, thereby promoting beneficial competition. Although Califano did not adopt the proposal as his own, Enthoven continued to promote it with a pair of 1978 articles in the *New England Journal of Medicine* and then a 1980 book.[32] Enthoven's proposals garnered significant attention in Washington; as one reviewer noted, "It is time we had a zesty book from the political Right. This is it, the song of a world of 'fair economic competition.'"[33]

Liberal economists did question whether competition could in fact provide all the benefits that its advocates promised. Economist Henry Aaron, who led ASPE under Carter, argued early in the Reagan administration that policymakers should view with "skepticism . . . the claims of those who espouse competition as *the* answer to excessive growth of expenditures on health care."[34] But this camp of economists, comfortable with using the market framework to think about medical care, nevertheless appreciated the potential benefits that competition might bring. Indeed, despite its note of caution, Aaron's editorial was titled "Orange Light for the Competitive Model."[35] Some liberal economists had in fact begun advocating for competition among health plans and removing restrictions on the tasks nonphysicians could perform as early as 1974.[36]

Policymakers and advocates who favored the social insurance approach, by contrast, saw the economic style as fundamentally in conflict with the vision of healthcare first and foremost as a right. And yet by 1979, even Ted Kennedy had compromised on his earlier proposals, introducing elements of competition into his latest attempt to secure universal coverage even as he retained the language of rights.[37] That year, Rashi Fein, an "architect of Medicare" and advocate of social insurance, issued a scathing warning about "the danger of looking to economics and economists to provide policy prescriptions" when "equity and distributive justice" were the real issues:

> Thus it is that the language of the marketplace—bottom line, marketing, sales, producer, and consumer—captivates our hospital administrators. Thus it is that the president—on grounds of efficiency—would replace elements of the Social Security system with means-tested programs in order to more effectively target expenditures. Thus the call for "technical answers, not political answers," for answers based on criteria of efficiency, not on considerations of social justice. . . . A pity, indeed, that national health insurance was not enacted in an earlier day when technicians (and economists) had not yet been elevated above politicians. We can be thankful that we are not now engaged in a great debate concerning the validity of the concept of free public education.[38]

Fein's language was strong, but the change he observed was real. Although champions remained, his vision of a world in which healthcare was too important to be left to the market had become increasingly difficult to defend.

The Decline of Populist Antitrust and Establishment of the Consumer Welfare Standard

The advance of the economic style proved increasingly constraining to those who wanted to make arguments from the left, regardless of the policy domain. In market governance, the institutionalization of economic reasoning gradually displaced the populist vision of antitrust that had been prominent since the New Deal, and which was committed to limiting market concentration and breaking up the biggest firms. This populist vision brought together a Jeffersonian affinity for small business, and a concern with the prices consumers paid, with a fear of the power big business might hold.

The Supreme Court was already supporting aggressive antitrust enforcement in the 1960s, reflecting its own interpretation of the purpose of antitrust law as balancing low prices for consumers with the protection of small business.[39] But liberal populists wanted to push antitrust policy even further. In 1972, Ralph Nader's group published a blistering report, *The Closed Enterprise System*. In Nader's own words, the study revealed how "corporate radicalism [is] so deeply insinuated into the politic-economic fabric of the society that a veritable revolution against citizens has occurred." He railed against the "terribly lagging, sometimes aiding and abetting" federal anti-trust enforcement establishment that had permitted it to happen and called for new legislation to "break up dominant firms in oligopolistic industries."[40]

These young consumerists were joined by some Democratic members of Congress, including old lion of New Deal populism Wright Patman (of the eponymous 1936 Robinson-Patman Act banning price discrimination) and Philip Hart, chair of the Senate Subcommittee on Antitrust and Monopoly. Hart hoped to take antitrust enforcement to the next level with his Industrial Reorganization Act, which proposed to break up industries with four-firm concentration ratios of over 50 percent.[41] Supporters of the 1972 bill justified this proposal not only on grounds that concentrated industries could avoid competition and keep prices high, but through explicit reference to corporate power, with Hart rejecting "the notion that we must allow the government to increasingly become the handmaiden of the corporations, that we must sit back and watch public government being replaced by private control."[42]

In the 1960s, liberal populists and liberal economists had found themselves largely in alliance on antitrust issues, despite caring most about different outcomes. While populists' priorities included the protection of small business and limiting corporate power, advocates of the economic style were concerned primarily with using antitrust policy to promote allocative efficiency. But economists understood efficiency as going hand in hand with the lowest possible prices for consumers, an outcome that the populists cared about as well.

When it came to turning those values into policy decisions, though, liberal economists were skeptical of simply presupposing that "bigness is (necessarily) badness," which they saw as a corollary of the populist tendency toward idealizing small business and fearing corporate power.[43] Instead, they preferred to evaluate how markets were performing on a case-by-case basis. But in the 1960s, when Harvard was the dominant school of industrial organization economics, most economists also believed that industries with high levels of market concentration would result in lower output and higher prices.[44] Even as they argued against using "Jeffersonian" antitrust to address "social power broadly defined," such economists tended to support levels of antitrust enforcement, including breaking up big firms, that from today's perspective seem exceptionally high.[45] Indeed, Johnson's Task Force on Antitrust Policy, which produced a 1968 report strongly grounded in structuralist economics, recommended firms be restricted to a market share of no more than 12 percent.[46]

This confidence that market concentration would produce inefficient outcomes led liberal economists to prefer policies that overlapped considerably with those of antitrust populists, even though the economists rejected the populists' concerns with small business and corporate power. The Industrial Reorganization Act even traced its origins to the draft legislation proposed by Harvard economists Carl Kaysen and Donald Turner in their 1959 book, *Antitrust Policy*.[47]

But in the early 1970s, liberal advocates of the economic style began questioning whether limiting consolidation would, in fact, promote efficiency. The structure-conduct-performance framework had found that industry concentration was associated with above-average profits, which structuralists took as an indicator that firms were exercising market power. In such cases, they believed, concentration should be reduced. By this time, though, Chicagoans were hammering away at these assumptions. They argued that size and profitability were often a result of efficiency, that high profits rarely lasted, and that even very large firms could rarely use market power, because doing so would attract new entrants.[48]

And increasingly, Harvard School economists accepted the Chicagoans' arguments. By 1974, Turner acknowledged disputes within the discipline on the "relationship between profits and concentration" and "how much [monopoly power] is attributable to economies of scale."[49] When he testified at hearings on the Industrial Reorganization Act, Turner said he had become "uneasy about using market share percentages as a presumptive test of substantial monopoly power." Given that he disagreed with other arguments for the bill—those based on promoting Jeffersonian ideals and limiting corporate power—Turner now "would recommend a considerably less ambitious program" than the one, based on Turner's own past recommendations, that Senator Hart had proposed.[50]

This did not mean that liberal economists across the board now agreed with the Chicago position that "antitrust enforcement should be concentrated against horizontal price fixing and regulatory barriers to entry"—a position even Richard Posner admitted "may seem a breathtaking constriction of the [Antitrust] Division's scope of activity."[51] But liberal adherents to the economic style nevertheless shared with Chicago a common framework for debate. Turner did not fully subscribe to Posner's conclusions. But he agreed with the presuppositions that led Posner there: that it was "proper, in fashioning antitrust goals, to exclude considerations other than economic efficiency, such as the merits of favoring small business or altering the distribution of income," and that the real issue was "how to choose among schools of economic thought that disagree on the consequences for efficiency of various market practices and conditions."[52] Harvard economists, like those from Chicago, believed that "populist goals should be given little or no independent weight in formulating antitrust rules and presumptions."[53]

The move of the liberal Harvard School away from populist antitrust helped justify a parallel shift in the courts. The late 1970s saw the Supreme Court move decisively in the direction of efficiency as the only legitimate goal of antitrust policy, and less enforcement as the way to achieve it. In 1977, in *Continental Television, Inc. v. GTE Sylvania, Inc.*, it rejected *per se* (that is, across-the-board) rules that prohibited manufacturers from placing resale restrictions on distributors.[54] While Chicagoans had long argued that resale restrictions could be efficiency-enhancing, Harvard had once seen them as a problematic exercise of market power. Now, though, the Harvard position had changed, and the court's decision drew extensively on a brief by Turner, as well as citing Chicagoans like Robert Bork and Posner.[55] Similarly, the court's *Brunswick* case that same year relied heavily on the arguments of Philip Areeda, Turner's colleague and collaborator, that "injury to a competitor is not a concern of the antitrust laws." In that case, the court narrowed the scope for private plaintiffs to claim treble damages and decisively rejected the protection of small business as an antitrust goal.[56]

By 1979, the Supreme Court had affirmatively embraced Bork's claim that the Sherman Act was intended as "a consumer welfare prescription." While "consumer welfare" might bring to mind Ralph Nader's concerns with corporate power as well as lower prices, Bork's great success was in redefining it, and persuading the courts to accept his redefinition, as synonymous with allocative efficiency.[57] The Antitrust Division and Federal Trade Commission were increasingly accepting the proposition that they should only enforce antitrust violations that reduced efficiency, and they had changed their decision-making processes accordingly.[58] In effect, the courts and the antitrust agencies reified a conception of antitrust policy that had been embraced by a bipartisan alliance of economists and allied legal scholars, marginalizing liberal populist conceptions of antitrust policy in the process.

Despite extensive hearings, the Industrial Reorganization Act never came to a vote. Wright Patman was ousted as chair of the House Banking Committee in 1975, and the Hart-Scott-Rodino Antitrust Improvements Act of 1976, passed in the year of both Patman's and Hart's deaths, reflected the "last gasp" of the populist antitrust tradition.[59] Hart-Scott-Rodino hardly upended antitrust; it authorized state attorneys general to bring treble-damages antitrust suits on behalf of their citizens and expanded agencies' ability to collect data from firms.[60] Yet even these modest provisions struggled to find their way through Congress, becoming law only in watered-down form.[61] Ironically, Hart-Scott-Rodino's most meaningful provision—the requirement that firms of a certain size must notify the Antitrust Division and FTC before conducting mergers—had an unintended anti-populist effect. Rather than challenge firms in the courts, the antitrust agencies shifted toward negotiating with firms prior to merger. Because such negotiation required the agencies to do more analysis of mergers before their consummation, rather than litigating them after, this move further strengthened the internal influence of economics.[62]

During the Carter years, some of the president's appointees—including Michael Pertschuk at the FTC and John Shenefield and Sanford Litvack at the Antitrust Division—were friendly to a broadly populist of antitrust policy.[63] As Pertschuk proclaimed in a 1977 speech, "Competition policy must sometimes choose between greater efficiency, which may carry with it the promise of lower prices, and other social objectives, such as the dispersal of power, which may result in marginally higher prices."[64] And Ted Kennedy, now chair of the Senate Judiciary Committee, in 1979 introduced a deconcentration bill that the New York Times described as "evok[ing] the ideals of Jeffersonian democracy and Adam Smith's model of perfectly competitive markets comprised of many small companies."[65]

These efforts quickly stalled out in a policymaking environment suffused with the economic style. Kennedy could barely get a much narrower antitrust reform bill out of committee, let alone pass a major attack on corporate concentration.[66] Carter's appointees had either limited success within their agencies (Shenefield and Litvack) or encountered sharp external pushback against their efforts (Pertschuk).[67] Later, Litvack would rail against the increasingly dominant view of "the [Antitrust] Division as a neutral arbiter of theoretical micro-economics."[68]

As economic reasoning became increasingly locked in as the appropriate way of thinking about antitrust policy, it became harder for other ways of thinking to even get a hearing—in law schools as well as in Washington. Areeda and Turner's three-volume 1978 treatise, Antitrust Law, would serve as the Harvard counterweight to Bork's Antitrust Paradox—the two immediately becoming "intellectual pillars of the U.S. antitrust system."[69] Yet as Louis Schwartz, a legal scholar not of the law-and-economics persuasion, noted in a review, the authors juxtaposed the goal of "populism" with that of "efficiency." "They present populism as a crude, confused yearning for income equalization, dispersion of economic and political power," he wrote, as "an aspiration for the virtues of yeomanry."[70] Economics, noted Schwartz, was not without value; it was one of many disciplines that "help, or seem to help, us comprehend or order the infinite chaos that would otherwise confront us."[71] Yet in rejecting competing values—like "fairness"—Schwartz suggested that economics betrayed a longer legacy.[72] "[T]his reviewer sees hope and portent in the history of populism's tenets which have become today's orthodoxies: antitrust laws, railroad regulation, regulation of stock and commodities markets, wage-hour legislation, protection of collective bargaining, child labor laws, and taxation of income at progressive rates."[73] The vision he upheld, though, was increasingly relegated to the sidelines.

The Spread of Cost-Benefit Analysis

The pattern held as well in social regulation. As the economic style of reasoning spread, it undermined moral lines of argument that had been successful for liberal Democrats advocating for more government control of health, safety, and the environment. Liberal advocates of the economic style soon found that their advocacy for an economic approach to regulatory decision-making unexpectedly aligned them with conservatives and industry interests. As the economic approach was gradually institutionalized across Washington, liberals who made noneconomic arguments had less and less room to politically maneuver.

The major wave of social regulation that began in the late 1960s had crested by the early 1970s. But the consumer, environmental, and public health advocates who had helped bring it to fruition were not resting on their laurels. Activists who had pushed Congress to create new regulatory agencies now focused on ensuring those agencies aggressively addressed the problems they were created to solve. Labor unions worked with Nader's Health Research Group, for example, to use legal means to force the Occupational Safety and Health Agency to set and enforce the standards required by law.[74] In other areas, advocacy groups demanded additional legislation to tackle important issues that had not yet been addressed. Environmentalists followed their early-1970s successes with a push to address hazardous waste, leading to the passage of several new laws in the second half of the decade.[75] And at least one movement effort—the Nader-led attempt to give consumers explicit voice in the regulatory process—sought to create another major new agency, the Consumer Protection Agency, as part of the regulatory mix.[76]

These liberal Democratic advocates for social regulation continued to work within a noneconomic framework. They based their arguments in the same basic theory of politics that produced the Occupational Safety and

Health Act and the Clean Air and Water Acts: that a safe and healthy environment (both natural and workplace) was a right and that acts that infringed upon those rights were moral offenses. The policy solutions they imposed similarly relied on a consensus about how best to address the dangers of regulatory capture, which they regarded as an ongoing risk to the public's health. Because they agreed that regulatory flexibility and cost considerations would lead to decisions that favored industry at the expense of the broader public, they preferred strict, often technology-based standards as a way to limit corporate influence.

By the mid-1970s, the business community was more effectively lobbying to fight back against what industry leaders portrayed as regulatory overreach. Even so, laws like the Safe Drinking Water Act (1974) and the Resource Conservation Recovery Act (1976) continued to exclude cost considerations as an explicit factor in deciding regulatory standards.[77] The courts, for the most part, interpreted statutes that did not specify the consideration of costs as not permitting it. *Tennessee Valley Authority v. Hill* (1978), for example, halted work on a $50 million dam that was 80 percent complete because it threatened the endangered snail darter; cost-benefit calculations did not factor in. Another Supreme Court case, *American Textile Manufacturers v. Donovan* (1981), rejected the argument that OSHA should have used cost-benefit analysis in setting the cotton dust standard, instead finding that Congress had already accepted that ensuring safe working environments would impose costs on employers.[78]

Liberal economists disagreed, unsurprisingly, with this approach, believing that good political decisions considered costs and trade-offs. Even during the first wave of environmental, health, and safety laws, economists criticized legislation that refused to take costs into account. Harvard economist Marc Roberts told the *National Journal* in 1972 that he was "a radical, a Democrat, and an ardent hater of Richard Nixon," yet continued, "There isn't a single respectable economist in the country who would back the no-discharge goal adopted by the Senate [in the Clean Water Act]. It will waste billions of dollars for no useful social or environmental purpose."[79] Having enshrined efficiency and cost-effectiveness as their core values, advocates of the economic style wanted neutral, apolitical evaluation of competing alternatives. They discounted the likelihood of capture and rejected the alternative view that neutral, technocratic decisions might simply be impossible when regulatory standards had tens or hundreds of millions of dollars of consequences.

In the domains of social policy and market governance, liberals took the lead in advocating for the economic style. They professed sympathy to the larger goal of using the government's power to improve the public welfare; they simply disagreed about the best way of achieving that goal. In social regulation, though, the initial push for economic analysis came from industry, which sought consideration of costs to limit new regulation.[80] Its early proponents within the Nixon and Ford administrations were conservative economists sympathetic to arguments limiting government intervention.[81] By the mid-1970s, however, liberal advocates of the economic style were vocally making a similar case, arguing that economic analysis was key to ensuring the cost-effectiveness of environmental, health, and safety regulation.

Charles Schultze, onetime champion of PPBS as director of Johnson's Budget Bureau, and by the mid-1970s a senior fellow at the Brookings Institution, was at the forefront of this move. Long concerned with the cost-effectiveness of government programs, Schultze built on the PPBS approach to make a liberal case for regulatory conservativism.[82] His 1975 book with fellow economist Allen Kneese, *Pollution, Prices, and Public Policy*, argued that "relying on a central regulatory bureaucracy to carry out social policy simply will not work" and advocated for a focus on incentives and market-like devices.[83] And as previously mentioned, his 1977 book, *The Public Use of Private Interest*, extended these arguments beyond environmental policy and introduced the pejorative "command-and-control" to describe what he saw as the inherently "ineffective and inefficient" regulatory paradigm then in place."[84] These arguments not only articulated a liberal argument for limiting social regulation (Schultze did believe that government had an important role to play in solving these problems), but also helped convince president-elect Carter to appoint him CEA chair.[85]

The Carter administration saw Schultze, working closely with Democratic economists like Alfred Kahn (chair of the Council on Wage and Price Stability [CWPS]), William Nordhaus (CEA member) and George Eads (Nordhaus's successor), push hard for cost-effectiveness analysis of agency regulations.[86] They spent political capital arguing against regulatory approaches that they thought could be made less expensive—pushing OSHA, for example, to loosen the proposed standard limiting cotton dust in textile mills, instead allowing workers to wear respirators as a way of lowering compliance costs.[87] Schultze and his allies exerted a great deal of energy working to increase White House oversight of rulemaking so that agencies would have to take costs into account.[88] His personal involvement in this process was considerable, as can be seen in the detailed notes he took on the academic literature regarding the health effects of ozone while overseeing review of an EPA-proposed standard for the pollutant.[89]

Schultze was not the only liberal economist to take the position that cost-effectiveness was critical to good regulatory policy. On the contrary, many of his peers found his approach intuitive. Yet that approach was also entirely continuous with that taken by Republican appointees under prior administrations. CWPS, for example, had initiated the process of commenting on proposed regulations to promote consideration of their costs and benefits during the Ford administration. Indeed, George Eads, who helped implement regulatory review as a Carter CEA member, had previously served as one of Ford's CWPS directors.[90] Moderate Republicans were friendly to this kind of regulatory reform, as were industry groups. Schultze's push to make textile-mill workers wear respirators, rather than force mills to invest in dust-reduction technology, was just what the textile industry had been advocating for since the Nixon administration.[91]

There were, of course, significant differences between liberal and conservative economists when it came to economic analysis of regulation. Liberals preferred cost-effectiveness analysis, which sought only to identify the least expensive way to achieve a specific regulatory goal; conservatives generally wanted full cost-benefit analysis, which evaluated whether the goals themselves were economically justifiable. Nevertheless, these two groups debated on the same intellectual field. They were more comfortable speaking to one another than to those using the noneconomic language of rights and moral absolutes.

The gap between Democratic economists and liberal advocacy groups went beyond lack of a shared language. Quite frequently, Carter's economists found themselves pitted directly against environmental and other movement groups that continued to advocate for regulation on different moral grounds. Such groups clashed repeatedly with Schultze's regulatory reviewers. They argued not only over cotton dust and ozone standards, but over rules around particulate emissions, strip-mining, benzene exposure, and water pollution—to highlight only a few.[92] Indeed, advocates of the economic style within the administration were often dismissive of the competing liberal approach to regulation. While both groups wanted a clean environment, safe workplaces, and health protections, as political scientist Susan Tolchin wrote, "in private interviews [White House economists] often do not conceal their disdain for the rigid approaches adopted by many of the agencies."[93] Seeing themselves as "partisan efficiency advocates," in Schultze's phrase, the economists struggled to take the activists seriously.[94]

As the economic approach became increasingly influential—both through the broad spread of economic reasoning and its specific instantiation in laws

and administrative rules—competing justifications for regulation, particularly justifications that intentionally bracketed cost considerations, became
harder for liberals to defend. By the end of the decade, an old-timer like
Senator Edmund Muskie, the driving force behind the Clean Air and Clean
Water Acts, was forced to defend his regulatory approach, railing against
"narrow, academic cost-benefit analysis" and the "group of economists . . .
set up in the White House to second-guess such regulations."[95] Other liberals committed to an environmental framework, like Tom Jorling, head of
EPA's water office, argued that "there is [no] magic in calling something an
incentive and not a regulation. . . . I think as a general matter that regulations are more effective from the standpoint of clarity and of administrative mechanisms to carry them out."[96] Liberal advocacy groups additionally
pointed out that cost-benefit analyses conducted by the businesses subject
to regulation were hardly to be trusted.[97]

By the end of the decade, such voices had become less central to political
debate. Law and the courts had only moved incrementally in the direction of
weighing costs during the Carter administration.[98] But administrative procedures had changed more significantly. The fact that new regulations would
henceforth be reviewed with a cost-benefit lens—and that the economic
style was increasingly represented within the agencies themselves—meant
that even those who rejected the economic approach were nearly always
forced to contend with it.[99]

The Larger Pattern

By the 1970s, the economic style of reasoning had become at least partially
institutionalized in a number of policy domains. Where it did, a pattern
emerged: in both Republican and Democratic administrations, liberal economists advocated for policies that tended to ally them with moderate Republicans, in opposition to liberal Democrats not invested in the economic style.
In healthcare, this meant economists supported an approach to universal
health insurance that centered cost-sharing and means-testing in service of
efficiency. In antitrust, they advocated for the exclusion of noneconomic
values from policymaking, so that corporate behavior could be challenged
only if it was efficiency-reducing. In environmental policy and other areas
of social regulation, they promoted a cost-effectiveness approach to analysis
that, environmentalists argued, made decisions too susceptible to industry
interests. In each of these domains, these economic arguments marginalized
liberal arguments based on rights, universalism, and equality.

While this pattern was not universal, it can be seen in other policy arenas as well. In antipoverty policy, for example, the trajectory followed one similar to that seen in health insurance debates. Here, too, liberal economists who cared deeply about efficiency as a policy value—even as they also wanted to use government to help solve social problems—ended up allying with the Nixon administration. With a strong commitment to the concept of a negative income tax as the most efficient solution to poverty, ASPE economists developed Nixon's Family Assistance Plan. Liberal advocates of the economic style generally supported this, even if they would have preferred the plan to be more generous. They preferred this approach to those grounded in logics that ran counter to the economic style, whether in the form of community action (now largely sidelined in the United States), family allowance (implemented in Canada, the U.K., and elsewhere, but which failed to get much traction in the United States at the time), or welfare rights (just reaching its moment of peak influence).[100]

By the time poverty returned to the political agenda under the Carter presidency, the Democratic policy space was almost completely constrained by the economic style. Antipoverty policy had become "welfare reform," and the two proposals that competed for position within the Carter administration essentially reflected an internal debate between two branches of the analytic camp: one from HEW's ASPE, which continued to advocate for reform in the negative income tax tradition, and one from the Department of Labor's ASPER, which centered on ensuring access to jobs. Both accepted the fundamental premise of the economic style, which held the goal of antipoverty policy to be getting income to people as cost-effectively as possible. The main point of contention was which direction would be more efficient: cash assistance or job provision. Technocrats fought the debate with competing microsimulation models.[101]

A slight variation on the pattern can be seen in transportation policy. Areas subject to economic regulation—price and entry controls—saw economists across the political spectrum ally with moderate Republicans and against a New Deal–era Democratic approach to regulation that prioritized market stability and equity of access. This alliance was already in evidence during the Nixon and Ford administrations and continued under Carter. In transportation policy, these groups also found a surprising new ally on the left in the form of Ralph Nader's consumer movement, which similarly supported deregulation. Unlike the economists, Naderites were not guided by efficiency as a core value of good policy; rather, they remained consistently concerned with political power and regulatory capture.[102] Their understanding of economic regulation as primarily benefiting producers led them to support transportation deregulation and economic deregulation more generally—a position that extended to support for limiting the professional power of doctors and promoting healthcare competition.[103]

Although the consumerist left allied with the economic style on deregulation, it pulled in different directions on other issues, because it was focused first and foremost on issues of power and capture, not efficiency. It strongly opposed the move toward cost-benefit analysis of social regulation, for example, on grounds that this would lead to weaker regulations that served industry interests.[104] And in telecommunications policy, the consumerist left agreed with economists that the AT&T regulated monopoly should be broken up, while parting ways with them on the public interest standard, which required broadcast stations to operate in the "public interest, convenience, and necessity."[105] Consumer advocates preferred that this standard be retained, rather than narrowing the definition of "public interest" to mean something closer to "efficiency" (as economists tended to prefer).[106]

More variations on this broad theme exist. Democratic advocates of the economic style allied with moderate Republicans on housing policy, where both favored a shift toward vouchers, and against liberal calls for more public housing.[107] In education, where the economic style took much longer to take hold, the pattern was less in evidence during the 1970s—but came to the forefront in the 1990s, when the center-left, economics-oriented Brookings Institution threw its weight behind the mostly conservative school choice movement.[108] The specific ways that this pattern played out differed across policy domains and was shaped by the relative strength of the economic style, the relative strength of the traditional left, and domain-specific politics. Yet the general trend held. In centering efficiency as a policy value, liberal economists and their allies advocated for policies that also resonated with moderate conservatives. Meanwhile liberals whose policies were grounded in noneconomic frameworks—like rights, equity, or power—found themselves opposed, and their arguments increasingly hard to defend.

The Economic Style and the Democratic Left

In the 1960s, liberal economists brought the economic style to Washington and advocated for its use. In many policy domains they were successful. The economic style was gradually institutionalized in policymaking circles through organizational change, integration into law and policy schools, and various forms of legal change. Sometimes, as in social policy domains and in environmental, health, and safety regulation, its success was facilitated by policymakers' desire to manage or control recent government expansion. Other times, as in market governance domains, it was the result of conscious institution-building. But while both liberal and conservative economists advanced the economic style, the effort was led primarily by Democratic appointees who wanted to use economic reasoning to improve government.

Even in the 1960s, advocates of the economic style—with its emphasis on efficiency as the ultimate measure of good policy—found themselves in conflict with more liberal Democrats, who wanted community action programs, populist antitrust policy, and strict, even punitive, environmental laws. But by the early 1970s, it was becoming clearer that Democratic adherents to the economic style were often more closely allied with moderate Republicans than with more liberal members of their own party. The liberal analytic establishment had a direct hand in several of Nixon's major policy proposals—including his comprehensive health insurance plan, his family assistance plan, and his housing voucher program—and broadly supported several of the administration's efforts in other policy domains, including attempts to improve healthcare through competition, to move away from a "bigness is badness" approach to antitrust, and to introduce cost analysis into regulatory decisions. At the same time, economists' core value of efficiency made them skeptical of proposals from liberal Democrats, including national health insurance, populist antitrust policies, and aggressive environmental regulations, that prioritized other goals.

By the time President Carter came into office, advocates of the economic style had established firm beachheads throughout the executive branch. Carter's policy proposals—a health reform plan that looked much like Nixon's, a strong push for transportation deregulation, a White House expansion of regulatory review—were heavily influenced by the economic style. Yet advocates of such an approach increasingly clashed with Democrats who advanced liberal positions on noneconomic grounds—including environmentalists who feared cost-benefit analysis would undermine hardwon protections, antitrust appointees who thought antitrust should do more than promote efficiency, and advocates of national health insurance who saw healthcare as a right. Although such voices could still be heard, they found it harder to defend their positions against the influence of the economic style.

Economists, and the economic style, are not the primary *reason* that Democratic policy positions moved away from the high liberalism associated with the Kennedy-Johnson era and the Great Society. The political mood of

the country was evolving for many reasons, ranging from the changing position of the United States in a global economy, to the economic stagflation
that proved so difficult to shake, to increased organization by conservative
groups from big business to the grassroots, to dissatisfaction that the government expansion of the previous decade had not always delivered on its
promises. While economists may have played some causal role in nudging
policy in this direction, the change itself seems overdetermined.

But what does matter is that economists, and the economic style, were
the *channel* through which this change took place within the Democratic
Party. As economic reasoning became increasingly influential and taken-for-
granted in policy circles, claims based on other values or ways of thinking
about policy—even ones that had been integral to liberal politics—struggled
to get a legitimate hearing. If they conflicted with the economic style, they
came to seem unreasonable, even irrational, and easy to dismiss. Although
economists themselves did not dominate the party (though they were
certainly influential advisors), policy solutions that seemed reasonable to
economists *did* come to define the scope of Democratic politics. This trend
was not limited to the Carter administration, but continued through the
Clinton and Obama eras as well.

Carter's presidency and subsequent Democratic administrations through
Obama's would show remarkable, ongoing deference to this technocratic,
efficiency-centered approach. Yet while Democrats would prove to be consistent supporters of the economic style for the next thirty-five years, allowing it to determine the space of political possibility, Republicans were not
nearly so committed to allowing the economic style to serve as their guide
to policy. While Nixon and even Ford may have been relatively friendly to
the economic style, the election of Ronald Reagan would usher in a new
Republican era—one in which the administration would use economics strategically, where it furthered existing political goals, rather than allowing its
goals to be defined by those of economics.

9

The Economic Style in the Age of Reagan

For two decades, the economic style of reasoning steadily expanded its footprint in Washington. From Robert McNamara's appointment of RAND economists to help run the Defense Department, to Charles Schultze's advocacy for economic analysis of regulations in the Carter White House, its impact steadily grew. Its broad approach to problems was partially institutionalized through its expansion into law and policy schools, through organizational changes within and around government, and through laws, regulations, court decisions, and administrative rules that made efficiency a central, and bipartisan, goal of public policy.

The election of Ronald Reagan to the presidency in November 1980 marked a turning point. Even as the most recent Republican administrations had aimed to limit government expansion, they nevertheless saw government as having a significant role to play in American life. Reagan rejected the premise. As he stated in his inaugural address, "[G]overnment is not the solution to the problem; government is the problem." Although he reassured his audience that "it's not my intention to do away with government," he emphasized that "[i]t is time to check and reverse the growth of government."[1] His economic program rested on the four pillars of reducing the growth of government spending, lowering tax rates, reducing regulation, and controlling growth of the money supply.[2]

Reagan lacked the antipathy to experts that, say, Nixon and even Johnson sometimes exhibited. But his relationship to expertise differed from that of his immediate predecessors in at least two ways. First and foremost, he was deeply committed to a well-developed set of political beliefs and saw experts primarily as sources of support for his own positions, not sources of new ideas. Second, he did not prioritize academic reputation in his preferred experts. The growth of a small but influential network of conservative think tanks in the 1970s provided him with a ready source of policy expertise that drew on experts from outside the academic mainstream as well as the usual university departments.[3]

Reagan's well-defined political ideals, combined with his view of experts as political tools rather than neutral technocrats, meant that his administration maintained a different relationship to the economic style of reasoning than had his predecessors. In some areas, the Reagan administration saw the economic style as operating counter to its broader goals. It saw the analytic offices in social policy domains like welfare, health, and housing, for example, as primarily existing to justify government programs. Their budgets were cut and their influence declined.[4] But in areas where the economic style could be used to support administration positions, the use of economic expertise continued to expand. In antitrust policy, for example, Chicago School arguments aligned with the administration's political preferences.[5] And while Reagan preferred "regulatory relief" to Carter's "regulatory reform," his administration nevertheless understood that expanding cost-benefit analysis was a useful way to achieve that goal and supported requirements for more of it.[6]

The Reagan administration's strategic use of the economic style in service of more fundamental political values, rather than as a source of such values, marked the beginning of a lasting divergence between the two parties—one that would become clearer when the Democrats returned to the presidency in 1992.

Limiting the Economic Style in Social Policy

The economic style of reasoning had flourished in social policy under presidents Nixon and Ford. The "most creative years" for policy analysis were 1964 to 1976, according to economist and onetime Office of Economic Opportunity analyst Walter Williams, and it "reached a high point in the Nixon administration" before "continu[ing] without notable change" under Carter.[7] In the face of a greatly expanded welfare state, and under administrations that were less adamantly opposed to social programs than Reagan's, economic analysis had been a useful tool even for Republican administrations to advocate for making government more cost-effective.

The Reagan administration, though, saw analysis in domains like anti-poverty and housing policy as existing in opposition to its overriding goal: reducing the size of the welfare state. As one of Reagan's less conservative cabinet members said of Edwin Meese, Reagan's chief policy advisor, "He viewed the ... presidency as a magnificent opportunity to smash the government programs that had created a 'welfare state.'"[8]

Policy analysis, by contrast, existed to make the welfare state more efficient, not to smash it. Accordingly, the Reagan administration dramatically scaled back its use of the economic style of reasoning in social policy. It cut support and staffing for the policy planning offices that were its main base within the executive branch and redirected the focus of much of their remaining work. This was particularly visible in the policy shops of the new Department of Health and Human Services (HHS) and the Department of Housing and Urban Development (HUD).[9]

The HHS Office of the Assistant Secretary of Planning and Evaluation (ASPE) had been one of the most robust analytic offices since its inception in the Johnson era. This had especially been the case since 1973, when OEO was shut down and its analytic office rolled into ASPE.[10] From a staff of about two dozen under William Gorham, who first led the office, ASPE grew to employ 150 professionals by 1975 and peaked with over 300 employees under President Carter.[11] By contrast, during the Reagan years staffing at ASPE fell from 165 to 75. For the first time, the office was headed by an appointee who was not part of the analytic community and indeed did not even value the analytic enterprise.[12] Nor was ASPE was the only policy office to experience such cutbacks. The Department of Labor's (DOL) policy planning office (which played an important role in Carter-era welfare reform debates), as well as HUD's Office of Policy Development and Research (PD&R), saw similar staffing drops: from 61 to 40 for DOL, and from 198 to 140 for HUD.[13]

What work continued in these analytic offices was redirected. In the 1970s, policy offices like ASPE and PD&R had partnered with organizations like RAND, the Urban Institute, and Mathematica to oversee major social experiments in poverty, health, and housing policy. These efforts already represented a deradicalization of the community-based political impulses behind the War on Poverty and the civil rights movement. But the Reagan administration was uninterested in a social scientific effort to identify the most effective forms of government intervention. Instead, the policy shops were required to open up their contracts beyond these familiar players to organizations that did not assume by default that government *should* be involved in solving social problems.[14]

The research questions prioritized by the policy planning offices also changed during the Reagan administration. The 1970s had seen the analytic establishment shift its focus from how to end poverty most efficiently to estimating the effects of government assistance on labor force participation. But now the emphasis changed once again, with a new concept—"welfare dependency"—occupying center stage.[15] Similarly, PD&R shifted its attention to studying the deregulation of housing production, in keeping with the administration's political priorities, rather than searching for the most efficient forms of housing assistance.[16]

Reagan also ended these offices' role in developing policy proposals for the administration. This had persisted across the last several presidencies, notably producing Nixon's not-so-conservative family assistance and health insurance plans. But by the end of the Reagan years, ASPE's role in proposing policy initiatives had declined dramatically.[17] Instead of serving as powerful champions of the economic style and a bipartisan source of policy ideas, as they had since 1965, the analytic offices now had much more limited influence. Their remaining efforts focused on research aligned with Reagan's goal of scaling back social policy programs.

It was not only the policy planning offices, though, that experienced cutbacks and a redirection of focus. A wider reduction of support for social policy research and evaluation had impacts on the whole policy research ecosystem that had grown up since the 1960s. Funding for evaluation, the lifeblood of policy research organizations, shrunk 37 percent in constant dollars from 1980 to 1984, and research awards in social policy domains declined as well.[18] The National Institute for Education, that "sparkling gem of rationality," dispersed 476 research awards in 1980; by 1985 that number was down to 168.[19] The Office of Research in the HHS Health Care Financing Administration, a newer source of support for economics, saw its research funding drop by nearly half over the course of Reagan's term.[20] And the number of contract awards given by the new Department of Education—which Reagan wanted to get rid of entirely—dropped from 119 to 25 during his first administration.[21]

All this meant fewer resources for the policy research organizations who conducted much of this work—and which played a critical role in reproducing the economic style. The Urban Institute had seen its budget climb from $10 million to nearly $20 million between 1972 and 1980. RAND's domestic policy budget, nearly zero before 1965, had grown to equal its defense research spending by the end of the 1970s.[22] The Reagan administration was not only antipathetic to social policy research, but saw these organizations—especially Urban—as fundamentally biased. Indeed, Urban, at the top of the administration's "enemies list" among the think tanks, saw $8 million in government funds evaporate during the first two years of Reagan's presidency.[23] Urban's overall budget dropped back to $10 million, not inflation-adjusted, by 1983.[24] RAND's overall budget was flat, but only because of its defense research: its work on domestic policy declined from half of its portfolio to 20 percent, in budgetary terms, by the late 1980s.[25] These organizations survived by relying on foundations (Ford was particularly generous), turning to state governments, and conducting more private research.[26]

As with the policy planning offices, this shift played out not only in budget cuts, but also in the standard of work being done. The General Accounting Office (GAO) found that while the number of evaluation studies declined only 3 percent between 1980 and 1984, "*[t]he same work was not being done in 1984 or in 1988 as had been done in 1980.*" Program evaluation had been built loosely on the principles of systems analysis. It attempted to accurately measure the quantitative effects of a particular policy or program, with an eye toward evaluating whether it was worth it. But with fewer resources, the studies became simpler and less precise—less consistent with the economic style. And with the flow of federal dollars turning into a trickle, some evaluation shops were getting out of the business entirely.[27]

External research, too, was focused in new directions, just as in the policy planning offices. ASPE's shift in priorities led the policy research ecosystem to emphasize new questions: not only whether the availability of welfare promoted "dependency," but whether single motherhood and teen pregnancy were encouraged by welfare use, and whether an urban "underclass" had become detached from the by labor market entirely—none of which had been previous priorities.[28] The approach that the research shops took to these questions was still largely consistent with the economic style. For the most part, they used econometric approaches to try to estimate the effects of particular policies on behaviors, although the emphasis was now more on unintended consequences than the efficient achievement of policy goals. But "welfare reform" had taken on a new meaning. The goal was no longer ending poverty as cost-effectively as possible, but instead limiting or restructuring welfare to ensure that recipients were incentivized to participate in the labor force.[29] A parallel shift took place in health services research, which had followed welfare policy in a technocratic direction, and away from policy advocacy, during the 1970s. The analytic establishment in health policy had little trouble reorienting itself from questions of how to efficiently provide medical care to more people, to how set rules that would promote competition and choice within the healthcare sector.[30]

While the Reagan administration turned away from the use of economic reasoning in social policy, this did not mean that all of the federal government abandoned it. Congress, in particular, remained supportive. The Congressional Budget Office, founded in 1975, had become a strong voice for economic reasoning in the legislative branch, and congressional support offices like the GAO and Congressional Research Service had become somewhat more analytic as well. These offices did not see staffing declines analogous to those that took place in the executive branch.[31] Congress also limited some of the funding cuts Reagan sought for program evaluation and social policy research.[32] Indeed, while in the early 1970s the analytic capacity in Congress had lagged far behind that of the executive branch, by the mid-1980s it had arguably outstripped it.

Reagan's weakening of the analytic capacity of the executive branch affected more than its short-term efficacy. By redirecting its research focus, his administration also shaped the long-term trajectory of the center-left analytic establishment. While Reagan unapologetically embraced ideology over technocracy, the analytic establishment was reasserting its objectivity and neutrality. Research became "exceedingly cautious [and] ideologically noncommittal."[33] Yet in their effort to remain neutral—not to mention funded—adherents to the economic style placed Reagan's issues at the center of their intellectual agenda. The new focus on welfare dependency, for example, produced work like Mary Jo Bane and David Ellwood's *The Dynamics of Dependence*, which made long-term receipt of welfare the policy problem to be solved, not poverty itself.[34] The authors identified as Democrats; indeed, they would later design Bill Clinton's approach to welfare reform. But even as they were more oriented toward providing alternatives than were Republicans, they accepted the conservative definition of the problem.[35]

As was the case for much of Reagan's agenda, the early and aggressive pursuit of policy goals—in this case, reductions in social welfare programs—was followed by a partial bounce back, undoing some of what had been achieved. Yet during both cutbacks and regrowth, the Reagan administration was consistent in its disinterest in using the economic style to inform social policy decisions. Instead, both here and elsewhere, Reagan led with his values—an approach that sometimes produced weak or highly debatable analysis, but that prevented the conservative goal of smaller government from being subsumed by the economist's goal of more efficient government.

Expanding the Economic Style in Market Governance

In social policy, where the economic style could potentially conflict with a more fundamental goal of scaling back the welfare state, the Reagan administration dramatically reduced federal agencies' reliance on the economic style and removed the resources that helped reproduce it. But in questions of market governance, the implications of the economic style—and especially its Chicago variant—aligned with the administration's values.

Reagan wanted to remove government restrictions on corporate behavior. Advocates of the economic style believed allocative efficiency should be the primary goal of market governance. To achieve this, such advocates wanted to remove economic regulation (price and entry controls) in most markets and to exclude consideration of noneconomic factors (like political power or effects on small business) from antitrust policy. Both goals moved in the direction the administration preferred, even though many advocates of the economic style—particularly in antitrust policy—did not fully agree with the Reagan position. Thus, in sharp contrast to its antipathy to economic reasoning in social policy, the Reagan administration embraced the economic style in market governance domains.

In some sectors, notably transportation deregulation, this approach involved dismantling the existing institutions that supported economic regulation. Restructuring governance of the air, rail, and trucking industries mainly meant removing rules and eliminating the agencies that enforced them rather than instituting a new regime based on economic reasoning.[36] Thus, while the administration's appointees to these agencies might be friendly to an economic approach, their long-term strategy did not depend on building capacity for economic analysis. In antitrust policy, though, the executive branch had considerable power to direct enforcement. Here, economic reasoning proved an important means through which the administration could not only achieve its political goals but also ensure that they would outlast the administration itself. By expanding and further institutionalizing the economic style at the Antitrust Division and Federal Trade Commission (FTC), Reagan locked in an efficiency-centered, consumer welfare vision of antitrust policy that has persisted for decades.

Economic reasoning in the antitrust agencies had steadily expanded under presidents Nixon, Ford, and Carter, but the expansion was not driven by the presidents themselves: Nixon's first antitrust chief was largely uninterested in economic reasoning, and Carter's appointees actively opposed many of economists' priorities. Instead, the economic style was advanced by the gradual expansion of industrial organization (I/O) economics into law, a slow institution-building process within the antitrust agencies, and Supreme Court decisions that recognized and reinforced a shift toward economic reasoning. But as of 1980, it was not yet clear how dominant allocative efficiency would become as a lens for the evaluation of antitrust policy.[37]

For the Reagan administration, though, economic reasoning—and particularly the Chicago School approach that was, for the moment, standard in industrial organization—aligned perfectly with preexisting political goals. Reagan was friendly to big business and held a strongly laissez-faire position on antitrust enforcement.[38] By the 1980s, the discipline of economics had evolved to the point that even Harvard School structuralists prescribed substantially more limited antitrust enforcement than had been the 1960s norm, and Chicagoans advised even less. Given this, the Reagan administration strongly supported the economic style in antitrust and worked to expand its use considerably.

At the Antitrust Division, this meant appointing Bill Baxter, an economics-friendly Stanford law professor, as assistant attorney general. Although he had once held interventionist beliefs, by the time his term began, Baxter had become a strong advocate of Chicago-style antitrust.[39] He opposed restrictions on vertical or conglomerate mergers entirely and thought horizontal mergers caused problems only at much higher levels of concentration than had historically been suggested. While he favored aggressive pursuit of price-fixing and cartel behavior, he believed other kinds of restraints generally encouraged efficiency and should not be challenged.[40] This perspective fit well with the Reagan administration's antitrust priorities.

As head of the Antitrust Division, Baxter oversaw, and even advocated for, substantial budget cuts at his own agency, including a 14 percent appropriations reduction for fiscal year 1982.[41] But this did not mean that he scaled back on economic analysis. While Baxter slashed the number of professional staff, cuts fell disproportionately on attorneys. Indeed, Baxter worked to expand the use of economics—and particularly its Chicago version—within the agency. He hired attorneys who were, like himself, oriented toward economics, and, in his own words, "commenced [mandatory] educational programs within the Division, several layers of elementary and more advanced economics courses for our lawyers."[42] He oversaw a major revision of Turner's 1968 merger guidelines that further increased the role of economic analysis and moved in the direction of Chicago criteria for evaluating mergers.[43] Baxter initiated a program to review past Antitrust Division judgments, which remained on the books as precedent, and vacate those not consonant with current economic reasoning.[44] He even began a project to identify private antitrust cases with the potential to shape legal doctrine in accordance with Chicago reasoning and filed amicus briefs in their support—although this behavior eventually earned the division a slap on the wrist from Congress.[45] In all these changes, the agency was moving toward institutionalizing allocative efficiency as the purpose of antitrust policy, with a Chicago-style perspective on what kind of market governance would best achieve that goal.

This trend continued under subsequent leadership. Law-and-economics scholar Douglas Ginsburg, who Baxter first brought to Washington, led a reorganization of the division that more fully integrated economics into litigation. His changes included elevating the director of the Economic Policy Office to the position of deputy assistant attorney general for economic analysis.[46] By the end of the Reagan administration, the division had shrunk considerably, increased its use of economic reasoning, and decreased its levels of enforcement. The DC-based professional staff declined from 352 to 166 between 1980 and 1986, but the proportion of economists in this mix nearly doubled.[47] And those attorneys remaining tended to have training in Chicago-style economics.[48]

Even the new, more relaxed merger guidelines were infrequently enforced during the Reagan administration.[49] A 1989 American Bar Association report found, "Division enforcement actions against conduct other than price-fixing and bid-rigging are extremely rare," with several types of enforcement having been abandoned entirely. Merger challenges declined considerably.[50] While subsequent administrations would hew less strictly to a Chicago view of economics, they retained an economic conception of antitrust policy.

Parallel developments took place at the FTC. In the late 1970s, the FTC had a split identity, with an increasingly strong Bureau of Economics, but with leaders like chair Michael Pertschuk committed to a populist, Naderite agenda that saw corporate size itself as a potential threat, regardless of efficiency implications.[51] Reagan, though, appointed Jim Miller, a Virginia economics PhD and a leader of the conservative deregulatory movement, to replace Pertschuk as FTC chair.[52] The first economist to hold the position, Miller used economics to lock in the new way of thinking about antitrust, while reducing the agency's size and refocusing it on deregulation.

Miller was highly critical of the FTC's antitrust efforts at the time of his arrival, arguing that it "seemed largely out of touch with emerging trends in legal and economic research."[53] To remedy this, he appointed Chicago-oriented economists and law-and-economics scholars to lead the FTC's three bureaus: Robert Tollison, a well-known public choice scholar, at the

Bureau of Economics; Thomas Campbell, a Chicago economics PhD and attorney, at the Bureau of Competition; and Timothy Muris, a law-and-economics scholar, at the Bureau of Consumer Protection.[54]

Miller oversaw a dramatic reduction in the FTC's budget, which he fully supported. When he left the agency in 1985, its budget was, after inflation, roughly half of what it had been when he started in 1981. Staffing declined accordingly, and—again paralleling the Antitrust Division—cuts disproportionately affected the noneconomic staff: the Bureau of Competition's staff was reduced by 15 percent, while the Bureau of Economics lost only 3 percent of its workforce.[55] As had Baxter at Antitrust, Miller increased economists' early involvement with cases, using economic analysis to decide which cases to enforce. As Miller himself wrote, he "saw to it that a large percentage of the commission's attorneys completed an intensive course in microeconomics, with emphasis on the economics of cartels, concentrated industries, prior discrimination, information theory, and horizontal mergers."[56]

The enforcement agenda of the FTC shifted accordingly, with its antitrust efforts focusing almost solely on large horizontal mergers and cartel-like behavior. Challenges to vertical and conglomerate mergers and vertical restraints disappeared almost entirely, and even challenges to horizontal mergers became rare. In the early 1980s, the nine biggest mergers ever found their way through FTC approval, setting the stage for continued merger-friendliness under Miller's successor, Daniel Oliver.[57] And, once again, while subsequent administrations might entertain a more expansive conception of what the FTC should do, the orientation toward economic reasoning, and to the efficiency-centered conception of antitrust, would persist.

Even before Reagan's appointees began to transform the judicial branch, the courts had shifted toward an economic view of antitrust policy. Law and economics was reaching its peak academic influence by 1980. By that point, Henry Manne's law-and-economics camp for judges had enrolled almost a fifth of the federal judiciary; by 1990, that number would reach 40 percent.[58] Court decisions like *NCAA v. Board of Regents of the University of Oklahoma* (1984), which reinforced Robert Bork's claim that promoting consumer welfare was the purpose of the Sherman Act, further locked in efficiency as the goal of antitrust.[59]

The combination of this judicial shift and the institutionalization of economic reasoning in the antitrust agencies ensured that the economic style would long outlast Reagan in economic regulation. While in social policy domains, Reagan decimated economic reasoning because it had the potential to justify the welfare state, in market governance his administration had no such objections. Indeed, in a policy domain like antitrust, where the executive branch was influential and institutionalization of the economic style was possible, the increased role for economics that his appointees achieved would last well beyond the administration itself.

Expansion with Limits in Social Regulation

The Reagan administration rejected economic analysis across the board in social policy while embracing it in market governance, and especially antitrust. But in social regulation—the rules governing environmental, health, and safety concerns—the administration took a slightly more nuanced approach. Reagan ran on a platform of deregulation, a position that was motivated more by a belief in limiting the scope of government than in making it efficient. For the most part, his administration saw economic analysis of social regulation—that is, cost-benefit analysis—as a tool to enact that goal and expanded its use accordingly.

Given that social regulation had expanded dramatically in the 1970s without paying much explicit attention to costs, it was a reasonable assumption that cost-benefit analysis would rein it in.[60] Certainly, regulated industries advocated for its use.[61] The fact that carrying out cost-benefit analysis depended on making a variety of assumptions and methodological choices that were themselves vulnerable to manipulation—for instance, about what counted as costs or benefits, about how they should be estimated, about how much to discount the future—meant that the approach could be massaged to produce the desired recommendations. Yet the administration was also aware that cost-benefit analysis might not always support its desired outcomes. When economic reasoning came into conflict with Reagan's underlying preference for less regulation, the administration prioritized less regulation over the mandate of efficiency.

President Carter had flown the banner of "regulatory reform"—cost-effectiveness analysis as a means to more efficiently achieve the goals of government—during his time in the White House. By contrast, on his first day in office, President Reagan appointed a task force on "regulatory relief."[62] While the effort to expand economic analysis in regulatory decision-making continued, the change in language from "reform" to "relief" reflected a change in philosophy. Carter's economists had been strong advocates for regulatory efficiency, but they assumed that the goals of government were legitimate, and that it had the potential to effectively achieve them. Reagan's deregulatory agenda, by contrast, started from a more fundamentally skeptical position about whether government could or should try to pursue such objectives.

Some of the people developing Reagan's regulatory agenda came out of the offices that had promoted regulatory reform under Ford and then Carter. Jim Miller (soon to be chair of the FTC) had led the Council on Wage and Price Stability (CWPS) office that had begun reviewing and commenting on the costs and benefits of major regulations under Ford. After Carter's election, Miller had become codirector of the Center for the Study of Government Regulation at the American Enterprise Institute (AEI), the new hub of deregulatory conversation in Washington.[63] Along with attorney C. Boyden Gray, Miller was in charge of developing a deregulatory plan in the lead-up to Reagan's inauguration.[64]

Miller asked fellow economists Jim Tozzi and Thomas Hopkins, also experienced regulatory reformers, to draft an executive order giving the Office of Management and Budget (OMB) authority to review regulations before they were issued. Tozzi had overseen the OMB Quality of Life Review of environmental regulations that had been introduced under Nixon, and Hopkins had served as Miller's deputy at CWPS.[65] The executive order they produced, signed by President Reagan a few weeks into his administration, made two changes that further advanced economic reasoning in social regulation.

First, Executive Order (EO) 12291 changed the type of economic analysis required in regulatory review. Instead of cost-effectiveness analysis, as the Carter administration had implemented, Reagan ordered full cost-benefit analysis (now renamed "Regulatory Impact Analysis") in areas where it was not statutorily prohibited. Agencies would no longer simply compare the relative cost-effectiveness of different methods of achieving a goal, but would have to show that the benefits of a new regulation actually outweighed its costs. If this could not be shown, the regulation would not move forward.[66]

Second, it centralized the regulatory review process along with strengthening it. EO 12291 eliminated existing White House groups with an interest in regulation, including CWPS, placing regulatory oversight in OMB's new Office of Information and Regulatory Affairs (OIRA).[67] OIRA was now given the authority to review *all* regulations before they were published, not just major ones. While the new responsibilities were assigned via executive order, the office itself had been established through legislation, which meant its existence could not be eliminated through presidential discretion alone. And, unlike previous efforts to establish regulatory oversight, the EO granted OIRA authority to actually hold up regulations that it did not approve.[68] Miller became OIRA's first administrator, Tozzi its deputy, and several of the CWPS economists transferred to the new office.[69]

Giving OIRA oversight authority helped institutionalize the economic analysis of social regulation. But the Reagan administration also recognized that only so much could be accomplished through executive order. David Stockman, Reagan's first OMB director, explained this before Reagan took office: to achieve its larger regulatory goals, the administration would need to propose a legislative reform package that would incorporate mandatory, cost-benefit analysis in the central suite of regulatory legislation, including the Clean Air and Clean Water Acts and the Occupational Safety and Health Act, lest administrative rulemaking fall to judicial review.[70] The administration never threw its full weight behind such a comprehensive package; as one insider noted, "[d]eregulation was clearly the lowest priority among the [four] major elements of the Reagan economic program."[71] Yet Reagan's efforts nevertheless produced some of the intended effects: the president rescinded or blocked 182 regulations in his first two years. None of the social regulatory agencies survived the first administration without at least some hit to their budgets.[72]

The Environmental Protection Agency (EPA) provides an illustrative example of how the expansion of the economic style under Reagan reverberated into future administrations. Although Reagan cut the budgets of many executive agencies, EPA was a particular target, hit with a 29 percent budget reduction between 1981 and 1983. The demoralized staff departed in droves, with almost a third leaving of their own volition in 1982.[73] Yet even as these drastic cuts were being implemented, the new requirement for regulatory impact analyses meant that the EPA needed more capacity for economic analysis. In response, the size and influence of the EPA's policy planning office was expanded. Reagan's first EPA administrator, Anne Gorsuch, was an outspoken critic of the agency and completely on board with Reagan's budget cuts. She had no particular respect for economists, yet the policy office gained influence during her tenure.[74] By 1984, one observer reported that "EPA has beefed up its economic analyses," and "a more rigorous internal review [of regulations] has developed."[75]

This expanded role for economics continued after Gorsuch's rocky time in office ended. Her successor, William Ruckelshaus, had served as the EPA's first administrator in the early 1970s and was much more supportive of the agency, but he, too, oversaw a further expansion of the economic style. During his second term as administrator, Ruckelshaus displayed an enthusiasm for cost-benefit analysis, taking seriously both the advice of EPA analysts and the regulatory impact statements they produced.[76] According to legal scholar Thomas McGarity, "[t]he analysts in the policy office achieved their zenith" under Ruckelshaus, and were "probably [the EPA's] most powerful institutional actors" at this time.[77]

The EPA was not the only regulatory agency to see its capacity for economic analysis expand even as budgets elsewhere were cut. The Occupational Safety and Health Administration (OSHA), for example, was among the slowest adopters of the economic style. Its enabling legislation disallowed cost-benefit tests, and the agency had dragged its feet on hiring economists.[78] But under Thorne Auchter, Reagan's first OSHA administrator, the agency developed a "stringent, fourfold cost-effectiveness test for health standards" that moved in the direction of economic reasoning.[79] Although OSHA, like its peer agencies, faced reductions in both budget and number of employees, Auchter was granted a request to hire additional economists. They would conduct analyses of the economic impact of regulatory standards for safe levels of lead and cotton dust in the workplace, and of rules to protect workers' hearing and to require labels on dangerous substances.[80] These organizational changes would continue to have effects even once deregulation was no longer at the top of OSHA's agenda.

While the Reagan administration generally expanded the use of economic reasoning in social regulation, it did not allow itself to be constrained by economics when it had a desired outcome in mind. Reagan's OIRA, for example, was criticized for serving not as a neutral arbiter, but as a backdoor through which industry could intervene in the regulatory process—the place where "regulations went to die."[81] As Jim Miller testified during his time as OIRA administrator, "I see no problem in off-the-record contacts with us"; he added that rejections of rules would be "communicated over the telephone," leaving no written record to justify their demise.[82]

At the EPA, too, economic analysis was often subservient to political goals. Gorsuch in particular had a reputation for taking policy analysts' advice when it advanced her deregulatory agency, and dismissing it when it did not.[83] Even conservative economists described a meeting with her to discuss market-based regulatory incentives as a "disaster," with an attendee reporting that Gorsuch "seemed disinterested [sic], as if we were politically irrelevant theorists she didn't have to bother with."[84] Thus even as economic analysis expanded within the EPA, analysts felt sidelined. Many believed their work was being used as window dressing for decisions higher-ups had already made for reasons of their own, rather than as meaningful inputs into such decisions.[85]

And despite its general advocacy of cost-benefit analysis, the Reagan administration did not ultimately support legislation to require it across the board—in part because it recognized the potential for such analysis to "backfire."[86] As Antonin Scalia, then coeditor of AEI's *Regulation* magazine, noted, "Regulatory reformers who do not recognize this fact and who continue to support the unmodified proposals of the past as though the fundamental game has not been altered, will be scoring points for the other team."[87] The decision of Reagan's Task Force on Regulatory Relief to revisit the standard on the lead content of gasoline backfired in just such a way. While the task force hoped to relax the standard, cost-benefit analysis instead showed that further limiting permissible amounts of lead would pay off tenfold: by lowering costs associated with the developmental consequences of lead exposure in children, its increasing of blood pressure in adults, and its acceleration of wear and tear on automobile components.[88]

Conservatives in Congress, following the administration's cues, stopped pursuing a bill that would impose across-the-board cost-benefit analysis.[89] Efforts to institute it piecemeal by amending existing legislation continued, but were still met with opposition from environmental activists. An administration push to amend the Clean Air Act in 1981, for example, was blocked by environmentalists who argued that "proposals for cost-benefit analysis of the [air quality] standards were smokescreens for gutting the 1970 act."[90]

Nor were the courts fully on board with the executive branch expansion of cost-benefit analysis. Many observers thought the Supreme Court would require cost-benefit analysis in *American Textile Manufacturers Institute, Inc. v. Donovan*, its 1981 decision on a textile industry challenge of OSHA's cotton dust standard, but it did not.[91] Instead, the court said, the law already "understood that worker protection would be costly and might reduce profits. Nonetheless, Congress decided that, in dealing with health standards at least, practicability was the only limiting criterion."[92] Even had it wanted to, the Reagan administration could not have simply required cost-benefit analysis across the board—at least without the support of Congress. But the administration's support for economic reasoning was more strategic than that: it expanded regulatory analysis as far as seemed politically useful, but was careful to not let it interfere with other, more fundamental, goals.

Values, Strategy, and the Economic Style

Whether one sees the Reagan administration as embracing the economic style of reasoning or rejecting it really depends on where one looks. In social policy domains, Reagan's is remembered as the "anti-analytic presidency." Reagan appointees rejected economic analysis designed to make government more efficient and effective and simply worked toward the goal of reducing the size and scope of government.[93] In other areas, like antitrust, his administration wholeheartedly embraced a mainstream Chicago orientation to policy and expanded the role of economics in lasting ways.[94] In still other domains, like social regulation, he supported the expansion of economic reasoning—in this case, cost-benefit analysis—up to the point at which it seemed likely to conflict with other political objectives, but no further.[95] And in policy areas beyond the scope of this book, Reagan was even willing to advocate for economic arguments that were rejected by the academic mainstream, like the Laffer-curve claim that cutting taxes would raise revenues.[96]

This highly selective approach to economic reasoning differed from how administrations of the previous two decades, whether Republican or Democratic, had approached it. The presidents of the 1960s and 1970s had varied in their affection for experts, and they certainly used expertise strategically to help them achieve political goals. But in general, the economic style slowly and steadily expanded its presence in policymaking circles over this period, gradually becoming adopted as the appropriate way of thinking about policy problems. Increasingly, efficiency, in its various forms, came to be seen as the measure of good public policy in domains from healthcare to transportation to the environment.

The growing influence of the economic style was not due solely to White House support. Economics was widely seen as a useful tool for decision-making across Washington. A given government office's embrace of economic tools often set off an analytical arms race in which other offices increased their own analytic capacity in order to keep up. The integration of economics into graduate programs in law and public policy also helped ensure a growing audience for its basic insights and a receptive environment for its increasing influence in Washington. As the economic style became anchored in the policy process through organizational, legal, and cultural change, it came to orient policymaking across both Democratic and Republican administrations—even when it conflicted with other political values.

But for the Reagan administration, the economic style was a means to an end, not an end in itself. While Democrats, and particularly those in the Carter administration, had increasingly come to see efficient, cost-effective government as a goal of its own, Reagan—to a greater extent than Nixon or Ford—saw government itself as the problem. Carter, taking the presidency at a time when the liberal wing of the Democratic Party was weakening, had found himself hamstrung by economic reasoning. His administration was unable or unwilling to pursue commitments to competing values—a right to healthcare, limits on corporate power, a right to clean air and water—that had historically been associated with Democrats. For Reagan, by contrast, economics served as a potentially useful but subservient tool to advance other, more fundamental, political values.

10

Conclusion

The partisan divergence in approach to the economic style that Reagan's presidency ushered in would persist for decades. Republicans continued to use the economic style strategically and flexibly, embracing it where it helped advance their goals and rejecting it when it conflicted with more fundamental values. Democrats, by contrast, consistently remained faithful to the economic style, much as they had under Jimmy Carter. They allowed the economic style to define the boundaries of legitimate policy debate.

Arguments that had, in the past, served Democrats well—that had been at the very heart of the New Deal and Great Society—were now off-limits. Claims about rights, equality, and power, among others, failed to gain traction in policy circles. They were seen as unrealistic or even naïve in their failure to recognize efficiency as the measure of good policy, and choice, competition, and incentives as the means to achieve that goal. Democrats' internalization of the economic style shaped the space of political possibility for them when they were in office.

The presidency of Bill Clinton, who advertised himself as a "New Democrat," illustrates the constraints of this approach particularly clearly. As was the case for Barack Obama, Clinton benefited from complete Democratic control of Congress during his first two years in office. Yet across the three broad domains covered in this book—social policy, market governance, and social regulation—Clinton advocated policies consistent with the economic style and rejected options that fundamentally challenged efficiency as the measure of good policy.

In healthcare reform, Clinton borrowed the title (Health Security Act) of Ted Kennedy's earlier efforts to create national health insurance. But rather than draw on the language of rights and the logic of social insurance—of a single system everyone paid into and benefited from—Clinton's plan was shaped by health policy frameworks that had come from economics. This approach sought to make healthcare more cost-effective and promoted choice and competition so that it would function more effectively as a market. Instead of proposing national health insurance, Clinton's plan paired the idea of "managed competition" under a global budget cap, an echo of the then-conservative proposal economist Alain Enthoven had set forth fifteen years earlier. Clinton's bill incentivized individuals and employers to take costs into account, promoted new kinds of competition among providers and insurers, and provided the uninsured with means-tested subsidies.[1]

In antitrust policy, where the economic style had been fully institutionalized through the consumer welfare standard, Clinton adhered to the new bipartisan consensus: that an efficiency-centered approach was the correct one to take, and that older approaches emphasizing political power or the protection of small business were fundamentally misguided.[2] As Joel Klein, Clinton's second assistant attorney general for antitrust, said during his tenure in Washington, "I'm not here to tackle big corporations or get in the way of economic efficiencies. . . . My thinking is mainstream economic thinking."[3] While some economists continued to advocate for stronger antitrust measures within the consumer welfare framework—game theory, for example, suggested that the strategic and dynamic nature of firm decisions could make anticompetitive actions rational, implying a need for more enforcement—their influence took place around the margins. By and large, the status quo remained intact.[4]

In environmental regulation, too, Clinton operated within the economic style. Clinton revoked the Reagan executive order that had required cost-benefit analysis where statute permitted, but he replaced it with a new executive order that was also consistent with the economic approach. Instead of requiring benefits to *exceed* costs, the new order required them to *justify* costs, and it introduced "distributive impacts" and "equity" as additional factors to be considered.[5] Clinton's approach here resembled Carter's, in that it favored economic analysis and the weighing of costs and benefits, but it emphasized cost-effectiveness over strict cost-benefit tests. He also added new considerations favored by economists, ordering federal agencies to examine regulatory alternatives like "economic incentives to encourage the desired behavior, such as user fees or marketable permits."[6] By the time of Clinton's presidency, older arguments about the need for inflexible pollution standards as a way to limit regulatory capture, or about the benefits of technology forcing, were seen as outdated.[7]

This broad commitment to the economic style—an agreement to limit the space of Democratic policy debate to positions that could be articulated from within it—remained intact into the Obama years. This was true despite a growing sense, after the 2008 financial crisis and then the Occupy Wall Street movement, that the status quo was failing many Americans. It would take the election of Donald Trump, who rejected all conventional forms of expertise and prompted much soul-searching among Democrats over their own path forward, for Democrats to question their ongoing commitment to the economic style and the kinds of policies it produced.

How We Got Here

This book explains how we got to this point of stasis—how we went from a world in which economics was not even seen as particularly relevant to domains like education, healthcare, or the environment, to one in which the economic style was integral to setting the terms of debate and providing a menu of policy options. It shows why this shift was of lasting importance, particularly for the left wing of the Democratic Party. Between 1960 and 1980, economists—particularly microeconomists, and particularly economists coming from the systems analytic and industrial organization communities—brought a distinct style of reasoning to Washington and provided new answers to old questions: How should government make decisions? How should we govern markets?

Their answer, in a phrase, was "to promote efficiency." This answer, and a tool kit of concepts and techniques for thinking about how to achieve it, was rooted in the neoclassical strain of microeconomics that came to dominate U.S. economics departments in the 1950s. From there, the economic style of reasoning made its way to Washington through the Planning-Programming-Budgeting System (PBBS), through the law and policy schools in which the style was eventually taught, and through networks centered at organizations like the Brookings Institution. It was partly institutionalized through organizational changes within government agencies, in the ecosystem of policy research organizations, and at universities. The economic style was also incorporated into the law via statutes, case law, and administrative rules that made efficiency a central value in policy.

This shift was initially led by center-left economists appointed by Democratic administrations, but continued under Republican presidents, all the way through the 1970s. Its rise was partly a product of the Great Society itself, as the expansion of government—through both social programs and environmental, health, and safety rules—increased its administrators' interest in rationalizing it and sometimes limiting its size. In fact, it was the expansion of government itself that provided financial resources for the offices and organizations that would lead the charge for its rationalization.

Although the spread of the economic style was uneven, its impact could be felt in domains from antitrust to antipoverty policy, from health to housing, from environment to transportation. Where it became influential, it centered efficiency and cost-effectiveness, choice and incentives, and competition and the market mechanism in its policy solutions. Its implicit theory of politics imagined that disinterested technocrats could make reasonably neutral, apolitical policy decisions. The economic style tended to downplay competing concerns about rights, equality, power, democratic process, and the politics of making policy, subordinating them to efficiency in ways that seemed justifiable from the economic perspective, but often seemed misguided to others.

In its centering of efficiency as the measure of good policy and its studious bracketing of politics itself, the economic style inevitably came into conflict with other approaches to politics. Advocates of the economic style found themselves at odds with those pushing for costly universal health insurance on the grounds that healthcare was a right, for an aggressive anti-merger policy driven by a desire to limit the power of big business, and for strong, inflexible environmental standards on the theory that anything less would open the door to corporate capture. As the economic style was institutionalized, these competing positions became more politically marginal. It became harder and harder for arguments that questioned the value of efficiency to be heard.

In theory, the prescriptions of the economic style could conflict with conservative approaches as well as liberal ones. If one believed that big government infringed on personal liberty, then one might object to efforts to improve the government's delivery of its social goals. But in practice, the center-left technocrats who advocated for the economic style repeatedly found themselves making common cause with moderate Republicans and lining up in opposition to more liberal Democrats. During the Nixon and Ford administrations, advocates of the economic style found common ground with Republicans on the desirability of cost-sharing in healthcare, of vouchers as a form of housing assistance, of a merger-friendly approach to antitrust, and of cost-benefit analysis of environmental regulations, among other policy positions.

By the end of the Carter administration, policy conversations within the Democratic Party were increasingly taking place within the more limited range of positions that seemed reasonable from the economic perspective. Welfare reform debates focused on the most cost-effective ways to deliver assistance. Transportation debates asked how far deregulation should go. Environmental policy weighed the most efficient path to achieve regulatory goals.

Many factors contributed to the decline of the Democratic left, only some of which can be attributed to the economic style. But the institutionalization of economic reasoning—whether through the presence and visibility in Washington offices of those committed to it, or through its actual incorporation into law, created long-term barriers for those who might wish to challenge it. The most extreme example involves the use of antitrust enforcement to pursue goals other than allocative efficiency. Once the Supreme Court recognized efficiency as the sole purpose of antitrust policy, enforcement in pursuit of any other goal effectively became illegal. Even where efficiency had not been integrated into law itself, the strength of the economic style within the federal bureaucracy and surrounding policy organizations made arguments grounded in other logics difficult to advance. This institutionalization made it harder for liberal Democrats to mount challenges to the newly dominant framework.

During the periods in which Democrats held the White House, and especially in the first two years of the Clinton and Obama administrations—when the range of policy possibilities should have been at their greatest—these limitations were constraining indeed. Even in these periods, Democrats largely limited their policy options to those that operated within the confines of the economic style.

Rethinking the 1970s and What Followed

For the better part of two decades now, historians and social scientists have sought to make sense of the political and economic transformation that took place in the United States during the 1970s. They have pointed to a range of factors to explain the "rise of neoliberalism," from global economic changes to on-the-ground social movements. The story told in this book adds a critical missing dimension to existing narratives—one that reorients how we think about the past, present, and future of U.S. politics.

The efficiency-centered, microeconomic style of reasoning that we have followed played an integral role in bringing public policy into the neoliberal era—one in which it came to seem, in Margaret Thatcher's famous phrase, that "there is no alternative." Thatcher was specifically referring to free markets and free trade, but the rise of the economic style eliminated a different set of alternatives. Arguments based on claims about absolute rights, which implied that cost should not be considered, lost legitimacy. So did positions that centered the impact of policy on community, or democracy, rather than cost-effectiveness. So did positions that valued equality or stability more highly than efficiency. Instead, policies that made sense in economic terms came to be seen as the only alternative.

Scholars' accounts of the role of economic ideas in the political turn of the 1970s have missed important parts of the story. The focus on policy paradigms—on the shift from Keynesianism to monetarism or supply-side economics—and on the accompanying policy advice given by economists has overemphasized both the role of macroeconomics and economists' importance as policy advisors. This is true of both early accounts of the shift and more recent ones that also cover the post-Reagan decades.[8] These narratives focus on overarching economic frameworks that have always been explicitly aligned with particular political stances, and that are widely acknowledged to be partisan as well as theoretical.

The economic style is subtler than this. It is a framework for decision-making whose influence is closely tied to its ability to claim political neutrality. It portrays itself merely as a technical means of decision-making that can be used with equal effectiveness by people with any political values. This, though, is a ruse: efficiency is a value of its own. And the diffuse adoption of this approach to policymaking—one that can be applied to almost any domain, not just monetary or fiscal or trade policy—has been at least as important as those overarching macroeconomic paradigms.

Existing narratives have also made conservatives and free-market ideology the main drivers of this political-economic transformation. Those emphasizing the ideas behind this change have focused heavily on the role of the Chicago School and its various allies (the Mont Pelerin Society, the conservative legal movement, conservative think tanks and foundations).[9] Even the details of debate—was neoliberalism a project of "rolling back" government or "rolling out" market-oriented modes of governance? has it limited state regulation of markets, or insulated the state from democratic impulses that might threaten the market order?—have taken place largely within this space.[10]

This book has shown, though, that center-left technocrats have a worldview of their own, one that is independently important for understanding the ideological underpinnings of the modern era. The central players in this story are economists (and their allies) who wanted to use economic reasoning to make government work better and more effectively, and who thought government had an important role to play in American life. Chicago Schoolers are on the stage, but they are not the stars. These "better-government" economists were already changing policymaking as Chicago was coming into its own, and their views, not those of people with strong ideological objections to government, were critical in changing how policymakers thought about social programs or market regulation. Any story that does not give them their full due is very much incomplete.

This story of center-left technocrats goes hand in hand with a focus on the state itself as a source of change. Government helped fund the development of the economic style—particularly its systems analytic piece at RAND—so it could carry out its functions more effectively. It was government expansion, in the form of Great Society programs and then the growth of social regulation that followed, that created the conditions for the spread of the economic style. And as the style gained traction, the state institutionalized it by expanding the government offices that came to reflect the economic style and by establishing funding streams that supported its reproduction in think tanks and policy research organizations.

As the economic style gained influence, assisted in various ways by the state, its values and techniques were sometimes instantiated in the state itself, and in various forms of law. From legislation requiring cost-benefit weighing, to Supreme Court decisions upholding the consumer welfare standard, to the creation of regulatory frameworks that enabled emissions trading, to the repeal of regulatory regimes that hindered market efficiency, the economic style was integrated into legal frameworks. In contrast to accounts that see the changes of the 1970s as something "done to" the state by outside actors, whether intellectual movements or political interest groups, in this story the call is coming from inside the house. The economic style that helps constrain the state is produced, and reproduced, by the state itself.

Last, this book helps flesh out an answer to a question that is still puzzling. In the mid-1970s, Democrats were the beneficiaries of a huge political scandal—Watergate—that might have helped them consolidate the gains they had made during the 1960s. But instead of succeeding on this front, they oversaw the collapse of the New Deal order and helped produce a new one in which government had a more limited role to play, and markets a much larger one, than Democrats had previously envisioned.

While we have accounts that explain Democrats' decline in the 1980s, and accounts that explain New Democrats' success in the 1990s, what I show here is how a new ideology that would become an alternative to postwar liberalism took hold.[11] This was more than just a rejection of the New Deal order. It was a positive alternative to that order that could tie together a range of Democrats who were no longer particularly committed to the old views. The gains of this economic ideology were incremental, but steady, and by the late 1970s it had a growing foothold among Democratic politicians. Already by the Carter administration, Democrats were increasingly "thinking like economists"—advocating for the policies they thought would be most efficient.[12] And the institutionalization of this worldview—in Democratic strongholds like Brookings, the Urban Institute, and policy schools, and in the state itself—helped ensure that it would be prominent for decades to come.

Lessons for the Practically Minded

This book also has lessons for those more interested in intervening in, rather than studying, politics and policy. I do not make specific policy recommendations here. But my account suggests insights that can inform political strategy. This may particularly be the case for progressives who have felt constrained by the confines of the economic style, perhaps without recognizing it as such.

The economic style, as a distinctive approach to policy problems, has become second nature in many Washington circles. Questioning its taken-for-grantedness requires recognizing its existence, characteristics, and political effectiveness. A large chunk of the Democratic Party has, until recently, dismissed many policies on progressive wish lists because those policies are not consistent with the economic style. For example, calls for robust antitrust enforcement to limit the power of big tech companies have been brushed off as fearmongering that fails to appreciate those companies' economic benefits. The prospect of national health insurance ("Medicare for All") has been dismissed as insufficiently cost-effective. Advocates for these policies have struggled to push back against the logic of the economic style, which feels natural to many who populate policy schools, think tanks, and similar locales.

Recognizing the appeal of the economic style is important to effectively articulating alternatives to it. The economic style is powerful in part because it appears to be a politically neutral tool kit. It is not. Understanding the assumptions and values embedded within it is key to denaturalizing it and successfully making other claims. Three of these—already hinted at in chapter 2—are particularly important.

First, the economic style does not allow for commitment to absolute principles—for moral values that are ends in themselves, rather than objectives to be evaluated in terms of costs, benefits, and trade-offs. Claims about rights, justice, or liberty do not start by weighing their costs. Such claims can be politically as well as morally powerful, as they start with a strong and uncompromising stance: if something is a right, we are obligated to provide it to every person. The question, then, is how best to do that.

In reality, American political institutions rarely treat rights, even those enshrined in law, as 100 percent absolute. For example, in the 1970s people with disabilities gained the right to access federally funded services, notably public transportation, on equal grounds.[13] But within the Carter administration, the economists responsible for reviewing cost-benefit analysis of regulations were particularly upset with the enormous price tag of retrofitting New York City subway stations. In their analysis, the costs of making these stations accessible was too high given the number of people who would be affected.[14] Despite the nominal right to transportation, many of these stations are still not wheelchair-accessible forty-plus years later.

But even if one recognizes that rights are rarely absolute in practice, starting with absolute claims is both morally powerful and politically useful. Too often, Democrats who have internalized the economic style begin their negotiations with a stance of "as much as is cost-effective." In contrast, their conservative counterparts begin with an absolute claim: a government program is an infringement on liberty, for example, and thus should not exist. This puts the former group in a weaker position right out of the gate.

Second, in making efficiency (in various forms) its core value, the economic style often treats efficiency as self-evidently good, rather than itself a choice that sometimes competes with other values, like equality or democracy. For example, antitrust policy has, for decades, been organized around the consumer welfare standard, which in practice is defined narrowly as allocative efficiency. This means that corporate behavior becomes an antitrust issue only if it threatens to increase prices charged above marginal cost.

While prohibiting monopoly prices sounds good, an approach to antitrust focused solely on what consumers pay excludes other values. Other powerful arguments for antitrust enforcement emphasize the outsized political influence of large corporations, the control of dominant platforms over speech, and the uneven playing field for small businesses and workers. Protecting democracy, free speech, and fair competition may at times be in direct conflict with ensuring the absolute lowest prices. But recognizing that efficiency is not the only value through which one can evaluate good policy is necessary before one can articulate why alternatives are worth defending.

Third, the economic style is based on a particular theory of how the world works—one in which, as a first-order approximation, individuals and firms respond rationally to incentives, markets are efficient allocators of resources, and political or practical barriers to creating economically logical policies are of secondary importance. In practice, this means that many adherents to the economic style maintain a deep commitment to policy solutions that have serious implementation challenges. The popular commitment in Democratic policy circles to cap-and-trade or carbon taxes as the only rational response to climate change is a pertinent example. While a strong version of either of these policies would be highly beneficial, the obstacles to enacting one effective enough to rein in climate change are formidable indeed. Carbon taxes have proven politically unpopular even in liberal jurisdictions like Washington State.[15] And while cap-and-trade programs have had some degree of success, so far their impact on greenhouse gas emissions in jurisdictions like the European Union and California has been relatively minor.[16]

Efficiency in theory does not necessarily mean efficiency in practice. Progressives who want to advocate for other approaches, like a Green New Deal, should start by clearly stating the grounds on which they think the economic style fails: in this case, an inadequate theory of politics.

Understanding the rhetorical power of, and the unstated assumptions behind, the economic style can be useful for challenging it. But doing so effectively also requires understanding how specific locations effectively reproduce the economic style, and where it has veto points in the policy process.

Much of this book has told an institutional story in which the economic style gained influence by becoming prominent in specific government offices (policy offices throughout the executive branch, the Congressional Budget Office), other policy-relevant organizations (think tanks like the Urban Institute, policy shops like Mathematica), and in professional schools (law, public policy) that train many of those who end up in Washington. Ensuring the influence of other perspectives means either expanding the kinds of expertise that such organizations draw upon or establishing equally influential alternatives to them.

Either of these is possible and—to a limited extent—is already taking place. This book, which provides a historical account, is not the best guide to which offices and organizations are currently the most important strongholds of the economic style (although the degree of continuity over time is significant). The key lesson is that, over the long run, it is crucial to have well-resourced organizational locations in which alternative frameworks can be incubated and spread. Those interested in the long-term ability of progressives to advocate for policies unconstrained by the economic style should devote resources to this—whether that means targeting government offices friendly to other perspectives, building their own network of think tanks, or supporting intellectual movements that provide alternatives within academia. Otherwise, they will have trouble converting grassroots support into real policy options.

In addition to building organizational homes for alternative perspectives, progressives should become aware of and, at times, target the economic style's veto points in law. The consumer welfare standard, which effectively excludes using antitrust policy to address issues other than efficiency, is a particularly clear example. But requirements for cost-benefit analysis in regulatory decision-making and even CBO scoring of the cost of legislation are also places where the economic style has effective veto power over policies inconsistent with it. (One might ask whether Medicare would have ever been created had the CBO existed in 1965.) In some cases, the best strategy might be to work within these techniques, rather than trying to eliminate them. Instead of eliminating cost-benefit analyses, for example, advocates might push for explicit requirements that such analyses address how regulation impacts different racial groups. But regardless of whether the strategy is to change how such veto points work, or eliminate them entirely, they must be acknowledged and addressed.

This points to a more general dilemma for those frustrated by the political constraints of the economic style: should the strategy be to reject it, or try to change it? While the economic style is not endlessly flexible, part of its power comes from its ability to incorporate new concerns within its framework. Indeed, much of the history of cost-benefit analysis is about finding new and clever ways to put prices on things Americans clearly value, but that are not explicitly priced—whether that valued thing is a safe work environment or the existence of the Grand Canyon.[17] There are always those working within the economic framework who are pushing it to better address inequality or other concerns it often neglects.

The history of efforts to integrate other frameworks into economics, though, suggests some limitations to this strategy of working from within. Two examples from environmental policy are telling.

As earlier chapters have discussed, ecological thinking was integral to the landmark environmental legislation passed between 1969 and 1973. These laws explicitly referred to the "biosphere" and "ecological systems."[18] As the economic style became more prominent in environmental policy during the 1970s and 1980s, though, the influence of ecological thinking waned. Those focused on ecology—the role of an individual species in the larger system, or how particular habitats helped regulate that system—grew frustrated that such interconnections were largely ignored by environmental economists, leading the latter to underweight the value of healthy ecosystems.[19]

In the 1990s, some ecologists, reacting to the dominance of economic reasoning, began taking a different tack. Biologist Gretchen Daly and others began to outline a new "ecosystem services" approach to thinking about the natural environment.[20] Ecosystem services sought to more fully quantify the economic contributions of ecological processes—not only the value of clean air as reflected in differential housing prices, as environmental economists might estimate, but also the economic contribution of wetlands in preventing floods. Using such an approach, ecological economist Robert Costanza and his colleagues made a splash with a 1997 article in *Nature* suggesting that the entire global ecosystem was worth something on the order of $33 trillion.[21]

Over the next decade, the federal government began to incorporate some of the language of ecosystem services into decision-making. It helped justify efforts like the U.S. Department of Agriculture's Conservation Reserve Program, which pays farmers not to use environmentally sensitive land.[22] But the impact of the ecosystem services approach has nevertheless remained limited, although it is more influential in transnational policy networks than domestic ones.[23] Even its advocates have critiqued it on a variety of practical grounds, including the very possibility of meaningfully quantifying the value of specific ecosystem services outside of a local environmental context: if bees offer the service of pollination, but nearby farmers switch to a self-pollinated crop, do the benefits of the bees simply disappear?[24] Others remain deeply uncomfortable with an approach that recognizes no value in the existence of a species unless it provides economic benefit.[25]

The environmental justice movement made its own attempt to integrate a noneconomic framework into economic reasoning. It originated in the early 1980s, when grassroots organizers began fighting back against the disproportionate impact of pollution on racialized communities. Led by Black Southerners and aligned with faith groups, what started as local activism against specific polluters and waste sites had, a decade later, coalesced into a national movement.[26] Drawing on the civil rights tradition, movement representatives "demand[ed] the right to participate as equal partners at every level of decision-making" and called for "the cessation of the production of all toxins, hazardous wastes, and radioactive materials."[27]

By the early 1990s, environmental justice activists had successfully pushed the Environmental Protection Agency (EPA) to establish an Environmental Equity Workgroup, charged with "review[ing] the evidence that racial minority and low-income communities bear a disproportionate environmental risk burden."[28] But as the EPA responded to environmental justice claims, it recast them in language compatible with its own economic understanding of environmental governance. The calls for justice and demands to end the production of toxic wastes were redefined as identifying "the relative risk burden borne by low-income and racial minority communities" and "factors that might give rise to differential risk reduction."[29]

Environmental justice advocates, unhappy with the EPA's act of translation, hoped for more when Bill Clinton was elected in 1992. Yet while the Clinton administration adopted some of the movement's terminology, it still defined environmental justice in terms compatible with, if expanding upon, economic reasoning: as "ensur[ing] that all people, regardless of race, national origin or income, are protected from disproportionate impacts of environmental hazards."[30] While all agencies were now explicitly tasked with addressing distributional effects in their regulatory decision-making, the language set up a "philosophical clash" between the grassroots movement and the EPA office that became the institutionalized home of environmental justice.[31] The specific inclusion of equity made no clear difference to policy, while translating movement concerns into economics-adjacent language excluded the movement's more fundamental critique and weakened the moral and political force of its claims.[32]

These examples are not reason to give up on efforts to expand the concerns addressed by the economic style. They do, though, suggest caution about how successful such strategies are likely to be.

Where We Are Now

As of this writing, six months into the Biden administration, it appears we may be at an inflection point with regard to the economic style. Some things have clearly changed. At the macroeconomic level, Democrats seem to have taken a lesson from 2008 that inadequate economic stimulus is a bigger risk than increased national debt. There is a new level of comfort with broad-based relief, including sending checks directly to Americans with limited means-testing. Some of the old guard of the economics elite—advisors like Larry Summers, who were influential under both the Clinton and Obama administrations—have lost their clout.

There are also signs of change in the policy domains where microeconomic reasoning is more relevant—the social policy, market governance, and regulatory domains examined in this book. Here, though, the picture is less clear. So far, Biden has been surprisingly responsive to the progressive wing of the Democratic Party, which is more influential and better-organized than it has been for decades. This has included offering tentative support for some policies that adherents to the economic style have consistently opposed, and appointing some strident critics of the old intellectual order. It is not yet evident, though, how significant or lasting this change is.

One dynamic at play is that the progressive wing of the party has openly embraced policies that are outside the bounds of the economic style, with significant support from other kinds of experts. This in turn is shaping the space of debate even among those committed to working within the style. These progressive "outsider" voices are pulling "insider" positions to the left—and encouraging insiders to think about, and deploy, the economic style in new ways. It remains to be seen whether the influence of "outsiders" will be lasting, whether it will produce durable movement within the style, or whether it will lead to policy change.

The debate over student loan forgiveness illustrates how this dynamic is playing out. The cancellation of student loan debt, outside of cases of explicit fraud, was almost politically unthinkable five years ago. Liberal economists and policy analysts have consistently opposed such a policy as both inefficient (because it would spend money on some people who could have paid off debt on their own) and regressive (because most student loan debt is held by households in the top half of the income distribution).

But advocates of student loan cancellation, buoyed by a small social movement ten years in the making and supported by experts coming from outside the Washington mainstream, have put this policy on the table. They have relied mostly on arguments incompatible with the economic style. Advocates make a moral case for unburdening borrowers, who are disproportionately young and face a difficult labor market. They point to racial disparities not only in borrowing, but also in the ability to repay. And they highlight the limitations of existing means of helping borrowers who struggle to repay, including the dysfunctional Public Service Loan Forgiveness program and complex income-based repayment options.[33]

This evolving political context has moved President Biden's position. While student debt cancellation is not a high priority for the administration, Biden has announced support for $10,000 of debt cancellation—well below the $50,000 proposed by Congressional Democrats, but a stance that would have been unimaginable under Obama. This political environment, along with changing evidence, has also led some liberal economists to reevaluate their position and support similar amounts of loan forgiveness. That said, such economists typically justify their changing position within the economic style. Student loan defaults are concentrated among borrowers with small amounts of debt, who are less likely to have finished degrees and thus received a wage boost; a modest degree of debt cancellation could help this population substantially while limiting the total cost of the program. Mounting evidence about the disproportionate impact of debt on Black borrowers, who have much lower levels of family wealth than white borrowers, is also shaping this shift.[34]

The larger point here is that we now see Democrats considering policy options that were, until recently, seen as beyond the bound of economic style. These policy proposals are being advanced along two separate pathways. On the one hand, support for policies at odds with the economic style are being driven by social movements, a broader progressive resurgence, and advocacy from experts with backgrounds in law, education, sociology, and other disciplines. On the other, this background of advocacy on noneconomic grounds is expanding the range of options seen as reasonable by those more actively committed to the economic style. The latter group has not abandoned its concern with efficiency, but it is reconsidering its interpretation of evidence in light of the changing political context.

Student loan policy is not the only place we see such dynamics. In antitrust policy, for example, we see a resurgent "New Brandeis" movement advocating for greater enforcement and rejection of the consumer welfare standard, to the dismay of an establishment that sees it as the most useful framework for evaluating antitrust harm. Yet as that movement has gained influence, those working within the economic style have also moved to the left. Economists are asking new questions about whether concentration is allowing employers to keep wages down and whether common ownership in concentrated industries—for example, a handful of large institutional investors control most of the shares of the few remaining U.S. airlines—is producing new forms of market power. Such questions are providing fresh justifications for greater antitrust enforcement, but in ways that remain consistent with the economic style.[35]

Similarly, increased concern by Democrats with climate change and systemic racism have begun to move the needle on regulatory policy. Most notably, on his first day of office Biden instructed the Office of Management and Budget to look for ways the regulatory review process can promote goals including not only equity (already officially a consideration) but "racial justice" and "the interests of future generations."[36] These will, presumably, encourage analysts to make at least some adjustments to how they calculate the costs and benefits of regulations, although such changes do not fundamentally challenge the economic style.

Moving beyond the limited policy choices of the Clinton and Obama years will require either shifting the range of options economists consider reasonable or bypassing the economic style entirely. Both of these options currently seem possible. The economic style of reasoning, and the discipline of economics itself, can evolve. Income inequality, a marginal topic in the discipline until the 2000s, has become a major focus of attention.[37] Groups like Economists for Inclusive Prosperity, established by academics in the mainstream of the discipline, have advocated for more attention to economic distribution.[38]

Yet as the student loan debate suggests, and as the history of the ecosystem services framework and the environmental justice movement reinforce, there are limits to the range of policy positions that can be made consistent with the economic style. Translating competing approaches to policy into economic terms can move the needle, but only up to a point. The internal dynamics of the discipline also tend to limit how far such change might go.

Where, then, does this leave those who want to restore an ambitious vision of how government might work differently—how it might produce a legal framework that would harness capitalism in service of everyone, how it might support a safety net and social institutions that would allow humans to fully flourish? Evolution of the economic style is certainly something to be encouraged. But lasting change will also require building intellectual frameworks that go beyond economics and building institutions that will help to support them. Such frameworks may center values like equality, racial justice, rights, and community. They will center questions of power and social structure. They will understand policy problems as political problems, not just technical ones.

Rebuilding the progressive movement is an all-hands-on-deck project. Allies within the economics discipline should be very welcome, as should the efforts of those interested in expanding the boundaries of the economic style. But the lesson for those unhappy with forty years of neoliberalism is clear. While we must be cautious not to undermine the value *of* expertise, it is more important than ever to recognize the values *within* expertise. When our values align with those of economics, we should embrace the many useful tools it has to offer. But when they conflict, we much be willing to advocate—without apology—for alternatives, rather than allowing our values to be defined by the values of economics.

ACKNOWLEDGMENTS

This book has been a long time in the making. So long, in fact, that rather than try to be exhaustive in my acknowledgments I will be brief, even though I know this means omitting many names.

I have been fortunate to work in two very collegial departments—first in the Department of Sociology at the University at Albany, SUNY, where I was employed until 2019, and then in Organizational Studies at the University of Michigan. Both have been wonderful places personally and professionally, and I deeply appreciate my friends and colleagues from each.

I am grateful for the work of many archivists and librarians who have helped me track down sources over the years. I also appreciate the comments, insights, and feedback of many audiences as this work developed, at conferences, departmental colloquia, and other events.

I was lucky to receive the Richard B. Fisher Membership of the Institute for Advanced Study in 2013–14, and spent a magical year in Princeton with my family, where the earliest parts of this book were written, and where I benefited from the insights of many brilliant colleagues.

This project benefited from the research assistance of many excellent graduate students at UAlbany over the years, including Nick Pagnucco, Jing Li, Laura Milanes-Reyes, Josh McCabe, Abby Stivers, Susana Muñiz-Moreno, Kenneth Chen, Yimang Zhou, and Jiwon Lee.

I am grateful for the comments of two extremely generous anonymous (although I have my guesses) reviewers from Princeton University Press, who helped to make the book so much better. I am also deeply appreciative of the comments of David Colander and Steve Medema, both of whom read the full manuscript, and who (I hope) saved me from making too much of a fool of myself writing about economics. Many others read chapters and provided comments along the way, and I am thankful for their time and feedback.

Danielle Allen, Roger Backhouse, Beatrice Cherrier, Henry Farrell, Mark Mizruchi, Dani Rodrik, Steve Teles, and Josh Whitford have each championed this project at critical moments in its development. Their collective support has meant a lot.

Meagan Levinson has been the world's most patient editor as I worked on this book, and worked on it, and worked on it. Recently, she recalled that mine was the first book contract she signed at Princeton; now that it's done I guess this means she's free to move on. Audra Wolfe has been involved in this project in some capacity for a long time, always striking the right balance between cheerleader and taskmaster. She played a critical role in the final round of editing, and I am so appreciative of her work. Jennifer Harris did such an exceptional job copyediting my first book that I was delighted to learn she was still working with the Press; her attention to this one has been no less meticulous. Kathleen Cioffi has ushered it smoothly through the production process.

I have been part of two writing groups as I worked on this book. The first, in Albany, included Jennifer Dodge, Abby Kinchy, and Kendra Smith-Howard, who provided moral support, writing feedback, and particular insight on environmental policy, in which we all share an interest. I miss them a great deal. The second is a motley crew that emerged from a mid-pandemic Twitter plea for others who wanted to write on Zoom at 7 am. "Writing with Randos"—a rotating cast of a dozen or fifteen—has been a highlight of my mornings for the last nine months. The Randos have become friends as well, and have gone above and beyond in helping me get through a personally challenging time. And speaking of Twitter, my larger cast of tweeps have been a source of enormous intellectual community, as well as distraction and bad memes. We all like to gripe about whether staying on is worth it, but for me it 100 percent is.

Although I am not sure Dan Hirschman has read this manuscript from beginning to end, he has commented on so many parts of it and we have had so many conversations about it that he is effectively a silent coauthor. Lisa Stampnitzky has been reading my work since we were in a dissertation group in grad school, and continues to be a generous colleague and friend. Aaron Major has always been willing to talk about the nuts and bolts of book-writing while serving as ad hoc running coach. And Abby Kinchy has gotten me through each day with morning e-mails, collegial griping, to-do lists, and friendship, for maybe a decade now. I'm not sure this book would be done without her.

Last, I am deeply grateful for my family—my husband, Daniel, and my children, Nova and Naomi—for making it possible for me to do this work, and giving me so much to live for beyond it.

This book draws on roughly three thousand primary and secondary sources, as well as archival sources consulted at nine different archives—many of which do not appear in the final product. It builds on considerable research on policy domains not discussed at length, as well as the five domains (poverty, healthcare, antitrust, transportation, and environmental policy) that receive most of the attention. Here, I discuss the archival sources the project uses, as well as highlighting other types of sources that were particularly useful in each chapter, emphasizing those (oral histories, dissertations, web resources) that might otherwise go overlooked.

I consulted the following archival collections in person:

Jimmy Carter Presidential Library, Atlanta, GA
    Charles L. Schultze Papers

University of Chicago Archives, Chicago, IL
    Department of Economics Records
    George Stigler Papers
    Aaron Director Papers

Cornell University Archives, Ithaca, NY
    Alfred E. Kahn Papers

Duke University Economists' Papers Archive, Durham, NC
    Juanita Kreps Papers
    Oskar Morgenstern Papers
    Albert E. Rees Papers
    Paul Samuelson Papers
    Leonard Silk Papers
    Robert Solow Papers
    William Volker Fund Records

Lyndon B. Johnson Presidential Library, Austin, TX
    Administrative Histories
    William Gorham Papers
    Oral Histories
    Donald F. Turner Papers
    White House Central Files

John F. Kennedy Presidential Library, Boston, MA
    Kermit Gordon Personal Papers
    Walter W. Heller Papers
    Oral Histories
    Adam Yarmolinsky Papers

National Archives, College Park, MD
    Records of the Bureau of the Budget
    Records of the Office of Economic Opportunity

RAND Corporation Archives, Santa Monica, CA
    Economics Department Papers
    Oral Histories
    Gus Shubert Papers

Rockefeller Archive Center, Sleepy Hollow, NY
    Nelson A. Rockefeller Personal Papers
    Rockefeller Special Studies Project
    Social Science Research Council Archives

In addition, I relied heavily on the Presidential Oral Histories collection at the University of Virginia's Miller Center, as well as drawing on oral history collections from the University of Wisconsin Oral History Program, Berkeley's Regional Oral History Office, the American Bar Association's Section on Antitrust Law, and the Environmental Protection Agency, among others.

Chapter 2 is based mostly on secondary sources. Here, Michael Bernstein's *A Perilous Progress: Economists and Public Purpose in Twentieth-Century America* was a key orienting point. The chapter is also heavily informed by the work of William Barber, Roger Backhouse, David Colander, Marion Fourcade, Mary Furner, Stephanie Mudge, Malcolm Rutherford, and Yuval Yonay.

For chapter 3, David Jardini's 1996 dissertation, "Out of the Blue Yonder: The RAND Corporation's Diversification into Social Welfare Research, 1946–1968" (self-published in 2013 as *Thinking through the Cold War*) was

NOTE ON SOURCES 237

absolutely critical, as was Stephanie Young's 2009 dissertation, "Power and the Purse: Defense Budgeting and American Politics, 1947–1972," which focuses heavily on PPBS. Although RAND archival material is cited to a limited extent, the story was significantly informed by RAND's internal publications, only some of which are available online, and particularly by the RAND organizational charts found in the papers of Gus Shubert. For the second half of chapter 3, archival records—particularly William Gorham's papers at the LBJ Library, the detailed administrative histories of each executive agency produced by the LBJ administration, and the records of the Evaluation Division of the Budget Bureau (which administered PPBS) at the National Archives—were key to untangling the story. Oral histories were also important throughout, including those with David Bell, Joseph Califano, William Capron, Alain Enthoven, Kermit Gordon, William Gorham, Charles Hitch, Robert Levine, David Novick, Edward Quade, Charles Schultze, Gus Shubert, Elmer Staats, and Charles Zwick.

Chapter 4 draws significantly on published primary sources for its narrative—particularly Kaysen and Turner's *Antitrust Policy* and John Meyer et al.'s *The Economics of Competition in the Transportation Industries*, but more generally a range of academic publications by economists and lawyers. De Jong and Shepherd's *Pioneers of Industrial Organization* is filled with short biographies of key figures in this field. Irwin Collier's online archival collection, "Economics in the Rear-View Mirror," was particularly helpful for information on mid-twentieth-century figures in Harvard industrial organization, including Edward Mason. The Eno Center for Transportation provides a similarly useful resource on the history of transportation policy in its Historical Documents Archive. Marc Eisner's *Antitrust and the Triumph of Economics* was a key orienting text, both here and in chapter 6. The Chicago story is informed by archival work at the University of Chicago, particularly the papers of George Stigler and Aaron Director; Eduardo Canedo's 2008 dissertation, "The Rise of the Deregulation Movement in Modern America," is also an important resource. I relied on oral histories and personal accounts by Alan Boyd, Stephen Breyer, Kermit Gordon, Ewald Grether, George Hay, Thomas Kauper, Carl Kaysen, Edward Mason, Joe Peck, and Charles Zwick, as well as the papers of Leonard Silk, which cover the Brookings Institution's program on government regulation of economic activity, and the magazine *Regulation*, housed online by the Cato Institute.

For chapter 5, Alice O'Connor's *Poverty Knowledge* was an early touchstone and continues to be one of my favorite works of history. Records from the LBJ Library, particularly the papers of William Gorham and the administrative history of the Department of Health, Education, and Welfare; the National Archives, particularly the Office of Economic Opportunity's Office of Planning, Research, and Evaluation; and Duke's Economists' Papers Archive, particularly the papers of Mathematica founder Oskar Morgenstern, were useful. In addition to some of the figures mentioned in chapter 3, chapter 5 draws on oral histories and interviews with Stuart Altman, Wilbur Cohen, Stuart Eizenstat, and Malcolm Peabody, along with the collection in Michael Gillette's volume, *Launching the War on Poverty*, and the Poverty and Urban Policy: Kennedy Library and Brandeis University Conference Oral History Interview. The material on health economics was substantially informed by Zach Griffen's dissertation research in progress on the economics of health and education and its influence on social policy.

In chapter 6, the antitrust sections rely particularly on Supreme Court cases to understand the evolution of legal standards. They were also informed by oral histories conducted by the America Bar Association's Section on Antitrust Law with Alfred Kahn, James C. Miller, Frederick Scherer, and Edwin Zimmerman (along with some individuals mentioned in chapter 4) and the Donald F. Turner Papers at the LBJ Library. The transportation section draws on archival work at Cornell University in the papers of Alfred Kahn. Paul Pautler's *A History of the FTC's Bureau of Economics*, published online, was very useful, as was David Reinecke's 2019 dissertation, "Network Struggles: Re-wiring U.S. Network Industries for Competition, 1970–2015." Initially, this chapter had a substantial section on governance of healthcare markets, which followed an analogous trajectory. Carl Ameringer's *The Health Care Revolution: From Medical Monopoly to Market Competition* was invaluable in understanding it, as was Laura Schmidt's 1999 dissertation, "The Corporate Transformation of American Health Care: A Study in Institution Building," and Paul Starr's classic, *The Social Transformation of American Medicine*. More generally, Martha Derthick and Paul Quirk's *The Politics of Deregulation* continues to be critical for understanding the story of deregulation.

Chapter 7 is informed by archival work in the voluminous papers of Charles Schultze at the Carter Library, as well as the web archives of the Council on Wage and Price Stability, which were housed at George Mason's Mercatus Center, but as of this writing are no longer available online. The chapter also draws on oral histories and memoirs of Doug Costle, William Reilly, William Ruckelshaus, Alan Schmid, and Jim Tozzi. Although I did not find it until after this chapter was drafted, Charles Halvorson's 2017 dissertation, "Valuing the Air: The Politics of Environmental Governance from the Clean Air Act to Carbon Trading," is particularly useful on the politics of emissions trading, as was Joe Green Conley's 2006 dissertation, "Environmentalism Contained: A History of Corporate Responses to the New Environmentalism," and Alan Carlin's online *History of Economic Research at the EPA*, now available via the Wayback Machine. The extended account of revising the ozone standard relies on Marc Landy, Marc Roberts, and Stephen Thomas's *The Environmental Protection Agency: Asking the Wrong Questions from Nixon to Clinton*; Brian Cook's *Bureaucratic Politics and Regulatory Reform: The EPA and Emissions Trading* covers the early development of emissions trading in detail.

Chapters 8 and 9 are based mostly on secondary and published primary sources, along with some of the oral histories already mentioned. Articles from the *National Journal* were particularly helpful with the day-to-day politics of regulatory reform, as was an online publication, "The Occupational Safety and Health Administration: A History of Its First Thirteen Years, 1971–1984." A published interview with William Baxter and memoirs by Michael Pertschuk and James Miller were also helpful.

Last, I want to acknowledge one book that shaped the entire project, and one that came out too late to shape it, but that covers overlapping ground. The first is Marion Fourcade's *Economists and Societies*. While I cite it only a handful of times, this entire project can be seen as a book-length expansion of about ten pages of *Economists and Societies*.

The other is Binyamin Appelbaum's *The Economists' Hour*, which came out in 2019, as I was writing the next-to-last draft of this book. Because it covers so much overlapping ground (Washington policy circles in the 1960s and 1970s), I held off reading it until I had finished my own account. Now that I have, I am happy to report that it is deeply informed and compellingly written—and that, much to my relief, I have not managed to write the same book.

NOTES

Chapter 1. Thinking like an Economist

1. Nagourney (2008).
2. Thrush (2010).
3. Brandon and Carnes (2014).
4. Brill (2015). See, for example, American Presidency Project (1972; 1976a).
5. Dennis (2010); Madrick (2010).
6. Crawford (2011).
7. Scheer (2010); Funk and Hirschman (2014); Bell (2009); White (2009).
8. H.R. 2454, officially known as the American Clean Energy and Security Act of 2009.
9. Sunstein (2018).
10. Seib (2008).
11. Hacking (1992).
12. These two sentences are paraphrased from Hirschman and Berman (2014: 794).
13. Also see Reay's (2012: 45) discussion of the "'core' of relatively simple ideas and techniques" used by practicing economists.
14. On policy stories, see Stone (1989).
15. Fleck (1979 [1935]). Fleck's older, more sociological conception of "thought styles" and Hacking's epistemological "styles of reasoning" overlap considerably (see Sciortino 2017 for a discussion); while I borrow Fleck's distinction between an esoteric and an exoteric circle, I use Hacking's terminology elsewhere.
16. Hallett and Gougherty (2018).
17. Fleck (1979 [1935]).
18. Enthoven (1963: 422); see also Klein (1988: 9), Reay (2012).
19. P.L. 91-190; P.L. 91-604; P.L. 92-500; Reorganization Plans No. 3 and 4 of 1970; Hays (1989); Kline (2007: chs. 6–7).
20. P.L. 91-190 §2; Milazzo (2006).
21. P.L. 91-604 §2.
22. Lowi (1969); Hoberg (1992: 72); P.L. 92-500; P.L. 91-604 §112.
23. The Council of Economic Advisers had suggested pollution taxes under both presidents Johnson and Nixon; see, for example, U.S. President (1965: 152; 1966: 120–21; 1970: 93).
24. See Mishan (1971); Solow (1971); Ruff (1970); Kneese and Schultze (1975) for contemporary discussions.
25. "Economist Favors" (1966).
26. Roberts (1980).
27. Kline (2007: 117–19); Regens and Rycroft (1988). Ironically, this was an unintended consequence of Clean Air Act restrictions that limited pollution locally but did not similarly restrict emissions that would travel farther away.

28. P.L. 91-190 §2, §101.

29. American Presidency Project (1990); Project 88 (1988: vii, 1).

30. Bryner (1995); Ellerman et al. (2005).

31. Dales (1968); Project 88 (1988); McCauley et al. (2008).

32. This reduction took place between 1990 and 2019, although the Acid Rain Program was not its only cause; see Grundler (2020).

33. Schmalensee and Stavins (2013).

34. Daily (1997); Costanza et al. (1997); Gómez-Baggethun (2010).

35. Bullard (1990); First National (1991).

36. Policy, Planning, and Evaluation (1992: 1).

37. First National (1991).

38. More details on the methodological approach can be found on the author's website.

39. Meyer et al. (1959: vi).

40. Schultze (1968: 96).

41. Alice Rivlin to Robert Grosse, 21 February 1966, folder "Programming," Box 1, Personal Papers of William Gorham, LBJ Presidential Library.

42. Boulding (1969).

43. Okun (1975).

44. Ginsburg (2008).

45. Winnick (1995: 96).

46. Steensland (2008).

47. Borstelmann (2011); Jacobs (2016); Mizruchi (2013); Waterhouse (2013); Stein (2011); Saez and Zucman (2016).

48. American Presidency Project (1980).

49. See, for example, the 1992 Democratic Party platform (Pear 1992) and Clinton's speech accepting the Democratic nomination (American Presidency Project 1992).

50. On global economic changes, see, for example, Duménil and Levy (2004); Harvey (2005); Glyn (2007); Cowie (2010); Stein (2011); Rosenfeld (2014); McCarthy (2017). On coalition fracture and realignment, see Phillips (2014 [1969]); Carter (1999); Baer (2000); Lassiter (2007); Kruse (2007); Miroff (2007); Martin (2008); Nelson (2014); Grossman and Hopkins (2016). On collective action, see Vogel (1989); Klatch (1999); McGirr (2001); Schulman and Zelizer (2008); Phillips-Fein (2009); Williams (2010); Dochuk (2011); Hacker and Pierson (2011); Mizruchi (2013); Waterhouse (2013).

51. Blyth (2002); Campbell and Pedersen (2014); Teles (2008); Mirowski and Plehwe (2009); Rodgers (2011); Medvetz (2012); Burgin (2012); Stedman Jones (2012); Stahl (2016); Slobodian (2018).

52. Mudge (2018).

53. Rodgers (2011); for work focused on macroeconomics, see, for example, Hall (1993); Bernstein (2001); Blyth (2002); Mudge (2018).

54. For example, Bernstein (2001); Conti-Brown (2016); Mudge (2018).

55. For example, Burgin (2012); MacLean (2017).

56. On policy streams, see Kingdon (1984).

57. Vogel (2017).

58. See, for example, the history of airline deregulation (Derthick and Quirk 1985).

59. Samuel DuBois Cook Center on Social Equity (2019); LPE Project (2017); Kramer (2018).

Chapter 2. The Economic Style and Its Antecedents

1. Bernstein (2001).

2. Fourcade (2009); see also Furner and Supple (1990).

3. Bernstein (2001); Fourcade (2009); Hawley (1990); Cuff (1989); Lacey and Furner (1993). See Furner (1975) on the early years of the AEA and Church (1974) on economists' role in public affairs before 1920.

4. Rutherford (2001; 2011a).

5. Hodgson (2003: 570).

6. Bernstein (2001); Mudge (2018).

7. Robbins (1932: 15); see Backhouse and Medema (2009a; 2009b) on the changing definitions of economics and on the reception of the Robbins definition in particular.

8. Samuelson (1961: vii); on consolidation in this period, see Medema (1998); Morgan and Rutherford (1998).

9. Koopmans (1947).

10. See especially Yonay (1998); Morgan and Rutherford (1998); Rutherford (2011a) on the history of institutional economics.

11. Although neoclassical economics and conservative economics are often associated with one another, Yonay (1998: ch. 3) argues that the conservative "old school" was primarily classical, while the "new school" of more interventionist economists included both neoclassical marginalists and historicists who were more direct antecedents of institutionalists.

12. Yonay (1998: ch. 3); Rutherford (2011a).

13. Rutherford (2001: 177–78).

14. Fourcade (2009: 81–84).

15. Yonay (1998: 16–17). The other two were Harvard and Chicago.

16. Hovenkamp (2015: 110); Medema (1998).

17. Cuff (1989).

18. Rutherford (2011a: 265)

19. Mudge (2018: 178–80).

20. The history of the development of GDP has been told in a number of places; see, for example, Carson (1975); Coyle (2014); Lepenies (2016); Hirschman (2016); Shenk (2016). On Kuznets's relationship with institutionalism, see Street (1988).

21. See, for example, Stapleford (2009) on the cost of living; Card (2011) and Duncan and Shelton (1978: 47) on the unemployment rate; Meade (2010) on input-output tables.

22. Anderson (2015); Igo (2007).

23. Leonard (2009: 127–28).

24. Barber (1985, especially 7–13; 1996); Bernstein (2001: 53–77).

25. These included Adolph Berle, John Maurice Clark, Morris Copeland, John Kenneth Galbraith, Gardiner Means, Robert Nathan, and Rexford Tugwell. See Bernstein (2001: 76); Barber (1996); Rutherford (2011a).

26. Pautler (2015: 2–4).

27. Hawley (1990: 293–99); McDean (1983); see Banzhaf (2006; 2010) and Rutherford (2011b) on the position of agricultural economics relative to institutional and neoclassical economics in this era.

28. U.S. Library of Congress (1995); Whyte (2017: 257). The director was Julius Klein.

29. Garraty (1981: 171–74); Rutherford (2001: 179–80). The Veblen student was Isador Lubin; the Commons student, Ewan Clauge.

30. Bernstein (2001: 76–77). Jacob Viner and Irving Fisher are examples of neoclassical economists of the era who were involved in policymaking.

31. Grossman (1982); Fogel et al. (2013).

32. Hodgson (2003: 570).

33. Biddle (1998).

34. CEA chairs Edwin Nourse, Leon Keyserling, Arthur Burns, and Raymond Saulnier reflected this institutionalist bent; see Pautler (2015: 111) on the FTC.

35. The economist was Winfield Riefler; see Conti-Brown (2016: 43). On Brookings's graduate school, see Smith (1991).

36. On Brookings, see Smith (1991).

37. Pautler (2015: 111).

38. Rutherford (2011b).

39. Coase (1984: 230).

40. Yonay (1998: 68).

41. Pautler (2015: 4).

42. The section title is from Roth (1986: 246). On "the political power of economic ideas," see, for example, Hall (1993); Blyth (2002); Campbell (1998). Mudge (2018) similarly centers macroeconomics in her study of economic experts and the political left, although her empirical focus is somewhat different.

43. Mudge (2018: 178–209).

44. Keynes (1936); see Carter (2020) for a recent biography.

45. See Meltzer (2003: 420) on Laughlin Currie's advocacy of countercyclical stimulus prior to Keynes's *General Theory*. See Rutherford (2001) and Conti-Brown (2016) on institutional economists in the Federal Reserve.

46. Mitchell's (1913) *Business Cycles* is one classic work in this genre. See Fogel et al. (2013) on NBER and its early work on business cycles.

47. Rutherford (2011a: 265).

48. Miller (2002); Backhouse (2017). Beyond his reputation as the "American Keynes," Hansen is best known for his theory of secular stagnation. On Hansen, see also Tobin (1976); Samuelson (1976).

49. Yonay (1998: 191–92).

50. Mudge (2018: 183–85).

51. Its author was Stanford economist Lorie Tarshis. See Lawson (2015); Backhouse (2017: ch. 26).

52. Colander and Landreth (1998); Mudge (2018: 183–91).

53. See Mirowski (1999); Wallis (1980) on Columbia's Statistical Research Group, which included Milton Friedman and George Stigler. Seven of the eighteen principal members of the statistical research group were primarily economists, according to Wallis. See Bartels (1983) on economists (including John Kenneth Galbraith) at the Office of Price Administration. And see Katz (1989: ch. 4) on economists at the Office of Strategic Services, led by Harvard's Edward Mason.

54. Edelstein (2001); Lacey (2011); Perlman (1987); Perlman and Marietta (2005).

55. Samuelson (1944: 298).

56. P.L. 79-304.

57. Hamby (1973: 60); see Bailey (1950) for the classic account of the passage of the Employment Act of 1946.

58. Wasem (2013).

59. Bernstein (2001: 113).

60. See Collins (1981; 1990; 2000) on "growthmanship" and the "commercial Keynesianism" that liberal businessmen embraced during the 1950s.

61. Meltzer (2003: 612, 633, 715).

62. Conti-Brown (2016) provides a nice overview of the Treasury-Fed Accord.

63. Fox (2014).

64. Conti-Brown (2016).

65. Bernstein (2001: 130); Collins (2000: ch. 1).

66. See Hatzis (1996) on the role of academics in setting Kennedy's policy agenda.

67. In addition to chair Walter Heller, Kennedy's CEA included James Tobin as a member, Robert Solow and Arthur Okun as staffers, and Paul Samuelson (who turned down an offer to serve as chair) as a behind-the-scenes advisor.

68. Romani (2018).

69. Bernstein (2001: 133–39); Berman and Pagnucco (2010); Collins (2000: ch. 2); Davis (1988).

70. Collins (2000: 52).

71. Schultz (1961); Brauer (1982); Holden and Biddle (2017).

72. On changing definitions of economics, see Backhouse and Medema (2009b; 2009a).

73. This is loosely adapted from Colander's (2000) definition of neoclassical economics.

74. Yonay (1998: ch. 2).

75. McCloskey and Trefethen (1954); Goodwin (1998: 64).

76. Thomas (2015).

77. Fourcade (2009: 84–87).

78. Backhouse (2015: 327).

79. Düppe and Weintraub (2014).

80. It tied for first place with Harvard; see Cherrier (2014: 34).

81. Cherrier (2014: 24); Backhouse (2017: ch. 25). In the 1955 edition of *Economics*, he began referring to this neoclassical micro/Keynesian macro approach as the "neoclassical synthesis"; see De Vroey and Garcia Duarte (2013) on the use and reception of the phrase.

82. Colander (2005: 253). William Nordhaus coauthored the 1985 and subsequent editions.

83. Samuelson (1948); see Erikson (2015) on the early development and reception of game theory.

84. Skousen (1997: 138).

85. Backhouse (1998: 105).

86. Although not referring to Hacking's "styles of reasoning," Morgan and Rutherford (1998: 20) also use the word "style" to "describe the differences implied in American economics as it emerged through the cold war world of the 1950s and 1960s." They prefer the term "tool-kit economics" to "neoclassical economics," emphasizing that "not all tools were associated with neoclassical economics," but there is clearly substantial overlap between the style they describe and the style discussed here.

87. Pearce (2000: 49–50); see Kaldor (1939); Hicks (1939; 1943) for the original work.

88. Monopoly was a long-recognized problem; although Marshall (1890) had identified externalities as well, they were seen as "exceptional" and "unimportant" until the 1960s. See Scitovsky (1954), quoted in Medema (2014a: 39).

89. A. C. Pigou proposed taxes as a way to address negative externalities as early as 1912 (Pigou 1912).

90. Banzhaf (2014).

91. For example, Becker (1957; 1968).

92. For example, Clawson (1959); Schelling (1968).

93. See chapters 3 and 4. Although less immediately relevant for this account, the economic style was also exported to business schools; see Khurana (2007).

94. See, for example, Colander (2000; 2005).

Chapter 3. How to Make Government Decisions

1. See Collins (2002); Jardini (1996: 24–44); Smith (1966: 38–60), among many sources on the origins of RAND.

2. Kaplan (1983: 86–87).

3. Hoag (1956: 1); systems analysis, and, before that, operations research, was commonly described as "quantitative common sense." See, for example, Amadae (2003: 63); National Research Council (1951: 2); Shrader (2008: 52).

4. Jardini (1996: 104–13).

5. "The Pentagon's Whiz Kids" (1962).

6. See, for example, Novick (1967 [1965]).

7. U.S. GAO (1969: 4, 11).

8. Mosher (1984: 124).

9. McCombe (1959: 103).

10. Smith (1966).

11. U.S. Air Force Project RAND (1948).

12. Jardini (1996: 82–91, 100); Thomas (2015: 112); see also Mirowski (2001: 210–11).

13. Jardini (1996: 82–91, 100).

14. Johnson (1997: 898); on the history of operations research, see Shrader (2006); Thomas (2015).

15. Hoag (1956: 1–2).

16. See Jardini (1996: 107–10) on how RAND's Economics Department used systems analysis to make itself more important to RAND, and Shrader (2006: 28, 48) on the limited presence of economists in wartime operations research. On RAND's first systems analysis, see Jardini (1996: 49–64) and Thomas (2015: ch. 23), among others.

17. Young (2009: 54).

18. On the Strategic Bombing Study, see Jardini (1996: 44–70); Collins (2002: ch. 5); Thomas (2015: 205–9).

19. Jardini (1996: 60–64). The Strategic Bombing Study was also politically insensitive to the Air Force's deep devotion to developing faster and more impressive planes.

20. Lindblom (1954: 1).

21. See, for example, Hitch (1952); Quade (1953); McKean (1953); Alchian and Kessel (1954); Lindblom (1954) for contributions to this debate.

22. Hitch (1958: 11–12).

23. Hitch (1952: 1–2).

24. Hitch (1952).

25. The argument in this and the previous paragraph draws heavily on Jardini (1996: 107–10).

26. Quade (1988: 37).

27. Smith (1966: 107, 109–10); see also Jardini (1996: 124–27).

28. Jardini (1996: 125).

29. Not all RAND economists were equally enamored of systems analysis; see, for example, Alchian and Kessel (1954); Klein (1958; 1960); Klein and Meckling (1958); Nelson (1958).

30. Haydon (1972).

31. RAND Corporation Archives, Gus Shubert Papers, Box 5, Organization Charts, Economics Department.

32. RAND Corporation Archives, Gus Shubert Papers, Box 5, Organization Charts, Economics Department.

33. Simon (1991: 116).

34. Shubert (1988: 42).

35. Herken (1985: 355–56).

36. McKean (1956: 53); see Porter (1995: ch. 7) on the development of cost-benefit analysis.

37. McKean (1955; 1956). See also DeHaven et al. (1953) and DeHaven and Hirshleifer (1957) for more work on water at RAND.

38. McKean (1958); Hoos (1972: 131). McKean's was one of three landmark books published that year that linked cost-benefit analysis of water resources to welfare economics; the other two were Eckstein (1958) and Krutilla and Eckstein (1958). See Hines (1959) for a review of all three.

39. Hitch (1988: 23).

40. Shubert (1992: 75); Kershaw and McKean (1959: iii). See also Kershaw and McKean (1960; 1962); McKean and Kershaw (1961). Kershaw would play a prominent role in applying the economic style of reasoning to the War on Poverty; see chapter 5.

41. Jardini (1996: 9, 133–34); Smith (1966: 164).

42. Jardini (1996: 128).

43. Jardini (1996: 155).

44. Enthoven (1971: 1); Jardini (1996: 156). See Enthoven (1971) more generally for an account of this period.

45. Kaplan (1983: 240–50); Wells (2001: 127, 153, 157).

46. Kaplan (1983: 250).

47. Hatzis (1996).

48. Byrne (1993).

49. Byrne (1993); Shrader (2008: 16–17).

50. Eisenhower (1961).

51. Novick, who by the time he developed his program budget was leading the spin-off Cost Analysis Department, had some graduate training in economics, but no PhD.

52. Novick (1966; 1988b: 31–34; 1988a); Novick (1954a: 14–15) contains an illustration.

53. See Mosher (1954; 1984); Schrader (2008: 26–30); Novick (1954a). Also see Novick (1966: 7; 1988b: 33; 1988a: 9) for brief accounts of this episode, and Novick (1954b; 1956; 1959) for further work in this direction at RAND.

54. Hitch and McKean (1960: xii).

55. The book is a single synthetic work, not an edited volume, but incorporated substantial previously published material by RAND economists Stephen Enke, Alain Enthoven, Malcolm Hoag, C. B. McGuire, and Albert Wohlstetter. Quotation is from Hitch and McKean (1960: v); italics in original.

56. Hitch and McKean (1960).

57. Jardini (1996: 210–12).

58. Enthoven (1971: 4). Although McNamara and Hitch had not met prior to this, McNamara was acquainted with John Williams, head of RAND's original Evaluation Section, during the war. See Thomas (2015: 114).

59. Jardini (1996: 212).

60. Enthoven (1971: 4). See Enthoven (1971) for his account of this period of events.

61. Jardini (1996: 166).

62. Jardini (1996: 165–66).

63. Jardini (1996: 167).

64. "The Pentagon's Whiz Kids" (1962).

65. Young (2009: 114); see also Jardini (1996: 214–15).

66. Jardini (1996: 216–17); Young (2009: 114–25). See also Novick (1962); Hitch (1965); Enthoven and Smith (1971) for firsthand accounts.

67. "Brains behind the Muscle" (1961a).

68. Jardini (1996: 220–21).

69. White (1963: 10), quoted in Jardini (1996: 222–23).

70. Jardini (1996: 221).

71. Jardini (1996: 221–22); Young (2009: 128–31; 147–48).

72. Young (2009: 149–63).

73. Enthoven (1963); Alsop (1962).
74. Novick (1954a: v).
75. Novick (1962: 1).
76. Bernstein (2001: 133–39); Berman (1979: 52, 54, 69).
77. Troy (2003).
78. Bell (1964: 76–78); Gordon (1969: 17–18).
79. Capron was at RAND from 1951 to 1956; see Hitch and Capron (1952) for a coauthored report. Capron joined the CEA staff in 1964, where he worked with Gordon and was deeply involved in developing the War on Poverty (O'Connor 2001; Schevitz 2002).
80. Jardini (1996: 339).
81. Jardini (1996: 342–43); Zwick (2000: 6). Zwick would follow Schultze as director in 1968.
82. Capron (1981). The fourth appointee was Elmer Staats, discussed later in this chapter.
83. Califano (1969: 17).
84. See, for example, Schultze (1968; 1969).
85. Jardini (1996: 339–41).
86. PPBS was required at nearly all executive agencies at the time; several other agencies were required to adopt PPBS in 1968. See U.S. GAO (1969: 4, 11, 12–13).
87. Novick (1967 [1965]); Jardini (1996: 343).
88. Mosher (1984: 124).
89. Another 1,442 FTEs were employed by the Defense Department; see U.S. GAO (1969: 48).
90. Harper et al. (1969: 628–29).
91. Belfer et al. (1968: 1).
92. Belfer et al. (1968: 1).
93. Mosher (1984: 124).
94. Wildavsky (1966; 1967); see also Hoos (1972).
95. Williams (1990: 42).
96. Harper et al. (1969); U.S. GAO (1969: 1).
97. Mosher (1984: 124); Schick (1973). A version of PPBS continues to be used in the Defense Department today.
98. U.S. GAO (1969: 4).
99. U.S. GAO (1969: 46).
100. U.S. GAO (1969: 46; see Appendix IV: 1 for a list of offices). These names were current ca. 1969, but changed over the years, often multiple times. For example, in 1969 the Department of Commerce had an Office of Programming, Planning and Research; Housing and Urban Development had an Office of Policy Analysis and Program Evaluation; and the Department of Justice had an Office of Planning and Evaluation. As of 2021, those agencies have, respectively, an Office of Policy and Strategic Planning; an Office of Policy Development and Research; and a Policy and Planning Staff.
101. Gorham (1986: 1–4).
102. Levine (1969: 2).
103. Levine (1969: 2).
104. Zwick (1969b: 6).
105. NRC (2008: 12); "Graduate School Notes" (1970).
106. Hjort (1968; 2016).
107. Harper et al. (1969: 624, 626).
108. Harper et al. (1969: 624).
109. Gorham (1986: 8–9); Departmental History, Office of the Assistant Secretary for Planning and Evaluation, pp. 3–4, folder "Assistant Secretary for Planning and Evaluation," Administrative History, Department of Health, Education, and Welfare, Volume I, Parts I & II, Box 1, Papers of Lyndon Baines Johnson, President, 1963–1969, LBJ Presidential Library.

110. Departmental History, Office of the Assistant Secretary for Planning and Evaluation, p. 16.

111. Gorham (1986: 14).

112. Harper et al. (1969); see also Doh (1971); Juncker (1968).

113. Lyons (1969: 220, 223).

114. Doh (1971: 68).

115. See O'Connor (2001: ch. 7) and Jardini (1996: 331–43) on how PPBS reshaped the Office of Economic Opportunity.

116. Harper et al. (1969); U.S. GAO (1969: 101).

117. O'Connor (2001: 203–10); U.S. DOL (1977); Lawlor (1979: 53–54); Weir (1993: 109).

118. Krueger (2014: 585); Kraemer et al. (1987).

119. See, for example, Eisner (1991); Nelson (1991); Kwerel (2000). For an exception, see Pugliaresi and Berliner (1989).

120. Kwerel (2000).

121. Cook (1988).

122. Nelson (1991: 139).

123. Rivlin (1971: 5).

124. "PPBS Education," Program Evaluation Staff report, 25 January 1966, unnamed folder, Box 1, RG 51 Bureau of the Budget, Series 62.10a, Evaluation Division 1962–68, National Archives at College Park, MD.

125. Memorandum from Peter L. Szanton to Mr. [Philip Samuel] Hughes, 1 September 1966, unnamed folder, Box 1, RG 51 Bureau of the Budget, Series 62.10a, Evaluation Division 1962–68, National Archives.

126. U.S. Civil Service Commission (1968: 4).

127. U.S. Civil Service Commission (1968: 2).

128. U.S. Civil Service Commission (1968: 34, 36).

129. "Training for PPB," report by Allen Schick, p. 1, March 1968, folder EPSA #3; and "Minutes of the Education Advisory Committee Meeting," p. 3, 2 May 1967, folder EPSA #2; Box 1, RG 51 Bureau of the Budget, Series 62.10a, Evaluation Division 1962–68, National Archives. The second year saw Chicago leave the program and University of California, Irvine, and MIT join it. Memorandum from Fred Hoffman to Charles Schultze, p. 2, 16 June 1967, folder EPSA #2, Box 1, RG 51.

130. "Minutes of the Education Advisory Committee Meeting," p. 3.

131. Hoffman to Schultze, p. 2.

132. "University Offerings in the Mid-Career Educational Program in Systematic Analysis," report by BOB and the National Institute of Public Affairs, December 1966, unnamed folder, Box 1, RG 51 Bureau of the Budget, Series 62.10a, Evaluation Division 1962–68, National Archives.

133. "Program Description of the Educational Program in Systematic Analysis for the 1960–1970 Class," folder EPSA, Box 5, RG 51 Bureau of the Budget, Series 62.10a, Evaluation Division 1962–68, National Archives.

134. "Training for PPB," pp. 13–14.

135. "Training for PPB," p. 15.

136. "Training for PPB," p. 14.

137. Allison (2006).

138. Fleishman (1990: 736); Allison (2006).

139. Miles (1967: 346); survey quoted in Campbell and Rawson (1981: 98).

140. Stokes (1986: 46); Fleishman (1990: 736–37).

141. Klein (1967: 15). See Miles (1967); Crecine (1982); and Walker (1976) for critiques of the state of public administration in the 1960s.

142. Fleishman (1990: 735).

143. Fleishman (1990: 733). These included programs at Michigan (1967), Harvard (1968), Berkeley (1969), SUNY Buffalo (1969), Carnegie Mellon (1979), Penn (1969), Ohio State (1969),

Minnesota (1970), Yale (1970) (Crecine 1971: 9) and RAND (1969), Texas (1970), and Duke (1971) (Fleishman 1990: 734). Yates (1977: 364) adds SUNY Stony Brook to this list.

144. Fleishman (1990: 733).

145. Crecine (1982: 2, 21).

146. Crecine et al. (1968).

147. RAND Corporation (2015).

148. Campbell and Rawson (1981: 103).

149. Stokes (1986: 46).

150. Crecine (1982: 3); see Fleishman (1990: 735) for another reference to the Air Bases Study.

151. Campbell and Rawson (1981: 91, 100); Allison (2006).

152. Jann (1991: 112).

153. Fleishman (1990: 750); Stock and Siegfried (2014: 4).

154. Walker (1976: 102).

155. Yates (1977: 369), quoting Edward Hamilton.

156. Allison (2006).

157. Fleishman (1990: 750).

158. Jenkins-Smith (1990: 51).

159. McLaughlin (1974: 79, 83).

160. McLaughlin (1974: ch. 3, 72–82); see also Rivlin (1971: 79–85).

161. McLaughlin (1974: 110).

162. Kraemer (1987: 128); see also Lynn and Whitman (1981) for a largely corroborating account.

163. Kraemer (1987: 35–42, 129–34).

164. Kraemer (1987: 134–36).

165. Kraemer (1987: 136).

166. Young (2009: 159).

167. See nine volumes of hearings (titled *Planning-Programming-Budgeting*) held by the U.S. Senate Committee on Government Operations' Subcommittee on National Security and International Operations in 1967 and 1968; see also Young (2009) and Fuller (1972).

168. Fenno (1968: 193).

169. Mosher (1979: 96–97, 104, 146).

170. Staats (1971: 15–18; 1987: 2, 23).

171. U.S. Senate (1968: 167).

172. Walker (1986: 47, 50); Mosher (1979: 175–76; 1984: 145).

173. Mosher (1979: 176); see also Thurber (1976: 207).

174. Mosher (1979: 191–92).

175. U.S. GAO (1978: 187).

176. Walker (1986: 97).

177. Walker (1986: 97).

178. Walker (1986: 41). See also Williams (1998: ch. 9) and Weiss (1992) for more on the CRS and OTA as analytic organizations.

179. See Saldin (2017: ch. 2); Pfiffner (1979).

180. Saldin (2017: 35).

181. Joyce (2011: 20).

182. Twogood (1997: 361).

183. Minor (1978: 101). Hughes spent most of his career at the Budget Bureau, where he eventually served as deputy to Charles Schultze. At the time of his consideration for the position of CBO director, he was Assistant Comptroller General under Elmer Staats (Gamarekian 1985; Estrada 2004).

184. Rivlin (1971); Joyce (2011: 20).

185. Minor (1978: 107).

186. These included Robert Reischauer, a Columbia PhD and her Brookings colleague; Robert Levine, Yale PhD, RAND alum, and former head of the OEO's PPO; Frank De Leeuw, Harvard PhD and former staffer at the Federal Reserve and Urban Institute; and James Blum, who had completed graduate coursework at Michigan and held leadership roles at Labor's ASPER and the Council on Wage and Price Stability (Duscha 1975; Minor 1978: 106; Day 2003).

187. Minor (1978: 114); Joyce (2011: 23).

188. Joyce (2011: 54, 59).

189. Joyce (2011: 123–28).

190. U.S. Congress (2021). The one exception is Dan L. Crippen, whose PhD is in public finance.

191. Twogood (1997: 361).

192. Minutes of Panel of Economic Advisers Meeting, 8 June 1977, folder "Congressional Budget Office 1975–1994," Box 23, Paul A. Samuelson Papers, Duke University Archives.

193. Minor (1978).

194. Mosher (1979: 276).

195. Haveman (1976: 235).

Chapter 4. How to Govern Markets

1. The term "workable competition" is from Clark (1940).

2. Frohnmayer (1969).

3. Meyer et al. (1959: vi).

4. See, for example, Hefleblower and Stocking (1958).

5. Grether (1970).

6. Chamberlin (1933). Cambridge's Joan Robinson published *The Economics of Imperfect Competition*, which took a very similar approach, the same year.

7. Shepherd (2007). For work covering the development of industrial organization economics from the 1930s to the 1950s from various angles, see Grether (1970); Peritz (1996); de Jong et al. (2007); and Hovenkamp (2009b), as well as many primary sources from Irwin Collier's website, "Economics in the Rear-View Mirror" (http://www.irwincollier.com/).

8. See, for example, Meyer et al. (1959); Nicholls (1951).

9. See, for example, Markham (1952).

10. Grether (1970: 84).

11. This was laid out in Bain's 1959 *Industrial Organization*, which would remain the dominant textbook into the 1970s; the American Economic Association called Bain, in 1983, "the undisputed father of modern Industrial Organization Economics" and referred to Chamberlin and Mason as its grandfathers (American Economic Review 1983).

12. See, for example Mason (1959); Kaysen and Turner (1959).

13. P.L. 51-647.

14. P.L. 63-212 §7.

15. P.L. 81-899.

16. See, for example, Kaysen and Turner (1959: 11–22) on policy goals from an economic perspective.

17. Mason had also served as doctoral advisor for both Kaysen and Turner. On the seminar, see Kaysen and Turner (1959: ii); Fisher (2012: 340–41).

18. Kaysen and Turner (1959: ch. 1).

19. Kaysen and Turner (1959: 75).

20. Kaysen and Turner (1959: ch. 3).

21. Kaysen and Turner (1959: 133).

22. See, for example, Edwards (1960); Fuchs (1960) for academic reviews.

23. Smith (1960).

24. See, for example, Grether (1993: 403–4).

25. Grether (1993: 403–4).

26. Peck (1988: 94–95). Although Meyer was not one of Mason's students, and is better known as the "father of transportation economics" (Glaeser 2009), the book's focus on industry and market structure place it squarely in the Harvard I/O tradition. The acknowledgments of the two books also highlight the connections between them: *Antitrust Policy* thanks Peck for his research assistance, while *Economics of Competition* thanks Kaysen for his manuscript comments.

27. Meyer et al. (1959: 17).

28. Meyer et al. (1959: 270).

29. Meyer et al. (1959: 1–2).

30. Meyer et al. (1959: vi).

31. Van Horn (2011); the pamphlet can be found as part of Simons (1948).

32. Van Horn (2009; 2011).

33. Van Horn (2009; 2011).

34. See, for example, Levi and Director (1956).

35. Van Horn (2011: 293). Nutter's 1949 PhD was published in 1951 as *The Extent of Enterprise Monopoly in the United States, 1899–1939*.

36. McGee (1958). See also Bork (1954) and Bowman (1957) for other contributions to this project.

37. Christophers (2016: 227–28).

38. Burgin (2012: 157).

39. For example, G. Warren Nutter went to the economics department of Yale and later Virginia, and John S. McGee to economics at the University of Washington, while Ward Bowman—along with Bork—was hired by Yale Law School.

40. Slobodian (2018).

41. Eisner (1991: 110).

42. Hovenkamp (2015: 110); see Rutherford (2011a) for legal realism from the institutional economics side.

43. Legal formalism was the previously dominant school.

44. Singer (1988); Hovenkamp (2015: ch. 6). See also Horwitz (1992); Schlegel (1995); Kalman (1986).

45. Hovenkamp (2015); Rutherford (2011a); Medema (1998).

46. Singer (1988: 505). The legal process school tried to split the difference between the principle-driven formalism that dominated during the *Lochner* era and the cause-effect realism that partially displaced it. See, for example, Sacks and Hart (1994 [1958]).

47. Hovenkamp (2015: 110).

48. Ellickson (1989: 27). Ellickson notes that neither Director nor Bowman held doctorates in economics, but were widely accepted as "full members of the [economists'] club."

49. Bok (1960).

50. Turner (1968).

51. Breyer (1996). Breyer was a 1964 Harvard Law School grad; although his early publications were mostly on regulated industries, he did teach antitrust at Harvard (Breyer 2008).

52. Coase (1960).

53. The exact nature of Coase's argument, which was not stated in formal terms, has been the subject of a great deal of legal exegesis; for discussions, see Medema (1996; 1999; 2011; 2020).

54. Medema (2014b).

55. Manne (1965); Landes (1968); Becker (1968).

56. University of Chicago (2020); Landes would, after a brief departure from the university, later return to the University of Chicago Law School.

57. Domnarski (2016). On Posner's influence, see Shapiro (2000).

58. Calabresi (1961); see Medema (2014b) on the importance of Yale (and specifically Calabresi) in drawing early attention to Coase's work.

59. Ellickson (1989: 28).

60. Ellickson (1989: 27).

61. Lovett (1974: 389–90).

62. Lovett (1974: 389–90). Only three of the rest did so at that point.

63. Lovett (1974: 393). The footnote to this description mentions that this is basically microeconomic theory with additional components from areas like industrial organization and public finance, and with less econometrics and macroeconomics than would be presented to graduate students in economics.

64. Posner (1973a).

65. Gellhorn and Robinson (1983: 247).

66. Eisner (1991: 16–17, 86–87).

67. Pautler (2015: 2–4); Markus (1962: 13–14).

68. Pautler (2015: 4, 40).

69. Pautler (2015: 40).

70. Grether (1993: 421).

71. Mueller (1962); Markus (1962: 17).

72. Shanahan (1966: 65).

73. Eisner (1991: 125–28). See also Weaver (1977: 134–35) and "U.S. Seeks" (1965c), in which Turner describes development of this unit as "[o]ne of his main projects."

74. Williamson (2002).

75. McLaren, an aggressive antitrust enforcer, ran afoul of Nixon when McLaren filed multiple suits against telecommunications giant ITT, despite ITT having been a major backer of the Nixon campaign. Nixon subsequently pushed him out. See Fligstein (1990: 206–10); Feldstein (2010: 226–29); Mueller (1983: 23–25); and Anderson (2000: 194–95) on this episode.

76. Smith (1972); Kauper (2007).

77. Williamson (2002); Kauper (2007); Hay (2008).

78. Hay (2008).

79. Eisner (1991: 138–39); Hay (2008).

80. Kauper (2007).

81. Harris and Milkis (1996: 163–67). One such report was from Ralph Nader's group (Cox et al. 1969); another was from the American Bar Association (1969).

82. Eisner (1991: 165).

83. Shepherd (1996: 948).

84. Eisner (1991: 166); Katzmann (1980: 40). According to Katzmann, only six of the forty professional staff who worked for the Bureau of Economics in 1970 remained by 1977.

85. See Eisner (2000) for an excellent history of regulation in the United States.

86. See, for example, Peltzman (1989), which equates the economic critique of regulation with the Chicago tradition.

87. See Keyes (1951); Meyer et al. (1959); Caves (1962) for contributions from Harvard; see Stigler and Friedland (1962) for a significant Chicago contribution. Stigler (1971) is often the canonical cite for the economic argument for deregulation, but by this point the argument reflected considerable consensus in economics. Averch and Johnson (1962) were writing from RAND; Paul

MacAvoy (1962; 1965), a 1960 Yale PhD whose first job was at MIT's business school, was also a key scholar who in some ways bridged the Harvard and Chicago networks.

88. See, for example, Huntington (1952); Bernstein (1955); Jaffe (1954).

89. For example, Buchanan and Tullock (1962); Downs (1957); Riker (1962); Kolko (1963). See Novak (2013) for an overview of 1950s and 1960s regulatory debates.

90. American Economic Review (1983).

91. Mason's recruits included Moses Abramowitz, Sidney Alexander, Paul Baran, Harold Barnett, Abram Bergson, Emile Despres, Carl Kaysen, Charles Kindleberger, Svend Larsen, Wassily Leontief, Walter Levy, Wilfred Malenbaum, Lloyd Metzler, Chandler Morse, Walt W. Rostow, Paul Sweezy, and Donald Wheeler (Katz 1989: ch. 4).

92. Mason (1973: 35).

93. Peck (1988: 94).

94. See Hatzis (1996) on Kennedy's use of academics.

95. Kaysen (1966).

96. John F. Kennedy Presidential Archives, Walter W. Heller papers, Box 3, General CEA records, Folder 3, "CEA general, 2/61–9/64." Peck (1988: 98) credits Gordon with serving as an advocate for transportation deregulation during the Kennedy administration. On Gordon's service under Kennedy and Johnson more generally, see Gordon (1964; 1969).

97. See U.S. President (1962: 196; 1963: 158) for lists of CEA consultants; on Caves, see Bianchi (2013); Peck (1988: 99); Caves (1962).

98. U.S. President (1963: xxii); see also Kennedy's transportation message to Congress in April 1962 (American Presidency Project 1962).

99. Benjamin Chinitz, Allen R. Ferguson, and James R. Nelson were the other three.

100. For Gordon's recommendations, see memorandum from Kermit Gordon to S. Douglass Cater, 22 June 1964, available at https://www.enotrans.org/wp-content/uploads/1964-06-22-Gordon-to-Cater.pdf (accessed 27 July 2021). The task force report, including a list of members, is available at https://www.enotrans.org/wp-content/uploads/membersOnly-1964-11-16-Transpo-Policy-Task-Force-Report.pdf (accessed 27 July 2021); quote is from p. ii. See also Peck (1988: 98); Rose et al. (2006: 136–39); Welborn (1993: 224) on the task force.

101. Zwick (1969a: 2). Zwick was tightly connected with both the Harvard I/O and the RAND networks; see Zwick (1969a: 4–9).

102. Zwick (1969a: 10).

103. Zwick (1969a: 10–12).

104. Boyer and Shepherd (1981: 359); Peck (1988: 100).

105. On the uneven, but generally pro-deregulation position of the Department of Transportation, see Derthick and Quirk (1985) and Rose et al. (2006); on Peck, see Peck (1988: 99).

106. Smith (1991: 88). It is worth noting that Gordon's most recent position before his stint on the CEA and as director of the Budget Bureau had been director of Ford's economic development and administration program (1961b).

107. Peck (1988: 101); "Studies in the Regulation of Economic Activity," p. 1, August 1969, folder "Regulation" #2, Box 10 A, Leonard Silk papers.

108. "Studies in the Regulation of Economic Activity," p. 1, August 1969, folder "Regulation" #2, Box 10 A, Leonard Silk papers.

109. "Studies in the Regulation of Economic Activity," pp. 24–25.

110. On transportation, see Friedlaender (1969); Eads (1971); Douglas and Miller (1974). On other topics, Capron (1971); Noll et al. (1973); Noll (1974); Breyer and MacAvoy (1974).

111. Smith (1991: 88–91).

112. "Studies in the Regulation of Economic Activity," p. 31. Harvard faculty included Phillip Areeda (law), Richard Caves (economics), Zvi Griliches (economics), Carl Kaysen (recently

NOTES TO CHAPTER 4

departed from the economics faculty), and Joe Peck (slightly less recently departed from the business school); Chicago's Phil Neal was a Harvard law alumnus; and Harvard economics PhDs included Joe Bain, Franklin Fisher, Burton Klein, James McKie, James Nelson, Richard Quandt, John Sheahan, and Peter Steiner. All but two of those were in economics; the others were legal scholars. At least half a dozen had studied under Edward Mason. The remaining advisory committee members as of 1969 were Paul MacAvoy, William Baxter, Richard Cyert, Jan Deutsch, Richard Heflebower, Edwin S. Mills, George Stigler, and Clair Wilcox.

113. "Studies in the Regulation of Economic Activity," p. 31. The antitrust-focused scholars included Phillip Areeda, William Baxter, Carl Kaysen, Phil Neal, and Louis B. Schwartz.

114. "Studies in the Regulation of Economic Activity," p. 31. William Baxter, an economics-oriented legal scholar who would later serve as Reagan's first antitrust chief, was another notable conservative.

115. These included figures like Paul MacAvoy and George Eads (CEA members under presidents Ford and Carter), Stephen Breyer (a key figure in airline deregulation, as well as future Supreme Court justice), and James C. Miller III (FTC chair and OMB director under Reagan). "Studies in the Regulation of Economic Activity," pp. 17, 31; Eads (1971); Breyer and MacAvoy (1974); Douglas and Miller (1974). Eads would also, in the early 1970s, serve as special economic advisor at the Antitrust Division.

116. Derthick and Quirk (1985: 38).

117. See Cox (1969); Esposito (1970); Zwick (1971); Green (1972) for examples of Nader critiques.

118. Stigler (1971: 17).

119. Domnarski (2016).

120. Kitch (1983: 184); Manne (2005: 310–11). For examples of this work, see Manne (1965; 1966).

121. Its economics faculty included Chicago's Harold Demsetz and UCLA's Armen Alchian.

122. Manne (2005); Lovett (1974: 400–401); Teles (2008).

123. On Chicago's patrons, see, for example, Van Horn and Mirowski (2009); Van Horn and Klaes (2011); Kitch (1983: 180–81); but also see Caldwell (2011). On the position of big business ca. 1970, see Collins (1981); Blyth (2002); Mizruchi (2013).

124. Teles (2008: 107–8).

125. Hovenkamp (2009a); for Johnson's report, see Neal et al. (1969).

126. Kauper (1984: 127).

127. Katzmann (1980: 38–39).

128. Kitch (1983); FTC (1974: ii); see Eisner (1991: 167–72) for one account of this period, as well as Klausner and Steel (1978); ABA Antitrust Section (1981).

129. Quoted in Ameringer (2008: 83).

130. Medvetz (2012: 101).

131. Stahl (2016: ch. 1); Smith (1991: 178–79).

132. See, for example, Cohen and Stigler (1971); Demsetz (1973); Posner (1973b); Peltzman (1974).

133. Stahl (2016: ch. 2).

134. Stahl (2016: 83).

135. Canedo (2008: 297).

136. Smith (1993: 179–80); Stahl (2016: 83–84).

137. See the masthead of early issues of *Regulation* (full text available at http://www.cato.org/regulation/archives) for information on the center's staffing.

138. "The Pentagon's Whiz Kids" (1962).

139. Hone (2016); Peck and Scherer (1962).

140. Zwick (1969a).

Chapter 5. The Economic Style and Social Policy

1. "Memorandum to Heads of Departments and Agencies," Lyndon B. Johnson, 25 August 1965, folder "FI Finance 12/1/64–8/25/65," Papers of Lyndon Baines Johnson, EX FI 11/22/63, Box 1, LBJ Archives.

2. Brown (1983: 17).

3. P.L. 88-452.

4. Blumenthal (1969); Moynihan (1969b).

5. O'Connor (2001: 167–73).

6. Cloward and Ohlin (2013 [1960]) is the classic example of this perspective.

7. "Poverty and Urban Policy: Kennedy Library and Brandeis University Conference Oral History Interview—JFK #1, 6/16/73," John F. Kennedy Presidential Library, pp. 217–18; Brauer (1982); Matusow (1984: 119–26); Gillette (2010); Huret (2018).

8. On the relationship between economists and other social scientists during the War on Poverty, see Fleury (2010) and Forget (2011); on human capital theory and the Heller CEA, see Holden and Biddle (2017). See also Gillette (2010: 6); Brauer (1982); Jardini (1996); O'Connor (2001); Huret (2018).

9. Berkowitz (1995); Oberlander (2003: 76–77); Jost (2003); Quadagno (2005).

10. Jeffrey (1978); Kantor (1991); Loss (2012).

11. Coan (1969); Pritchett (2008: 2).

12. "Memorandum to Heads of Departments and Agencies," LBJ Archives.

13. Jardini (1996: 339–42); Schultze (1969). On Schultze's view of PPBS, see also Schultze (1968).

14. Wildavsky (1966: 305).

15. On the backgrounds of the men leading these offices, see Gorham (1986: 1–4) and Levine (1969: 2). See Harper et al. (1969) and Doh (1971) on the relative success of these PPBS offices.

16. Blumenthal (1969); Moynihan (1969a).

17. O'Connor (2001: 168–69); Administrative History, Office of Economic Opportunity, Volume I, Box 1, LBJ Archives, pp. 59–62.

18. Larochelle (2019).

19. Jardini (1996: 339–41).

20. The 8 October 1964 memo, "Is There a Hitch in OEO's Future?" is quoted in Jardini (1996: 335–36).

21. Greenstone and Peterson (1973); Quadagno (1994); Cazenave (2007); Larochelle (2019).

22. Cazenave (2007: 151–52); see also Franklin (1965) and the oral histories in Gillette (2010: ch. 9).

23. October 1965 memo quoted in Cazenave (2007: 152); emphasis in original. See also Stossel (2004: 411); Lemann (1988); Califano (1991: 79); Bauman (2008).

24. U.S. GAO (1969: 4); Hinton (2016: 68–72). See Bauman (2007: 281–83) on how the failure of War on Poverty funds to reach the community was a contributor to Watts.

25. Jardini (1996: 334–40); O'Connor (2001: 176).

26. See folder "Definition of Poverty," Box 2, OEO Office of Planning, Research and Evaluation Subject File, 1964–1972, Records of Agencies for Economic Opportunity and Legal Services, RG 381, NARA. Watts (1968) nicely captures the two conceptualizations.

27. O'Connor (2001: 178–79).

28. Williams (1971: 6–7).

29. See Friedman (1962); Brauer (1982: 108).

30. Folder "Negative Income Taxation—1965," Box 4, OEO Office of Planning, Research and Evaluation Subject File, 1964–1972, Records of Agencies for Economic Opportunity and

Legal Services, RG 381, NARA. See O'Connor (2001: 186–87) on the challenges of evaluating Community Action programs.

31. Memorandum from Shriver to Schultze, "National Anti-Poverty Plan" (n.d.), folder "OEO Five-Year Plan Cal. 1965," Box 3, OEO Office of Planning, Research and Evaluation Subject File, 1964–1972, Records of Agencies for Economic Opportunity and Legal Services, RG 381, NARA.

32. On Shriver, see Levine (1969: 7); Stossel (2004).

33. Memorandum from Shriver to Schultze, "National Anti-Poverty Plan."

34. American Presidency Project (1965).

35. "Justification for Revisions in Budget Bureau Proposed OEO Budget under $1.5 Billion Ceiling," 19 December 1965, folder "OEO Five-Year Plan Cal. 1965," Box 3, OEO Office of Planning, Research and Evaluation Subject File, 1964–1972, Records of Agencies for Economic Opportunity and Legal Services, RG 381, NARA.

36. Herbert J. Kramer, quoted in Gillette (2010: 405).

37. O'Connor (2001: 179–81).

38. O'Connor (2001: 187–90).

39. On the congressional battle, see Gillette (2010: 361–66); on Shriver's departure, see Gillette (2010: 395–99).

40. O'Connor (2001: 190–91).

41. "The Department of Health, Education, and Welfare during the Administration of President Lyndon B. Johnson," pp. 1–2, folder "Volume I, Part I, Office of the Secretary, Assistant Secretary for: Administration, Comptroller, Planning and Evaluation, Education, Health and Scientific Affairs," Administrative History, Department of Health, Education, and Welfare Volume I, Part I & II, Box 1, LBJ Archives.

42. Gorham (1986: 1–4).

43. Gorham (1986: 6); Departmental History, Office of the Assistant Secretary for Planning and Evaluation, pp. 3–4, folder "Assistant Secretary for Planning and Evaluation," Administrative History, Department of Health, Education, and Welfare, Volume I, Parts I & II, Box 1, LBJ Archives.

44. Gorham (1986: 24).

45. Williams (1971: 174).

46. See Rivlin (1969) on the lack of program information faced by ASPE, as well as Drew (1967: 11–13). Gorham (1986: 8); "Sharpening the Knife That Cuts the Public Pie," lecture dated 20 December 1967, folder "Articles by William Gorham," Box 1, Personal Papers of William Gorham, LBJ Archives.

47. Departmental History, Office of the Assistant Secretary for Planning and Evaluation, p. 16; see also chapter 3 of this book.

48. Departmental History, Office of the Assistant Secretary for Planning and Evaluation, p. 6.

49. Alice Rivlin to Robert Grosse, 21 February 1966, folder "Programming," Box 1, Personal Papers of William Gorham, LBJ Presidential Library.

50. Rivlin, quoted in Botner (1970: 426).

51. Gorham (1986: 7).

52. Gorham (1986: 14); see also Drew (1967).

53. Gladieux and Wolanin (1976: 37).

54. Gladieux and Wolanin (1976: 39).

55. The administration was following the lead of a 1966 task force led by University of North Carolina president William Friday and heavily weighted with leaders of universities, which produced a report that strongly leaned toward institutional aid (Kerr 1984: 42–49). Also see Graham (1984) on the politics leading up to and following the Higher Education Act of 1965.

56. See Gladieux and Wolanin (1976: 48–49) for some discussion of economists' position on student aid.

57. Kerr (1984: 49).

58. Kerr (1984: 48–51). On Rivlin's replacement of Gorham, see Departmental History, Office of the Assistant Secretary for Planning and Evaluation, p. 4.

59. Kerr (1984: 51–52); U.S. HEW (1969).

60. Gladieux and Wolanin (1976: 59–60).

61. O'Connor (2001: 226); Doh (1971: 70); Williams (1990: 44–45); Falkson (1980: 5); Steensland (2008: 87–89).

62. U.S. GAO (1969: 101); Harper et al. (1969: 624).

63. U.S. DOL (1977); Lawlor (1979: 53–54); Weir (1993: 109); Breslau (1998: ch. 2).

64. Breslau (1998: ch. 2). Economists in leadership positions at ASPER during the 1970s included Orley Ashenfelter (Princeton 1970), George E. Johnson (Berkeley 1966), Ernst W. Stromsdorfer (Washington 1962), Frank P. Stafford (Chicago 1968), Alan L. Gustman (Michigan 1969), and Daniel S. Hamermesh (Yale 1969) (Breslau 1998: 57; Krueger 2014: 585).

65. O'Connor (2001: 238); Kraemer et al. (1987: 134–36).

66. P.L. 89-174.

67. Weaver received his economics PhD in 1933; Pritchett (2008: 30).

68. Pritchett (2008: 120); National Research Council (2008: 12); Harper et al. (1969: 625, 627, 631).

69. National Research Council (2008: 13).

70. National Research Council (2008: 12); U.S. DHUD (2016: 6); Lamb (2005: ch. 3); Bonastia (2006: ch. 4).

71. Orlebeke (2000); Arias (2013).

72. O'Connor (2001: 217–19).

73. McLaughlin (1974: v, 3).

74. McLaughlin (1974: 1–3).

75. Samuel Halperin, quoted in McLaughlin (1974: 3).

76. Gorham (1967: 8).

77. Gorham (1967: 6).

78. McLaughlin (1974: 35); see also Rivlin (1971: 79–85).

79. Rossi and Lyall (1976: 10, 169); Ennis (1979).

80. Levine (1975: 21).

81. "Mathematica," folder "Miscellaneous 1959, 1960, ND," Box 91, Oskar Morgenstern Papers, David M. Rubenstein Rare Book and Manuscript Library, Duke University.

82. Frumkin and Francis (2015: 413); "Mathematica, Inc.," folder "Introduce Mathematica, 1963–1971," Box 91, Oskar Morgenstern Papers.

83. Rossi and Lyall (1976: 8).

84. Rossi and Lyall (1976: 11).

85. "Mathematica, Inc.," folder "Introduce Mathematica, 1963–1971."

86. Just before the NIT study, Mathematica's principal staff included three mathematics PhDs, four economics PhDs, an MS in management engineering, and Oskar Morgenstern, a game theorist whose doctorate was actually in political science. "Mathematica," folder "Mathematica, 1969, 1975, 1977, N.D.," Box 91, Oskar Morgenstern Papers. NAS report is quoted in O'Connor (2001: 219).

87. Rossi and Lyall (1976: 10, 171).

88. Rossi and Lyall (1976: 171).

89. O'Connor (2001: ch. 9).

90. Contextual clues suggest the bill was likely the Child Health Act.

91. Gorham (1986: 9–10). Gorham's account can be found in several places—see also Lei (2014); Frumkin and Francis (2015: 404–5); Rich (2004: 48)—but I have not seen corroborating evidence that he was the original source of the set-aside.

92. U.S. GAO (1973: 41–53).

93. Buchanan and Wholey (1972).

94. McLaughlin (1974: 82), quoting an interview with Joseph Froomkin, head of the Office of Program Planning and Evaluation, the Office of Education's analytic office.

95. Jardini (1996: 358).

96. Jardini (1996: 358–59).

97. Quoted in Jardini (1996: 400).

98. Departmental History, Office of the Assistant Secretary for Planning and Evaluation, p. 4; see also Gorham (1986: 22–25) on his decision to leave ASPE, which he viewed as having by then secured PPBS's future at HEW, to lead Urban.

99. Smith (1993: 153); Light (2005: 224).

100. Gorham (1986: 24–25); Smith (1993: 152); Jardini (1996: 404–5).

101. Frumkin and Francis (2015: 408).

102. Jardini (1996: 417).

103. Carroll et al. (1972), especially chs. 3 and 4; see also Gramlich and Koshel (1975).

104. Munnell (1986: 1–2).

105. President's Committee on Urban Housing (1968: 72); Hays (2012: 101–18).

106. Lowry (1982: 22).

107. Orlebeke (2000: 503); Arias (2013: 52, 57–58).

108. Newhouse (1993: 4); Manning et al. (1987: 272); Greenberg et al. (2003: 72–73); see also Welfare Reform Academy (2014).

109. Gueron and Rolston (2013: 23–28).

110. While founding director Mitchell Sviridoff was not an economist, most of the Supported Work Advisory Committee that became MDRC's board of directors were, as was MDRC's research director (Gueron and Rolston 2013: 28, 92).

111. Wholey (1970).

112. See, for example, Rossi and Wright (1984); Weiss (1987); House (1990); Shadish et al. (1991); Alkin (2012); Frumkin and Francis (2015).

113. "UOS Division Report: January, 1974," folder "Mathematica: Projects, 1970–1977," and "Mathematica Expects Record 1975 Revenues, Flat Income Before Extraordinary Items," folder "Memoranda 1974–1977," Box 91, Oskar Morgenstern Papers.

114. Frumkin and Francis (2015).

115. Schorr (1966b); Steensland (2008: 85); McCabe and Berman (2016); McCabe (2018).

116. Cohen and Friedman (1972: 12).

117. Friedman (1962); O'Connor (2001).

118. Tobin (1966); Schorr (1966a).

119. Schorr (1966a); Tobin (1966); see also Tobin (1967) for another argument against family allowance on efficiency grounds, as well as Kershaw (1970); Levine (1970); and Rivlin (1971).

120. Burke and Burke (1974: 38).

121. Burke and Burke (1974: 38).

122. Burke and Burke (1974: 38).

123. Steensland (2008: 79–80); see also Burke and Burke (1974).

124. The following account draws particularly on Burke and Burke (1974); Hoff-Wilson (1991); and Steensland (2008); all of which cover the development and trajectory of Nixon's Family Assistance Plan in some detail. See Hoff-Wilson (1991: 91); Steensland (2008: 87).

125. Departmental History, Office of the Assistant Secretary for Planning and Evaluation, pp. 3–4, folder "Assistant Secretary for Planning and Evaluation," Administrative History, Department of Health, Education, and Welfare, Volume I, Parts I & II, Box 1, Papers of Lyndon Baines Johnson, President, 1963–1969, LBJ Presidential Library; Hoff-Wilson (1991: 92–93); Steensland (2008: 88). Bateman, who was only thirty at the time, later became a vice president of the Urban Institute (Burke and Burke 1974: 53).

126. Hoff-Wilson (1991: 100).

127. Hoff-Wilson (1991: 93).

128. Burke and Burke (1974: 39).

129. Williams (1975: 434); Moynihan (1973: 554); Steensland (2008: 153–55). See Williams more generally for an evaluation of the role of policy analysis across competing accounts of the Nixon's Family Assistance Program.

130. O'Connor (2001: 141–42).

131. Both were passed as the Social Security Amendments of 1965, P.L. 89-97. See Oberlander (2003: 30–31) and Quadagno (2005: 33–34) as well as Berkowitz (1995: ch. 10) for a detailed account of the legislative battle leading up to the passage of Medicare.

132. Oberlander (2003: 24, 30–31); Quadagno (2005: 73–75); see also Starr (1982: 363–78) for coverage of this period.

133. Oberlander (2003: 24).

134. Quadagno (2005: ch. 3); Smith (2016).

135. Derickson (2002); Hoffman (2012).

136. Zelizer (1998).

137. Jost (2007: ch. 6); D. M Fox (1979); Klarman (1979); Melhado (1998).

138. Arrow (1963); Fleury (2012: 13–14).

139. Social Security Administration (1968).

140. U.S. Department of Health, Education, and Welfare (1967).

141. U.S. Department of Health, Education, and Welfare (1967); Social Security Administration (1968); Institute of Medicine (1979: 76).

142. Quadagno (2005: 112).

143. Quadagno (2005: 112–13). See the *Congressional Record*, 25 January 1971, 284–313, for the text of the bill.

144. Greenberg et al. (2003: 72–73); Welfare Reform Academy (2014).

145. Pauly (1968).

146. Pauly (1968); Levins (2017).

147. See, for example, Arrow (1968) for a respectful response; see Hoffman (2006) for a broader history of cost-sharing in U.S. healthcare.

148. Melhado (1998: 247).

149. Interim results were first published in Newhouse et al. (1981).

150. Newhouse (1993: 4); Manning et al. (1987: 272); Greenberg et al. (2003: 72–73); see also Welfare Reform Academy (2014).

151. On the HIE's impact, see Jost (2007).

152. Nyman (2007: 760); he points to Feldstein (1973) as well as Pauly (1968).

153. Falkson (1980: 5).

154. Falkson (1980: 10).

155. Falkson (1980: 10).

156. Brown (1983: 18).

157. Brown (1983: 17).

158. Falkson (1980); Brown (1983); see also Starr (1982).

159. Quadagno (2005: 118–20); Wainess (1999).

160. Altman (2003: 13–16).

161. Rivlin (1974).

162. Altman and Shachtman (2011: ch. 1).

163. Altman and Shachtman (2011: 54, 47). See also Morrill 2013 for an account of ASPE during this period.

164. See, for example, Freed and Das (2015) for a comparison of Nixon's plan with Obama's Affordable Care Act.

165. Smith (2016); Ward (2017); Hoffman (2012: ch. 7); Derickson (2002).

166. *Congressional Record*, 25 January 1971, 288.

167. See Melhado (1998: 233) for an extensive list of citations to sources critical of cost-sharing ca. 1967–71.

168. Melhado (1998: 236); Greenberg et al. (2003: 73); Hoffman (2012: 163).

169. Rivlin (1974).

170. Orlebeke (2000); Hays (2012); von Hoffman (2012).

171. Olsen (1969); Arias (2013); Winnick (1995).

172. Johnson (2016: 75); Bonastia (2006); Mason (2014).

173. On economic analysis at HUD's Office of Policy Development and Research, see National Research Council (2008: 13); Lstiburek (2010); U.S. Department of Housing and Urban Development (2016). On EHAP, see Struyk and Bendick (1981); Winnick (1995); Johnson (2016); and especially Arias (2013). On Section 8, see Kim (2016); Hays (2012); von Hoffman (2012); Johnson (2016).

174. Lamb (2005); Pedriana and Stryker (2017).

175. Coan (1969); Pritchett (2008: 2). See Rosen (2020) for an examination of this policy in the current period.

176. Gladieux and Wolanin (1976); Thomas and Brady (2005).

177. For example, see Pincus (1971); Carroll et al. (1972); Pascal and Pincus (1973) for reviews of RAND's early work on education.

178. On education as a production function, see Bowles (1970); Hanushek (1972); on choice and competition, see Weiler (1972); Hall (1972).

179. P.L. 92-318 § 405; Gladieux and Wolanin (1976: 70, 117).

180. Sproull et al. (1978: 28–32, 45, 72, 117); Timpane (1982).

181. Sproull et al. (1978: 28, 91–93, 113–14, 117); Atkinson and Jackson (1992: 59–60); Lagemann (2000: ch. 6).

182. Atkinson and Jackson (1992: 53).

183. See, for example, Lagemann (2000); Mosteller and Boruch (2002); Angrist (2004: 202); Rudalevige (2009).

Chapter 6. The Economic Style and Market Governance

1. On the dialectic relationship between antitrust and intellectual property, see Christophers (2016).

2. Medvetz (2012).

3. Brown (1983: 17).

4. 15 U.S.C. §§ 1–7.

5. For various takes on the Sherman Act, see Bork (1978); Lande (1982); Millon (1988); Levinson (2011); Orbach (2013); Dameron (2016); Christophers (2016: 149–53).

6. Levinson (2011); 15 U.S.C. § 13.

7. Peritz (1996: ch. 3); Vaheesan (2014).

8. 310 U.S. 496.

9. Fligstein (1990: 196).

10. 370 U.S. 294 (1962); see also *Von's Grocery Co. et al.* (384 U.S. 270 [1966]) and *Utah Pie Co. v. Continental Baking Co.* (386 U.S. 685 [1967]) for other examples of aggressive enforcement.

11. 370 U.S. 294 (1962); see also, for example, *United States v. Von's Grocery et al.*, 384 U.S. 270 (1966).

12. 374 U.S. 321 (1963); see Kaysen and Turner (1959) for the economic theory.

13. 374 U.S. 321 (1963).

14. Hemphill and Posner (2015).

15. 74 U.S. 321 (1963).

16. Turner (1964: 1324).

17. Domnarski (2016).

18. Bork and Bowman (1965: 368).

19. Eisner (1991: 16–17).

20. Williamson (1995: 63).

21. Hurley (2006); Gaughan (2017).

22. P.L. 63-212 §7; "Sound Antitrust Advice" (1965b); Fligstein (1990: ch. 6).

23. U.S. DOJ (1968: 1–2).

24. Greene (2006); Newborn and Snider (1992).

25. Weaver (1977: 134).

26. Weaver (1977: 132–35); Fligstein (1990: 207).

27. On conglomerate mergers generally in this era, see Hurley (2006); Gaughan (2017); for Turner's position, see Turner (1964).

28. Fligstein (1990: 206–10).

29. Quoted in Mueller (1983: 23–25).

30. Feldstein (2010: 226–29); Anderson (2000: 194–95).

31. Feldstein (2010: 226–29).

32. Smith (1972); Kauper (2007). See Kauper (1969) for a statement of his views shortly before the appointment.

33. Kauper (1977; 1980; 2007); Posner (1971).

34. Eisner (1991: 135–38); Kauper (1984; 2007); Hay (2008).

35. Kauper (2007).

36. Sims and Herman (1997); see also Eisner (1991: 144).

37. Eisner (1991: 138–39).

38. Eisner (1991: 172).

39. FTC (1971: ii); Decker et al. (1972: 56); Eisner (1991: 168).

40. FTC (1974: ii); Kitch (1983).

41. Eisner (1991: 167).

42. Quoted in Eisner (1991: 168–69).

43. Eisner (1991: 169–71); see also Klausner and Steel (1978); ABA Antitrust Section (1981).

44. Cowan (1978; 1979).

45. Cowan (1979; 1980).

46. Litvack (1982a: 850).

47. Pertschuk quoted in Eisner (1991: 175).

48. Pertschuk (1983); Eisner (1991: 171, 174–79); Pautler (2003: 49–54).

49. Eisner (1991: 179).

50. Peritz (1996: 221–28); the cases were *United States v. Arnold, Schwinn & Co.* (386 U.S. 568 [1967]); *FTC v. Procter & Gamble Co.* (388 U.S. 365 [1967]); and *Utah Pie Co. v. Continental Baking Co.* (386 U.S. 685 [1967]).

51. 374 U.S. 321 (1963).

52. See, for example, *United States v. General Dynamics Corp. et al.* (415 U.S. 486 [1974]) and *United States v. Marine Bancorporation, Inc., et al.* (418 U.S. 602 [1974]).

53. 429 U.S. 477 (1977).

54. 433 U.S. 36 (1977); Lehman and Phelps (2005). The 1967 decision was *United States v. Arnold, Schwinn & Co.* (388 U.S. 365 [1967]).

55. 433 U.S. 36 (1977).

56. Bork (1978: 14).

57. 442 U.S. 330 (1979).

58. See, for example, Crane (2014); Barak (2014); Dameron (2016); Vaheesan (2014); Orbach (2013); Meese (2010).

59. Eisner (1991: 188).

60. Eisner (2000).

61. These included the Motor Carrier Act of 1935 and the Civil Aeronautics Act of 1938. See Eisner (2000); Horwitz (1991: 73–74).

62. Bernstein (1955); Huntington (1952); Jaffe (1954).

63. Kolko (1963); Weinstein (1968); Sklar (1988); see Novak (2013) for an overview.

64. Fellmeth et al. (1970).

65. Johnson (1965); on "foreshadowings of deregulation" during the Johnson administration, see Welborn (1993: 220–27).

66. Rose et al. (2006: 152–56).

67. Rose et al. (2006: 158); Derthick and Quirk (1988: 38–39).

68. Rose et al. (2006: 158), bracketed text in original quote.

69. Rose et al. (2006: 160–61).

70. Seevers (1975: 201).

71. Derthick and Quirk (1985: 40); Breyer (2008). See also Kauper (2007) for a similar list of locations housing deregulation advocates by the mid-1970s.

72. U.S. DOL (2021).

73. See Economists Conference on Inflation (1974: 6–7, 14–15) for a list of attendees.

74. Moore (1972); Economists Conference on Inflation (1974: 11–13).

75. Economists Conference on Inflation (1974: 11–13). The goals included removing price, entry, and trade restrictions in the transportation, energy, banking, and agricultural sectors.

76. Economists Conference on Inflation (1974: 157–58).

77. Ford (1974); see also Mieczkowski (2005: 184–87).

78. Rose et al. (2006: 160).

79. Derthick and Quirk (1985: 48–49).

80. Breyer and MacAvoy (1974); see also Breyer (1973).

81. Derthick and Quirk (1985: 40); see also Breyer's account (2008). See also Kauper (2007) pointing to the reasoning behind choosing airlines as the first target for deregulation.

82. Derthick and Quirk (1985: 43).

83. Derthick and Quirk (1985: 43); Breyer (2008).

84. Breyer (2008).

85. Rose et al. (2006: 169–76); see also Mieczkowski (2005: 185–87).

86. American Presidency Project (1976b).

87. Derthick and Quirk (1985: 58–59, 66).

88. Derthick and Quirk (1985: 88, 90); Behrman (1980: 103–8).

89. Rose et al. (2006: 179–81).

90. Rose et al. (2006: 186); Derthick and Quirk (1985: 53). In contrast, Biven (2002: 218) plays up his support during the campaign. Carter signed the Airline Deregulation Act (P.L. 95-504) in 1978, and the Motor Carrier Act (P.L. 96-296) and the Staggers Rail Act (P.L. 96-448) in 1980.

91. Derthick and Quirk (1985: 54).

92. Rose et al. (2006: 191); Derthick and Quirk (1985: 66).

93. Derthick and Quirk (1985: 66–67, 99).

94. Rose et al. (2006: 188–89).

95. Derthick and Quirk (1985: 104).

96. See Derthick and Quirk (1985: 121) on the near-unanimity of economists' position.

97. Schultze (1977b).

98. See, for example, Nordhaus and Litan (1983) and Eads and Fix (1984b) for their respective takes on regulation. Eads in particular was part of the Brookings I/O network and had published on the airline industry; see, for example, Eads (1971).

99. For example, see Canedo (2008: 214–15) on CWPS's role in drafting of an airline deregulation proposal under Ford, along with the CEA, Office of Management and Budget, and the Antitrust Division.

100. Derthick and Quirk (1985: 69).

101. McCraw (1986: 231); see, for example, Dirlam and Kahn (1954) versus Kahn (1970).

102. McCraw (1986: 233–37); Kahn (1970; 1971).

103. McCraw (1986: 242–59).

104. Breyer (2008).

105. McCraw (1986: 224).

106. Derthick and Quirk (1985: 78–79); Levine (1965).

107. Shepherd (1996: 948).

108. American Presidency Project (1977); Johnson (1984).

109. McCraw (1986: 275).

110. Derthick and Quirk (1985: 149).

111. Rose et al. (2006: 187–88).

112. Derthick and Quirk (1985: 82).

113. Derthick and Quirk (1985: 70–82).

114. Rose et al. (2006: 200–201, 205); Derthick and Quirk (1985: 149).

115. Derthick and Quirk (1985: 148–51).

116. P.L. 95-504; P.L. 96-296; P.L. 96-448. See Derthick and Quirk (1985: 97–98) on the Motor Carrier Act, and Rose et al. (2006: 208) on the Staggers Rail Act.

117. Rose et al. (2006: 218–19).

118. Horwitz (1991: 12–13).

119. See, for example, Economides (2005: 52) on economists' interpretation of the public interest in telecommunications regulation.

120. Horwitz (1991: 225–33); Derthick and Quirk (1985: 6–7, 19, 59–60).

121. Eisner (2000: 186); Derthick and Quirk (1985: 79); Jung (1996: 26); Reinecke (2019: 429).

122. On telecommunications regulation and deregulation to 1990, Horwitz (1991) is definitive; see Reinecke (2019: 293–753) for a thorough treatment of the 1970s to early 2000s.

123. See, for example, O'Neill et al. (1992); DeLor (2014); Vietor (1996); Vanatta (2015); Krippner (2011); Funk and Hirschman (2014); Suárez and Kodolny (2011); Dobbin and Jung (2010); Kwak (2013); MacKenzie (2006).

124. Starr (1982); Quadagno (2005); Klarman (1979); D. M. Fox (1979).

125. For RAND examples, see Enthoven (1978b; 1978a; 1980); Newhouse (1993). For Chicago examples, see Havighurst (1970a; 1970b; 1977; 2004); Greenberg (1978). For a workshop representing both, see National Research Council (1975). For a review, see Melhado (1988; 1998).

126. Brown (1983: 17) adapts the phrase from Schultze (1977: 13).

127. Many of the principles of managed competition are laid out in Enthoven (1978b; 1978a; 1980), but the term comes from Enthoven (1988).

128. Schmidt (1999); Brown (1983); Ameringer (2008).

129. Starr (1982); Melhado (1988); Ameringer (2008).

Chapter 7. The Economic Style and Social Regulation

1. P.L. 92-500.

2. Carson (1962); Kline (2007: 73–75).

3. Nader (1965).

4. MacLaury (1981).

5. See, for example, Noble (1986: 79).

6. Wilson (1984: 211).

7. NHTSA was initially called the National Traffic Safety Bureau; see P.L 89-563.

8. Halvorson (2017: 42–43).

9. Mashaw and Harfst (1991: 59–61).

10. Noble (1986: 89–90).

11. Mashaw and Harfst (1991: 63–65).

12. Hays (1989: 30).

13. Marcus (1980a: 272); Milazzo (2006: 221).

14. Merrill (1997: 1061–62); see, for example, Cox et al. (1969); Esposito and Silverman (1970); Fellmeth et al. (1970); Zwick and Benstock (1971); Green (1972) for various Naderite critiques.

15. Marcus (1980a); Wilson (1984).

16. Lowi (1969). See chapter 4 on the cross-disciplinary emergence of critiques of regulatory capture.

17. Wilson (1984: 211–12); see also Marcus (1980a: 268–69), regarding environmental policy in particular.

18. Noble (1986: 89–90); P.L. 91-596 § 6(b)(5).

19. P.L. 92-500; P.L. 92-516.

20. Hoberg (1992: 72).

21. See, for example, Roberts (1980) for a critique of the Clean Water Act from an economic perspective.

22. U.S. President (1965: 152); see also U.S. President (1966: 120–21); U.S. President (1970: 93). The Nixon administration, prompted by its economists, sought a tax on lead additives (U.S. House 1970).

23. Based on a review of all hearings listed in the legislative history of the Clean Air Act in ProQuest Congressional; see U.S. Senate (1970) for the exception, and White (1976) for supporting evidence. A review of the nine-part hearings on the Clean Water Act, *Water Pollution Control Legislation*, showed similarly limited influence of economists.

24. Roberts (1980: 97).

25. Roberts (1980: 105).

26. Liroff (1976); P.L. 91-190.

27. Culhane (1990: 685); see also Bartlett (1986) on the "ecological rationality" of NEPA.

28. Andrews (1984: 53). Early CEQ reports consistently treat pollution as an externality, and many devote whole chapters to "the economic costs of pollution and pollution abatement."

29. Liroff (1976: 11); Jackson quoted in Fishman (1973: 210).

30. Diver (1981: 409, 411).

31. On the history of cost-benefit analysis, see especially Porter (1995: ch. 7), but also Boland et al. (2009: 85–87); Pearce (2000: 49–50); Hammond (1960: 3–6); Hanley and Splash (1993: 4–8); Holmes (1972; 1979).

32. For work tying cost-benefit analysis to welfare economics, see McKean (1958); Eckstein (1958); Krutilla and Eckstein (1958). Among other connections, Charles Hitch, head of RAND's

Economics Department in the 1950s, was on the board of RFF (Krutilla and Eckstein 1958: v) and would later become its president (Resources for the Future 1977: viii). On the history of RFF, see Resources for the Future (1977). See Banzhaf (2010) on the competing RAND and RFF traditions in cost-benefit analysis.

33. P.L. 92-516 §102.

34. Culhane (1990: 686).

35. *Calvert Cliffs' Coordinating Committee, Inc., v. AEC*, 449 F.2d 1109 (1971).

36. Burmeister (1972: 1092); Buntain (1974); Fishman (1973: 221–27).

37. Buntain (1974: 542).

38. Buntain (1974).

39. See Burmeister (1972) for a relatively early discussion linking *Calvert Cliffs* and other early court decisions more explicitly to the formal welfare economics tradition of cost-benefit analysis.

40. Andrews (1984: 46–47); Bromley (2000: 7–8).

41. Ford Vice President John S. Bugas, quoted in Conley (2006: 145).

42. Conley (2006: 155–56).

43. Tozzi (2011: 42).

44. Schmid (2008: 15).

45. Schmid (1969: 589).

46. Tozzi (2011: 42).

47. Executive Order 11523.

48. Conley (2006: 160), quoting Steck (1975: 266).

49. Conley (2006: 160).

50. Quarles (1976: 32).

51. Roberts (1980: 99); Landy et al. (1994: 34, 25–26); Cook (1988: 60).

52. Halvorson (2017: 81).

53. Halvorson (2017: 80–81); Marcus (1980b: 102–7). Alain Enthoven, a key disseminator of PPBS, helped develop the plan for how EPA would be structured (Marcus 1980b: 276–77).

54. Halvorson (2017: 84).

55. Steck (1975: 268).

56. Eads and Fix (1984b: 47).

57. Domestic Council Study Memorandum quoted in Conley (2006: 161–62).

58. Eads and Fix (1984b: 48); see also Conley (2006: 163–64); Percival (1991); Halvorson (2017: 114–16) as well as Tozzi (2011) for a firsthand account.

59. Tozzi (2011: 46–47). Tozzi's resume is available at http://www.thecre.com/pdf/TOZZI _Resume.pdf (accessed 27 July 2021).

60. Tozzi (2011: 43) mentions Robert Harrison and Jim Tang as other staffers who moved from the Army SAG to OMB.

61. Conley (2006: 165); Eads and Fix (1984b: 49).

62. Conley (2006: 165).

63. Quoted in Conley (2006: 165); see also Eads and Fix (1984b: 46–50). Tozzi (2011: 45) argues that claims that the Quality of Life Review was "a modest effort" relative to regulatory review under Carter or Reagan "underestimate [its] significance."

64. Eads and Fix (1984b: 50).

65. Eads and Fix (1984b: 49).

66. Costle (2001); see also Halvorson (2017: 81).

67. Eads and Fix (1984b: 50–53).

68. Eads (1971); Miller (2011a). Eads would later serve as a member of Carter's CEA; Miller would lead OMB's Office of Information and Regulatory Affairs, the FTC, and OMB itself at different points in the Reagan administration.

69. Eads and Fix (1984b: 53); see also Sabin (2016: 11).

70. Eads and Fix (1984b: 52).

71. Hopkins et al. (1981).

72. Eads (1971); Douglas and Miller (1974).

73. Letter from George Eads to Roger Strelow, 9 May 1975, online CWPS archives, available at http://cwps.mercatus.org/wp-content/uploads/1-0301.pdf (accessed 15 September 2016; no longer accessible).

74. Remarks of James C. Miller III before the American Management Association's First National Form on Business, Government and the Public Interest, 2 December 1976, online CWPS archives, available at http://cwps.mercatus.org/wp-content/uploads/6-0401.pdf (accessed 15 September 2016; no longer accessible).

75. See Hopkins et al. (1981: A1–A7).

76. Noble (1986: 166).

77. Noble (1986: 191).

78. Carlin (2006).

79. Mashaw and Harfst (1991: 189–90).

80. Mashaw and Harfst (1991: 191).

81. Sabin (2016).

82. On Schultze's selection by Carter, see Biven (2002: 54–55); on Schultze's role as budget director, see chapter 3.

83. Kneese and Schultze (1975); Schultze (1977a); see also Schultze (1968).

84. Eads and Fix (1984b: 55–60).

85. Executive Order 12044.

86. "Regulatory Reform: President Carter's Program," n.d., folder "Regulatory Reform [6]," Box 75, Charles L. Schultze Subject Files, Jimmy Carter Presidential Library.

87. Eads and Fix (1984b: 55–60).

88. The "big five" included ozone standards (EPA), surface mining rules (Interior), carcinogens (OSHA), handicapped retrofitting (Transportation), and sulfur emissions from new power plants (EPA). See "Certain Regulatory Problems," 1 December 1978, folder "Regulatory Reform [2]," Box 75, Charles L. Schultze Subject Files, Jimmy Carter Presidential Library. See Hopkins et al. (1981: A1–A7) for a complete list of regulations reviewed.

89. These included George Eads, who returned to the White House as a CEA member in 1979; CEA staffers Robert Litan and Lawrence J. White, who conducted many of the analyses; and Alfred Kahn, who became chairman of CWPS after his time at the Civil Aeronautics Board. See, for example, Eads and Fix (1984b); Litan (1983); White (1981); McCraw (1986).

90. Mashaw and Harfst (1991: 165).

91. Tolchin (1979).

92. Clark (1978).

93. Landy et al. (2007); Miller (1977: 18).

94. Quoted in Sabin (2016: 11), emphasis in original.

95. Cook (1988: 70); see also Costle (2001).

96. Mashaw and Harfst (1991: 166–73; 200–201).

97. Noble (1986: 191).

98. Sabin (2016: 23); Noble (1986: 164); see *Natural Resource Defense Council v. Schultze* (U.S. District Court for the District of Columbia, Civil Action 79–153) and *Sierra Club v. Costle* (D.C. Court of Appeals, Civil Action 79–1565).

99. On disability rights, see Katzmann (1986); Berkowitz (1989); O'Brien (2001); Switzer (2003); Pettinicchio (2019). One of the "big five" social regulations RARG was concerned with was the requirement that public transportation systems be made accessible regardless of what could sometimes (as in the case of the New York City subway) be extraordinary cost.

100. The other four were carbon monoxide, nitrogen dioxide, sulfur dioxide, and particulates; lead was added a few years later.

101. Quoted in Halvorson (2017: 49).

102. P.L. 91-604.

103. P.L. 91-604; Landy et al. (1994: 49–50, 66); Halvorson (2017: 245–49).

104. Landy et al. (1994: 63–64, 67).

105. Landy et al. (1994: 67–68).

106. Memo from Barber to Hawkins quoted in Landy et al. (1994: 68).

107. Landy et al. (1994: 63, 70).

108. Landy et al. (1994: 69, 71–73).

109. Quoted in Landy et al. (1994: 75–76).

110. P.L. 91-604 §111.

111. Gerard and Lave (2007: 8).

112. Cook (1988: 64–65).

113. Cook (1988: 64–65); Landy et al. (1994); Halvorson (2017: ch. 5). Quotation is from U.S. EPA (1975: 58116).

114. Cook (1988: 65); Liroff (1986: 109–10); Levin (1982: 69). Cook attributes EPA's willingness to create a bubble option to the pressure it was under from the Quality of Life Review.

115. The use of "command and control" to refer to regulation appears to originate with Schultze (1977a), although the phrase was previously used in a military context.

116. Pigou (1912); see also Kumekawa (2017).

117. For example, U.S. Congress (1971a); U.S. Congress (1971b); Cook (1988: 40–41); Haveman (2014); Kneese and Schultze (1975); Schultze (1977a).

118. Crocker (1966); Dales (1968). See also Mishan (1967) for an early discussion of the concept.

119. Cook (1988: 45–46); see also Levin (1982: 68–70).

120. Cook (1988: 68–70).

121. Costle (2001); Kearns et al. (2014); Bornstein (1998; 2004).

122. Drayton (1980: 2).

123. Landy et al. (1994: 55); Cook (1988: 70).

124. Cook (1988: 127).

125. Cook (1988: 73–74, 77–78); Levin (1982: 71); Landy et al. (1994: 215–19).

126. Landy et al. (1994: 215–17); Levin (1982: 65).

127. Halvorson (2017: 227–29).

128. Levin (1982: 75); Cook (1988: 75).

129. Cook (1988: 71–72, 78); Levin (1982).

130. Liroff (1986: 51); Levin (1982: 92).

131. Cook (1988: 78); Meidinger (1985: 476).

132. Halvorson (2017: 230–32).

133. Mashaw and Harfst (1991: 59–61).

134. The National Traffic and Motor Vehicle Safety Act, P.L. 89-563 §102(2). On the dominance of engineering, see Mashaw and Harfst (1991: 172).

135. Mashaw and Harfst (1991: 114–15, 165–66, 191–93). See also Vinsel (2019) for a detailed discussion of competing forms of expertise in automotive regulation.

136. The Occupational Safety and Health Act, P.L. 91-596; see Noble (1986: 94).

137. Noble (1986: 96, 106–107); see *Industrial Union Department v. Hodgson*, 499 F.2d 467 (D.C. Cir. 1974).

138. Clark (1978); Tolchin (1979); Noble (1986: 174–75, 191).

139. Noble (1986: 172, 191).

140. The Federal Insecticide, Fungicide, and Rodenticide Act, rewritten in 1972, required EPA to "weigh the environmental and health risks [of pesticides] against the economic benefits of agricultural production"; Andrews (1999: 243), quoted in Conley (2006: 197). The Toxic Substances Control Act explicitly stated that, in regulating chemical substances that might impose health or environmental risks, the EPA "Administrator shall consider the environmental, economic, and social impact of any action"; P.L. 94-469 §2(c). See Morgenstern (1997: 8–9) for a review of cost-benefit considerations as addressed in major environmental laws up to the mid-1990s.

141. On NSPS, see Davis et al. (1977: 14); 486 F.2d 375 (1973). On endangered species, see Sinden (2005); Cannon (2010); 437 U.S. 153 (1978). On cotton dust, see Fisher (1984); 452 U.S. 490 (1981).

Chapter 8. How the Economic Style Replaced the Democratic Left

1. On the passage of Medicare and Medicaid, see (among others) Berkowitz (1995); Oberlander (2003); Quadagno (2005).

2. Quadagno (2005: 112–13); see *Congressional Record*, 25 January 1971, pp. 284–313, for the text of the bill.

3. Starr (1982: 382); Lyons (1971).

4. See, for example, U.S. DHEW (1967); Social Security Administration (1968); Davis (1975); Institute of Medicine (1979). The moral hazard literature begins with Pauly (1967); see Jost (2007: ch. 6); D. M. Fox (1979); Klarman (1979); Melhado (1998) for various accounts of the history of health economics.

5. Falkson (1980: 5); see chapter 5 on the creation of ASPE.

6. Altman (2003: 13–16). His title was deputy assistant secretary of planning and evaluation for health.

7. Altman and Shachtman (2011: ch. 1).

8. Wainess (1999: 312–15).

9. See, for example, Rivlin (1974).

10. Davis (1975: 162).

11. Wainess (1999); Altman and Shachtman (2011: ch. 1).

12. Starr (1982: 411); Quadagno (2005: 124).

13. Starr (1982: 413); Finbow (1998).

14. Davis (1975: 110).

15. Finbow (1998: 173); Quadagno (2005: 129).

16. Starr (1982: 413).

17. See, for example, Friedman and Kuznets (1945); Kessel (1958); Moore (1961).

18. Havighurst (2004: 109).

19. Havighurst (1970a: 232).

20. Starr (1982: 395).

21. Havighurst (2004: 109); Havighurst (1970c).

22. See Havighurst (1970a; 1970b) for the introduction to two special issues on healthcare; see Havighurst (1974) for an American Enterprise Institute conference featuring (among others) Johnson-era ASPE economist Robert N. Grosse and RAND Health Insurance Experiment director Joseph Newhouse, along with Mark Pauly ("moral hazard") and the ubiquitous Richard Posner. Other attendees included Stuart Altman of HEW, Yale law and economics scholar Guido Calabresi, future HEW deputy assistant secretary Karen Davis, and Chicago economist Reuben Kessel.

23. Ameringer (2008: 72–76, 92–93); *Goldfarb v. Virginia State Bar*, 421 U.S. 773 (1975).

24. Ameringer (2008: 100–101).

25. See Signs (2015) for a brief review of the FTC's activity in this area, as well as Ameringer (2008) and Greenberg (1978) for the conference proceedings.

26. Greenberg (1978: iv–vi).

27. See, for example, Weisbrod (1978) for an example of such arguments.

28. See, for example, U.S. Senate (1974a; 1974c; 1974b); Pertschuk (1983); Ameringer (2008: 88–90).

29. Finbow (1998: 173).

30. Melhado (1988: 87).

31. Enthoven (1978a: 709–10; 1978b: 653); see Enthoven (1988) for the term "managed competition."

32. Enthoven (1978b; 1978a; 1980).

33. Stevens (1981: 1159); see Oliver (1991) on the fate of several bills proposing plans modeled on Enthoven's.

34. Aaron (1983: 284), italics in original.

35. Aaron (1983).

36. See Fuchs (1974: 149–51). Fuchs, a strong advocate of universal comprehensive insurance, helped establish health economics as a field by creating programs at both the Ford Foundation and NBER in the 1960s (Fleury 2012: 13–14).

37. Shabecoff (1979).

38. Marquard (2014); Fein (1979: 353–54); see also Fein (1982) for a similar critique. Fein defined himself as an economist, but received his PhD in 1956 in what he called "political economy" (Fein 1994) and was a critic of the modern economic style.

39. See chapter 6.

40. Green (1972: ix); see also Cox et al. (1969) for Nader's report on the FTC.

41. Hart (1972); "Industrial Reorganization Act" (1973); see U.S. Senate (1973) and seven more volumes for hearings. The four-firm concentration ratio is the percentage of a given market controlled by the four largest firms within it.

42. Hart (1972: 40–41).

43. See, for example, "Antitrust Nominee" (1965a).

44. Neal et al. (1969: 24).

45. Kaysen and Turner (1959).

46. Neal et al. (1969); Hovenkamp (2009a).

47. Kaysen and Turner (1959); on the lineage of the bill, see "Industrial Reorganization Act" (1973); Hart (1972); Harris (1971); Neal et al. (1969).

48. See McGee (1971); Goldschmidt et al. (1974); Posner (1979) for summaries of some of these arguments.

49. Goldschmid et al. (1974: 339–40).

50. U.S. Senate (1973: 275–76).

51. Posner (1971: 513, 508).

52. Posner (1971: 501).

53. Areeda and Turner (1978: 110).

54. 433 U.S. 36 (1977).

55. Kovacic (2020: 470), citing Gavil (2002); see also Niefer (2018).

56. Kovacic (2007: 52–62).

57. 442 U.S. 330 (1979); see also Bork (1978); Crane (2014).

58. Eisner (1991); Katzmann (1980); see also chapter 6.

59. Stoller (2019: 341–347); Sims and Herman (1997: 876).

60. P.L. 94-435.

61. Sims and Herman (1997: 873–77).

62. Sims and Herman (1997); Eisner (1991: 144–45).

63. See, for example, Cowan (1978; 1979; 1980).

64. Averitt (2018).

65. Cowan (1979).

66. Cowan (1979). Kennedy's other bill would have "restore[d] the standing in law of consumers to bring civil price-fixing suits against companies" after the 1977 *Illinois Brick* Supreme Court decision eliminated it; although the bill made it out of committee, it did not become law.

67. For Pertschuk's account of these years, see Pertschuk (1983).

68. Litvack (1982b: 650).

69. Kovacic (2020: 471).

70. Schwartz (1979: 246).

71. Schwartz (1979: 267).

72. Schwartz (1979: 251).

73. Schwartz (1979: 247); see also E. M. Fox (1979) for a similar review of Areeda and Turner.

74. Noble (1986: ch. 5).

75. These included the Resource Conservation and Recovery Act (RCRA, 1976), the Toxic Substances Control Act (1976), and the Comprehensive Environmental Response, Compensation, and Liability Act, better known as Superfund (1980). See Wagner (2004).

76. Glickman (2009: 298).

77. See Baram (1980) and Fraas (1991) for discussions of which laws incorporated cost considerations and in what ways; see Blaise (2000) for an overview of this shift, and Cinti (1990) for cost-benefit debates in the context of RCRA specifically.

78. 437 U.S. 153 (1978); 452 U.S. 490 (1981); Schwartz (1981); Cannon (2010).

79. Barfield (1972); see also Ruff (1970) for an early articulation of this position.

80. Steck (1975).

81. Conley (2006); Percival (1991); Tozzi (2011); Miller (1977).

82. On program cost-effectiveness, see Schultze (1968; 1969).

83. Kneese and Schultze (1975: 117).

84. Schultze (1977a: 6, 29). "Command-and-control" is first introduced on p. 6 and is used several other times throughout the book.

85. Schultze (1977a); Rhoads (1985: 39).

86. Sabin (2016).

87. Sabin (2016: 12–13); Clark (1978: 1283–84).

88. Sabin (2016).

89. Notes, folder "Regulation: Ozone [1]," Box 74, Charles L. Schultze's Subject Files, Carter Presidential Library.

90. Hopkins and Stanley (2015); see also Eads (1982); Eads and Fix (1984b).

91. Clark (1978: 1283). See Landy et al. (1994) for similar dynamics around ozone standards.

92. Sabin (2016: 17–18); DeMuth (1980).

93. Tolchin (1979).

94. Schultze (1968: 96); see also Schultze (1982: 62).

95. Edmund Muskie speech at the University of Michigan, 14 February 1979, folder "Regulation," Box 73, Charles L. Schultze's Subject Files, Carter Presidential Library.

96. Kirschten (1979: 1526).

97. Letter from twenty-five groups on behalf of Public Citizen to President Carter, 2 November 1979, folder "Briefing Book: Regulatory Reform, 11/79 [3]," Box 130, Charles L. Schultze Briefing Book Files, Carter Presidential Library.

98. Baram (1980); Fraas (1991); Blaise (2000); Schwartz (1981); Cannon (2010).

99. On representation in the agencies, see Cook (1988: 70); Mashaw and Harfst (1991); Noble (1986: 191).

100. Burke and Burke (1974); Hoff-Wilson (1991); O'Connor (2001); Steensland (2008).

101. O'Connor (1998: 120–21); see also Lynn and Whitman (1981); Kraemer et al. (1987: 35–42, 128–36).

102. Derthick and Quirk (1985); Canedo (2008).

103. Ameringer (2008).

104. See, for example, Noble (1986); Mashaw and Harfst (1991); Conley (2006).

105. P.L. 73-416 §312.

106. Horwitz (1991); Jung (1996); Reinecke (2019).

107. Winnick (1995).

108. Lagemann (2000). While written by political scientists, Chubb and Moe's (1990) *Politics, Markets, and America's Schools*, published by the Brookings Institution, was very compatible with the economic style. Not all liberal economists agreed with its proposal for vouchers, but its argument for choice and competition appealed to many.

Chapter 9. The Economic Style in the Age of Reagan

1. American Presidency Project (1981).

2. Niskanen (1988).

3. Troy (2003: ch. 7); Williams (1990: ch. 4). The administration's embrace of Arthur Laffer and his arguments that lowering taxes would raise revenues is perhaps the best-known example; while Laffer was an economics PhD and once a junior faculty member at the University of Chicago, almost no academic economists agreed with his empirical claims (Berman and Milanes-Reyes 2013).

4. Williams (1990).

5. Eisner (1991).

6. Eads and Fix (1984a; 1984b).

7. Williams (1990: 41).

8. Terrel Bell, Reagan's first education secretary, quoted in Williams (1990: 13).

9. Education was hived off as its own department in 1980, but was less analytic from the start.

10. O'Connor (2001: 194).

11. Gorham (1986: 24); Williams (1990: 45); Radin (1991: 146). Radin implies that the unusually large number of staff under Carter was owing to "[e]xtensive use . . . of temporary appointment authority."

12. Williams (1990: 71); O'Connor (2001: 245, 344). The figures are for 1980 and 1988, respectively.

13. Williams (1990: 71).

14. O'Connor (2001: 244).

15. O'Connor (2001: 251).

16. U.S. Department of Housing and Urban Development (2016).

17. Radin (1991: 147).

18. U.S. GAO (1988: 9).

19. Sproull et al. (1978: 45); Williams (1990: 71).

20. Klarman (1979: 378); Williams (1990: 71).

21. Williams (1990: 70–71).

22. Frumkin and Francis (2015: 408–10).

23. O'Connor (2001: 244, 246).

24. Frumkin and Francis (2015: 408).

25. Frumkin and Francis (2015: 409–10).

26. O'Connor (2001: 245–46).

27. U.S. GAO (1988: 10), emphasis in original.

28. O'Connor (2001: 251).

29. O'Connor (2001: 251).

30. Fox (1991: 190).

31. Joyce (2011); Malbin (1979); Williams (1990: 71–72).

32. Williams (1990: 70); O'Connor (2001: 245).

33. O'Connor (2001: 246).

34. Bane and Ellwood (1983).

35. O'Connor (2001: 252–56).

36. The Interstate Commerce Commission, for example, saw an inflation-adjusted 54 percent reduction in its budget between 1980 and 1985, while the Civil Aeronautics Board experienced an 86 percent cut (Litan 1985: 23).

37. Decisions like *Continental Television v. GTE Sylvania* and *Reiter v. Sonotone* gained importance only through their subsequent use as precedent; as William Kovacic argues, they could have turned out to be outliers (Kovacic 1990: 1437).

38. See, for example, Mizruchi (2013); Waterhouse (2013).

39. Baxter was a signatory to the aggressively pro-enforcement Neal Report of the Johnson Task Force on Antitrust Policy in 1969 (Neal et al. 1969). Baxter discussed his change of views in Whiting et al. (1985: 33).

40. For descriptions of Baxter's views, see Baxter (1981; 1982); Bickel (1983); Cohen (1981); Kramer (1981); Eisner (1991: 188–89, 201).

41. Kramer (1981: 1298).

42. Eisner (1991: 190); Baxter et al. (1982: 24).

43. Pautler (2003: 95); U.S. DOJ (1982). See Edwards et al. (1981); Fox (1982); Turner (1982); Hills et al. (1982); Kauper (1983); Ordover and Willig (1983) for discussions of the revised guidelines.

44. Eisner (1991: 204–5).

45. Eisner (1991: 207–8).

46. Marcus and Kamen (1987); Eisner (1991: 193–94).

47. Eisner (1991: 190). Attorneys still made up a substantial majority, however; the ratio increased from 1.5:10 to 2.9:10.

48. Eisner (1991: 190).

49. A second minor revision took place in 1984; see U.S. DOJ (1984).

50. Millstein et al. (1989: 755–56).

51. See, for example, Pautler (2015); Pertschuk (1983).

52. Fox (1987: 33). Miller advanced economic analysis of regulation under Ford as head of the Government Operations and Research Office at the Council on Wage and Price Stability; see chapter 7 and next section.

53. Miller (1989: 43).

54. Eisner (1991: 212–14).

55. Eisner (1991: 215, 218).

56. Miller (1989: 43).

57. Eisner (1991: 221–24); Oliver (1986).

58. Ellickson (1989); Barbash (1980); Teles (2008: 113). See Ash et al. (2019) on the causal effects of Manne camp attendance on judicial decisions.

59. 468 U.S. 85 (1984); see also Kovacic (1990: 1447) on the lower courts.

60. The budgets of the regulatory agencies (including both social and economic regulation) tripled in real terms between 1970 and 1981; see Litan (1985: 22).

61. See, for example, Noble (1986: 113–14).

62. Eads and Fix (1984b: 108–9).

63. Miller (2011a); Stahl (2016: 83–85).

64. Miller (2011b: 96–97). C. Boyden Gray served as counsel to George H. W. Bush during his time as vice president and president.

65. Tozzi (2011: 63).

66. Eads and Fix (1984b: 109).

67. OIRA was established by the Paperwork Reduction Act (P.L. 96-511), passed at the end of the Carter administration, but EO 12291 gave the office its role in regulatory review.

68. Percival (1991: 149); Eads and Fix (1984b: 298–99).

69. Miller (2011b: 97); Tozzi (2011: 63).

70. Stockman (1980).

71. Niskanen (1988).

72. Noble (1986: 160). Cuts ranged from less than 5 percent (in inflation-adjusted terms) between 1980 and 1985 at EPA (though this reflected recovery from deeper initial cuts) to 10 percent at the Occupational Safety and Health Administration and 22 percent at the National Highway Traffic Safety Administration, among others; see Litan (1985: 23).

73. Lash et al. (1984: 59).

74. On Gorsuch's relationship with economists, see Lash et al. (1984: 7–14); see also McGarity (1991: 260).

75. Olson (1984: 49).

76. Cook (1988: 143).

77. McGarity (1991: 260).

78. P.L. 91-596; Noble (1986: 191); Eisner (2000).

79. Noble (1986: 194).

80. MacLaury (1984: Ch. 5).

81. Revesz and Livermore (2011: 189).

82. Quoted in Lash et al. (1984: 23).

83. McGarity (1991: 260).

84. Lash et al. (1984: 28–29).

85. McGarity (1991: 260).

86. Noble (1986: 67).

87. Quoted in Noble (1986: 67); see also Jim Miller's statement to "congressional staffers that an omnibus regulatory reform bill could create 'impediments to the kind of work that needs to be done.'"

88. Nichols (1997).

89. Noble (1986: 67).

90. Congressional Quarterly (1985: 26).

91. 452 U.S. 490 (1981).

92. Quoted in Noble (1986: 169–70).

93. Williams (1990).

94. Eisner (1991).

95. Noble (1986: 67).

96. Berman and Milanes-Reyes (2013).

Chapter 10. Conclusion

1. Hacker (1997), especially p. 156; Starr (1992); Skocpol (1996: 67–70).

2. Balto (1999); Litan and Shapiro (2002).

3. Segal (1998).

4. Giocoli (2014); Kovacic and Shapiro (2000: 56); U.S. DOJ (1993); see Blumenthal (1993); U.S. DOJ and FTC (1992) for another example of game theoretic influence.

5. Executive Order 12866.

6. Executive Order 12866; for discussions, see Weidenbaum (1997); OIRA (1997); Hahn et al. (2003).

7. For other discussions of Clinton-era social regulation, see Pildes and Sunstein (1995); Duffy (1997); Kagan (2001); Shapiro (2005).

8. Hall (1993) is a classic early account; Mudge (2018) is an excellent recent one.

9. For example, Mirowski and Plehwe (2009); Burgin (2012); Teles (2008); Hollis-Brusky (2015); Stahl (2016).

10. See, for example, Peck and Tickell (2002); Slobodian (2018).

11. See, for example, Pacewicz (2016); Mudge (2018).

12. I thank a reviewer for helping to articulate this contribution clearly.

13. Pettinicchio (2019).

14. Memorandum for the President from Stu Eizenstat, Fred Kahn, Jim McIntyre, Charlie Schultze, 20 November 1978, folder "Regulatory Reform [3]," Box 75, Charles L. Schultze's Subject Files, Carter Presidential Library.

15. Schimel (2019).

16. The EU Emissions Trading Scheme has long been criticized for being structured in a way that places a low price on carbon (Carrington 2013), but more recently prices have hit record highs (Chestney 2021). Evaluating its overall success is complex; recent evidence suggests it has modestly reduced EU emissions relative to the counterfactual (Bayer and Aklin 2020), although it seems unlikely that this is significant enough to curb global warming. California's cap-and-trade system has been subject to similar critiques (Roberts 2018). See Cullenward and Victor (2020) for a broader review of the political limitations of market-based climate policy.

17. On valuing safety, see Hood (2017); for an early statement on existence value, see Krutilla (1967).

18. P.L. 91-190. See also Marcus (1980b); Liroff (1976); Milazzo (2006); Caldwell (1982) on the role of ecological thinking in the passage of environmental laws in this era.

19. Gómez-Baggethun (2010: 1212–13). See also Russell and Sagoff (2005; 2009) on the different, and often incompatible, concerns of ecologists and economists.

20. For example, Daily (1997); see Gómez-Baggethun (2010) for a history.

21. Costanza et al. (1997).

22. See, for example, Schaefer et al. (2015) for a review of ecosystem services in the U.S. government and Costanza et al. (2017) for a discussion of the progress of the ecosystem services approach in its first two decades.

23. See Schomers and Matzdorf (2013) for a global review.

24. Other practical questions include whether treating ecosystems in economic ways—that is, instrumentally, with no moral obligation to conserve—runs the risk of harming the environment more than relying on ethical appeals alone. See Gómez-Baggethun (2010: 1215–16); Child (2009); McCauley (2006); Sagoff (2011).

25. See, for example, Child (2009: 241); McCauley (2006: 28).

26. Bullard (1990); U.S. GAO (1983); Commission for Racial Justice (1987); Policy, Planning, and Evaluation (1992).

27. First National (1991).

28. Policy, Planning, and Evaluation (1992: 90, i).

29. Policy, Planning, and Evaluation (1992: 1).

30. Holifield (2001: 80).

31. Holifield (2001: 80). EPA created an Office of Environmental Equity in 1992, under President George H. W. Bush; Clinton renamed it the Office of Environmental Justice in 1994.

32. Hahn et al. (2003: 405). See also Harrison (2019) on the difficulty of advancing environmental justice claims within EPA and other regulatory agencies.

33. See Jones (2020); Lowrey (2020); Singer and Sussman (2020) for examples of such arguments.

34. See, for example, Scott-Clayton (2018).

35. See, for example, Dube et al. (2020); Azar et al. (2018).

36. "Modernizing Regulatory Review," Memorandum for the Heads of Executive Departments and Agencies, 20 January 2021.

37. Hirschman (forthcoming).

38. Economists for Inclusive Prosperity (2019).

BIBLIOGRAPHY

Aaron, Henry J. 1983. "Orange Light for the Competitive Model." *Journal of Health Economics* 2(2): 281–84.

ABA Antitrust Section. 1981. *The FTC as an Antitrust Enforcement Agency: Its Structures, Powers and Procedures, Volume II*. Chicago: American Bar Association.

Alchian, Armen A., and Reuben A. Kessel. 1954. *A Proper Role of Systems Analysis*. Santa Monica, CA: RAND Corporation, D-2057. As of May 20, 2021: https://www.rand.org/pubs/documents/D2057.html.

Alkin, Marvin (Ed.). 2012. *Evaluation Roots: A Wider Perspective of Theorists' Views and Influences*. Thousand Oaks, CA: SAGE Publications.

Allison, Graham. 2006. "Emergence of Schools of Public Policy: Reflections by a Founding Dean." Pp. 58–79 in *The Oxford Handbook of Public Policy*, edited by Michael Moran and Martin Rein. Oxford: Oxford University Press.

Alsop, Stewart. 1962. "Our New Strategy: The Alternatives to Total War." Pp. 13–17 in *Saturday Evening Post*, 1 December.

Altman, Stuart. 2003. "Interview with Stuart Altman." Oral history conducted by Judy Moore and David Smith. Baltimore, MD: Centers for Medicare and Medicaid Services. As of 28 July 2021: https://www.cms.gov/About-CMS/Agency-Information/History/Downloads/CMSOralHistoryBiosInterviews.zip.

Altman, Stuart, and David Shachtman. 2011. *Power, Politics, and Universal Health Care: The Inside Story of a Century-Long Battle*. Amherst, NY: Prometheus Books.

Amadae, S. M. 2003. *Rationalizing Capitalist Democracy: The Cold War Origins of Rational Choice Liberalism*. Chicago: University of Chicago Press.

American Bar Association. 1969. *Report of the ABA Commission to Study the Federal Trade Commission*. Chicago: American Bar Association.

American Economic Review. 1983. "Joe S. Bain: Distinguished Fellow 1982." *American Economic Review* 73(3): n.p.

American Presidency Project. 1962. "John F. Kennedy: Special Message to the Congress on Transportation." University of California, Santa Barbara. As of 28 July 2021: https://www.presidency.ucsb.edu/documents/special-message-the-congress-transportation.

———. 1965. "Lyndon B. Johnson: 388—The President's News Conference, July 28, 1965." University of California, Santa Barbara. As of 28 July 2021: https://www.presidency.ucsb.edu/documents/the-presidents-news-conference-1038.

———. 1972. "1972 Democratic Party Platform." University of California, Santa Barbara. As of 28 July 2021: https://www.presidency.ucsb.edu/documents/1972-democratic-party-platform.

———. 1976a. "1976 Democratic Party Platform." University of California, Santa Barbara. As of 28 July 2021: https://www.presidency.ucsb.edu/documents/1976-democratic-party-platform.

———. 1976b. "Gerald R. Ford: Statement on the Railroad Revitalization and Regulatory Reform Act of 1976." University of California, Santa Barbara. As of 28 July 2021: https://www

.presidency.ucsb.edu/documents/statement-the-railroad-revitalization-and-regulatory-reform-act-1976.

———. 1977. "Jimmy Carter, Civil Aeronautics Board Nomination of Elizabeth E. Bailey to Be a Member." University of California, Santa Barbara. As of 28 July 2021: https://www.presidency.ucsb.edu/documents/civil-aeronautics-board-nomination-elizabeth-e-bailey-be-member.

———. 1980. "Ronald Reagan: Address Accepting the Presidential Nomination at the Republican National Convention in Detroit." University of California, Santa Barbara. As of 28 July 2021: https://www.presidency.ucsb.edu/documents/address-accepting-the-presidential-nomination-the-republican-national-convention-detroit.

———. 1981. "Ronald Reagan: Inaugural Address." University of California, Santa Barbara. As of 28 July 2021: https://www.presidency.ucsb.edu/documents/inaugural-address-11.

———. 1990. "George Bush: Statement on Signing the Bill Amending the Clean Air Act." University of California, Santa Barbara. As of 28 July 2021: https://www.presidency.ucsb.edu/documents/statement-signing-the-bill-amending-the-clean-air-act.

———. 1992. "William J. Clinton: Address Accepting the Presidential Nomination at the Democratic National Convention in New York." University of California, Santa Barbara. As of 28 July 2021: https://www.presidency.ucsb.edu/documents/address-accepting-the-presidential-nomination-the-democratic-national-convention-new-york.

Ameringer, Carl F. 2008. *The Health Care Revolution: From Medical Monopoly to Market Competition.* Berkeley: University of California Press.

Anderson, Jack, with Daryl Gibson. 2000. *Peace, War, and Politics: An Eyewitness Account.* New York: Macmillan.

Anderson, Margo J. 2015. *The American Census: A Social History.* New Haven, CT: Yale University Press.

Andrews, Richard N. L. 1984. "Economics and Environmental Decisions, Past and Present." Pp. 43–85 in *Environmental Policy under Reagan's Executive Order: The Role of Benefit-Cost Analysis,* edited by V. Kerry Smith. Chapel Hill: University of North Carolina.

———. 1999. *Managing the Environment, Managing Ourselves: A History of American Environmental Policy.* New Haven, CT: Yale University Press.

Angrist, Joshua D. 2004. "American Education Research Changes Tack." *Oxford Review of Economic Policy* 20(2): 198–212.

"Antitrust Nominee Is Questioned on Views of Business 'Bigness.'" 1965. *New York Times,* 11 June.

Areeda, Phillip E., and Donald F. Turner. 1978. *Antitrust Law: An Analysis of Antitrust Principles and Their Application.* New York: Aspen Law & Business.

Arias, Melanie Kayser Schmidt. 2013. "Experimental Citizens: The Experimental Housing Allowance Program and Housing Vouchers as American Social Policy in the 1970s and 1980s." PhD diss., University of California, Los Angeles.

Arrow, Kenneth. 1963. "Uncertainty and the Welfare Economics of Medical Care." *American Economic Review* 53(5): 941–73.

———. 1968. "The Economics of Moral Hazard: Further Comment." *American Economic Review* 58(3): 537–39.

Ash, Elliot, Daniel L. Chen, and Suresh Naidu. 2019. "Ideas Have Consequences: The Effect of Law and Economics on American Justice." Unpublished working paper. As of 28 July 2021: https://users.nber.org/~dlchen/papers/Ideas_Have_Consequences.pdf.

Atkinson, Richard C., and Gregg B. Jackson (Eds.). 1992. *Research and Education Reform: Roles for the Office of Educational Research and Improvement.* Washington, DC: National Academy of Sciences.

Averch, Harvey, and Leland Johnson. 1962. "Behavior of the Firm under Regulatory Constraint." *American Economic Review* 52: 1052–69.

Averitt, Neil. 2018 "Neil Averitt Commentary: Let Us Now Remember Michael Pertschuk's Famous Speech." *FTC Watch*. As of 28 July 2021: https://www.mlexwatch.com/articles/3029/print?section=ftcwatch.

Azar, José, Martin C. Schmalz, and Isabel Tecu. 2018. "Anticompetitive Effects of Common Ownership." *Journal of Finance* 73(4): 1513–65.

Backhouse, Roger E. 1998. "The Transformation of U.S. Economics, 1920–1960, Viewed through a Survey of Journal Articles." *History of Political Economy* 30: 85–107.

———. 2015. "Revisiting Samuelson's *Foundations of Economic Analysis*." *Journal of Economic Literature* 53(2): 326–50.

———. 2017. *Founder of Modern Economics: Paul A. Samuelson*. Oxford: Oxford University Press.

Backhouse, Roger E., and Steven G. Medema. 2009a. "Defining Economics: The Long Road to Acceptance of the Robbins Definition." *Economica* 76: 805–20.

———. 2009b. "Retrospectives: On the Definition of Economics." *Journal of Economic Perspectives* 23: 221–34.

Baer, Kenneth S. 2000. *Reinventing Democrats: The Politics of Liberalism from Reagan to Clinton*. Lawrence: University Press of Kansas.

Bailey, Stephen Kemp. 1950. *Congress Makes a Law: The Story behind the Employment Act of 1946*. New York: Columbia University Press.

Balto, David A. 1999. "Antitrust Enforcement in the Clinton Administration." *Cornell Journal of Law and Public Policy* 9(1): 61–132.

Bane, Mary Jo, and David Ellwood. 1983. *The Dynamics of Dependence: The Routes to Self-Sufficiency*. Cambridge, MA: Urban Systems Research and Engineering.

Banzhaf, H. Spencer. 2006. "The Other Economics Department: Demand and Value Theory in Early Agricultural Economics." *History of Political Economy* 38(Annual Supplement): 9–31.

———. 2010. "Consumer Surplus with Apology: A Historical Perspective on Nonmarket Valuation and Recreation Demand." *Annual Review of Resource Economics* 2: 183–207.

———. 2014. "The Cold-War Origins of the Value of Statistical Life." *Journal of Economic Perspectives* 28(4): 213–26.

Baram, Michael S. 1980. "Cost-Benefit Analysis: An Inadequate Basis for Health, Safety, and Environmental Regulatory Decisionmaking." *Ecology Law Quarterly* 8(3): 473–531.

Barbash, Fred. 1980. "Big Corporations Bankroll Seminars for U.S. Judges." *Washington Post*, 20 January.

Barber, William J. 1985. *From New Era to New Deal: Herbert Hoover, the Economists, and American Economic Policy, 1921–1933*. Cambridge: Cambridge University Press.

———. 1996. *Designs within Disorder: Franklin D. Roosevelt, the Economists, and the Shaping of American Economic Policy, 1933–1945*. Cambridge: Cambridge University Press.

Barfield, Claude E. 1972. "Economic Arguments May Force Retreat from Senate Water-Quality Goals." Pp. 136–47 in *National Journal*, 22 January.

Bartlett, Robert V. 1986. "Rationality and the Logic of the National Environmental Policy Act." *Environmental Professional* 8(2): 105–11.

Bauman, Robert. 2007. "The Black Power and Chicano Movements in the Poverty Wars in Los Angeles." *Journal of Urban History* 33(2): 277–95.

———. 2008. *Race and the War on Poverty: From Watts to East L.A.* Norman: University of Oklahoma Press.

Baxter, William F., Harvey M. Applebaum, E. William Barnett, Allen C. Holmes, and Earl E. Pollock. 1981. "Panel Discussion: Interview with William F. Baxter Assistant Attorney General Antitrust Division." *Antitrust Law Journal* 50: 151–71.

Baxter, William F., E. William Barnett, Carla A. Hills, Harvey M. Applebaum, and Earl E. Pollock. 1982. "Interview with William F. Baxter, Assistant Attorney General Antitrust Division." *Antitrust Law Journal* 51: 23–40.

Bayer, Patrick, and Michaël Aklin. 2020. "The European Union Emissions Trading System Reduced CO_2 Emissions Despite Low Prices." *Proceedings of the National Academy of Sciences* 117(16): 8804–12.

Becker, Gary. 1957. *The Economics of Discrimination*. Chicago: University of Chicago Press.

———. 1968. "Crime and Punishment: An Economic Approach." *Journal of Political Economy* 76(2): 169–217.

Behrman, Bradley. 1980. "Civil Aeronautics Board." Pp. 75–120 in *The Politics of Regulation*, edited by James Q. Wilson. New York: Basic Books.

Belfer, Donald A., Jonathan D. Casher, Peter G. Gerstberger, Cyrus F. Gibson, Paul W. MacAvoy, and Quentin S. Meeker. 1968. *A Planning Programming Budgeting System for the United States Geological Survey*. Cambridge, MA: Alfred P. Sloan School of Management, MIT.

Bell, David E. 1964. "David E. Bell, Oral History Interview—JFK#1, 7/11/1964." Oral history conducted by Robert C. Turner. Boston, MA: John F. Kennedy Presidential Library and Museum.

Bell, Jacqueline. 2009. "No Antitrust Cure-All for 'Too Big to Fail': Experts." Law360. As of 28 July 2021: https://www.law360.com/articles/94528/no-antitrust-cure-all-for-too-big-to-fail -experts.

Berkowitz, Edward D. 1989. *Disabled Policy: America's Programs for the Handicapped*. Cambridge: Cambridge University Press.

———. 1995. *Mr. Social Security: The Life of Wilbur J. Cohen*. Lawrence: University Press of Kansas.

Berman, Elizabeth Popp, and Laura M. Milanes-Reyes. 2013. "The Politicization of Knowledge Claims: The 'Laffer Curve' in the U.S. Congress." *Qualitative Sociology* 36: 53–79.

Berman, Elizabeth Popp, and Nicholas Pagnucco. 2010. "Economic Ideas and the Political Process: Debating Tax Cuts in the U.S. House of Representatives, 1962–1981." *Politics and Society* 38: 347–72.

Berman, Larry. 1979. *The Office of Management and Budget and the Presidency: 1921–1979*. Princeton, NJ: Princeton University Press.

Bernstein, Marver. 1955. *Regulating Business by Independent Commission*. Princeton, NJ: Princeton University Press.

Bernstein, Michael A. 2001. *A Perilous Progress: Economists and Public Purpose in Twentieth-Century America*. Princeton, NJ: Princeton University Press.

Bianchi, Patrizio. 2013. "Bain and the Origins of Industrial Economics." *European Review of Industrial Economics and Policy* 7. As of 28 July 2021: http://revel.unice.fr/eriep/?id=3608.

Bickel, David R. 1983. "The Antitrust Division's Adoption of a Chicago School Economic Policy Calls for Some Reorganization: But Is the Division's New Policy Here to Stay?" *Houston Law Review* 20: 1083–1127.

Biddle, Jeff. 1998. "Institutional Economics: A Case of Reproductive Failure?" *History of Political Economy* 30(4): 108–33.

Biven, W. Carl. 2002. *Jimmy Carter's Economy: Policy in an Age of Limits*. Chapel Hill: University of North Carolina Press.

Blaise, Lynn E. 2000. "Beyond Cost/Benefit: The Maturation of Economic Analysis of the Law and Its Consequences for Environmental Policymaking." *University of Illinois Law Review* 2000: 237–53.

Blumenthal, Richard. 1969. "The Bureaucracy: Antipoverty and the Community Action Program." Pp. 129–79 in *American Political Institutions and Public Policy*, edited by Allan P. Sindler. Boston: Little, Brown.

Blumenthal, William. 1993. "Thirty-One Merger Policy Questions Still Lingering after the 1992 Guidelines." *Antitrust Bulletin* 38(3): 593–641.

Blyth, Mark. 2002. *Great Transformations: Economic Ideas and Institutional Change in the Twentieth Century*. Cambridge: Cambridge University Press.

Bok, Derek. 1960. "Section 7 of the Clayton Act and the Merging of Law and Economics." *Harvard Law Review* 74: 226–355.

Boland, John J., Nicholas Flores, and Charles W. Howe. 2009. "The Theory and Practice of Cost-Benefit Analysis." Pp. 82–135 in *The Evolution of Water Resource Planning and Decision Making*, edited by Clifford S. Russell and Duane D. Baumann. Cheltenham, UK: Edward Elgar.

Bonastia, Christopher. 2006. *Knocking at the Door: The Federal Government's Attempt to Desegregate the Suburbs*. Princeton, NJ: Princeton University Press.

Bork, Robert. 1954. "Vertical Integration and the Sherman Act: The Legal History of an Economic Misconception." *University of Chicago Law Review* 22: 157–201.

———. 1978. *The Antitrust Paradox: A Policy at War with Itself*. New York: Free Press.

Bork, Robert, and Ward S. Bowman, Jr. 1965. "The Goals of Antitrust: A Dialogue on Policy." *Columbia Law Review* 65(3): 363–76.

Bornstein, David. 1998. "Changing the World on a Shoestring." *The Atlantic*, 1 January.

———. 2004. *How to Change the World: Social Entrepreneurs and the Power of New Ideas*. Oxford: Oxford University Press.

Borstelmann, Thomas. 2011. *The 1970s: A New Global History from Civil Rights to Economic Inequality*. Princeton, NJ: Princeton University Press.

Botner, Stanley. 1970. "Four Years of PPBS: An Appraisal." *Public Administration Review* 30(4): 423–31.

Boulding, Kenneth. 1969. "Economics as a Moral Science." *American Economic Review* 59: 1–12.

Bowles, Samuel. 1970. "Towards an Educational Production Function." Pp. 11–70 in *Education, Income, and Human Capital*, edited by W. Lee Hansen. Cambridge, MA: NBER.

Bowman, Jr., Ward S. 1957. "Tying Arrangements and the Leverage Problem." *Yale Law Journal* 67: 19–36.

Boyer, Kenneth D., and William G. Shepherd (Eds.). 1981. *Economic Regulation: Essays in Honor of James R. Nelson*. Lansing: Michigan State University.

"Brains behind the Muscle." 1961. *Time*, 7 April.

Brandon, William P., and Keith Carnes. 2014. "Federal Health Insurance and 'Exchanges': Recent History." *Journal of Health Care for the Poor and Underserved* 25(1): xxxii–lvii.

Brauer, Carl M. 1982. "Kennedy, Johnson, and the War on Poverty." *Journal of American History* 69: 98–119.

Breslau, Daniel. 1998. *In Search of the Unequivocal: The Political Economy of Measurement in U.S. Labor Policy*. Westport, CT: Greenwood Publishing Group.

Breyer, Stephen. 1996. "Donald F. Turner." *Antitrust Bulletin* 41(4): 725–27.

———. 2008. "Interview with Stephen Breyer." Oral history conducted by James Sterling Young. Charlottesville: Miller Center, University of Virginia.

Breyer, Stephen, and Paul W. MacAvoy. 1973. "The Natural Gas Shortage and the Regulation of Natural Gas Producers." *Harvard Law Review* 86(6): 941–87.

———. 1974. *Energy Regulation by the Federal Power Commission*. Washington, DC: Brookings Institution.

Brill, Steven. 2015. *America's Bitter Pill: Money, Politics, Backroom Deals, and the Fight to Fix Our Broken Healthcare System*. New York: Random House.

Bromley, Daniel W. 2000. "Program Evaluation and the Purpose of Rivers." *Journal of Contemporary Water Research and Education* 116(1): 7–10.

Brown, Lawrence. 1983. *Politics and Health Care Organization: HMOs as Federal Policy*. Washington, DC: Brookings Institution.

Bryner, Gary C. 1995. *Blue Skies, Green Politics: The Clean Air Act of 1990 and Its Implementation*. Washington, DC: Congressional Quarterly.

Buchanan, Garth N., and Joseph S. Wholey. 1972. "Federal Level Evaluation." *Evaluation* 1(1): 17–22.

Buchanan, James M., and Gordon Tullock. 1962. *The Calculus of Consent: Logical Foundations of Constitutional Democracy*. Ann Arbor: University of Michigan Press.

Bullard, Robert. 1990. *Dumping in Dixie: Race, Class, and Environmental Quality*. Boulder, CO: Westview Press.

Buntain, David R. 1974. "Judicial Review of Cost-Benefit Analysis under NEPA." *Nebraska Law Review* 53(4): 540–80.

Burgin, Angus. 2012. *The Great Persuasion: Reinventing Free Markets since the Depression*. Cambridge, MA: Harvard University Press.

Burke, Vincent J., and Vee Burke. 1974. *Nixon's Good Deed: Welfare Reform*. New York: Columbia University Press.

Burmeister, Jr., Edward D. 1972. "Cost-Benefit Analysis and the National Environmental Policy Act of 1969." *Stanford Law Review* 24(6): 1092–1116.

Byrne, John A. 1993. *The Whiz Kids: The Founding Fathers of American Business—and the Legacy They Left Us*. New York: Doubleday Business.

Calabresi, Guido. 1961. "Some Thoughts on Risk Distribution and the Law of Torts." *Yale Law Journal* 70(4): 499–553.

Caldwell, Bruce. 2011. "The Chicago School, Hayek, and Neoliberalism." Pp. 301–34 in *Building Chicago Economics: New Perspectives on the History of America's Most Powerful Economics Program*, edited by Robert Van Horn, Philip Mirowski, and Thomas A. Stapleford. Cambridge: Cambridge University Press.

Caldwell, Lynton Keith. 1982. *Science and the National Environmental Policy Act*. Tuscaloosa: University of Alabama Press.

Califano, Joseph A. 1969. "Joseph A. Califano, Jr., Oral History Interview I." Oral history conducted by Joe B. Frantz. Austin, TX: Lyndon B. Johnson Presidential Library.

———. 1991. *The Triumph and Tragedy of Lyndon Johnson: The White House Years*. New York: Simon & Schuster.

Campbell, John L. 1998. "Institutional Analysis and the Role of Ideas in Political Economy." *Theory and Society* 27: 377–409.

Campbell, John L., and Ove K. Pedersen. 2014. *The National Origins of Policy Ideas: Knowledge Regimes in the United States, France, Germany, and Denmark*. Princeton, NJ: Princeton University Press.

Campbell, Richard W., and George E. Rawson. 1981. "The 'New' Public Policy Programs and Their Effect on the Professional Status of Public Administration." *Southern Review of Public Administration* 5(1): 91–113.

Canedo, Eduardo. 2008. "The Rise of the Deregulation Movement in Modern America, 1957–1980." PhD diss., Columbia University.

Cannon, Jonathan. 2010. "The Sounds of Silence: Cost-Benefit Canons in *Entergy Corp. v. Riverkeeper, Inc.*" *Harvard Environmental Law Review* 34: 425–60.

Capron, William M. (Ed.). 1971. *Technological Change in Regulated Industries*. Washington, DC: Brookings Institution.

———. 1981. "William M. Capron Oral History Interview I." Oral history conducted by Michael Gillette. Austin, TX: Lyndon B. Johnson Presidential Library.

Card, David. 2011. "Origins of the Unemployment Rate: The Lasting Legacy of Measurement without Theory." *American Economic Review* 101: 552–57.

Carlin, Alan. 2006. "History of Economic Research at the EPA." National Center for Environmental Economics, Environmental Protection Agency. As of 28 July 2021: https://web.archive.org/web/20151004032244/http://yosemite.epa.gov/ee/epa/eed.nsf/00000000000000000000 000000000000/2f68aa9ffb75364b8525779700781a24!OpenDocument.

Carrington, Damian. 2013. "EU Carbon Price Crashes to Record Low." *The Guardian*, 24 January.

Carroll, Stephen J., George R. Hall, John A. Pincus, and Daniel Weiler. 1972. *Rand Work in Elementary and Secondary Education: A Representative Selection*. Santa Monica, CA: RAND Corporation, R-1052. As of May 20, 2021: https://www.rand.org/pubs/reports/R1052.html.

Carson, Carol. 1975. "The History of the United States National Income and Product Accounts: The Development of an Analytical Tool." *Review of Income and Wealth* 21: 153–81.

Carson, Rachel. 1962. *Silent Spring*. New York: Houghton Mifflin.

Carter, Dan T. 1999. *From George Wallace to Newt Gingrich: Race in the Conservative Counterrevolution, 1963–1994*. Baton Rouge: Louisiana State University Press.

Carter, Zachary D. 2020. *The Price of Peace: Money, Democracy, and the Life of John Maynard Keynes*. New York: Random House.

Caves, Richard. 1962. *Air Transport and Its Regulators*. Cambridge, MA: Harvard University Press.

Cazenave, Noel A. 2007. *Impossible Democracy: The Unlikely Success of the War on Poverty Community Action Programs*. Albany: State University of New York Press.

Chamberlin, Edward. 1933. *The Theory of Monopolistic Competition: A Re-Orientation of the Theory of Value*. Cambridge, MA: Harvard University Press.

Cherrier, Béatrice. 2014. "Toward a History of Economics at MIT, 1940–72." *History of Political Economy* 46: 15–44.

Chestney, Nina. 2021. "EU Carbon Price Hits Record High above 45 Euros a Tonne." *Reuters*, 20 April.

Child, Matthew F. 2009. "The Thoreau Ideal as a Unifying Thread in the Conservation Movement." *Conservation Biology* 23(2): 241–43.

Christophers, Brett. 2016. *The Great Leveler: Capitalism and Competition in the Court of Law*. Cambridge, MA: Harvard University Press.

Chubb, John E., and Terry M. Moe. 1990. *Politics, Markets, and America's Schools*. Washington, DC: Brookings Institution.

Church, Robert L. 1974. "Economists as Experts: The Rise of an Academic Profession in the United States, 1870–1920." Pp. 571–609 in *The University in Society*, edited by Lawrence Stone. Princeton, NJ: Princeton University Press.

Cinti, Thomas A. 1990. "The Regulator's Dilemma: Should Best Available Technology or Cost Benefit Analysis Be Used to Determine the Applicable Hazardous Waste Treatment, Storage, and Disposal Technology." *Rutgers Computer and Technology Law Journal* 16: 145–67.

Clark, J. M. 1940. "Toward a Concept of Workable Competition." *American Economic Review* 30(2): 241–56.

Clark, Timothy B. 1978. "When the President Tries to Regulate." Pp. 2029 in *National Journal*, 16 December.

Clawson, Marion. 1959. *Methods of Measuring the Demand for and Value of Outdoor Recreation*. Washington, DC: Resources for the Future.

Cloward, Richard A., and Lloyd E. Ohlin. 2013 [1960]. *Delinquency and Opportunity: A Study of Local Gangs*. New York: Routledge.

Coan, Jr., Carl A. S. 1969. "The Housing and Urban Development Act of 1968: Landmark Legislation for the Urban Crisis." *Urban Lawyer* 1(1): 1–33.

Coase, Ronald. 1960. "The Problem of Social Cost." *Journal of Law and Economics* 3: 1–44.

———. 1984. "The New Institutional Economics." *Journal of Institutional and Theoretical Economics* 140: 229–31.

Cohen, Manuel Frederick, and George J. Stigler. 1971. *Can Regulatory Agencies Protect Consumers?* Washington, DC: American Enterprise Institute.

Cohen, Wilbur J., and Milton Friedman. 1972. *Social Security: Universal or Selective?* Washington, DC: American Enterprise Institute.

Colander, David. 2000. "The Death of Neoclassical Economics." *Journal of the History of Economic Thought* 22(2): 127–43.

———. 2005. "What Economists Teach and What Economists Do." *Journal of Economic Education* 36(3): 249–60.

Colander, David, and Harry Landreth. 1998. "Political Influence on the Textbook Keynesian Revolution: God, Man, and Laurie Tarshis at Yale." Pp. 59–72 in *Keynesianism and the Keynesian Revolution in America*, edited by O. F. Hamouda and Betsey B. Price. Cheltenham, UK: Edward Elgar.

Collins, Martin J. 2002. *Cold War Laboratory: RAND, the Air Force, and the American State, 1945–1950*. Washington, DC: Smithsonian Institution.

Collins, Robert M. 1981. *The Business Response to Keynes, 1929–1964*. New York: Columbia University Press.

———. 1990. "The Emergence of Economic Growthmanship in the United States: Federal Policy and Economic Knowledge in the Truman Years." Pp. 138–170 in *The State and Economic Knowledge: The American and British Experiences*, edited by Mary O. Furner and Barry Supple. Cambridge: Cambridge University Press.

———. 2000. *More: The Politics of Economic Growth in Postwar America*. Oxford: Oxford University Press.

Commission for Racial Justice, United Church of Christ. 1987. *Toxic Wastes and Race*. New York: United Church of Christ.

Congressional Quarterly. 1985. "Environmental Policy." *Congress and the Nation, 1981–1984 (Vol. 6)*. Washington, DC: CQ Press. As of 28 July 2021: https://sk.sagepub.com/cqpress/congress-and-the-nation-vi/n8.xml.

Conley II, Joe Greene. 2006. "Environmentalism Contained: A History of Corporate Responses to the New Environmentalism." PhD diss., Princeton University.

Conti-Brown, Peter. 2016. *The Power and Independence of the Federal Reserve*. Princeton, NJ: Princeton University Press.

Cook, Brian J. 1988. *Bureaucratic Politics and Regulatory Reform: The EPA and Emissions Trading*. Westport, CT: Greenwood Publishing Group.

Costanza, Robert, Ralph d'Arge, Rudolf de Groot, Stephen Farber, Monica Grasso, Bruce Hannon, Karin Limburg, Shahid Naeem, Robert V. O'Neill, Jose Paruelo, Robert G. Raskin, Paul Sutton, and Marjan van den Belt. 1997. "The Value of the World's Ecosystem Services and Natural Capital." *Nature* 387(15 May): 253–60.

Costanza, Robert, Rudolf de Groot, Leon Braat, Ida Kubiszewski, Lorenzo Fioramonti, Paul Sutton, Steve Farber, and Monica Grasso. 2017. "Twenty Years of Ecosystem Services: How Far Have We Come and How Far Do We Still Need to Go?" *Ecosystem Services* 28: 1–16.

Costle, Douglas. 2001. "Douglas M. Costle: Oral History Interview." Oral history conducted by Dennis Williams. Washington, DC: U.S. Environmental Protection Agency.

Cowan, Edward. 1978. "Law for Size Limits on Mergers Sought." Pp. 25–26 in *New York Times*, 30 December.

———. 1979. "Popularity for 'Big Is Bad' Idea Fades in Key Places." Pp. E3 in *New York Times*, 13 May.

———. 1980. "New Antitrust Chief Faces Policy Dispute." Pp. D1, D3 in *New York Times*, 21 January.

———. 1981. "Antitrust Nominee Is Reported." Pp. 33 in *New York Times*, 7 February.

Cowie, Jefferson R. 2010. *Stayin' Alive: The 1970s and the Last Days of the Working Class*. New York: New Press.

Cox, Edward Finch, Robert C. Fellmeth, and John E. Schulz. 1969. *The Nader Report on the Federal Trade Commission*. New York: Richard W. Baron Publishing Company.

Coyle, Diane. 2014. *GDP: A Brief but Affectionate History*. Princeton, NJ: Princeton University Press.

Crane, Daniel A. 2014. "The Tempting of Antitrust: Robert Bork and the Goals of Antitrust Policy." *Antitrust Law Journal* 79(3): 835–53.

Crawford, Corinne. 2011. "The Repeal of the Glass-Steagall Act and the Current Financial Crisis." *Journal of Business and Economics Research* 9(1): 127–33.

Crecine, John P. 1971. "University Centers for the Study of Public Policy: Organizational Viability." *Policy Sciences* 2(1): 7–32.

———. 1982. "Introduction and Overview." Pp. 1–23 in *The New Educational Programs in Public Policy: The First Decade*, edited by John P. Crecine. Greenwich, CT: JAI Press Inc.

Crecine, John P., H. Ayers Brinser, R. Lee Brummet, Robert S. Friedman, Floyd Mann, John H. Romani, Frederic M. Scherer, Guy E. Swanson, and Robert Vinter. 1968. *Public Policy Research and Administration: A Proposal for Educational Innovation.* Santa Monica, CA: RAND Corporation, P-3824. As of May 20, 2021: https://www.rand.org/pubs/papers/P3824.html.

Crocker, Thomas D. 1966. "The Structuring of Atmospheric Pollution Control Systems." Pp. 61–86 in *The Economics of Air Pollution*, edited by H. Wolozin. New York: W. W. Norton.

Cuff, Robert D. 1989. "Creating Control Systems: Edwin F. Gay and the Central Bureau of Planning and Statistics, 1917–1919." *Business History Review* 63(3): 588–613.

Culhane, Paul J. 1990. "NEPA's Effect on Agency Decision Making." *Environmental Law* 20: 681–702.

Cullenward, Danny, and David G. Victor. 2020. *Making Climate Policy Work.* Cambridge, UK: Polity Press.

Daily, Gretchen (Ed.). 1997. *Nature's Services: Societal Dependence on Natural Ecosystems.* Washington, DC: Island Press.

Dales, J. H. 1968. *Pollution, Property and Prices: An Essay in Policy-Making and Economics.* Toronto: University of Toronto Press.

Dameron, Charles S. 2016. "Present at Antitrust's Creation: Consumer Welfare in the Sherman Act's State Statutory Forerunners." *Yale Law Journal* 125(4): 796–1149.

Davis, Amy Elisabeth. 1988. "Politics of Prosperity: The Kennedy Presidency and Economic Policy." PhD diss., Columbia University.

Davis, Christopher, Jeffrey Kurtock, James P. Leape, and Frank Magill. 1977. "The Clean Air Act Amendments of 1977." *Harvard Environmental Law Review* 2: 1–103.

Davis, Karen. 1975. *National Health Insurance: Benefits, Costs, and Consequences.* Washington, DC: Brookings Institution.

Day, Dwayne A. 2003. *Gourmet Chefs and Short Order Cooks: A Policy History of the Congressional Budget Office.* Unpublished work. As of 28 July 2021: https://szgerzensee.ch/fileadmin /Dateien_Anwender/Dokumente/Conferences/Swiss_Debt_Brake/BAnderson_Nov_2012 .pdf.

Decker, Richard K., Lee N. Abrams, Ernest G. Barnes, Philip Elman, Robert A. Hammond III, Allen C. Holmes, and Lawrence G. Meyer. 1972. "Panel Discussion: New Directions for the Federal Trade Commission." *Antitrust Law Journal* 42(1): 55–77.

DeHaven, James C., and Jack Hirshleifer. 1957. "Feather River Water for Southern California." *Land Economics* 33(3): 198–209.

DeHaven, James C., Jack Hirshleifer, and Linn A. Gore. 1953. *A Brief Survey of the Technology and Economics of Water Supply.* Santa Monica, CA: RAND Corporation, R-258-RC. As of 20 May 2021: https://www.rand.org/pubs/reports/R0258.html.

de Jong, Henry W., and William G. Shepherd (Eds.). 2007. *Pioneers of Industrial Organization: How the Economics of Competition and Monopoly Took Shape.* Northampton, MA: Edward Elgar.

DeLor, Michael J. 2014. "The Regulatory Response to Crisis: Crisis, Congress, and the Federal Energy Regulatory Commission." PhD diss., Virginia Tech.

Demsetz, Harold. 1973. *The Market Concentration Doctrine.* Washington, DC: American Enterprise Institute.

DeMuth, Christopher C. 1980. "The White House Review Programs." Pp. 13–26 in *Regulation* (Jan.–Feb.). As of 28 July 2021: https://www.cato.org/sites/cato.org/files/serials/files/regulation/1980/3/v4n2-6.pdf.

Dennis, Brady. 2010. "Congress Passes Financial Reform Bill." *Washington Post*, 16 July.

Derickson, Alan. 2002. "'Health for Three-Thirds of the Nation': Public Health Advocacy of Universal Access to Medical Care in the United States." *American Journal of Public Health* 92: 180–90.

Derthick, Martha, and Paul J. Quirk. 1985. *The Politics of Regulation.* Washington, DC: Brookings Institution Press.

De Vroey, Michel, and Pedro Garcia Duarte. 2013. "In Search of Lost Time: The Neoclassical Synthesis." *BE Journal of Macroeconomics* 13(1): 965–96.

Director, Aaron, and Edward H. Levi. 1956. "Law and the Future: Trade Regulation." *Northwestern University Law Review* 51: 281–96.

Dirlam, Joel B., and Alfred E. Kahn. 1954. *Fair Competition: The Law and Economics of Antitrust Policy.* Ithaca, NY: Cornell University Press.

Diver, Colin S. 1981. "Policymaking Paradigms in Administrative Law." *Harvard Law Review* 95(2): 393–434.

Dobbin, Frank, and Jiwook Jung. 2010. "The Misapplication of Mr. Michael Jensen: How Agency Theory Brought Down the Economy and Why It Might Again." *Research in the Sociology of Organizations* 30B: 29–64.

Dochuk, Darren. 2011. *From Bible Belt to Sunbelt: Plain-Folk Religion, Grassroots Politics, and the Rise of Evangelical Conservatism.* New York: Norton.

Doh, Joon Chien. 1971. *The Planning-Programming-Budgeting System in Three Federal Agencies.* New York: Praeger Publishers.

Domnarski, William. 2016. *Richard Posner.* Oxford: Oxford University Press.

Douglas, George W., and James C. Miller III. 1974. *Economic Regulation of Domestic Air Transport: Theory and Policy.* Washington, DC: Brookings Institution.

Downs, Anthony. 1957. *An Economic Theory of Democracy.* New York: Harper.

Drayton, William. 1980. "Economic Law Enforcement." *Harvard Environmental Law Review* 4: 1–40.

Drew, Elizabeth B. 1967. "PPBS: HEW Grapples with PPBS." Pp. 9–29 in *Public Interest* (Summer).

Dube, Arindrajit, Jeff Jacobs, Suresh Naidu, and Siddharth Suri. 2020. "Monopsony in Online Labor Markets." *American Economic Review: Insights* 2(1): 33–46.

Duffy, Robert J. 1997. "Regulatory Oversight in the Clinton Administration." *Presidential Studies Quarterly* 27(1): 71–90.

Duménil, Gérard, and Dominique Lévy. 2004. *Capital Resurgent: Roots of the Neoliberal Revolution.* Cambridge, MA: Harvard University Press.

Duncan, Joseph W., and William C. Shelton. 1978. *Revolution in United States Government Statistics 1926–1976.* Washington, DC: U.S. Government Printing Office.

Düppe, Till, and E. Roy Weintraub. 2014. "Siting the New Economic Science: The Cowles Commission's Activity Analysis Conference of June 1949." *Science in Context* 27(3): 453–83.

Duscha, Julius. 1975. "Budget Expert for the Congress." Pp. 155 in *New York Times*, 8 June.

Eads, George. 1971. *The Local Service Airline Experiment.* Washington, DC: Brookings Institution.

———. 1982. "White House Oversight of Executive Branch Regulation." Pp. 177–200 in *Social Regulation: Strategies for Reform*, edited by Eugene Bardach and Robert Kagan. Piscataway, NJ: Transaction.

Eads, George C., and Michael Fix (Eds.). 1984a. *The Reagan Regulatory Strategy: An Assessment.* Washington, DC: Urban Institute.

———. 1984b. *Relief or Reform? Reagan's Regulatory Dilemma.* Washington, DC: Urban Institute.

Eckstein, Otto. 1958. *Water Resource Development: The Economics of Project Evaluation.* Cambridge, MA: Harvard University Press.

Economides, Nicholas. 2005. "Telecommunications Regulation: An Introduction." Pp. 48–76 in *The Limits of Market Organization*, edited by Richard R. Nelson. New York: Russell Sage Foundation.

"Economist Favors Pollution Charge." 1966. *New York Times*, 15 June.

Economists Conference on Inflation. 1974. *The Economists Conference on Inflation*. Washington, DC: U.S. Government Printing Office.

Economists for Inclusive Prosperity. 2019. "Economists for Inclusive Prosperity." As of 28 July 2021: https://econfip.org/policy-briefs/economics-for-inclusive-prosperity-an-introduction/.

Edelstein, Michael. 2001. "The Size of the U.S. Armed Forces during World War II: Feasibility and War Planning." *Research in Economic History* 20: 47–97.

Edwards, Corwin D. 1960. "Antitrust Policy, an Economic and Legal Analysis." *American Economic Review* 50(5): 1102–8.

Edwards, Steven M., Robert D. Joffe, William J. Kolasky, John J. McGowan, Carlos E. Mendez-Penate, Janusz A. Ordover, Phillip A. Proger, Louis M. Solomon, and Utz P. Toepke. 1981. "Proposed Revisions of the Justice Department's Merger Guidelines." *Columbia Law Review* 81: 1543–81.

Eisenhower, Dwight D. 1961. "Farewell Address." As of 28 July 2021: https://www.ourdocuments.gov/doc.php.

Eisner, Marc Allen. 1991. *Antitrust and the Triumph of Economics: Institutions, Expertise, and Policy Change*. Chapel Hill: University of North Carolina Press.

———. 2000. *Regulatory Politics in Transition*. Baltimore, MD: Johns Hopkins University Press.

Ellerman, A. Denny, Paul Joskow, Richard Schmalensee, Juan-Pablo Montero, and Elizabeth M. Bailey. 2005. *Markets for Clean Air: The U.S. Acid Rain Program*. Cambridge: Cambridge University Press.

Ellickson, Robert C. 1989. "Bringing Culture and Human Frailty to Rational Actors." *Chicago-Kent Law Review* 65: 23–55.

Ennis, Thomas W. 1979. "David Kershaw Dead; Executive Was Expert on Welfare Reform." Pp. B23 in *New York Times*, 13 December.

Enthoven, Alain C. 1963. "Economic Analysis in the Department of Defense." *American Economic Review* 53: 413–23.

———. 1971. "Alain C. Enthoven Oral History Interview—JFK#1, 06/04/1971." Oral history conducted by William W. Moss. Boston, MA: John F. Kennedy Presidential Library and Museum.

———. 1978a. "Consumer-Choice Health Plan—A National-Health-Insurance Proposal Based on Regulated Competition in the Private Sector." *New England Journal of Medicine* 298: 709–20.

———. 1978b. "Consumer-Choice Health Plan—Inflation and Inequity in Health Care Today: Alternatives for Cost Control and an Analysis of Proposals for National Health Insurance." *New England Journal of Medicine* 298: 650–58.

———. 1980. *Health Plan: The Only Practical Solution to the Soaring Cost of Medical Care*. Boston, MA: Addison-Wesley.

———. 1988. "Managed Competition: An Agenda for Action." *Health Affairs* 7(3): 25–47.

Enthoven, Alain C., and K. Wayne Smith. 1971. *How Much Is Enough? Shaping the Defense Program 1961–1969*. Santa Monica, CA: RAND Corporation, CB-403. As of May 20, 2021: https://www.rand.org/pubs/commercial_books/CB403.html.

Erickson, Paul. 2015. *The World the Game Theorists Made*. Chicago: University of Chicago Press.

Esposito, John C., and Larry J. Silverman. 1970. *Vanishing Air: The Ralph Nader Study Group Report on Air Pollution*. New York: Grossman Publishers.

Estrada, Louie. 2004. "Federal Election Official Phillip 'Sam' Hughes Dies." Pp. C11 in *Washington Post*, 20 June.

Falkson, Joseph. 1980. *HMOs and the Politics of Health System Reform*. Chicago: American Hospital Association.

Federal Trade Commission. 1971. *Annual Report of the Federal Trade Commission for the Fiscal Year Ended June 30, 1971*. Washington, DC: Federal Trade Commission.

———. 1974. *Annual Report of the Federal Trade Commission for the Fiscal Year Ended June 30, 1974*. Washington, DC: Federal Trade Commission.

Fein, Rashi. 1979. "Commentary." *Milbank Quarterly* 57(3): 353–57.

———. 1982. "What Is Wrong with the Language of Medicine?" *New England Journal of Medicine* 306: 863–64.

———. 1994. "Economists and Health Reform." *PS: Political Science & Politics* 27(2): 192–94.

Feldstein, Mark. 2010. *Poisoning the Press: Richard Nixon, Jack Anderson, and the Rise of Washington's Scandal Culture*. New York: Macmillan.

Feldstein, Martin S. 1973. "The Welfare Loss of Excess Health Insurance." *Journal of Political Economy* 81(2): 251–80.

Fellmeth, Robert C. 1970. *The Interstate Commerce Omission, the Public Interest and the ICC: The Ralph Nader Study Group Report on the Interstate Commerce Commission and Transportation*. New York: Grossman Publishers.

Fenno, Richard F. 1968. "The Impact of PPBS on the Congressional Appropriations Process." Pp. 175–94 in *Information Support, Program Budgeting, and the Congress*, edited by Robert Lee Chartrand, Kenneth Janda, and Michael Hugo. New York: Spartan Books.

Finbow, Robert. 1998. "Presidential Leadership or Structural Constraints? The Failure of President Carter's Health Insurance Proposals." *Presidential Studies Quarterly* 28(1): 169–86.

First National People of Color Environmental Leadership Summit. 1991. "The Principles of Environmental Justice." As of 28 July 2021: https://www.ejnet.org/ej/principles.html.

Fisher, Bruce D. 1984. "Controlling Government Regulation: Cost-Benefit Analysis before and after the Cotton-Dust Case." *Administrative Law Review* 36(2): 179–207.

Fisher, Franklin M. 2012. "Carl Kaysen: 5 March 1920–8 February 2010." *Proceedings of the American Philosophical Society* 156: 340–46.

Fishman, Steven B. 1973. "A Preliminary Assessment of the National Environmental Policy Act of 1969." *Urban Law Annual* 1973: 209–41.

Fleck, Ludwik. 1979 [1935]. *Genesis and Development of a Scientific Fact*. Chicago: University of Chicago Press.

Fleishman, Joel L. 1990. "A New Framework for Integration: Policy Analysis and Public Management." *American Behavioral Scientist* 33(6): 733–54.

Fleury, Jean-Baptiste. 2010. "Drawing New Lines: Economists and Other Social Scientists on Society in the 1960s." *History of Political Economy* 42: 315–42.

———. 2012. "Poverty and the Scope of Economics in the Sixties."

Fligstein, Neil. 1990. *The Transformation of Corporate Control*. Cambridge, MA: Harvard University Press.

Fogel, Robert William, Enid M. Fogel, Mark Guglielmo, and Nathaniel Grotte. 2013. "The Early History of the NBER." Pp. 21–48 in *Political Arithmetic: Simon Kuznets and the Empirical Tradition in Economics*, edited by Robert William Fogel, Enid M. Fogel, Mark Guglielmo, and Nathaniel Grotte. Chicago: University of Chicago Press.

Ford, Gerald R. 1974. "'Whip Inflation Now' Speech." Miller Center, University of Virginia. As of 28 July 2021: https://millercenter.org/the-presidency/presidential-speeches/october-8-1974-whip-inflation-now-speech.

Forget, Evelyn L. 2011. "A Tale of Two Communities: Fighting Poverty in the Great Society (1964–68)." *History of Political Economy* 43: 199–223.

Fourcade, Marion. 2009. *Economists and Societies: Discipline and Profession in the United States, Britain, and France, 1890s to 1990s*. Princeton, NJ: Princeton University Press.

Fox, Daniel M. 1979. "From Reform to Relativism: A History of Economists and Health Care." *Milbank Quarterly* 57(3): 297–336.

———. 1991. "The 'Milbank Quarterly' and Health Services Research, 1977–1990." *Milbank Quarterly* 69(2): 185–97.

Fox, Eleanor M. 1979. "A Clarion Universe of Microeconomic Policy." *New York University Law Review* 54: 446–66.

———. 1982. "The 1982 Merger Guidelines: When Economists Are Kings?" *California Law Review* 71: 281–302.

———. 1987. "Chairman Miller, the Federal Trade Commission, Economics, and *Rashomon*." *Law and Contemporary Problems* 50(4): 33–55.

Fox, Justin. 2014. "How Economics PhDs Took Over the Federal Reserve." *Harvard Business Review*. As of 28 July 2021: https://hbr.org/2014/02/how-economics-phds-took-over-the-federal-reserve.

Fraas, Arthur. 1991. "The Role of Economic Analysis in Shaping Environmental Policy." *Duke Law Journal* 54(4): 113–25.

Franklin, Ben A. 1965. "Mayors Shelve Dispute on Poor." Pp. 20 in *New York Times*, 2 June.

Freed, Gary L., and Anup Das. 2015. "Nixon or Obama: Who Is the Real Radical Liberal on Health Care?" *Pediatrics* 136(2): 211–14.

Friedlaender, Ann F. 1969. *The Dilemma of Freight Transport Regulation*. Washington, DC: Brookings Institution.

Friedman, Milton. 1962. *Capitalism and Freedom*. Chicago: University of Chicago Press.

Friedman, Milton, and Simon Kuznets. 1945. *Income from Independent Professional Practice*. New York: National Bureau of Economic Research.

Frohnmayer, Otto J. 1969. "Dwight D. Eisenhower, 1890–1969." *American Bar Association Journal* 55: 550.

Frumkin, Peter, and Kimberly Francis. 2015. "Constructing Effectiveness: The Emergence of the Evaluation Research Industry." Pp. 397–426 in *LBJ's Neglected Legacy: How Lyndon Johnson Reshaped Domestic Policy and Government*, edited by Robert H. Wilson, Norman J. Glickman, and Laurence E. Lynn, Jr. Austin: University of Texas Press.

Fuchs, Ralph F. 1960. "Antitrust Policy: An Economic and Legal Analysis." *University of Pennsylvania Law Review* 109: 146–52.

Fuchs, Victor R. 1974. *Who Shall Live? Health, Economics, and Social Choice*. New York: Basic Books.

Fuller, Jon Wayne. 1972. "Congress and the Defense Budget: A Study of the McNamara Years." PhD diss., Princeton University.

Funk, Russell, and Daniel Hirschman. 2014. "Derivatives and Deregulation: Financial Innovation and the Demise of Glass–Steagall." *Administrative Science Quarterly* 59: 690–704.

Furner, Mary O. 1975. *Advocacy and Objectivity: A Crisis in the Professionalization of American Social Science, 1865–1905*. Lexington: University of Kentucky.

Furner, Mary O., and Barry Supple. 1990. "Ideas, Institutions, and State in the United States and Britain: An Introduction." Pp. 1–39 in *The State and Economic Knowledge: The American and British Experiences*, edited by Mary O. Furner and Barry Supple. Cambridge: Cambridge University Press.

Gamarekian, Barbara. 1985. "A Career of Power and Anonymity." *New York Times*, 15 June.

Garraty, John A. 1981. *The Cost of Living in America, 1800–1980: A Graphic Treatment*. Cambridge: Cambridge University Press.

Gaughan, Patrick A. 2017. *Mergers, Acquisitions, and Corporate Restructurings*. New York: Wiley.

Gavil, Andrew I. 2002. "A First Look at the Powell Papers: Sylvania and the Process of Change in the Supreme Court." *Antitrust* 17: 8–13.

Gellhorn, Ernest, and Glen O. Robinson. 1983. "The Role of Economic Analysis in Legal Education." *Journal of Legal Education* 33: 247–73.

Gerard, David, and Lester Lave. 2007. "Experiments in Technology Forcing: Comparing the Regulatory Processes of U.S. Automobile Safety and Emissions Regulations." *International Journal of Technology, Policy, and Management* 7(1): 1–14.

Gillette, Michael L. 2010. *Launching the War on Poverty: An Oral History*. Oxford: Oxford University Press.

Ginsburg, Douglas H. 2008. "Judge Bork, Consumer Welfare, and Antitrust Law." *Harvard Journal of Law and Public Policy* 31: 449–54.

Giocoli, Nicola. 2014. *Predatory Pricing in Antitrust Law and Economics: A Historical Perspective*. New York: Routledge.

Gladieux, Lawrence E., and Thomas R. Wolanin. 1976. *Congress and the Colleges: The National Politics of Higher Education*. Lexington, MA: Lexington Books.

Glaeser, Edward L. 2009. "Remembering the Father of Transportation Economics." *New York Times*, 27 October.

Glickman, Lawrence B. 2009. *Buying Power: A History of Consumer Activism in America*. Chicago: University of Chicago Press.

Glyn, Andrew. 2007. *Capitalism Unleashed: Finance, Globalization, and Welfare*. Oxford: Oxford University Press.

Goldschmid, Harvey J., H. Michael Mann, and J. Fred Weston (Eds.). 1974. *Industrial Concentration: The New Learning*. New York: Little, Brown.

Gómez-Baggethun, Erik, Rudolf de Groot, Pedro L. Lomas, and Carlos Montes. 2010. "The History of Ecosystem Services in Economic Theory and Practice: From Early Notions to Markets and Payment Schemes." *Ecological Economics* 69: 1209–18.

Goodwin, Craufurd D. 1998. "The Patrons of Economics in a Time of Transformation." *History of Political Economy* 30(Annual Supplement): 53–81.

Gordon, Kermit. 1964. "Kermit Gordon, Oral History Interview—JFK#1, 7/12/1964." Oral history conducted by Robert C. Turner. Boston, MA: John F. Kennedy Presidential Library and Museum.

———. 1969. "Oral History." Oral history conducted by David McComb. Austin, TX: Lyndon B. Johnson Presidential Library.

Gorham, William. 1967. "Notes of a Practitioner." Pp. 4–8 in *Public Interest* (Summer).

———. 1986. "William Gorham Oral History Interview I." Oral history conducted by Janet Kerr-Tener. Austin, TX: Lyndon B. Johnson Presidential Library.

"Graduate School Notes." 1970. *Princeton Alumni Weekly*, 29 September.

Graham, Hugh Davis. 1984. *The Uncertain Triumph: Federal Education Policy in the Kennedy and Johnson Years*. Chapel Hill: University of North Carolina Press.

Gramlich, Edward M., and Patricia P. Koshel. 1975. *Educational Performance Contracting*. Washington, DC: Brookings Institution.

Green, Mark J. 1972. *The Closed Enterprise System: Ralph Nader's Study Group Report on Antitrust Enforcement*. New York: Bantam Books.

Greenberg, David H., Donna Linksz, and Marvin Mandell. 2003. *Social Experimentation and Public Policymaking*. Washington, DC: Urban Institute Press.

Greenberg, Warren (Ed.). 1978. *Competition in the Health Care Sector: Past, Present, and Future: Proceedings of a Conference Sponsored by the Bureau of Economics, Federal Trade Commission, March 1978*. Washington, DC: Beard Books.

Greene, Hillary. 2006. "Guideline Institutionalization: The Role of Merger Guidelines in Antitrust Discourse." *William and Mary Law Review* 48: 771–857.

Greenstone, J. David, and Paul E. Peterson. 1973. *Race and Authority in Urban Politics: Community Participation in the War on Poverty*. New York: Russell Sage Foundation.

Grether, Ewald T. 1970. "Industrial Organization: Past History and Future Problems." *American Economic Review* 60(2): 83–89.

———. 1993. "Ewald T. Grether: Dean of UCB School of Commerce, Industry, and Labor Administration." Oral history conducted by Harriet Nathan. Berkeley: Oral History Center, Bancroft Library, University of California.

Grossman, David M. 1982. "American Foundations and the Support of Economic Research, 1913–29." *Minerva* 20(1/2): 59–82.

Grossmann, Matt, and David A. Hopkins. 2016. *Asymmetric Politics: Ideological Republicans and Group Interest Democrats*. Oxford: Oxford University Press.

Grundler, Christopher. 2020. "The Acid Rain Program: A Success Story." EPA Blog. As of 28 July 2021: https://blog.epa.gov/2020/05/21/the-acid-rain-program-a-success-story/.

Gueron, Judith, and Howard Rolston. 2013. *Fighting for Reliable Evidence*. New York: Russell Sage Foundation.

Hacker, Jacob S. 1997. *The Road to Nowhere: The Genesis of President Clinton's Plan for Health Security*. Princeton, NJ: Princeton University Press.

Hacker, Jacob S., and Paul Pierson. 2011. *Winner-Take-All Politics: How Washington Made the Rich Richer—and Turned Its Back on the Middle Class*. New York: Simon & Schuster.

Hacking, Ian. 1992. "Statistical Language, Statistical Truth, and Statistical Reason: The Self-Authentification of a Style of Scientific Reasoning." *Social Dimensions of Science* 3: 130–57.

Hahn, Robert W., Sheila M. Olmstead, and Robert N. Stavins. 2003. "Environmental Regulation in the 1990s: A Retrospective Analysis." *Harvard Environmental Law Review* 27: 377–415.

Hall, George R. 1972. "The RAND/HEW Study of Performance Contracting: A Brief Summary of Findings." Pp. 14–22 in *Rand Work in Elementary and Secondary Education: A Representative Selection*, edited by Stephen J. Carroll, George R. Hall, John A. Pincus, and Daniel Weiler. Santa Monica, CA: RAND Corporation.

Hall, Peter A. 1993. "Policy Paradigms, Social Learning and the State: The Case of Economic Policymaking in Britain." *Comparative Politics* 25: 275–96.

Hallett, Tim, and Matt Gougherty. 2018. "Making Policy Professionals: Economics and Socialization in a Masters of Public Affairs Program." Paper presented at the European Group for Organization Studies Meetings, Tallinn, Estonia.

Halvorson, George Charles. 2017. "Valuing the Air: The Politics of Environmental Governance from the Clean Air Act to Carbon Trading." PhD diss., Columbia University.

Hamby, Alonzo. 1973. *Beyond the New Deal: Harry S. Truman and American Liberalism*. New York: Columbia University Press.

Hammond, Richard J. 1960. *Benefit-Cost Analysis and Water-Pollution Control*. Stanford, CA: Food Research Institute of Stanford University.

Hanley, Nick, and Clive L. Splash. 1993. *Cost-Benefit Analysis and the Environment*. Cheltenham, UK: Edward Elgar.

Hanushek, Eric A. 1972. *Education and Race: An Analysis of the Educational Production Process*. New York: Lexington Books.

Harper, Edwin, Fred A. Kramer, and Andrew M. Rouse. 1969. "Implementation and Use of PPB in Sixteen Federal Agencies." *Public Administration Review* 1969(November/December): 623–32.

Harris, Fred R. 1971. "The 'New Populism' and Industrial Reform: The Case for a New Antitrust Law." *Antitrust Law and Economics Review* 4: 9–46.

Harris, Richard A., and Sidney M. Milkis. 1996. *The Politics of Regulatory Change: A Tale of Two Agencies*. Oxford: Oxford University Press.

Harrison, Jill Lindsey. 2019. *From the Inside Out: The Fight for Environmental Justice within Government Agencies*. Cambridge, MA: MIT Press.

Hart, Philip A. 1972. "Restructuring the Oligopoly Sector: The Case for a New Industrial Reorganization Act." *Antitrust Law and Economics Review* 5: 35–70.

Harvey, David. 2005. *A Brief History of Neoliberalism*. Oxford: Oxford University Press.

Hatzis, Panagiotis. 1996. "The Academic Origins of John F. Kennedy's New Frontier." Master's thesis, Concordia University. As of 28 July 2021: https://www.collectionscanada.gc.ca/obj /s4/f2/dsk2/ftp04/mq25959.pdf.

Haveman, Robert H. 1976. "Policy Analysis and the Congress: An Economist's View." *Policy Analysis* 2(2): 235–50.

———. 2014. "Curriculum Vitae." As of 28 July 2021: https://lafollette.wisc.edu/images /publications/facstaff/haveman/haveman-robertCV.pdf.

Havighurst, Clark C. 1970a. "Health Care: Part I: Forward." *Law and Contemporary Problems* 35(Spring): 229–32.

———. 1970b. "Health Care: Part II: Forward." *Law and Contemporary Problems* 35(Spring): 667–68.

———. 1970c. "Health Maintenance Organizations and the Market for Health Services." *Law and Contemporary Problems* 35: 716–95.

——— (Ed.). 1974. *Regulating Health Facilities Construction: Proceedings of a Conference on Health Planning, Certificates of Need, and Market Entry*. Washington, DC: American Enterprise Institute for Public Policy Research.

———. 1977. "Controlling Health Care Costs: Strengthening the Private Sector's Hand." *Journal of Health Politics, Policy and Law* 1(4): 471–98.

———. 2004. "I've Seen Enough! My Life and Times in Health Care Law and Policy." *Health Matrix: The Journal of Law-Medicine* 14(1): 107–30.

Hawley, Ellis W. 1990. "Economic Inquiry and the State in New Era America; Antistatist Corporatism and Positive Statism in Uneasy Coexistence." Pp. 287–324 in *The State and Economic Knowledge*, edited by Mary O. Furner and Barry Supple. Cambridge: Cambridge University Press.

Hay, George H. 2008. "Oral History." Conducted by Ky P. Ewing. American Bar Association, Section of Antitrust Law, Public Education and Oral History Committee. Available from the author upon request.

Haydon, Brownlee W. 1972. *Histogram of RAND Departmental Growth*. Santa Monica, CA: RAND Corporation Archives, IN-21377-1.

Hays, R. Allen. 2012. *The Federal Government and Urban Housing*. Albany: SUNY Press.

Hays, Samuel P. 1989. "Three Decades of Environmental Politics: The Historical Context." Pp. 19–80 in *Government and Environmental Politics: Essays on Historical Developments since World War Two*, edited by Michael J. Lacey. Washington, DC: Woodrow Wilson Center Press.

Hefleblower, Richard B., and George W. Stocking. 1958. *Readings in Industrial Organization and Public Policy*. Homewood, IL: American Economic Association.

Hemphill, Scott, and Richard A. Posner. 2015. "*Philadelphia National Bank* at 50: An Interview with Judge Richard Posner." *Antitrust Law Journal* 80: 205–17.

Herken, Gregg. 1985. *Counsels of War*. New York: Alfred A. Knopf.

Hicks, J. R. 1939. "The Foundations of Welfare Economics." *Economic Journal* 49: 696–712.

———. 1943. "The Four Consumer's Surpluses." *Review of Economic Studies* 11(1): 31–41.

Hills, Carla A., William F. Baxter, Thomas J. Campbell, and Donald F. Turner. 1982. "Panel Discussion: The New Merger Guidelines." *Antitrust Law Journal* 51: 317–35.

Hines, L. G. 1959. "The Economists Discover Water Resources." *Journal of Soil and Water Conservation* 14: 125–26.

Hinton, Elizabeth. 2016. *From the War on Poverty to the War on Crime*. Cambridge, MA: Harvard University Press.

Hirschman, Daniel. 2016. "Inventing the Economy, or: How We Learned to Stop Worrying and Love the GDP." PhD diss., University of Michigan.

———. Forthcoming. "Rediscovering the 1%: Knowledge Infrastructures and the Stylized Facts of Inequality." *American Journal of Sociology*.

Hirschman, Daniel, and Elizabeth Popp Berman. 2014. "Do Economists Make Policies? On the Political Effects of Economics." *Socio-Economic Review* 12(4): 779–811.

Hitch, Charles. 1952. *Suboptimization in Operations Problems*. Santa Monica, CA: RAND Corporation. P-326, 1952. As of 21 May 2021: https://www.rand.org/pubs/papers/P326.html.

———. 1958. *Economics and Military Operations Research*. Santa Monica, CA: RAND Corporation, P-1250. As of 21 May 2021: https://www.rand.org/pubs/papers/P1250.html.

———. 1965. *Decision-Making for Defense*. Berkeley: University of California Press.

———. 1988. "Rand History Project Interview." Oral history conducted by Martin Collins and Joe Tatarewicz. Washington, DC: The NASM-RAND History Project, National Air and Space Museum, Smithsonian Institution.

Hitch, Charles, and William M. Capron. 1952. *Implications of Potential Weapon Developments for Strategic Bombing and Air Defense: A Preliminary Study*. Santa Monica, CA: RAND Corporation, RM-868. As of 21 May 2021: https://www.rand.org/pubs/research_memoranda/RM868.html.

Hitch, Charles, and Roland McKean. 1960. *The Economics of Defense in the Nuclear Age*. Cambridge, MA: Harvard University Press.

Hjort, Howard. 1968. "Discussion: Public Land Policy in the Context of Planning-Programming-Budgeting Systems." *American Journal of Agricultural Economics* 50(5): 1685–87.

———. 2016. "Howard Hjort." LinkedIn. As of 12 May 2016: https://www.linkedin.com/in/howard-hjort-13369220.

Hoag, Malcolm W. 1956. *An Introduction to Systems Analysis*. Santa Monica, CA: RAND Corporation, RM-1678-PR. As of 21 May 2021: https://www.rand.org/pubs/research_memoranda/RM1678.html.

Hoberg, George. 1992. *Pluralism by Design: Environmental Policy and the American Regulatory State*. Westport, CT: Greenwood Publishing Group.

Hodgson, Geoffrey M. 2003. "John R. Commons and the Foundations of Institutional Economics." *Journal of Economic Issues* 37(3): 547–76.

Hoff-Wilson, Joan. 1991. "Outflanking the Liberals on Welfare." Pp. 85–106 in *Richard M. Nixon: Politician, President, Administrator*, edited by Leon Friedman and William F. Levantrosser. Santa Barbara, CA: ABC-CLIO.

Hoffman, Beatrix. 2012. *Health Care for Some: Rights and Rationing in the United States since 1930*. Chicago: University of Chicago Press.

Holden, Laura, and Jeff Biddle. 2017. "The Introduction of Human Capital Theory into Education Policy in the United States." *History of Political Economy* 49(4): 537–74.

Holifield, Ryan. 2001. "Defining Environmental Justice and Environmental Racism." *Urban Geography* 22(1): 78–90.

Hollis-Brusky, Amanda. 2015. *Ideas with Consequences: The Federalist Society and the Conservative Counterrevolution*. Oxford: Oxford University Press.

Holmes, Beatrice Hort. 1972. *A History of Federal Water Resources Programs, 1800–1960*. Washington, DC: Economic Research Service, U.S. Department of Agriculture.

———. 1979. *A History of Federal Water Resources Programs and Policies, 1960–1970*. Washington, DC: Economic Research Service, U.S. Department of Agriculture.

Hone, Thomas C. 2016. "The Historiography of Programming and Acquisition Management since 1950, with a Focus on the Navy." Naval History and Heritage Command. As of 28 July 2021:

https://www.history.navy.mil/research/library/online-reading-room/title-list-alphabetically/n/needs-opportunities-modern-history-us-navy/historiography-programming-acquisition-management-hone.html.

Hood, Katherine. 2017. "The Science of Value: Economic Expertise and the Valuation of Human Life in U.S. Federal Regulatory Agencies." *Social Studies of Science* 47(4): 441–65.

Hoos, Ida Russakoff. 1972. *Systems Analysis in Public Policy: A Critique.* Berkeley: University of California Press.

Hopkins, Thomas, Thomas M. Lenard, John F. Morrall III, and Elizabeth A. Pinkston. 1981. "A Review of the Regulatory Interventions of the Council on Wage and Price Stability 1974–1980." Unpublished paper, Council on Wage and Price Stability, Washington, DC. As of 14 February 2016: http://cowps.mercatus.org/wp-content/uploads/CWPS%20Review%201974-1980.pdf. Available from the author upon request.

Hopkins, Thomas, and Laura Stanley. 2015. "The Council on Wage and Price Stability: A Retrospective." *Journal of Benefit-Cost Analysis* 6(2): 400–431.

Horwitz, Morton J. 1992. *The Transformation of American Law, 1870–1960: The Crisis of Legal Orthodoxy.* Oxford: Oxford University Press.

Horwitz, Robert Britt. 1991. *The Irony of Regulatory Reform: The Deregulation of American Telecommunications.* Oxford: Oxford University Press.

House, Ernest R. 1990. "Trends in Evaluation." *Educational Researcher* 19(3): 24–28.

Hovenkamp, Herbert. 2009a. "Introduction to the Neal Report and the Crisis in Antitrust." *Competition Policy International* 5: 217–83.

———. 2009b. "United States Competition Policy in Crisis: 1890–1955." *Minnesota Law Review* 94: 311–67.

———. 2015. *The Opening of American Law: Neoclassical Legal Thought, 1870–1970.* Oxford: Oxford University Press.

Huntington, Samuel P. 1952. "The Marasmus of the ICC: The Commission, the Railroads, and the Public Interest." *Yale Law Journal* 61: 467–509.

Huret, Romain. 2018. *The Experts' War on Poverty.* Ithaca, NY: Cornell University Press.

Hurley, Timothy M. 2006. "The Urge to Merge: Contemporary Theories on the Rise of Conglomerate Mergers in the 1960s." *Journal of Business and Technology Law* 1(1): 185–205.

Igo, Sarah E. 2007. *The Averaged American: Surveys, Citizens, and the Making of a Mass Public.* Cambridge, MA: Harvard University Press.

"The Industrial Reorganization Act: An Antitrust Proposal to Restructure the American Economy." *Columbia Law Review* 73(3): 635–76.

Institute of Medicine. 1979. *Health Services Research: Report of a Study.* Washington, DC: National Academy of Sciences.

Jacobs, Meg. 2016. *Panic at the Pump: The Energy Crisis and the Transformation of American Politics in the 1970s.* New York: Hill and Wang.

Jaffe, Louis L. 1954. "The Effective Limits of the Administrative Process: A Reevaluation." *Harvard Law Review* 67(7): 1105–35.

Jann, Werner. 1991. "From Policy Analysis to Political Management? An Outside Look at Public-Policy Training in the United States." Pp. 110–30 in *Social Sciences and Modern States: National Experiences and Theoretical Crossroads*, edited by Peter Wagner, Carol Hirschon Weiss, Björn Wittrock, and Hellmut Wollman. Cambridge: Cambridge University Press.

Jardini, David R. 1996. "Out of the Blue Yonder: The RAND Corporation's Diversification into Social Welfare Research, 1946–1968." PhD diss., Carnegie Mellon University.

Jeffrey, Julie Roy. 1978. *Education for Children of the Poor: A Study of the Origins and Implementation of the Elementary and Secondary Education Act of 1965.* Columbus: Ohio State University Press.

Jenkins-Smith, Hank C. 1990. *Democratic Politics and Policy Analysis.* Pacific Grove, CA: Brooks/Cole Publishing.

Johnson, Jeremy. 2016. "Housing Vouchers: A Case Study of the Partisan Policy Cycle." *Social Science History* 40: 63–91.

Johnson, Kirk. 1984. "Technology's Dean: Elizabeth E. Bailey." *New York Times*, 26 August.

Johnson, Lyndon B. 1965. "January 4, 1965: State of the Union." Miller Center, University of Virginia. As of 28 July 2021: https://millercenter.org/the-presidency/presidential-speeches/january-4-1965-state-union.

Johnson, Stephen B. 1997. "Three Approaches to Big Technology: Operations Research, Systems Engineering, and Project Management." *Technology and Culture* 38(4): 891–919.

Jones, Daniel Stedman. 2012. *Masters of the Universe: Hayek, Friedman, and the Birth of Neoliberal Politics*. Princeton, NJ: Princeton University Press.

Jones, Sarah. 2020. "Student-Loan Debt Is Immoral." *New York Magazine*, 16 November. As of 28 July 2021: https://nymag.com/intelligencer/2020/11/biden-student-loan-forgiveness-plan-college-debt-is-immoral.html.

Jost, Timothy. 2003. *Disentitlement? The Threats Facing Our Public Health-Care Programs and a Rights-Based Response*. Oxford: Oxford University Press.

———. 2007. *Health Care at Risk: A Critique of the Consumer-Driven Movement*. Durham, NC: Duke University Press.

Joyce, Philip G. 2011. *The Congressional Budget Office: Honest Numbers, Power, and Policymaking*. Washington, DC: Georgetown University Press.

Juncker, Carl Frederick. 1968. "Establishing Planning-Programming Budgeting Systems in Two Non-Defense Departments." PhD diss., George Washington University.

Jung, Donald J. 1996. *The Federal Communications Commission, the Broadcast Industry, and the Fairness Doctrine, 1981–1987*. Lanham, MD: University Press of America.

Kagan, Elena. 2001. "Presidential Administration." *Harvard Law Review* 114(8): 2245–2385.

Kahn, Alfred. 1970. *The Economics of Regulation, Vol. I: Economic Principles*. Cambridge, MA: MIT Press.

———. 1971. *The Economics of Regulation, Vol. II: Institutional Issues*. Cambridge, MA: MIT Press.

Kaldor, Nicholas. 1939. "Welfare Propositions of Economics and Interpersonal Comparisons of Utility." *Economic Journal* 49(195): 549–52.

Kalman, Laura. 1986. *Legal Realism at Yale, 1927–1960*. Durham: University of North Carolina Press.

Kantor, Harvey. 1991. "Education, Social Reform, and the State: ESEA and Federal Education Policy in the 1960s." *American Journal of Education* 100(1): 47–83.

Kaplan, Fred. 1983. *The Wizards of Armageddon*. Stanford, CA: Stanford University Press.

Katz, Barry M. 1989. *Foreign Intelligence: Research and Analysis in the Office of Strategic Services, 1942–1945*. Cambridge, MA: Harvard University Press.

Katzmann, Robert A. 1980. *Regulatory Bureaucracy: The Federal Trade Commission and Antitrust Policy*. Cambridge, MA: MIT Press.

———. 1986. *Institutional Disability: The Saga of Transportation Policy for the Disabled*. Washington, DC: Brookings Institution Press.

Kauper, Thomas E. 1969. "The 'Warren Court' and the Antitrust Laws: Of Economics, Populism, and Cynicism." *Michigan Law Review* 67: 325–42.

———. 1977. "New Approaches to the Old Problem." *Antitrust Law Journal* 46: 435–47.

———. 1980. "The Goals of United States Antitrust Policy—The Current Debate." *Zeitschrift für die gesamte Staatswissenschaft* 136: 408–34.

———. 1983. "The 1982 Horizontal Merger Guidelines: Of Collusion, Efficiency, and Failure." *California Law Review* 71: 497–534.

———. 1984. "The Role of Economic Analysis in the Antitrust Division Before and After the Establishment of the Economic Policy Office: A Lawyer's View." *Antitrust Bulletin* 29: 111–32.

———. 2007. "Oral History." Oral history conducted by Donald C. Klawiter, American Bar Association, Section of Antitrust Law, Public Education and Oral History Committee. Available from the author upon request.

Kaysen, Carl. 1966. "Carl Kaysen Oral History Interview—JFK #1, 7/11/1966." Oral history conducted by Joseph E. O'Connor. Boston, MA: John F. Kennedy Presidential Library and Museum.

Kaysen, Carl, and Donald F. Turner. 1959. *Antitrust Policy: An Economic and Legal Analysis.* Cambridge, MA: Harvard University Press.

Kearns, Kevin P., Dillon Moore, Rebecca Jeudin, Srivastava Kodavatiganti, and Lydia McShane. 2014. "Bill Drayton and Ashoka." *Johnson Institute for Responsible Leadership Case Study Series* (Fall). As of 28 July 2021: http://citeseerx.ist.psu.edu/viewdoc/download?doi=10.1.1.684 .3685&rep=rep1&type=pdf.

Kerr, Janet C. 1984. "From Truman to Johnson: Ad Hoc Policy Formulation in Higher Education." *Review of Higher Education* 8: 15–54.

Kershaw, Joseph A., and Roland McKean. 1959. *Systems Analysis and Education.* Santa Monica, CA: RAND Corporation, RM-2473-FF. As of 21 May 2021: https://www.rand.org/pubs/research _memoranda/RM2473.html.

———. 1960. *Decision-Making in the Schools: An Outsider's View.* Santa Monica, CA: RAND Corporation, P-1886. As of 21 May 2021: https://www.rand.org/pubs/papers/P1886.html.

———. 1962. *Teacher Shortages and Salary Schedules.* Santa Monica, CA: RAND Corporation, RM-3009-FF. As of 21 May 2021: https://www.rand.org/pubs/research_memoranda/RM3009.html.

Kershaw, Joseph A., with the assistance of Paul N. Courant. 1970. *Government against Poverty.* Washington, DC: Brookings Institution.

Kessel, Reuben A. 1958. "Price Discrimination in Medicine." *Journal of Law and Economics* 1: 20–53.

Keyes, Lucile S. 1951. *Federal Control of Entry into Air Transportation.* Cambridge, MA: Harvard University Press.

Keynes, John Maynard. 1936. *The General Theory of Employment, Interest and Money.* London: Harcourt, Brace.

Khurana, Rakesh. 2007. *From Higher Aims to Hired Hands: The Social Transformation of American Business Schools and the Unfulfilled Promise of Management as a Profession.* Princeton, NJ: Princeton University Press.

Kim, Anne. 2016. "The Monthly Interview: The Man Who Reinvented Public Housing." *Washington Monthly,* 30 June. As of 28 July 2021: https://washingtonmonthly.com/2016/06/30/the -monthly-interview-the-man-who-reinvented-public-housing/.

Kingdon, John W. 1984. *Agendas, Alternatives, and Public Policies.* New York: HarperCollins Publishers.

Kirschten, Dick. 1979. "Tom Jorling—The Lament of a Former Regulator." Pp. 1526–28 in *National Journal,* 15 September.

Kitch, Edmund W. 1983. "The Fire of Truth: A Remembrance of Law and Economics at Chicago, 1932–1970." *Journal of Law and Economics* 26(1): 163–234.

Klarman, Herbert E. 1979. "Health Economics and Health Economics Research." *Milbank Quarterly* 57(3): 371–79.

Klatch, Rebecca E. 1999. *A Generation Divided: The New Left, the New Right, and the 1960s.* Berkeley: University of California Press.

Klausner, Manuel, and Shawn Steel. 1978. "Spotlight: Agency Activist." *Reason* (May). As of 28 July 2021: https://reason.com/1978/05/01/spotlight-agency-activist/.

Klein, Burt. 1988. "Oral History Interview." Oral history conducted by Joe Tatarewicz. Washington, DC: The NASM-RAND History Project, National Air and Space Museum.

Klein, Burton H. 1958. *What's Wrong with Military R and D?* Santa Monica, CA: RAND Corporation, P-1267.

———. 1960. *The Decision-Making Problem in Development*. Santa Monica, CA: RAND Corporation, P-1916. As of 20 May 2021: https://www.rand.org/pubs/papers/P1916.html.

———. 1967. *Public Administration and the Contemporary Economic Revolution*. Santa Monica, CA: RAND Corporation, P-3586. As of 20 May 2021: https://www.rand.org/pubs/papers/P3586.html.

Klein, Burton H., and William Meckling. 1958. *Application of Operations Research to Development Decisions*. Santa Monica, CA: RAND Corporation, P-1054. As of 21 May 2021: https://www.rand.org/pubs/papers/P1054.html.

Kline, Benjamin. 2007. *First along the River: A Brief History of the U.S. Environmental Movement*. Lanham, MD: Rowman & Littlefield.

Kneese, Allen V., and Charles L. Schultze. 1975. *Pollution, Prices, and Public Policy*. Washington, DC: Brookings Institute Press.

Kolko, Gabriel. 1963. *The Triumph of Conservatism: A Reinterpretation of American History, 1900–1916*. New York: Free Press.

Koopmans, Tjalling C. 1947. "Measurement without Theory." *Review of Economics and Statistics* 29(3): 161–72.

Kovacic, William E. 1990. "The Antitrust Paradox Revisited: Robert Bork and the Transformation of Modern Antitrust Policy." *Wayne Law Review* 36: 1413–71.

———. 2007. "The Intellectual DNA of Modern U.S. Competition Law for Dominant Firm Conduct: The Chicago/Harvard Double Helix." *Columbia Law School* 2007: 1–80.

———. 2020. "The Chicago Obsession in the Interpretation of U.S. Antitrust History." *University of Chicago Law Review* 87(2): 459–94.

Kovacic, William E., and Carl Shapiro. 2000. "Antitrust Policy: A Century of Legal and Economic Thinking." *Journal of Economic Perspectives* 14: 43–60.

Kraemer, Kenneth L., Siegfried Dickhoven, Susan Fallows Tierney, and John Leslie King. 1987. *Datawars: The Politics of Modeling in Federal Policymaking*. New York: Columbia University Press.

Kramer, Larry. 2018. "Beyond Neoliberalism: Rethinking Political Economy." Hewlett Foundation, 26 April. As of 28 July 2021: https://hewlett.org/library/beyond-neoliberalism-rethinking-political-economy/.

Kramer, Victor H. 1981. "Antitrust Today: The Baxterization of the Sherman and Clayton Acts." *Wisconsin Law Review* 1981: 1287–1302.

Krippner, Greta. 2011. *Capitalizing on Crisis: The Political Origins of the Rise of Finance*. Cambridge, MA: Harvard University Press.

Krueger, Alan B. 2014. "The Department of Labor at the Intersection of Research and Policy." *ILR Review* 67(Supplement): 584–93.

Kruse, Kevin. 2007. *White Flight: Atlanta and the Making of Modern Conservatism*. Princeton, NJ: Princeton University Press.

Krutilla, John V. 1967. "Conservation Reconsidered." *American Economic Review* 57(4): 777–86.

Krutilla, John V., and Otto Eckstein. 1958. *Multiple Purpose River Development: Studies in Applied Economic Analysis*. Baltimore, MD: Resources for the Future, Inc., by Johns Hopkins University Press.

Kumekawa, Ian. 2017. *The First Serious Optimist: A. C. Pigou and the Birth of the Welfare Economics*. Princeton, NJ: Princeton University Press.

Kwak, James. 2013. "Cultural Capture and the Financial Crisis." Pp. 71–98 in *Preventing Regulatory Capture: Special Interest Influence and How to Limit It*, edited by Daniel Carpenter and David A. Moss. Cambridge: Cambridge University Press.

Kwerel, Evan R., and Gregory L. Rosston. 2000. "An Insiders' View of FCC Spectrum Auctions." *Journal of Regulatory Economics* 17(3): 253–89.

Lacey, Jim. 2011. *Keep from All Thoughtful Men: How U.S. Economists Won World War II*. Annapolis, MD: Naval Institute Press.

Lacey, Michael J., and Mary O. Furner (Eds.). 1993. *The State and Social Investigation in Britain and the United States*. Cambridge: Cambridge University Press.

Lagemann, Ellen Condiffe. 2000. *An Elusive Science: The Troubling History of Educational Research*. Chicago: University of Chicago Press.

Lamb, Charles M. 2005. *Housing Segregation in Suburban America since 1960: Presidential and Judicial Politics*. Cambridge: Cambridge University Press.

Lande, Robert H. 1982. "Wealth Transfers as the Original and Primary Concern of Antitrust: The Efficiency Interpretation Challenged." *Hastings Law Journal* 34: 65–151.

Landes, William M. 1968. "The Economics of Fair Employment Laws." *Journal of Political Economy* 76(4): 507–52.

Landy, Marc K., Martin A. Levin, and Martin M. Shapiro (Eds.). 2007. *Creating Competitive Markets: The Politics of Regulatory Reform*. Cambridge: Cambridge University Press.

Landy, Marc K., Marc J. Roberts, and Stephen R. Thomas. 1994. *The Environmental Protection Agency: Asking the Wrong Questions from Nixon to Clinton*. Oxford: Oxford University Press.

Larochelle, Ryan. 2019. "Reassessing the History of the Community Action Program, 1963–1967." *Journal of Policy History* 31(1): 126–64.

Lash, Jonathan, Katherine Gillman, and David Sheridan. 1984. *A Season of Spoils: The Reagan Administration's Attack on the Environment*. New York: Pantheon Books.

Lassiter, Matthew D. 2007. *The Silent Majority: Suburban Politics in the Sunbelt South*. Princeton, NJ: Princeton University Press.

Lawlor, Edward F. 1979. "Income Security." Pp. 11–59 in *Studies in the Management of Social R&D: Selected Policy Areas*, edited by Laurence E. Lynn, Jr. Washington, DC: National Academy of Sciences.

Lawson, Catherine. 2015. "The 'Textbook Controversy': Lessons for Contemporary Economics." *Journal of Academic Freedom* 6. As of 28 July 2021: https://www.aaup.org/JAF6/%E2%80%9Ctextbook-controversy%E2%80%9D-lessons-contemporary-economics.

Lehman, Jeffrey, and Shirelle Phelps. 2005. *West's Encyclopedia of American Law*. New York: Thomson/Gale.

Lei, Serena. 2014. "Research's Role in the War on Poverty: A Q&A with William Gorham, Founding President of the Urban Institute." Washington, DC: Urban Institute.

Lemann, Nicholas. 1988. "The Unfinished War." Pp. 37–56 in *Atlantic Monthly*, December.

Leonard, Thomas C. 2009. "American Economic Reform in the Progressive Era: Its Foundational Beliefs and Their Relation to Eugenics." *History of Political Economy* 41(1): 109–41.

Lepenies, Philipp. 2016. *The Power of a Single Number: A Political History of GDP*. New York: Columbia University Press.

Levin, Michael H. 1982. "Getting There: Implementing the 'Bubble' Policy." Pp. 59–92 in *Social Regulation: Strategies for Reform*, edited by Eugene Bardach and Robert Kagan. Piscataway, NJ: Transaction.

Levine, Michael E. 1965. "Is Regulation Necessary? California Air Transportation and National Regulatory Policy." *Yale Law Journal* 74: 1416–47.

Levine, Robert A. 1969. "Oral History." Oral history conducted by Stephen Goodell. Austin, TX: Lyndon B. Johnson Presidential Library.

———. 1970. *The Poor Ye Need Not Have with You: Lessons from the War on Poverty*. Cambridge, MA: MIT Press.

———. 1975. "How and Why the Experiment Came About." Pp. 15–24 in *Work Incentives and Income Guarantees: New Jersey Negative Income Tax Experiment*, edited by Joseph A. Pechman and P. Michael Timpane. Washington, DC: Brookings Institution.

Levins, Hoag. 2017. "Penn's Nationally Renowned Accidental Health Economist." Leonard Davis Institute of Health Economics, University of Pennsylvania. As of 28 July 2021: https://ldi.upenn.edu/news/penns-nationally-renowned-accidental-health-economist.

Levinson, Marc. 2011. *The Great A&P and the Struggle for Small Business in America*. New York: Hill & Wang.

Light, Jennifer S. 2005. *From Warfare to Welfare: Defense Intellectuals and Urban Problems in Cold War America*. Baltimore, MD: Johns Hopkins University Press.

Lindblom, C. E. 1954. *On Criteria: The Last Prose of the Summer*. Santa Monica, CA: RAND Corporation Archives, D-2424.

Liroff, Richard A. 1976. *A National Policy for the Environment: NEPA and Its Aftermath*. Bloomington: Indiana University Press.

———. 1986. *Reforming Air Pollution Regulation: The Toil and Trouble of EPA's Bubble*. Washington, DC: Conservation Foundation.

Litan, Robert E. 1985. "Regulatory Policy in the Second Reagan Term." *Brookings Review* 3(3): 21–27.

Litan, Robert E., and Carl Shapiro. 2002. "Antitrust Policy in the Clinton Administration." Pp. 435–85 in *American Economic Policy in the 1990s*, edited by Jeffrey A. Frankel and Peter R. Orszag. Cambridge, MA: MIT Press.

Litan, Robert E., and William Nordhaus. 1983. *Reforming Federal Regulation*. New Haven, CT: Yale University Press.

Litvack, Sanford M. 1982a. "The Ebb and Flow of Antitrust Enforcement: The Reagan and Carter Administrations." *Brigham Young University Law Review* 1982: 849–56.

———. 1982b. "Government versus Antitrust Policy: Theory versus Practice and the Role of the Antitrust Division." *Texas Law Review* 60: 649–70.

Loss, Christopher P. 2012. *Between Citizens and the State: The Politics of American Higher Education in the 20th Century*. Princeton, NJ: Princeton University Press.

Lovett, William A. 1974. "Economic Analysis and Its Role in Legal Education." *Journal of Legal Education* 26: 385–421.

Lowi, Theodore. 1969. *The End of Liberalism*. New York: W. W. Norton.

Lowrey, Annie. 2020. "Go Ahead, Forgive Student Debt." *The Atlantic*, November. As of 28 July 2021: https://www.theatlantic.com/ideas/archive/2020/11/why-biden-should-forgive-student-loan-debt/617171/.

Lowry, Ira S. 1982. *Looking Back on the Housing Assistance Supply Experiment*. Santa Monica, CA: RAND Corporation, P-6785. As of 21 May 2021: https://www.rand.org/pubs/papers/P6785.html.

LPE Project. 2017. "Toward a Manifesto." Law and Political Economy Project, Yale University. As of 28 July 2021: https://lpeproject.org/lpe-manifesto/.

Lstiburek, Joseph. 2010. "BSI-030: Advanced Framing." Building Science Corporation. As of 28 July 2021: https://www.buildingscience.com/documents/insights/bsi-030-advanced-framing.

Lynn, Jr., Laurence E., and David deF. Whitman. 1981. *The President as Policymaker: Jimmy Carter and Welfare Reform*. Philadelphia: Temple University Press.

Lyons, Gene M. 1969. *The Uneasy Partnership: Social Science and the Federal Government in the Twentieth Century*. New York: Russell Sage Foundation.

Lyons, Richard D. 1971. "Americans Now Favor a National Health Plan." Pp. 1 in *New York Times*, 9 August.

MacAvoy, Paul W. 1962. *Price Formation in Natural Gas Fields: A Study of Competition, Monopoly, and Regulation*. New Haven, CT: Yale University Press.

———. 1965. *The Economic Effects of Regulation: The Trunkline Railroad Cartels and the Interstate Commerce Commission Before 1900*. Cambridge, MA: MIT Press.

MacKenzie, Donald. 2006. *An Engine, not a Camera: How Financial Models Shape Markets*. Cambridge, MA: MIT Press.

MacLaury, Judson. 1981. "The Job Safety Law of 1970: Its Passage Was Perilous." U.S. Department of Labor. As of 28 July 2021: https://www.dol.gov/general/aboutdol/history/osha.

———. 1984. "The Occupational Safety and Health Administration: A History of Its First Thirteen Years, 1971–1984." U.S. Department of Labor. As of 28 July 2021: https://www.dol.gov/general/aboutdol/history/mono-osha13introtoc.

MacLean, Nancy. 2017. *Democracy in Chains: The Deep History of the Radical Right's Stealth Plan for America*. New York: Penguin.

Madrick, Jeff. 2010. "Obama's Risky Business." *New York Review*, 15 July.

Malbin, Michael J. 1979. *Unelected Representatives*. New York: Basic Books.

Manne, Henry G. 1965. "Mergers and the Market for Corporate Control." *Journal of Political Economy* 73(2): 110–20.

———. 1966. *Insider Trading and the Stock Market*. New York: Free Press.

———. 2005. "How Law and Economics Was Marketed in a Hostile World: A Very Personal History." Pp. 309–27 in *The Origins of Law and Economics: Essays by the Founding Fathers*, edited by Francesco Parisi and Charles K. Rowley. Cheltenham, UK: Edward Elgar Publishing.

Manning, Willard G., Joseph P. Newhouse, Naihua Duan, Emmett B. Keeler, Arleen Leibowitz, and M. Susan Marquis. 1987. "Health Insurance and the Demand for Medical Care: Evidence from a Randomized Experiment." *American Economic Review* 77(3): 251–77.

Marcus, Alfred. 1980a. "Environmental Protection Agency." Pp. 267–303 in *The Politics of Regulation*, edited by James Q. Wilson. New York: Basic Books.

———. 1980b. *Promise and Performance: Choosing and Implementing an Environmental Policy*. Westport, CT: Greenwood Press.

Marcus, Ruth, and Al Kamen. 1987. "Reagan Selects Conservative Appeals Judge for High Court." *Washington Post*, 30 October.

Markham, Jr., Jesse W. 1952. *Competition in the Rayon Industry*. Cambridge, MA: Harvard University Press.

Markus, Lewis. 1962. "The Role of Economics in Department of Justice Enforcement of the Antitrust Laws." *ABA Antitrust Section* 20: 13–19.

Marquard, Bryan. 2014. "Rashi Fein, 88; Economist Was an Architect of Medicare." *Boston Globe*, 11 September.

Marshall, Alfred. 1890. *Principles of Economics*. London: Macmillan.

Martin, Isaac William. 2008. *The Permanent Tax Revolt: How the Property Tax Transformed American Politics*. Stanford, CA: Stanford University Press.

Mashaw, Jerry L., and David L. Harfst. 1991. *The Struggle for Auto Safety*. Cambridge, MA: Harvard University Press.

Mason, Edward S. (Ed.). 1959. *The Corporation in Modern Society*. Cambridge, MA: Harvard University Press.

———. 1973. "Oral History Interview with Edward S. Mason." Oral history conducted by Richard D. McKinzie. Independence, MO: Harry S. Truman Library.

Mason, Robert. 2014. *Richard Nixon and the Quest for a New Majority*. Chapel Hill: University of North Carolina Press.

Matusow, Allen J. 1984. *The Unraveling of America: A History of Liberalism in the 1960s*. New York: Harper & Row.

McCabe, Joshua. 2018. *The Fiscalization of Social Policy: How Taxpayers Trumped Children in the Fight against Child Poverty*. Oxford: Oxford University Press.

McCabe, Joshua, and Elizabeth Popp Berman. 2016. "American Exceptionalism Revisited: Tax Relief, Poverty Reduction, and the Politics of Child Tax Credits." *Sociological Science* 3: 540–67.

McCarthy, Michael A. 2017. *Dismantling Solidarity: Capitalist Politics and American Pensions since the New Deal*. Ithaca, NY: Cornell University Press.

McCauley, Douglas J. 2006. "Selling Out on Nature." *Nature* 443(7 September): 27–28.

McCauley, Kathy, Bruce Barron, and Morton Coleman. 2008. *Crossing the Aisle to Cleaner Air: How the Bipartisan "Project 88" Transformed Environmental Policy.* Pittsburgh: Institute of Politics, University of Pittsburgh.

McCloskey, J. F., and Florence N. Trefethen. 1954. *Operations Research for Management.* Baltimore, MD: Johns Hopkins University Press.

McCombe, Leonard. 1959. "Valuable Batch of Brains: An Odd Little Company Called RAND Plays Big Role in U.S. Defense." Pp. 101–7 in *Life,* 11 May.

McCraw, Thomas K. 1986. *Prophets of Regulation: Charles Francis Adams, Louis D. Brandeis, James M. Landis, Alfred E. Kahn.* Cambridge, MA: Belknap Press.

McDean, Harry C. 1983. "Professionalism, Policy, and Farm Economists in the Early Bureau of Agricultural Economics." *Agricultural History* 57(1): 64–82.

McGarity, Thomas O. 1991. *Reinventing Rationality: The Role of Regulatory Analysis in the Federal Bureaucracy.* Cambridge: Cambridge University Press.

McGee, John S. 1958. "Predatory Price Cutting: The Standard Oil (N.J.) Case." *Journal of Law and Economics* 1: 137–69.

———. 1971. *In Defense of Industrial Concentration.* New York: Praeger Publishers.

McGirr, Lisa. 2001. *Suburban Warriors: The Origins of the New American Right.* Princeton, NJ: Princeton University Press.

McKean, Roland N. 1953. *Suboptimization Criteria and Operations Research.* Santa Monica, CA: RAND Corporation, P-386. As of 20 May 2021: https://www.rand.org/pubs/papers/P386.html.

———. 1955. *Criteria for the Selection of Water-Resource Projects.* Santa Monica, CA: RAND Corporation, P-689. As of 21 May 2021: https://www.rand.org/pubs/papers/P689.html.

———. 1956. "Criteria for the Selection of Water-Resource Projects." *Operations Research* 4(1): 52–60.

———. 1958. *Efficiency in Government through Systems Analysis: With Emphasis on Water Resource Development.* New York: John Wiley & Sons, CB-125.

McKean, Roland, and Joseph A. Kershaw. 1962. *The Solution for Teacher Shortages.* Santa Monica, CA: RAND Corporation, P-2458-1. As of 21 May 2021: https://www.rand.org/pubs/papers/P2458-1.html.

McLaughlin, Milbrey Wallin. 1974. *Evaluation and Reform: The Elementary and Secondary Education Act of 1965, Title I.* Santa Monica, CA: RAND Corporation, R-1292-RC. As of 21 May 2021: https://www.rand.org/pubs/reports/R1292.html.

Meade, Douglas S. 2010. "The U.S. Benchmark IO Table: History, Methodology, and Myths." Paper presented at the 18th Inforum World Conference, Hikone, Japan. As of 28 July 2021: http://www.inforum.umd.edu/papers/conferences/2010/Meade.pdf.

Medema, Steven G. 1996. "Of Pangloss, Pigouvians and Pragmatism: Ronald Coase and Social Cost Analysis." *Journal of the History of Economic Thought* 18(1): 96–114.

———. 1998. "Wandering the Road from Pluralism to Posner: The Transformation of Law and Economics in the Twentieth Century." *History of Political Economy* 30: 202–24.

———. 1999. "Legal Fiction: The Place of the Coase Theorem in Law and Economics." *Economics & Philosophy* 15(2): 209–33.

———. 2011. "A Case of Mistaken Identity: George Stigler, 'The Problem of Social Cost,' and the Coase Theorem." *European Journal of Law and Economics* 31(1): 11–38.

———. 2014a. "The Curious Treatment of the Coase Theorem in the Environmental Economics Literature, 1960–1979." *Review of Environmental Economics and Policy* 8(1): 39–57.

———. 2014b. "Debating Law's Irrelevance: Legal Scholarship and the Coase Theorem in the 1960s." *Texas A&M Law Review* 2: 159–213.

———. 2020. "The Coase Theorem at Sixty." *Journal of Economic Literature* 58(4): 1045–1128.

Medvetz, Thomas. 2012. *Think Tanks in America.* Chicago: University of Chicago Press.

Meese, Alan J. 2010. "Debunking the Purchaser Welfare Account of Section 2 of the Sherman Act: How Harvard Brought Us the Total Welfare Standard and Why We Should Keep It." *New York University Law Review* 85(3): 659–737.

Meidinger, Errol. 1985. "On Explaining the Development of 'Emissions Trading' in U.S. Air Pollution Regulation." *Law & Policy* 7(4): 447–79.

Melhado, Evan M. 1988. "Competition versus Regulation in American Health Policy." Pp. 15–102 in *Money, Power, and Health Care*, edited by Evan M. Melhado, Walter Feinberg, and Harold M. Swartz. Ann Arbor, MI: Health Administration Press.

———. 1998. "Economists, Public Provision, and the Market: Changing Values in Policy Debate." *Journal of Health Politics, Policy and Law* 23(2): 215–63.

Meltzer, Allan H. 2003. *A History of the Federal Reserve, Volume 1: 1913–1951*. Chicago: University of Chicago Press.

Merrill, Thomas W. 1997. "Capture Theory and the Courts: 1967–1983." *Chicago-Kent Law Review* 72(4): 1039–1117.

Meyer, John R., Merton J. Peck, John Stenason, and Charles J. Zwick. 1959. *The Economics of Competition in the Transportation Industries*. Cambridge, MA: Harvard University Press.

Mieczkowski, Yanek. 2005. *Gerald Ford and the Challenges of the 1970s*. Lexington: University Press of Kentucky.

Milazzo, Paul Charles. 2006. *Unlikely Environmentalists: Congress and Clean Water, 1948–1972*. Lawrence: University of Kansas Press.

Miles, Jr., Rufus E. 1967. "The Search for Identity of Graduate Schools of Public Affairs." *Public Administration Review* 27(4): 343–56.

Miller III, James C. 1977. "Lessons of the Economic Impact Statement Program." Pp. 41–21 in *Regulation* (July/Aug.).

———. 1989. *The Economist as Reformer: Revamping the FTC, 1981–1985*. Washington, DC: American Enterprise Institute.

———. 2011a. "Curriculum Vitae." As of 28 July 2021: http://www.jimmiller.org/Jim_vitae.html.

———. 2011b. "The Early Days of Reagan Regulatory Relief and Suggestions for OIRA's Future." *Administrative Law Review* 63: 93–101.

Miller, John E. 2002. "From South Dakota Farm to Harvard Seminar: Alvin H. Hansen, America's Prophet of Keynesianism." *Historian* 64(34): 603–22.

Millon, David K. 1988. "The Sherman Act and the Balance of Power." *Southern California Law Review* 61: 1219–92.

Millstein, Ira M., Lloyd Constantine, Richard J. Favretto, Donald L. Flexner, Warren S. Grimes, Thomas E. Kauper, Mark Leddy, Paul W. MacAvoy, J. Paul McGrath, Barbara A. Reeves, John H. Shenefield, Joe Sims, Stephen D. Susman, Lawrence J. White, and Diane P. Wood. 1989. "Report of the ABA Antitrust Section Task Force on the Antitrust Division of the U.S. Department of Justice." *Antitrust Law Journal* 58: 737–93.

Minor, Harry Francis. 1978. "Policy Analysis and the Congress: An Organizational Study of the Congressional Budget Office." PhD diss., Massachusetts Institute of Technology.

Miroff, Bruce. 2007. *The Liberals' Moment: The McGovern Insurgency and the Identity Crisis of the Democratic Party*. Lawrence: University Press of Kansas.

Mirowski, Philip. 2001. *Machine Dreams: Economics Becomes a Cyborg Science*. Cambridge: Cambridge University Press.

Mirowski, Philip, and Dieter Plehwe (Eds.). 2009. *The Road from Mont Pelerin: The Making of the Neoliberal Thought Collective*. Cambridge, MA: Harvard University Press.

Mishan, E. J. 1967. *The Costs of Economic Growth*. New York: Frederick A. Praeger.

———. 1971. "The Postwar Literature on Externalities: An Interpretive Essay." *Journal of Economic Literature* 9(1): 1–28.

Mitchell, Wesley Clair. 1913. *Business Cycles*. Berkeley: University of California Press.

Mizruchi, Mark. 2013. *The Fracturing of the American Corporate Elite*. Cambridge, MA: Harvard University Press.

Moore, Thomas. 1961. "The Purpose of Licensing." *Journal of Law and Economics* 4: 93–117.

———. 1972. *Freight Transportation Regulation, Surface Freight, and the Interstate Commerce Commission*. Washington, DC: American Enterprise Institute.

Morgan, Mary S., and Malcolm Rutherford. 1998. "American Economics: The Character of the Transformation." *History of Political Economy* 30(5): 1–26.

Morgenstern, Richard D. 1997. *Economic Analyses at EPA: Assessing Regulatory Impact*. Washington, DC: Resources for the Future.

Mosher, Frederick C. 1954. *Program Budgeting: Theory and Practice, with Particular Reference to the U.S. Department of the Army*. Chicago: Public Administration Service.

———. 1979. *The GAO: Quest for Accountability in American Government*. Boulder, CO: Westview Press.

———. 1984. *A Tale of Two Agencies: A Comparative Study of the General Accounting Office and the Office of Management and Budget*. Baton Rouge: Louisiana State University Press.

Mosteller, F., and R. Boruch (Eds.). 2002. *Evidence Matters: Randomized Trials in Education Research*. Washington, DC: Brookings Institution.

Moynihan, Daniel P. 1969a. *Maximum Feasible Misunderstanding: Community Action in the War on Poverty*. New York: Free Press.

——— (Ed.). 1969b. *On Understanding Poverty: Perspectives from the Social Sciences*. New York: Basic Books.

———. 1973. *The Politics of a Guaranteed Income: The Nixon Administration and the Family Assistance Plan*. New York: Vintage Books.

Mudge, Stephanie L. 2018. *Leftism Reinvented: Western Parties from Socialism to Neoliberalism*. Cambridge, MA: Harvard University Press.

Mueller, Willard F. 1962. "The Role of Economics in Antitrust Enforcement at the Federal Trade Commission." *ABA Antitrust Section* 20: 20–28.

———. 1983. "The Anti-Antitrust Movement." *Industrial Organization, Antitrust, and Public Policy*: 19–40.

Munnell, Alicia H. (Ed.). 1986. *Lessons from the Income Maintenance Experiments: Proceedings of a Conference Held in September 1986*. Boston: Federal Reserve Bank of Boston and Brookings Institution.

Nader, Ralph. 1965. *Unsafe at Any Speed: The Designed-In Dangers of the American Automobile*. New York: Grossman Publishers.

Nagourney, Adam. 2008. "Obama Wins Election." *New York Times*, 4 November.

National Research Council, Committee on Operations Research. 1951. *Operations Research with Special Reference to Non-Military Applications: A Brochure*. Washington, DC: National Academies Press.

National Research Council, Committee to Evaluate the Research Plan of the Department of Housing and Urban Development. 2008. *Rebuilding the Research Capacity at HUD*. Washington, DC: National Research Council.

Neal, Phil C., William F. Baxter, Robert H. Bork, Carl H. Fulda, William K. Jones, Dennis G. Lyons, Paul W. MacAvoy, James W. McKie, Lee E. Preston, James A. Rahl, Richard E. Sherwood, and S. Paul Posner. 1969. "Report of the White House Task Force on Antitrust Policy." *Antitrust Law and Economics Review* 2: 11–52.

Nelson, Richard. 2014. *Resilient America: Electing Nixon in 1968, Channeling Dissent, and Dividing Government*. Lawrence: University Press of Kansas.

Nelson, Richard R. 1958. *Procrastination, Commitment, and the Optimum Time for Decision: Some Applications to the Use of Systems Analysis in R. and D. Decision Making*. Santa Monica, CA: RAND Corporation Archives, D-5508.

Nelson, Robert H. 1991. "The Office of Policy Analysis in the Department of the Interior." Pp. 122–43 in *Organizations for Policy Analysis: Helping Government Think*, edited by Carol H. Weiss. Thousand Oaks, CA: Sage.

Newborn, Steven A., and Virginia L. Snider. 1992. "The Growing Judicial Acceptance of the Merger Guidelines." *Antitrust Law Journal* 60: 849–56.

Newhouse, Joseph P. 1993. *Free for All? Lessons from the RAND Health Insurance Experiment*. Cambridge, MA: Harvard University Press.

Newhouse, Joseph P., Willard G. Manning, Carl N. Morris, Larry L. Orr, Naihua Duan, Emmett B. Keeler, Arleen Leibowitz, Kent H. Marquis, M. Susan Marquis, Charles E. Phelps, and Robert H. Brook. 1981. "Some Interim Results from a Controlled Trial of Cost Sharing in Health Insurance." *New England Journal of Medicine* 305: 1501–7.

Nicholls, William H. 1951. *Price Policies in the Cigarette Industry: A Study of 'Concerted Action' and Its Social Control, 1911–50*. Nashville, TN: Vanderbilt University Press.

Nichols, Albert L. 1997. "Lead in Gasoline." Pp. 49–86 in *Economic Analyses at EPA: Assessing Regulatory Impact*, edited by Richard D. Morgenstern. Washington, DC: Resources for the Future.

Niefer, Mark J. 2018. "Donald Turner, Vertical Restraints, and the Inhospitality Tradition of Antitrust." *Antitrust Law Journal* 82(2): 389–433.

Niskanen, William A. 1988. "Reaganomics." Library of Economics and Liberty. As of 28 July 2021: https://www.econlib.org/library/Enc1/Reaganomics.html.

Noble, Charles. 1986. *Liberalism at Work: The Rise and Fall of OSHA*. Philadelphia: Temple University Press.

Noll, Roger G. (Ed.). 1974. *Government and the Sports Business*. Washington, DC: Brookings Institution.

Noll, Roger G., Merton J. Peck, and John J. McGowan (Eds.). 1973. *Economic Aspects of Television Regulation*. Washington, DC: Brookings Institution.

Novak, William J. 2013. "A Revisionist History of Regulatory Capture." Pp. 25–48 in *Preventing Regulatory Capture: Special Interest Influence and How to Limit It*, edited by Daniel Carpenter and David A. Moss. Cambridge: Cambridge University Press.

Novick, David. 1954a. *Efficiency and Economy in Government through New Budgeting and Accounting Procedures*. Santa Monica, CA: RAND Corporation, R-254. As of 20 May 2021: https://www.rand.org/pubs/reports/R254.html.

———. 1954b. *Which Program Do We Mean in Program Budgeting?* Santa Monica, CA: RAND Corporation, P-530. As of 21 May 2021: https://www.rand.org/pubs/papers/P0530.html.

———. 1956. *A New Approach to the Military Budget: A Working Paper*. Santa Monica, CA: RAND Corporation. RM-1759-PR.

———. 1959. *The Federal Budget as an Indicator of Government Intentions and the Implications of Intentions*. Santa Monica, CA: RAND Corporation, P-1803. As of 21 May 2021: https://www.rand.org/pubs/papers/P1803.html.

———. 1962. *Program Budgeting: Long-Range Planning in the Department of Defense*. Santa Monica, CA: RAND Corporation, RM-3359-ASDC. As of 21 May 2021: https://www.rand.org/pubs/research_memoranda/RM3359.html.

——— (Ed.). 1967 [1965]. *Program Budgeting: Program Analysis and the Federal Budget*. Cambridge, MA: Harvard University Press.

———. 1988a. *Beginning of Military Cost Analysis 1950–1961*. Santa Monica, CA: RAND Corporation, P-7425. As of 21 May 2021: https://www.rand.org/pubs/papers/P7425.html.

———. 1988b. "Rand History Project Interview." Oral history conducted by Martin Collins. Washington, DC: The NASM-RAND History Project, National Air and Space Museum, Smithsonian Institution.

Nutter, G. Warren. 1951. *The Extent of Enterprise Monopoly in the United States, 1899–1939: A Quantitative Study of Some Aspects of Monopoly.* Chicago: University of Chicago Press.

Nyman, John. 2007. "American Health Policy: Cracks in the Foundation." *Journal of Health Politics, Policy and Law* 32(5): 759–83.

Oberlander, Jonathan. 2003. *The Political Life of Medicare.* Chicago: University of Chicago Press.

O'Brien, Ruth. 2001. *Crippled Justice: The History of Modern Disability Policy in the Workplace.* Chicago: University of Chicago Press.

O'Connor, Alice. 1998. "The False Dawn of Poor-Law Reform: Nixon, Carter, and the Quest for a Guaranteed Income." *Journal of Policy History* 10(1): 99–129.

———. 2001. *Poverty Knowledge: Social Science, Social Policy, and the Poor in Twentieth-Century U.S. History.* Princeton, NJ: Princeton University Press.

Office of Information and Regulatory Affairs, Office of Management and Budget. 1997. *Report to Congress on the Costs and Benefits of Federal Regulations.* Washington, DC: U.S. GPO.

Okun, Arthur M. 1975. *Equality and Efficiency: The Big Tradeoff.* Washington, DC: Brookings Institution.

Oliver, Daniel. 1986. "Statement before the American Bar Association Antitrust Law Section." As of 28 July 2021: https://www.ftc.gov/system/files/documents/public_statements/692451/19860812_oliver_statement_before_the_american_bar_association_antitrust_law_section.pdf.

Oliver, Thomas R. 1991. "Health Care Market Reform in Congress: The Uncertain Path from Proposal to Policy." *Political Science Quarterly* 106(3): 453–77.

Olsen, Edgar O. 1969. *An Efficient Method of Improving the Housing of Low Income Families.* Santa Monica, CA: RAND Corporation, P-4258. As of 21 May 2021: https://www.rand.org/pubs/papers/P4258.html.

Olson, Erik D. 1984. "The Quiet Shift of Power: Office of Management and Budget Supervision of Environmental Protection Agency Rulemaking Under Executive Order 12,291." *Virginia Journal of Natural Resources Law* 4: 1–80b.

O'Neill, Richard P., Charles S. Whitmore, and Gary J. Mahrenholz. 1992. "A Comparison of Electricity and Natural Gas Markets and Regulation in the USA." *Utilities Policy* 2(3): 204–27.

Orbach, Barak. 2013. "How Antitrust Lost Its Goal." *Fordham Law Review* 81: 2253–77.

———. 2014. "Was the Crisis in Antitrust a Trojan Horse?" *Antitrust Law Journal* 79(3): 881–902.

Ordover, Janusz A., and Robert D. Willig. 1983. "The 1982 Department of Justice Merger Guidelines: An Economic Assessment." *California Law Review* 71: 535–74.

Orlebeke, Charles J. 2000. "The Evolution of Low-Income Housing Policy, 1949 to 1999." *Housing Policy Debate* 11(2): 489–520.

Pacewicz, Josh. 2016. *Partisans and Partners: The Politics of the Post-Keynesian Society.* Chicago: University of Chicago Press.

Pascal, Anthony H., and John A. Pincus. 1973. *RAND's Education and Human Resources Program, 1973.* Santa Monica, CA: RAND Corporation, P-5058. As of 20 May 2021: https://www.rand.org/pubs/papers/P5058.html.

Pauly, Mark V. 1967. "Efficiency in Public Provision of Medical Care." PhD diss., University of Virginia.

———. 1968. "The Economics of Moral Hazard: Comment." *American Economic Review* 58(3): 531–37.

Pautler, Paul A. (Ed.). 2003. *FTC History: Bureau of Economics Contributions to Law Enforcement, Research, and Economic Knowledge and Policy.* Washington, DC: Federal Trade Commission.

———. 2015. "A History of the FTC's Bureau of Economics." American Antitrust Institute Working Paper No. 15-03. As of 28 July 2021: https://www.antitrustinstitute.org/wp-content/uploads/2018/08/FTC-Bureau-of-Economics-History_0.pdf.

Pear, Robert. 1992. "The 1992 Campaign: Platform; In a Final Draft, Democrats Reject a Part of Their Past." Pp. A13 in *New York Times*, 26 June.

Pearce, David. 2000. "Cost-Benefit Analysis and Environmental Policy." Pp. 48–74 in *Environmental Policy: Objectives, Instruments, and Implementation*, edited by Dieter Helm. Oxford: Oxford University Press.

Peck, Jamie, and Adam Tickell. 2002. "Neoliberalizing Space." *Antipode* 34: 380–404.

Peck, Merton J. 1988. "Deregulation of the Transportation Industry." Pp. 93–106 in *Effective Social Science: Eight Cases in Economics, Political Science, and Sociology*, edited by Bernard Barber. New York: Russell Sage Foundation.

Peck, Merton J., and Frederic M. Scherer. 1962. *The Weapons Acquisition Process: An Economic Analysis*. Boston: Harvard Business School.

Pedriana, Nicholas, and Robin Stryker. 2017. "From Legal Doctrine to Social Transformation? Comparing U.S. Voting Rights, Equal Employment Opportunity, and Fair Housing Legislation." *American Journal of Sociology* 123: 86–135.

Peltzman, Sam. 1974. *Regulation of Pharmaceutical Innovation: The 1962 Amendments*. Washington, DC: American Enterprise Institute.

Peltzman, Sam, Michael E. Levine, and Roger G. Noll. 1989. "The Economic Theory of Regulation after a Decade of Deregulation." *Brookings Papers on Economic Activity: Microeconomics* 1989: 1–59.

"The Pentagon's Whiz Kids." 1962. *Time*, 3 August.

Percival, Robert V. 1991. "Checks without Balance: Executive Office Oversight of the Environmental Protection Agency." *Law and Contemporary Problems* 54(4): 127–204.

Peritz, Rudolph J. R. 1996. *Competition Policy in America: History, Rhetoric, Law*. New York: Oxford University Press.

Perlman, Mark. 1987. "Political Purpose and the National Accounts." Pp. 133–51 in *The Politics of Numbers*, edited by William Alonso and Paul Starr. New York: Russell Sage Foundation.

Perlman, Mark, and Morgan Marietta. 2005. "The Politics of Social Accounting: Public Goals and the Evolution of the National Accounts in Germany, the United Kingdom and the United States." *Review of Political Economy* 17(2): 211–30.

Pertschuk, Michael. 1983. *Revolt against Regulation: The Rise and Pause of the Consumer Movement*. Berkeley: University of California Press.

Pettinicchio, David. 2019. *Politics of Empowerment: Disability Rights and the Cycle of American Policy Reform*. Stanford, CA: Stanford University Press.

Pfiffner, James P. 1979. *The President, the Budget, and Congress: Impoundment and the 1974 Budget Act*. Boulder, CO: Westview Press.

Phillips-Fein, Kim. 2009. *Invisible Hands: The Making of the Conservative Movement from the New Deal to Reagan*. New York: W.W. Norton.

Phillips, Kevin. 2014 [1969]. *The Emerging Republican Majority*. Princeton, NJ: Princeton University Press.

Pigou, A. C. 1912. *Wealth and Welfare*. London: Macmillan and Co.

Pildes, Richard H., and Cass R. Sunstein. 1995. "Reinventing the Regulatory State." *University of Chicago Law Review* 62(1): 1–129.

Pincus, John. 1971. "Policy Studies at RAND: Education and Human Resources." Santa Monica, CA: RAND Corporation, P-4721. As of 21 May 2021: https://www.rand.org/pubs/papers/P4721.html.

Policy, Planning, and Evaluation, U.S. Environmental Protection Agency. 1992. *Environmental Equity: Reducing Risk for All Communities, Volume 1: Workgroup Report to the Administrator*. Washington, DC: U.S. Environmental Protection Agency.

Porter, Theodore M. 1995. *Trust in Numbers*. Princeton, NJ: Princeton University Press.

Posner, Richard A. 1971. "A Program for the Antitrust Division." *University of Chicago Law Review* 38: 500–536.

———. 1973a. *Economic Analysis of Law*. Boston: Little, Brown.

———. 1973b. *Regulation of Advertising by the FTC*. Washington, DC: American Enterprise Institute.

———. 1979. "The Chicago School of Antitrust Analysis." *University of Pennsylvania Law Review* 127: 925–48.

President's Committee on Urban Housing (Kaiser Committee). 1968. *A Decent Home*. Washington, DC: U.S. Government Printing Office.

Pritchett, Wendell. 2008. *Robert Clifton Weaver and the American City: The Life and Times of an Urban Reformer*. Chicago: University of Chicago Press.

Project 88. 1988. *Project 88: Harnessing Market Forces to Protect Our Environment: Initiatives for the New President*. Unpublished report to Senators Timothy E. Wirth and John Heinz. Washington, DC. As of 28 July 2021: https://scholar.harvard.edu/files/stavins/files/project_88-1.pdf.

Pugliaresi, Lucian, and Diane T. Berliner. 1989. "Policy Analysis at the Department of State: The Policy Planning Staff." *Journal of Policy Analysis and Management* 8(3): 379–94.

Quadagno, Jill. 1994. *The Color of Welfare: How Racism Undermined the War on Poverty*. Oxford: Oxford University Press.

———. 2005. *One Nation, Uninsured: Why the U.S. Has No National Health Insurance*. New York: Oxford University Press.

Quade, E. S. 1953. *The Proposed RAND Course in Systems Analysis*. Santa Monica, CA: RAND Corporation Archives, D-1991.

Quade, Edward. 1988. "Rand History Project Interview." Oral history conducted by Martin Collins. Washington, DC: The NASM-RAND History Project, National Air and Space Museum, Smithsonian Institution.

Quarles, John. 1976. *Cleaning Up America: An Insider's View of the Environmental Protection Agency*. Boston: Houghton Mifflin.

Quirk, Paul J. 1988. "In Defense of the Politics of Ideas." *Journal of Politics* 50(1): 31–41.

Radin, Beryl A. 1991. "Policy Analysis in the Office of the Assistant Secretary for Planning and Evaluation in HEW/HHS: Institutionalization and the Second Generation." Pp. 144–60 in *Organizations for Policy Analysis: Helping Government Think*, edited by Carol H. Weiss. Thousand Oaks, CA: Sage.

RAND Corporation. 2015. "Henry S. Rowen, Second President of RAND, Dies at 90." Press release, 16 November. As of 27 May 2021: https://www.rand.org/news/press/2015/11/16.html.

Reay, Michael J. 2012. "The Flexible Unity of Economics." *American Journal of Sociology* 118: 45–87.

Regens, James L., and Robert W. Rycroft. 1988. *The Acid Rain Controversy*. Pittsburgh: University of Pittsburgh Press.

Reinecke, David. 2019. "Network Struggles: Re-wiring U.S. Network Industries for Competition, 1970–2015." PhD diss., Princeton University.

Resources for the Future. 1977. *Resources for the Future: The First 25 Years, 1952–1977*. Washington, DC: Resources for the Future.

Revesz, Richard L., and Michael A. Livermore. 2011. *Retaking Rationality: How Cost-Benefit Analysis Can Better Protect the Environment and Our Health*. Oxford: Oxford University Press.

Rhoads, Steven E. 1985. *The Economist's View of the World*. Cambridge: Cambridge University Press.

Rich, Andrew. 2004. *Think Tanks, Public Policy, and the Politics of Expertise*. Cambridge: Cambridge University Press.

Riker, William H. 1962. *The Theory of Political Coalition*. New Haven, CT: Yale University Press.

Rivlin, Alice M. 1969. "The Planning, Programming, and Budgeting System in the Department of Health, Education, and Welfare: Some Lessons from Experience." Pp. 909–22 in *The Analysis and Evaluation of Public Expenditures: The PPB System, Volume 3,* edited by Joint Economic Committee U.S. Congress, Subcommittee on Economy in Government. Washington, DC: U.S. Government Printing Office.

———. 1971. *Systematic Thinking for Social Action.* Washington, DC: Brookings Institution Press.

———. 1974. "Agreed: Here Comes National Health Insurance." Pp. 206 in *New York Times,* 21 July.

Robbins, Lionel. 1932. *An Essay on the Nature and Significance of Economic Science.* London: Macmillan.

Roberts, David. 2018. "California's Cap-and-Trade System May Be Too Weak to Do Its Job." *Vox,* 13 December. As of 28 July 2021: https://www.vox.com/energy-and-environment/2018/12 /12/18090844/california-climate-cap-and-trade-jerry-brown.

Roberts, Marc J. 1980. "The Political Economy of the Clean Water Act of 1972: Why No One Listened to the Economists." Pp. 97–119 in *The Utilisation of the Social Sciences in Policy Making in the United States: Case Studies,* edited by OECD. Paris: OECD.

Robinson, Joan. 1933. *The Economics of Imperfect Competition.* London: Macmillan.

Rodgers, Daniel T. 2011. *Age of Fracture.* Cambridge, MA: Belknap Press of Harvard University Press.

Romani, Roberto. 2018. "On Science and Reform: The Parable of the New Economics, 1960s–1970s." *European Journal of the History of Economic Thought* 25(2): 295–326.

Rose, Mark H., Bruce E. Seely, and Paul F. Barrett. 2006. *The Best Transportation System in the World: Railroads, Trucks, Airlines, and American Public Policy in the Twentieth Century.* Philadelphia: University of Pennsylvania Press.

Rosen, Eva. 2020. *The Voucher Promise: "Section 8" and the Fate of an American Neighborhood.* Princeton, NJ: Princeton University Press.

Rosenfeld, Jake. 2014. *What Unions No Longer Do.* Cambridge, MA: Harvard University Press.

Rossi, Peter H., and Katharine Lyall. 1976. *Reforming Public Welfare: A Critique of the Negative Income Tax Experiment.* New York: Russell Sage Foundation.

Rossi, Peter H., and James D. Wright. 1984. "Evaluation Research: An Assessment." *Annual Review of Sociology* 10(1984): 331–52.

Roth, Alvin E. 1986. "Laboratory Experimentation in Economics." *Economics and Philosophy* 2: 245–73.

Rudalevige, Andrew. 2009. "Juggling Act: The Politics of Science in Education Research." *Education Next* 9(1): 34–41.

Ruff, Larry E. 1970. "The Economic Common Sense of Pollution." Pp. 69–85 in *Public Interest* (Spring).

Russell, Clifford S., and Mark Sagoff. 2005. "Why Is Meaningful Collaboration between Ecologists and Economists So Difficult?" *Journal of Contemporary Water Research and Education* 131: 13–20.

———. 2009. "On the Collaboration of Ecologists and Economists." Pp. 188–219 in *The Evolution of Water Resource Planning and Decision Making,* edited by Clifford S. Russell and Duane D. Baumann. Cheltenham, UK: Edward Elgar.

Rutherford, Malcolm. 2001. "Institutional Economics: Then and Now." *Journal of Economic Perspectives* 15(3): 173–94.

———. 2011a. *The Institutionalist Movement in American Economics, 1918–1947: Science and Social Control.* Cambridge: Cambridge University Press.

———. 2011b. "The USDA Graduate School: Government Training in Statistics and Economics, 1921–1945." *Journal of the History of Economic Thought* 33(4): 419–47.

Sabin, Paul. 2016. "'Everything Has a Price': Jimmy Carter and the Struggle for Balance in Federal Regulatory Policy." *Journal of Policy History* 28(1): 1–47.

Sacks, Albert, and Hart, Jr., Henry M. 1994 [1958]. *The Legal Process: Basic Problems in the Making and Application of Law.* Westbury, NY: Foundation Press.

Saez, Emmanuel, and Gabriel Zucman. 2016. "Wealth Inequality in the United States since 1913: Evidence from Capitalized Income Tax Data." *Quarterly Journal of Economics* 131(2): 519–78.

Sagoff, Mark. 2011. "The Quantification and Valuation of Ecosystem Services." *Ecological Economics* 70: 497–502.

Saldin, Robert P. 2017. *When Bad Policy Makes Good Politics: Running the Numbers on Health Reform*. Oxford: Oxford University Press.

Samuel DuBois Cook Center on Social Equity. 2019. "Baby Bonds: A Universal Path to Ensure the Next Generation Has the Capital to Thrive." Samuel DuBois Cook Center on Social Equity, Duke University. As of 28 July 2021: https://socialequity.duke.edu/portfolio-item/baby-bonds -a-universal-path-to-ensure-the-next-generation-has-the-capital-to-thrive/.

Samuelson, Paul A. 1944. "Unemployment Ahead: A Warning to the Washington Expert." Pp. 297–99 in *New Republic*, 11 September.

———. 1948. *Economics: An Introductory Analysis*. First edition. New York: McGraw-Hill.

———. 1961. *Economics: An Introductory Analysis*. Fifth edition. New York: McGraw-Hill.

———. 1976. "Alvin Hansen as a Creative Economic Theorist." *Quarterly Journal of Economics* 90(1): 24–31.

Schaefer, Mark, Erica Goldman, Ann M. Bartuska, Ariana Sutton-Grier, and Jane Lubchenco. 2015. "Nature as Capital: Advancing and Incorporating Ecosystem Services in United States Federal Policies and Programs." *Proceedings of the National Academy of Sciences* 112(24): 7383–89.

Scheer, Robert. 2010. "McCain Gets It, Obama Doesn't." *The Nation*, 11 January.

Schelling, Thomas. 1968. "The Life You Save May Be Your Own." Pp. 127–62 in *Problems in Public Expenditure Analysis*, edited by Samuel B. Chase, Jr. Washington, DC: Brookings Institution.

Schevitz, Tanya. 2002. "William Capron—LBJ Aide, Professor." *San Francisco Chronicle*, 12 October.

Schick, Allen. 1973. "A Death in the Bureaucracy: The Demise of Federal PPB." *Public Administration Review* 33: 146–56.

Schimel, Kate. 2019. "A Carbon Tax in Washington State Seemed Like a Sure Thing: What Went Wrong?" *Mother Jones*, 23 January. As of 28 July 2021: https://www.motherjones.com /environment/2019/01/a-carbon-tax-in-washington-state-seemed-like-a-sure-thing-what -went-wrong/.

Schlegel, John Henry. 1995. *American Legal Realism and Empirical Social Science*. Durham: University of North Carolina Press.

Schmalensee, Richard, and Robert N. Stavins. 2013. "The SO_2 Allowance Trading System: The Ironic History of a Grand Policy Experiment." *Journal of Economic Perspectives* 27(1): 103–22.

Schmid, A. Allan. 1969. "Effective Public Policy and the Government Budget: A Uniform Treatment of Public Expenditures and Regulatory Rules." Pp. 579–91 in *The Analysis and Evaluation of Public Expenditures: The PPB System*, edited by Joint Economic Committee U.S. Congress, Subcommittee on Economy in Government. Washington, DC: U.S. Government Printing Office.

———. 2008. "My Work as an Institutional Economist." Center for Regulatory Effectiveness. As of 28 July 2021: https://thecre.com/pdf/20131229_My_work_as_an_Insitutional_Economist .pdf.

Schmidt, Laura Anne. 1999. "The Corporate Transformation of American Health Care: A Study in Institution Building." PhD diss., University of California, Berkeley.

Schomers, Sarah, and Bettina Matzdorf. 2013. "Payments for Ecosystem Services: A Review and Comparison of Developing and Industrialized Countries." *Ecosystem Services* 6: 16–30.

Schorr, Alvin L. 1966a. "Against a Negative Income Tax." Pp. 110–19 in *The Public Interest* (Fall).

———. 1966b. *Poor Kids: A Report on Children in Poverty*. New York: Basic Books.

Schulman, Bruce J., and Julian Zelizer (Eds.). 2008. *Rightward Bound: Making America Conservative in the 1970s*. Cambridge, MA: Harvard University Press.

Schultz, Theodore W. 1961. "Investment in Human Capital." *American Economic Review* 51: 1–17.

Schultze, Charles L. 1968. *The Politics and Economics of Public Spending*. Washington, DC: Brookings Institution.

———. 1969. "Charles L. Schultze, Oral History Interview." Oral history conducted by David McComb. Austin, TX: Lyndon B. Johnson Presidential Library.

———. 1977a. *The Public Use of Private Interest*. Washington, DC: Brookings Institution.

———. 1977b. "The Public Use of Private Interest." *Regulation* 1(2): 10–14.

———. 1982. "The Roles and Responsibilities of the Economist in Government." *American Economic Review* 72(2): 62–66.

Schwartz, Bernard. 1981. "The Court and Cost-Benefit Analysis: An Administrative Law Idea Whose Time Has Come—or Gone?" *Supreme Court Review* 1981: 291–307.

Schwartz, Louis B. 1979. "On the Uses of Economics: A Review of the Antitrust Treatises." *University of Pennsylvania Law Review* 128: 244–68.

Sciortino, Luca. 2017. "On Ian Hacking's Notion of Style of Reasoning." *Erkenntnis* 82(2): 243–64.

Scott-Clayton, Judith. 2018. "The Looming Student Loan Default Crisis Is Worse Than We Thought." Washington, DC: Brookings Institution.

Seevers, Gary L. 1975. "Prospects for Regulatory Reform." Pp. 201–4 in *Perspectives on Federal Transportation Policy*, edited by James C. Miller III. Washington, DC: American Enterprise Institute for Public Policy Research.

Segal, David. 1998. "Joel Klein, Hanging Tough." *Washington Post*, 24 March.

Seib, Gerald F. 2008. "In Crisis, Opportunity for Obama." *Wall Street Journal*, 21 November.

Shabecoff, Philip. 1979. "Kennedy Offers Broad Health Plan and Challenges Carter to Support It." *New York Times*, 15 May.

Shadish, William R., Thomas D. Cook, and Laura C. Leviton. 1991. *Foundations of Program Evaluation: Theories of Practice*. Thousand Oaks, CA: SAGE.

Shanahan, Eileen. 1966. "Antitrust Chief with a Sophisticated View." Pp. 61, 65 in *New York Times*, 29 June.

Shapiro, Fred R. 2000. "The Most-Cited Legal Scholars." *Journal of Legal Studies* 29(S1): 409–26.

Shapiro, Stuart. 2005. "Unequal Partners: Cost-Benefit Analysis and Executive Review of Regulations." *Environmental Law Reporter* 35(7): 10433–44.

Shenk, Timothy. 2016. "Inventing the American Economy." PhD diss., Columbia University.

Shepherd, William G. 1996. "Donald Turner and the Economics of Antitrust." *Antitrust Bulletin* 41(Winter): 935–48.

———. 2007. "Edward S. Mason." Pp. 209–10 in *Pioneers of Industrial Organization: How the Economics of Competition and Monopoly Took Shape*, edited by Henry W. de Jong and William G. Shepherd. Northampton, MA: Edward Elgar.

Shrader, Charles R. 2006. *History of Operations Research in the United States Army: Volume I: 1942–62*. Washington, DC: U.S. Government Printing Office.

———. 2008. *History of Operations Research in the United States Army: Volume II: 1961–1973*. Washington, DC: U.S. Government Printing Office.

Shubert, Gustave. 1988. "Oral History Interview." Oral history conducted by Joseph Tatarewicz. Santa Monica, CA: RAND Corporation Archives.

———. 1992. "Oral History Interview." Oral history conducted by James Digby. Santa Monica, CA: RAND Corporation Archives.

Signs, Kelly. 2015. "FTC Milestone: A New Age Dawns for the FTC's Competition Work." Competition Matters, Federal Trade Commission. As of 28 July 2021: https://www.ftc.gov/news-events/blogs/competition-matters/2015/02/ftc-milestone-new-age-dawns-ftcs-competition-work.

Simon, Herbert. 1991. *Models of My Life*. New York: Basic Books.

Simons, Henry C. 1948. *Economic Policy for a Free Society*. Chicago: University of Chicago Press.

Sims, Joe, and Deborah P. Herman. 1997. "The Effect of Twenty Years of Hart-Scott-Rodino on Merger Practice: A Case Study in the Law of Unintended Consequences Applied to Antitrust Legislation." *Antitrust Law Journal* 65: 865–904.

Sinden, Amy. 2005. "In Defense of Absolutes: Combating the Politics of Power in Environmental Law." *Iowa Law Review* 90: 1405–1511.

Singer, Hal, and Shaoul Sussman. 2020. "Six Stupid Arguments against Forgiving Student Loan Debt." *American Prospect*, 1 December. As of 28 July 2021: https://prospect.org/day-one -agenda/six-stupid-arguments-against-forgiving-student-loan-debt/.

Singer, Joseph William. 1988. "Legal Realism Now." *California Law Review* 76(2): 465–544.

Sklar, Martin J. 1988. *The Corporate Reconstruction of American Capitalism, 1890–1916*. Cambridge: Cambridge University Press.

Skocpol, Theda. 1996. *Boomerang: Health Care Reform and the Turn against Government*. New York: W. W. Norton.

Skousen, Mark. 1997. "The Perseverance of Paul Samuelson's *Economics*." *Journal of Economic Perspectives* 11(2): 137–52.

Slobodian, Quinn. 2018. *Globalists: The End of Empire and the Birth of Neoliberalism*. Cambridge, MA: Harvard University Press.

Smith, Bruce L. R. 1966. *The Rand Corporation: Case Study of a Nonprofit Advisory Corporation*. Cambridge, MA: Harvard University Press.

Smith, David Barton. 2016. *The Power to Heal: Civil Rights, Medicare, and the Struggle to Transform America's Health System*. Nashville, TN: Vanderbilt University Press.

Smith, James Allen. 1991. *Brookings at Seventy-Five*. Washington, DC: Brookings Institution Press.

———. 1993. *The Idea Brokers: Think Tanks and the Rise of the New Policy Elite*. New York: Free Press.

Smith, Richard Austin. 1960. "What Antitrust Means under Mr. Bicks." *Fortune*, March.

Smith, Robert M. 1972. "Antitrust Division Chief Quits; Professor Is Named Successor." Pp. 16 in *New York Times*, 10 June.

Social Security Administration. 1968. "History of SSA during the Johnson Administration 1963–1968." As of 28 July 2021: https://www.ssa.gov/history/ssa/lbjmedicare1.html.

Solow, Robert M. 1971. "The Economist's Approach to Pollution and Its Control." *Science* 173: 498–503.

"Sound Antitrust Advice." 1965. *Wall Street Journal*, 16 February.

Sproull, Lee, Stephen Weiner, and David Wolf. 1978. *Organizing an Anarchy: Belief, Bureaucracy, and Politics in the National Institute of Education*. Chicago: University of Chicago Press.

Staats, Elmer. 1971. "Oral History: Interview I." Oral history conducted by T. H. Baker. Austin, TX: Lyndon B. Johnson Presidential Library.

———. 1987. "Elmer B. Staats: Comptroller General of the United States 1966–1981." Oral history conducted by Henry Eschwege, Werner Grosshans, Donald J. Horan, and Elizabeth Poel. Washington, DC: United States General Accounting Office.

Stahl, Jason. 2016. *Right Moves: The Conservative Think Tank in American Political Culture since 1945*. Chapel Hill: University of North Carolina Press.

Stapleford, Thomas A. 2009. *The Cost of Living in America: A Political History of Economic Statistics, 1880–2000*. Cambridge: Cambridge University Press.

Starr, Paul. 1982. *The Social Transformation of American Medicine: The Rise of a Sovereign Profession and the Making of a Vast Industry*. New York: Basic Books.

———. 1992. *The Logic of Health-Care Reform*. Knoxville, TN: Whittle Communications.

Steck, Henry J. 1975. "Private Influence on Environmental Policy: The Case of the National Industrial Pollution Control Council." *Environmental Law* 5: 241–81.

Steensland, Brian. 2008. *The Failed Welfare Revolution: America's Struggle over Guaranteed Income Policy*. Princeton, NJ: Princeton University Press.

Stein, Judith. 2011. *Pivotal Decade: How the United States Traded Factories for Finance in the Seventies*. New Haven, CT: Yale University Press.

Stevens, Rosemary. 1981. "Review: Health Plan: The Only Practical Solution to the Soaring Cost of Medical Care by Alain C. Enthoven." *Medical Care* 19(11): 1159–61.

Stigler, George J. 1971. "The Theory of Economic Regulation." *Bell Journal of Economics and Management Science* 2: 3–21.

Stigler, George J., and Claire Friedland. 1962. "What Can Regulators Regulate? The Case of Electricity." *Journal of Law and Economics* 5: 1–16.

Stock, Wendy A., and John J. Siegfried. 2014. "15 Years of Research on Graduate Education in Economics: What Have We Learned?" *Research in Economic Education* 45(4): 287–303.

Stockman, Dave. 1980. "The Stockman Manifesto." *Washington Post*, 14 December.

Stokes, Donald E. 1986. "Political and Organizational Analysis in the Policy Curriculum." *Journal of Policy Analysis and Management* 6(1): 45–55.

Stoller, Matt. 2019. *Goliath: The 100-Year War between Monopoly Power and Democracy*. New York: Simon & Schuster.

Stone, Deborah A. 1989. "Causal Stories and the Formation of Policy Agendas." *Political Quarterly* 104: 281–300.

Stossel, Scott. 2004. *Sarge: The Life and Times of Sargent Shriver*. Washington, DC: Smithsonian Books.

Street, James H. 1988. "The Contribution of Simon S. Kuznets to Institutionalist Development Theory." *Journal of Economic Issues* 22(2): 499–509.

Struyk, Raymond J., and Bendick, Jr., Marc (Eds.). 1981. *Housing Vouchers for the Poor: Lessons from a National Experiment*. Washington, DC: Urban Institute Press.

Suárez, Sandra, and Robin Kolodny. 2011. "Paving the Road to 'Too Big to Fail': Business Interests and the Politics of Financial Deregulation in the United States." *Politics and Society* 39(1): 74–102.

Sunstein, Cass R. 2018. "Changing Climate Change, 2009–2016." *Harvard Environmental Law Review* 42(1): 231–85.

Switzer, Jacqueline Vaughn. 2003. *Disabled Rights: American Disability Policy and the Fight for Equality*. Washington, DC: Georgetown University Press.

Teles, Steven M. 2008. *The Rise of the Conservative Legal Movement: The Battle for Control of the Law*. Princeton, NJ: Princeton University Press.

Thomas, Janet Y., and Kevin P. Brady. 2005. "The Elementary and Secondary Education Act at 40: Equity, Accountability, and the Evolving Federal Role in Education." *Review of Research in Education* 29: 51–67.

Thomas, William. 2015. *Rational Action: The Sciences of Policy in Britain and America, 1940–1960*. Cambridge, MA: MIT Press.

"Three Members of the Council of Economic Advisers." 1961. *New York Times*, 3 February.

Thrush, Glenn. 2010. "Left to Obama: We're Not Happy." *Politico*, 7 June. As of 28 July 2021: https://www.politico.com/story/2010/06/left-to-obama-were-not-happy-038222.

Thurber, James A. 1976. "Congressional Budget Reform and New Demands for Policy Analysis." *Policy Analysis* 2(2): 197–214.

Timpane, P. Michael. 1982. "Federal Progress in Education Research." *Harvard Educational Review* 52(4): 540–48.

Tobin, James. 1966. "The Case for an Income Guarantee." Pp. 31–41 in *The Public Interest* (Summer).

———. 1967. "Do We Want Children's Allowances?" Pp. 16–18 in *New Republic*, 25 November.

———. 1976. "Hansen and Public Policy." *Quarterly Journal of Economics* 90(1): 32–37.

Tolchin, Susan J. 1979. "Presidential Power and the Politics of RARG." Pp. 44–49 in *Regulation* (July/Aug.).

Tozzi, Jim. 2011. "OIRA's Formative Years: The Historical Record of Centralized Regulatory Review Preceding OIRA's Founding." *Administrative Law Review* 63: 37–69.

Troy, Tevi. 2003. *Intellectuals and the American Presidency: Philosophers, Jesters, or Technicians?* New York: Rowman & Littlefield.

Turner, Donald F. 1964. "Conglomerate Mergers and Section 7 of the Clayton Act." *Harvard Law Review* 78: 1313–95.

———. 1968. "*Antitrust Analysis: Problems, Text, Cases* by Phillip Areeda." *Harvard Law Review* 81(4): 913–15.

———. 1982. "Observations on the New Merger Guidelines and the 1968 Merger Guidelines." *Antitrust Law Journal* 51: 307–15.

Twogood, R. Philip. 1997. "Reconciling Politics and Budget Analysis: The Case of the Congressional Budget Office." Pp. 359–70 in *Public Budgeting and Finance*, edited by Robert T. Golembiewski and Jack Rabin. New York: Marcel Dekker.

U.S. Air Force Project RAND. 1948. *New York Conference of Social Scientists: September 14 to 19, 1947.* Santa Monica, CA: RAND Corporation, R-106. As of 20 May 2021: https://www.rand.org/pubs/reports/R106.html.

U.S. Civil Service Commission. 1968. *A Follow-Up Study of the Three-Week Residential Seminar in PPBS.* Washington, DC: Bureau of Training.

U.S. Congress, Congressional Budget Office. 2021. "History." As of 28 July 2021: https://www.cbo.gov/about/history.

U.S. Congress, Joint Economic Committee, Subcommittee on Economy in Government. 1971a. *Economic Analysis and the Efficiency of Government, Part 6: Economic Incentives to Control Pollution.* Washington, DC: U.S. Government Printing Office.

U.S. Congress, Joint Economic Committee, Subcommittee on Priorities and Economy in Government. 1971b. *Economics of National Priorities.* Washington, DC: U.S. Government Printing Office.

U.S. Department of Health, Education, and Welfare. 1967. *A Report to the President on Medical Care Prices (Gorham Report).* Washington, DC: U.S. Department of Health, Education and Welfare.

U.S. Department of Health, Education, and Welfare, Office of the Assistant Secretary for Planning and Evaluation. 1969. *Toward a Long-Range Plan for Federal Financial Support for Higher Education: A Report to the President (Rivlin Report).* Washington, DC: U.S. Government Printing Office.

U.S. Department of Housing and Urban Development, Office of Policy Development and Research. 2016. *PD&R: A Historical Investigation at (Almost) 50.* Washington, DC: U.S. Department of Housing and Urban Development.

U.S. Department of Justice, and Federal Trade Commission. 1992. *Horizontal Merger Guidelines.* Washington, DC: U.S. Government Printing Office.

U.S. Department of Justice, Antitrust Division. 1968. *1968 Merger Guidelines.* Washington, DC: U.S. Government Printing Office.

———. 1982. *1982 Merger Guidelines.* Washington, DC: U.S. Government Printing Office.

———. 1984. *1984 Merger Guidelines.* Washington, DC: U.S. Government Printing Office.

———. 1993. *Corporate Leniency Policy.* Washington, DC: U.S. Government Printing Office.

U.S. Department of Labor. 1977. "Overview of the Nixon-Ford Administration at the Department of Labor 1969–1977." As of 28 July 2021: https://www.dol.gov/general/aboutdol/history/webid-nixonford.

U.S. Department of Labor, Bureau of Labor Statistics. 2021. "Consumer Price Index (CPI)." As of 28 July 2021: https://www.bls.gov/cpi/.

U.S. Environmental Protection Agency. 1975. "Standards of Performance for New Stationary Sources: Modification, Notification, and Reconstruction." *Federal Register* 40: 58416–20.

U.S. General Accounting Office. 1969. *Survey of Progress in Implementing the Planning-Programming-Budgeting System in Executive Agencies.* Washington, DC: U.S. Government Printing Office.

———. 1973. *Program Evaluation: Legislative Language and a User's Guide to Selected Sources.* Washington, DC: U.S. General Accounting Office.

———. 1978. *1977 Annual Report of the Comptroller General of the United States.* Washington, DC: U.S. Government Printing Office.

———. 1983. *Siting of Hazardous Waste Landfills and Their Correlation with Racial and Economic Status of Surrounding Communities.* Washington, DC: General Accounting Office.

———. 1988. *Program Evaluation Issues.* Washington, DC: U.S. Government Publishing Office.

U.S. House, Committee on Ways and Means. 1970. "Tax Recommendations of the President." Washington, DC: U.S. Government Printing Office.

U.S. Library of Congress. 1995. "Data as Product and the Growth of the Social Sciences." Coolidge-Consumerism Collection. As of 28 July 2021: http://lcweb2.loc.gov:8081/ammem/amrlhtml /insocsci.html.

U.S. President. 1962. *The Economic Report of the President.* Washington, DC: U.S. Government Printing Office.

———. 1963. *The Economic Report of the President.* Washington, DC: U.S. Government Printing Office.

———. 1965. *The Economic Report of the President.* Washington, DC: U.S. Government Printing Office.

———. 1966. *The Economic Report of the President.* Washington, DC: U.S. Government Printing Office.

———. 1970. *The Economic Report of the President.* Washington, DC: U.S. Government Printing Office.

"U.S. Seeks to Map Antitrust Guides." 1965. *New York Times,* 17 July.

U.S. Senate, Committee on Government Operations, Subcommittee on National Security and International Operations. 1968. *Planning-Programming-Budgeting: Part 3.* Washington, DC: U.S. Government Printing Office.

U.S. Senate, Committee on Public Works, Subcommittee on Air and Water Pollution. 1970. *Air Pollution, 1970: Part 4.* Washington, DC: U.S. Government Printing Office.

U.S. Senate, Committee on the Judiciary, Subcommittee on Antitrust and Monopoly. 1973. *Industrial Reorganization Act: Part I: General Views.* Washington, DC: U.S. Government Printing Office.

———. 1974a. *Competition in the Health Services Market: Part 1.* Washington, DC: U.S. Government Printing Office.

———. 1974b. *Competition in the Health Services Market: Part 2.* Washington, DC: U.S. Government Printing Office.

———. 1974c. *Competition in the Health Services Market: Part 3.* Washington, DC: U.S. Government Printing Office.

University of Chicago Law School. 2020. "William M. Landes." As of 28 July 2021: https://www .law.uchicago.edu/faculty/landes.

Vaheesan, Sandeep. 2014. "The Evolving Populisms of Antitrust." *Nebraska Law Review* 93(2): 370–428.

Vanatta, Sean H. 2015. "Citibank, Credit Cards, and the Local Politics of National Consumer Finance, 1968–1991." *Business History Review* 90(1): 57–80.

Van Horn, Robert. 2009. "Reinventing Monopoly and the Role of Corporations." Pp. 204–37 in *The Road from Mont Pelerin: The Making of the Neoliberal Thought Collective,* edited by Philip Mirowski and Dieter Plehwe. Cambridge, MA: Harvard University Press.

———. 2011. "Jacob Viner's Critique of Chicago Neoliberalism." Pp. 279–300 in *Building Chicago Economics: New Perspectives on the History of America's Most Powerful Economics Program,* edited by Robert Van Horn, Philip Mirowski, and Thomas A. Stapleford. Cambridge: Cambridge University Press.

Van Horn, Robert, and Matthias Klaes. 2011. "Intervening in Laissez-Faire Liberalism: Chicago's Shift on Patents." Pp. 180–207 in *Building Chicago Economics: New Perspectives on the History of America's Most Powerful Economics Program*, edited by Robert Van Horn, Philip Mirowski, and Thomas A. Stapleford. Cambridge: Cambridge University Press.

Van Horn, Robert, and Philip Mirowski. 2009. "The Rise of the Chicago School of Economics and the Birth of Neoliberalism." Pp. 139–78 in *The Road from Mont Pelerin: The Making of the Neoliberal Thought Collective*, edited by Philip Mirowski and Dieter Plehwe. Cambridge, MA: Harvard University Press.

Vietor, Richard. 1996. *Contrived Competition: Regulation and Deregulation in America*. Cambridge, MA: Belknap Press.

Vinsel, Lee. 2019. *Moving Violations: Automobiles, Experts, and Regulations in the United States*. Baltimore, MD: Johns Hopkins University Press.

Vogel, David. 1989. *Fluctuating Fortunes: The Political Power of Business in America*. New York: Basic Books.

Vogel, Kenneth P. 2017. "Google Critic Ousted from Think Tank Funded by the Tech Giant." *New York Times*, 30 August.

von Hoffman, Alexander. 2012. "History Lessons for Today's Housing Policy: The Politics of Low-Income Housing." *Housing Policy Debate* 22(3): 321–76.

Wagner, Travis. 2004. "Hazardous Waste: Evolution of a National Environmental Problem." *Journal of Policy History* 16(4): 306–31.

Wainess, Flint. 1999. "The Ways and Means of National Health Care Reform, 1974 and Beyond." *Journal of Health Politics, Policy and Law* 24(2): 305–33.

Walker, Jack L. 1976. "The Curriculum in Public Policy Studies at the University of Michigan: Notes on the Ups and Downs of IPPS." *Journal of Urban Analysis* 3(2): 89–103.

Walker, Wallace E. 1986. *Changing Organizational Culture: Strategy, Structure and Professionalism in the U.S. General Accounting Office*. Knoxville: University of Tennessee Press.

Ward, Jr., Thomas J. 2017. *Out in the Rural: A Mississippi Health Center and Its War on Poverty*. Oxford: Oxford University Press.

Wasem, Ruth Ellen. 2013. *Tackling Unemployment: The Legislative Dynamics of the Employment Act of 1946*. Kalamazoo, MI: W. E. Upjohn Institute for Employment Research.

Waterhouse, Benjamin C. 2013. *Lobbying America: The Politics of Business from Nixon to NAFTA*. Princeton, NJ: Princeton University Press.

Watts, Harold W. 1968. "An Economic Definition of Poverty." Institute for Research on Poverty Discussion Paper. Madison, WI: Institute for Research on Poverty. As of 28 July 2021: https://www.irp.wisc.edu/publications/dps/pdfs/dp568.pdf.

Weaver, Suzanne. 1977. *Decision to Prosecute: Organization and Public Policy in the Antitrust Division*. Cambridge, MA: MIT Press.

Weidenbaum, Murray. 1997. "Regulatory Process Reform: From Ford to Clinton." Pp. 20–26 in *Regulation* (Winter).

Weiler, Daniel. 1972. "The OEO Elementary Education Voucher Demonstration." Pp. 23–30 in *Rand Work in Elementary and Secondary Education: A Representative Selection*, edited by Stephen J. Carroll, George R. Hall, John A. Pincus, and Daniel Weiler. Santa Monica, CA: RAND Corporation, R-1052. As of 20 May 2021: https://www.rand.org/pubs/reports/R1052.html.

Weinstein, James. 1968. *The Corporate Ideal in the Liberal State, 1900–1918*. Boston: Beacon Press.

Weir, Margaret. 1993. *Politics and Jobs: The Boundaries of Employment Policy in the United States*. Princeton, NJ: Princeton University Press.

Weisbrod, Burton A. 1978. "Comment." Pp. 49–55 in *Competition in the Health Care Sector: Past, Present, and Future: Proceedings of a Conference Sponsored by the Bureau of Economics, Federal Trade Commission, March 1978*, edited by Warren Greenberg. Frederick, MD: Beard Books.

Weiss, Carol H. 1987. "Evaluating Social Programs: What Have We Learned?" *Society* 25(1): 40–45.

———. 1992. *Organizations for Policy Analysis: Helping Government Think.* Thousand Oaks, CA: Sage.

Welborn, David M. 1993. *Regulation in the White House: The Johnson Presidency.* Austin: University of Texas Press.

Welfare Reform Academy, School of Public Policy, University of Maryland. 2014. "2014 Rossi Award Winner Larry Orr." As of 28 July 2021: http://welfareacademy.org/rossi/2014_orr.shtml.

Wells, Tom. 2001. *Wild Man: The Life and Times of Daniel Ellsberg.* New York: Palgrave Macmillan.

White, Lawrence J. 1976. "Effluent Charges as a Faster Means of Achieving Pollution Abatement." *Public Policy* 24(1): 111–25.

———. 1981. *Reforming Regulation: Processes and Problems.* Hoboken, NJ: Prentice Hall PTR.

———. 2009. "Financial Regulation and the Current Crisis: A Guide for the Antitrust Community." American Antitrust Institute. As of 28 July 2021: https://www.antitrustinstitute.org/wp-content/uploads/2018/08/AAI-White-COmmentary-fin-reg-and-antitrust_061120092144.pdf.

White, Thomas D. 1963. "Strategy and the Defense Intellectuals." Pp. 10–11 in *Saturday Evening Post*, 4 May.

Whiting, Richard A., Phillip Areeda, William F. Baxter, Robert H. Bork, and Frederick M. Rowe. 1985. "Panel Discussion." *Antitrust Law Journal* 54(1): 31–37.

Wholey, Joseph S., John W. Scanlon, Hugh G. Duffy, James S. Fukumoto, and Leona M. Vogt. 1970. *Federal Evaluation Policy: Analyzing the Effects of Public Programs.* Washington, DC: Urban Institute.

Whyte, Kenneth. 2017. *Hoover: An Extraordinary Life in Extraordinary Times.* New York: Alfred A. Knopf.

Wildavsky, Aaron. 1966. "The Political Economy of Efficiency: Cost-Benefit Analysis, Systems Analysis, and Program Budgeting." *Public Administration Review* 26: 292–310.

———. 1967. "The Political Economy of Efficiency." *Public Interest* (Summer).

Williams, Daniel K. 2010. *God's Own Party: The Making of the Christian Right.* Oxford: Oxford University Press.

Williams, Walter. 1971. *Social Policy Research and Analysis: The Experience in the Federal Social Agencies.* New York: American Elsevier.

———. 1975. "The Continuing Struggle for a Negative Income Tax: A Review Article." *Journal of Human Resources* 10(4): 427–44.

———. 1990. *Mismanaging America: The Rise of the Anti-Analytic Presidency.* Lawrence: University Press of Kansas.

———. 1998. *Honest Numbers and Democracy: Social Policy Analysis in the White House, Congress and in Federal Agencies.* Washington, DC: Georgetown University Press.

Williamson, James R. 1995. *Federal Antitrust Policy during the Kennedy-Johnson Years.* Westport, CT: Greenwood Publishing Group.

Williamson, Oliver E. 2002. "The Merger Guidelines of the U.S. Department of Justice—In Perspective." Paper presented at the 20th Anniversary of the 1982 Merger Guidelines: The Contribution of the Merger Guidelines to the Evolution of Antitrust Doctrine, Washington, DC. As of 28 July 2021: https://www.justice.gov/atr/hmerger/11257.htm.

Wilson, Graham K. 1984. "Social Regulation and Explanations of Regulatory Failure." *Political Studies* 32: 203–25.

Winnick, Louis. 1995. "The Triumph of Housing Allowance Programs: How a Fundamental Policy Conflict Was Resolved." *Cityscape* 1(3): 95–121.

Yates, Jr., Douglas T. 1977. "The Mission of Public Policy Programs: A Report on Recent Experience." *Policy Sciences* 8(3): 363–73.

Yonay, Yuval. 1998. *The Struggle over the Soul of Economics: Institutionalist and Neoclassical Economists in America between the Wars*. Princeton, NJ: Princeton University Press.

Young, Stephanie. 2009. "Power and the Purse: Defense Budgeting and American Politics, 1947–1972." PhD diss., University of California, Berkeley.

Zelizer, Julian. 1998. *Taxing America: Wilbur D. Mills, Congress, and the State, 1945–1975*. Cambridge: Cambridge University Press.

Zwick, Charles J. 1969a. "Oral History: Interview I." Oral history conducted by David McComb. Austin, TX: Lyndon B. Johnson Presidential Library.

———. 1969b. "Oral History: Interview II." Oral history conducted by David McComb. Austin, TX: Lyndon B. Johnson Presidential Library.

———. 2000. "Oral History." Oral history conducted by Cynthia Barnett. Gainesville: Florida Growth Management Oral History Collection, University of Florida.

Zwick, David, and Marcy Benstock. 1971. *Water Wasteland: The Ralph Nader Study Group Report on Water Pollution*. New York: Grossman Publishers.

INDEX

Foundations of Economic Analysis (Samuelson), 36
Fourcade, Marion, 24
Fox, Peter D., 123
FPC (Federal Power Commission), 142
Freeman, Orville, 61
Free Market Study Project, 79
Friday, William, 257n55
Friedman, Milton, 80, 104, 144
FTC (Federal Trade Commission), 11,
    29–30, 74, 85–88, 94–97, 136–39, 147–51,
    190–91, 206–12
Fuchs, Victor, 120, 270n36

Galbraith, John Kenneth, 144
game theory, 218, 258n86
GAO (General Accounting Office), 56, 58,
    67–68, 205–6
Gaskins, Darius, 147–48
Gay, Edwin, 27–28
*General Theory of Employment, Interest, and
    Money* (Keynes), 31–32
Ginsburg, Douglas, 209
Glass-Steagall Act, 2
Glenmede Trust, 95
Glennan, Thomas K., 125
Goldwater, Barry, 56
Google, 21
Gordon, Kermit, 55, 89–91, 144
Gorham, William, 59–60, 102, 106–8, 111,
    113–14, 118, 183, 203
Gorham Report, 120, 123
Gorsuch, Anne, 213–15
Gougherty, Matt, 5
government, 9; centralized authority and,
    102–10; decision-making protocols of,
    6–7, 11–12, 15–18, 35–38, 41–44, 56–58,
    81–84, 110–16, 131–32, 138–39, 178–79,
    193–94, 196–98, 222; shrinking of, as goal,
    12–13, 15–18, 92–95, 132, 153, 161–62,
    180–81, 189, 195–96, 201–6; technocratic
    improvement goals and, 3–4, 11, 19–22, 51,
    56, 99, 123–32, 142–43, 166–68, 179–82,
    216–23; well-functioning markets and,
    6, 9–11, 38, 71, 75–81, 88–97, 129–32,
    141–53, 206–11, 221–22. *See also* antitrust
    policy; economic style of reasoning;
    markets
Government Operations and Research
    Office (CWPS), 165
grassroots organizing, 21–23
Gray, C. Boyden, 212
Great Depression, 32, 130
Great Recession, 1–3, 219

Great Society programs, 12, 34, 55–56,
    98–110, 116–28, 157, 199, 220, 223
greenhouse gas emissions, 10
Green New Deal, 22
Greenspan, Alan, 69
Grosse, Robert, 106
growth (as macroeconomic issue), 33–34
Gustman, Alan, 61

Hacking, Ian, 5, 245n86
Hahn, John, 170
Hale, Robert, 82
Hallett, Tim, 5
Halperin, Samuel, 111
Hamermesh, Daniel, 61
Hamilton, William, 82
Hansen, Alvin, 32
Harfst, David, 157
Hart, Philip, 188–89
Hart-Scott-Rodino Antitrust Improvement
    Act, 137, 190–91
Harvard Business School, 62–63
Harvard Law School, 83–84
Harvard School (of I/O economists), 11,
    73–84, 89–97, 131–35, 139–43, 153,
    188–90. *See also specific people*
Harvard University, 27–28, 41, 64–65,
    75–79, 82, 91
Havighurst, Clark, 185
Hawkins, David, 170–71, 175
Hay, George, 87, 137
Hayek, Friedrich, 80
healthcare policy, 1–2, 10–17, 119–24,
    130, 151–52, 182–87, 197, 199, 205–6,
    211–19. *See also* ACA (Affordable Care
    Act); HMOs (health maintenance organizations); Medicaid; Medicare (program);
    social insurance
Health Maintenance Act, 122
Health Research Group, 192
Health Security bill (Kennedy), 123–24,
    182–84, 218
Heller, Walter, 34, 69, 144
HEW (Department of Health, Education,
    and Welfare), 16, 59–69, 101–15, 118–25,
    151, 183–84, 186, 197–98
Hewlett Foundation, 22
HHS (Department of Health and Human
    Services), 203–4
HIE (Health Insurance Experiment), 115,
    121–24
higher education, 17, 107–10, 257n55
Higher Education Act, 55–56, 98–100,
    107–8, 257n55

Ingram Content Group UK Ltd.
Milton Keynes UK
UKHW010626120723
424988UK00003B/87